OBJECT LESSONS

....

Robyn Wiegman

DUKE UNIVERSITY PRESS   DURHAM & LONDON   2012

© 2012 Duke University Press
All rights reserved
Printed in the United States of
America on acid-free paper ∞
Designed by Amy Ruth Buchanan
Typeset in Garamond Premier Pro
by Westchester Book Group
Library of Congress Cataloging-in-
Publication Data appear on the
last printed page of this book.

OBJECT LESSONS

NEXT WAVE: NEW DIRECTIONS IN WOMEN'S STUDIES

A series edited by Inderpal Grewal, Caren Kaplan, and Robyn Wiegman

CONTENTS

....

ACKNOWLEDGMENTS

....

The people who must be thanked should also be forgiven for my inability to make this book into everything they might have wanted from it. Numerous readers gave their time and energy to help me develop various parts of it: Eva Cherniavsky, Antonio Viego, Madelyn Detloff, Robert Corber, Zahid Chaudhary, Michael Hardt, Tyler Curtain, Karla Holloway, Janice Radway, George Haggerty, Molly McGarry, Toril Moi, Linda Zerilli, Lauren Berlant, Judith Kegan Gardiner, and Rey Chow. Others took up discussions with me at pivotal points, often changing my entire direction; these include Clare Hemmings, Janet Halley, Inderpal Grewal, Caren Kaplan, Minoo Moallem, Bill Maurer, Brian Carr, Carla Freccero, Laurie Shannon, Elizabeth Grosz, Donatella Izzo, Liam Kennedy, Jennifer Brody, Sarah Franklin, Anne Firor Scott, Karen Krahulik, Carolyn Allen, Patricia Clough, Janet Jakobsen, Annamarie Jagose, Elizabeth A. Wilson, Tom Foster, Steven Angelides, Ara Wilson, Ranjana Khanna, Meg Wesling, Katrin Sieg, Ralph Litzinger, Deborah Thomas, Birte Christ, and Sabine Sielke. My thanks to the feminist scholars of the 2005 "Think Again" workshop for their many insights and inspirations, especially those not already named: Paola Bacchetta, Tani Barlow, Tina Campt, Kavita Philip, Priti Ramamurthy, Juana María Rodríguez, Jenny Terry, Kathi Weeks, and Laura Wexler.

This book would not have been possible without the assistance of many people—from graduate researchers who delivered me from both small and large mistakes to the absolutely irreplaceable women on the staff of Women's

Studies at Duke University who allowed me to continue to write while serving as program director. On the former, I thank Kyle Julien, Brian Carr, Cybelle McFadden Wilkens, Eden Osucha, Elizabeth Clift, Paul Lai, Netta Van Vliet, Jesse Shaw, Amalle Dublon, Rizvana Bradley, Carolyn Laubender, and Lisa Klarr. To the latter, Gwen Rogers, Lillian Spillers, and Cassandra Harris: I appreciate not just the dedication, but the way each of you made our work fun. In addition, I would like to thank graduate students at the University of North Carolina and Duke who moved through my feminist theory and American Studies courses and helped me think about the labor that identity performs in the culture of professional training.

Audiences at various universities and conferences helped me hone my arguments. I am especially grateful for discussions at University of Aberdeen, University of Bonn, Columbia University, Norwegian University of Science and Technology, University of Kansas, Duke University, University of California–Davis, Yale University, University of Illinois, Harvard University, University of California–Los Angeles, University of Iowa, University of California–Riverside, University of California–Berkeley, University of California–San Diego, Pennsylvania State University, Melbourne Center for Research on Women and Gender, University of Alabama–Birmingham, West Virginia University, the Center for American Studies in Rome and the Italian Association for North American Studies, the Dartmouth Futures of American Studies Institute, the Pembroke Center for Research on Women, the German Network of American Studies Workshop, the Nordic American Studies Association Conference, and the Australia and New Zealand American Studies Association Conference. In the final stages, I received invaluable feedback from audiences at Washington University, Yale University, the Clinton Institute for American Studies, and Indiana University.

My interest in identity and institutionalization first took shape at Syracuse University, where Tom Yingling, Bill Readings, Steven Melville, Steve Mailloux, and Linda Alcoff were extraordinary colleagues and friends whose commitments to the social life of theory and to transformed university cultures affected me profoundly. My seven-year sojourn as a codirector of the Futures of American Studies Institute at Dartmouth College gave me the opportunity to consider the collision between literary and historical projects on one hand and cultural theory on the other. I am in long-standing debt to Donald E. Pease for innumerable conversations, both there and elsewhere, and to the institute itself, which has enabled me to sustain relationships to a group of thoughtful interlocutors, including Elizabeth Dillon, Eric Lott, Winifred Fluck, Hamilton Carroll, Marty Favor, and Cindi Katz. At Duke University, I have had the great reward of a community of passionate critical theorists to think and work with, especially Wahneema Lubiano and Michael Hardt, who may not know how much they have influenced me.

To Eva, I am grateful for the long walks and the home cooking and for moving to Seattle when I needed it. To Laurie for quick wit, serious scholarship, and excellent e-mail repartee. To Tyler for vigilant friendship and the daily news. To Rob for travel itineraries and anti-oedipal sibling love. To Karla for having my back and forgetting the dress. To Mad for the last minute rescue. And finally, let me thank those who wanted me to say what my project was in languages more closely resembling their own: Bret Nelson, Michael Schultheis, Ann Schuessler, Cathy DeSmet, Sharon Wiegman, Kimber Schnepf, and especially Lana Nesmith, who is relieved, I'm sure, to be holding this book in her hands. To each of you, I can only promise to do better.

....

"Doing Justice with Objects" had several incarnations before appearing here in a massively revised form. It was published originally as "Object Lessons: On Men, Masculinity, and the Sign of 'Women'" in *Signs* 26.2 (Winter 2001): 355–88. It was revised as "Unmaking: Men and Masculinity in Feminist Theory," in *Masculinity Studies and Feminist Theory: New Directions*, ed. Judith Kagan Gardiner (New York: Columbia University Press, 2002): 31–59; and as "The Progress of Gender: Whither 'Women'?" in *Women's Studies on Its Own*, ed. Robyn Wiegman (Durham, NC: Duke University Press, 2002): 106–40.

"Telling Time" began its print career as "Dear Ian" in the *Duke Journal of Gender, Law and Policy* 11 (Spring 2004): 93–120.

"The Political Conscious" appeared as "Whiteness Studies and the Paradox of Particularity," *boundary 2* 26.3 (Fall 1999): 115–50 and was reprinted under the same title in *The Futures of American Studies*, ed. Donald E. Pease and Robyn Wiegman (Durham, NC: Duke University Press, 2002): 269–304, and *Interdisciplinarity and Social Justice*, ed. Joe Parker, Mary Romero, and Ranu Samantrai (Albany: State University of New York Press, 2010): 217–43; and as "'My Name Is Forrest, Forrest Gump': Whiteness Studies and the Paradox of Particularity," in *Multiculturalism, Postcoloniality, and Transnational Media*, ed. Ella Shohat and Robert Stam (New Brunswick, NJ: Rutgers University Press, 2003): 227–55.

"Refusing Identification" appeared initially as "Outside American Studies: On the Unhappy Pursuits of Non-Complicity," *Rivista di Studi Americani* 19 (2008): 35–78, and was published in shorter form under the same title in *American Studies/Shifting Gears*, ed. Birte Christ and Christian Kloeckner (Heidelberg: Winter, 2010): 39–63. It also appeared in an earlier version as "Romancing the Future: Internationalization as Symptom and Wish," in *American Studies: An Anthology*, ed. Kevin Gaines, Janice Radway, Barry Shank, and Penny Von Eschen (Malden, MA: Blackwell, 2008): 578–87.

"Critical Kinship" first appeared under the title "Intimate Publics: Race, Property, and Personhood," *American Literature* 74.4 (December 2002): 859–85, in a special issue, "Literature and Science: Cultural Forms, Conceptual Exchanges," ed. Wai Chee Dimock and Priscilla Wald; and was reprinted as "Intimate Publics: Race, Property, and Personhood," in *Race, Nature, and the Politics of Difference*, ed. Donald Moore, Jake Kosek, and Anand Pandian (Durham, NC: Duke University Press, 2003): 296–319.

"The Vertigo of Critique" was first published as "Heteronormativity and the Desire for Gender," *Feminist Theory* 7 (April 2006): 89–103; and later revised as "The Desire for Gender" for *A Companion to LGBT/Q Studies*, ed. George Haggerty and Molly McGarry (Malden, MA: Blackwell, 2006): 217–36.

How to Read This Book

If *Object Lessons* accomplishes what I want, it will offer readers a way to see both inside and across the critical habits and political ambitions of identity knowledges in their current institutional and intellectual formations in the contemporary United States.[1] It will orient them—and you, I hope— toward understanding the overlapping and divergent distinctions that attend the study of race, gender, sexuality, and nation. The book will not

---

1. I use the phrase "identity knowledges" to reference the many projects of academic study that were institutionalized in the U.S. university in the twentieth century for the study of identity. The scholarship that analyzes the history of these formations, along with the debates that have challenged their institutional coherency and political import, is vast. For a selective review, see Champagne and Stauss, *Native American Studies in Higher Education*; Kidwell and Velie, *Native American Studies*; Ono, *Asian American Studies after Critical Mass* and *A Companion to Asian American Studies*; Gordon and Gordon, *A Companion to African-American Studies*; Bobo et al., *The Black Studies Reader*; Poblete, *Critical Latin American and Latino Studies*; Flores and Rosaldo, *A Companion to Latina/o Studies*; Chabram-Dernersesian, *The Chicana/o Cultural Studies Reader*; Kennedy and Beins, *Women's Studies for the Future*; Scott, *Women's Studies on the Edge*; Maddox, *Locating American Studies*; Pease and Wiegman, *The Futures of American Studies*; Radway et al., *American Studies*; Rowe, *A Concise Companion to American Studies*; Abelove et al., *The Lesbian and Gay Studies Reader*; Corber and Valocchi, *Queer Studies*; and Haggerty and McGarry, *A Companion to Lesbian, Gay, Bisexual, Transgender, and Queer Studies*.

make sense as a compendium for such knowledges, no matter how much it comments on the academic entities that have emerged as a consequence of the rise of identity as a social force in the twentieth century.[2] It is not an encyclopedia of what various identity-based fields are doing, nor a status report on their current political authority or institutional health. It is not comprehensive, as numerous identity-based fields of study are not taken up at all, and some are recurrent much more often than others. My uneven attention to the terrain of identity knowledge is not an "oversight"—I have sought to be neither inclusive nor representative—nor is it a statement about the value I attribute to some fields over others. But it does reveal a core belief that travels throughout these pages, which is that the legitimacy of any study of identity is not finally contingent on the legibility of all identity forms within it. This remark is pointedly set against the demand of intersectional analysis, which calls for scholars in identity studies to offer cogent and full accounts of identity's inherent multiplicity in ways that can exact specificity about human experience without reproducing exclusion.[3] In its broadest stroke, *Object Lessons* aims to interrupt faith in

2. There are multiple names for these entities. A survey of institutional projects for the study of *race and ethnicity* reveals: Ethnic Studies, Comparative Ethnic Studies, African American Studies, African and African American Studies, Black Studies, African Diaspora Studies, Africana Studies, Asian American Studies, Asian/Pacific/American Studies, Asian and Asian American Studies, Chicano/a Studies, Chicano/Latino Studies, Puerto Rican/Latino Studies, Latin American and Latino Studies, Hispanic and Latino Studies, Mexican American Studies, Native American Studies, American Indian Studies, Native Studies, First Nations Studies, and Indigenous Studies; for *sexuality:* Sexuality Studies, Gay/Lesbian Studies, Lesbian/Gay/Bisexual/Transgender Studies, Sexual Diversity Studies, Queer Studies, and Multicultural Queer Studies; for *gender*: Women's Studies, Women and Gender Studies, Critical Gender Studies, and Feminist Studies; and for *nation*: American Studies, American Cultural Studies, Critical U.S. Studies, and North American Studies. Universities have also combined these fields into singular administrative units, as in the Department of Social and Cultural Analysis, Critical Cultural Studies, Culture and Theory, Liberation Studies, and Justice Studies.

3. The critical genealogy for intersectional analysis is often traced to Kimberlé Crenshaw's "Demarginalizing the Intersection of Race and Sex" and "Mapping the Margins." Today it is ubiquitous in identity-based fields of study and across the disciplines. But as Julie S. Jordan-Zachery writes, "Researchers employ the term in myriad ways and oftentimes inconsistently and ambiguously" (255). Some researchers, including Jordan-Zachery, locate intersectional commitments in the discourse of political rights by and for black women in the United States in the nineteenth and twentieth centuries, well

just such a critical leap in order to attend to the daunting hope that under-lies it: that if only we find the right discourse, object of study, or analytic tool, our critical practice will be adequate to the political commitments that inspire it. Intersectionality is not alone in posing and then providing an answer to this, the fundamental conundrum and animating question of identity studies. Other keywords—transgender, diaspora, transnational, normativity, interdisciplinary—have all been used in recent years to evoke the possibility of doing justice to and with objects of study or the analytics developed to name and explicate them. But while each of these terms can tell us something specific about how the question has been answered, it is the first—indeed the singular—task of *Object Lessons* to study the answer's ardent pursuit.

In the chapters that follow, I explore a range of identity knowledges—Women's Studies, Ethnic Studies, Queer Studies, Whiteness Studies, and American Studies—in order to consider what they have wanted from the objects of study they assemble in their self-defining critical obligation to so-cial justice.[4] I focus on identity fields of study not because they are absolutely

before Crenshaw's theoretical use of the term. See Jordan-Zachery, "Am I a Black Woman or a Woman Who Is Black?"; and Brah and Phoenix, "Ain't I a Woman." Others differentiate the analytic origin of the concept from its articulation as a method or the-ory. See especially Yuval-Davis, "Intersectionality and Feminist Politics"; McCall, "The Complexity of Intersectionality"; and Davis, "Intersectionality as Buzzword." For a dis-cussion about the intersectional metaphor, see Brown, "The Impossibility of Women's Studies"; Villarejo, "Tarrying with the Normative"; and Valentine, "Theorizing and Re-searching Intersectionality." For an important consideration of the nonanalogous status of identity, see Barrett, "Identities and Identity Studies."

4. Throughout this study, I use the phrase "social justice" as a generic figure of the political destination of identity knowledges, knowing that its meaning is precisely what is at stake in the different disciplinary and critical relations that generate identity-based scholarship. For some scholars and in some disciplinary traditions, social justice will always be measured by a state-oriented outcome, with the transformation of laws and policies signifying its political resolution. In others, the juridical solution is absolutely rejected, along with the terms by which dissent is managed in a liberal social order, such that justice is always excessive of constitutional orders and governmentality of any kind, being the eternally postponed figure of what is to come. While each chapter pays close attention to how justice is configured in a specific field-forming debate, *Object Lessons* is ultimately less interested in measuring the strength and weaknesses of different under-standings than in exploring the way that identity knowledges take their commitment to some version of justice as a self-constituting fact.

different from other academic domains, but because they invest so much in making explicit what other fields do not explicitly name by framing their modes and manners of analysis as world-building engagements aimed at social change. All of the fields that I write about identify themselves in both historical and theoretical terms according to their proud avowal of political intentions. Each field thus engages in intense debate over the ways in which its objects of study, methodological practices, and theoretical discourses foster (or don't) contemporary political transformation. In some contexts, as in Ethnic and Women's Studies, transformation is figured by claiming for minoritized subjects the right to study themselves and to make themselves the object of their study.[5] In other fields, justice is sought by refusing identification with the field's primary object of study, as when scholars set out to "unmake" the universalism of whiteness in Whiteness Studies or to expose and contest the imperial nation in American Studies. In all of these fields, political claims are routinely attributed to methodological priorities. Interdisciplinarity, for instance, is often forwarded as the means to transcend the proclaimed limitations and fragmented perspectives of the disciplines while live subject research is taken to undermine objectification by emphasizing the subjectivity and agency of the object of study. While the relationship between American Studies and minoritized identity forms will be addressed in due course, the resonant point here is that identity knowledges are animated by powerful political desires, and that each has sought quite explicitly to know itself and to assess its self-worth by situating its object relations as a living habit of—and for—social justice.

The first questions that frame my inquiry, then, are these: What has enabled or emboldened, allowed or encouraged scholars to believe that justice can be achieved through the study of identity?[6] How have identity

5. In using the word "minoritized" instead of "minority" throughout this study, I want to indicate social processes, not statistical populations. Both women and people of color as groups—each statistically a global majority—are minoritized within patriarchal, colonial, and capitalist formations, and only in some contexts do either of these categories indicate a numerical minority.

6. In *Object Lessons*, the "study of identity" is intended to reference the scope of approaches that have accompanied identity's academic sojourn, whether affirmative or critical of identity. This means that those trajectories that limn the antihumanist impulses of postmodern thought and have been understood to be anti-identitarian are part

objects of study been imbued with political value, and what does "the political" mean in those academic domains that take critical practice as the means and measure for pursuing justice? What kind of power is invested in the act of thinking, and what kind of thinking is considered most capable of acting, such that the political commitments and critical itineraries of identity knowledges can be fulfilled? On what critical terms, with which cultural materials, methodological priorities, and theoretical discourses has the study of identity been given disciplinary shape, and how has belief in its political agency been produced and sustained? While it is hardly possible to answer such questions comprehensively, *Object Lessons* sets out to address them by foregrounding the diversity of aim and ambition that attends the ways in which objects of study are politically arrayed across various identity knowledge domains. By considering the epistemological and affective force of political claims, I meditate in each of the following chapters on the object relations at stake and on the critical subjectivities honed by and for them. My attention thus turns to the rhetorical forms of critical argument as much as to the object content of various fields to explore not only the kinds of questions that motivate critical practices but the forms their answers take, along with the modes of reading and interpretation they simultaneously invite and prohibit. As readers will see, nearly all of the chapters of *Object Lessons* dwell on the political investments and aspirations of identity knowledges by attending to the disciplinary practices that comprise and define them.

While other essays and books on the topic often act as a defense of identity studies, my project explores the shape of the conversations they stage and sustain—or deflect and avoid—about themselves from within. Hence this book expends no effort on amassing evidence for the legitimacy of identity as the focus or foundation for academic study, nor is it a deconstructive exercise propelled by a covert intention to dissuade their ongoing generation. Instead, *Object Lessons* proceeds from the assumption that identity studies as we currently know them emerged into critical legibility in the U.S. university in the second half of the twentieth century through the convergence of various social forces, such that new practices of governmentality, social protest, and institutional attachments rewrote the discourse

---

of identity knowledges. Indeed, as I will discuss in chapter 2, the ongoing critique of identity helps sustain the disciplinary reproduction of identity-based fields.

of the university's responsibilities, constituencies, and function. I write from the position of those who entered the rank of full professor in the past decade who never experienced a university culture devoid of identity knowledges and the social concerns that attend them. As we carved out academic positions, my generation fought less for the emergence of our fields than for their extension and expansion, for more institutional legitimacy and power, and for the right to self-governance and self-assessment. We sought to more fully institutionalize what had been tangential or tentative or underorganized or unresourced. While some have been tempted to take the story about the founding of identity knowledges as the most important—or only—story to be told, I am interested in the distance traveled from the inaugural moment to the languages, affects, and debates that comprise its contemporary form. Let "multiculturalism" speak volumes about the scope and tenor of the divergences in historical contexts and institutional politics that have accompanied identity's arrival, and let "globalization" foreground the current epistemological challenge of revising the politically powerful but at times nationally focused horizons in which identity studies were largely born.[7] While it is certainly naive to assume that there is no ongoing inaugural struggle, *Object Lessons* positions its investigations on the side of institutionalization that takes it as an established fact.[8] By institutionalization, I do not mean departmentalization

7. In the early 1990s, Gayatri Spivak referenced the terms of a debate that has become increasingly heated in recent years by saying, "The United States is certainly a multiracial culture, but its parochial multicultural debates, however animated, are not a picture of globality. . . . [W]e must negotiate between nationalism (uni- or multicultural) and globality . . . by keeping nation and globe distinct as [we study] their relationship" (279). Spivak's comments were not directly aimed at identity knowledges, but similar charges have been made against what I call their "democratic nationalism," by which I mean their rhetorical invocation of numerous tropes, histories, and horizons of U.S. national political life. Today, of course, every identity studies domain is being rewritten by the internationalizing imperative that is now reshaping the U.S. academy. On the internationalization of the U.S. university, see Kolasch, *The Internationalisation of the Higher Education Industry*, and Li, *Globalization and the Humanities*; and on the impact of postnational frameworks for U.S. identity knowledges, see Cherniavsky, "Subaltern Studies in a US Frame." For Spivak, see "Scattered Speculations on the Question of Cultural Studies."

8. The inaugural struggle is certainly not over in Arizona, which banned Ethnic Studies classes in public schools in 2010 because they "are designed primarily for pupils of a

per se, no matter how often this administrative structure is a favored connotation. Institutionalization points instead to the generative influence of identity knowledges across the disciplines and to the many courses, conferences, publications, and academic organizations that now comprise their intellectual and organizational formations.

This side of institutionalization is where it becomes possible, then, to consider how identity knowledges have been transformed by their transit through the university, such that today's dilemmas might rightly be said to have been inconceivable at the start. Take the problem of the coherency identity knowledges have had to confer on themselves and their objects of study under the auspices of taking representation and speech as the founding notes of political value. How strange it is that in closing the distance, itself conceived of as epistemic violence, between the subject and object of knowledge, identity studies are now sworn to an increasingly unsettling convergence: that to legitimately speak for an identity object of study one must be able to speak *as* it, even as such speaking threatens to strip subjects of epistemological authority over everything they are not. The price of the gain in self-representation is often paid by the service that follows, as one is repeatedly asked to appear dressed in identity clothes. It is sometimes easier, of course, to forgo resentment when you know your role on a committee is simply to be its black, gay, brown, or female member—that familiar representative function that has little purchase on who you actually are. But it is often harder to bear the psychic burdens of maneuvering between the aspirations and disappointments that accompany critical practices understood as political acts of self-defense. How much goodness, after all, must one attribute to her identity objects of study to withstand what it means to both represent and be represented by them? Given that subjects of knowledge are never fully commensurate with the objects they seek to authorize, what tactic is on offer from within identity knowledges to handle the contradictions between the educated elite and the subalterns we study and represent? *I* will always speak for more people than it has a right to, even when its right is conferred by being one among the very group of people *I* cites. And then there are other compelling problems that arise,

---

particular ethnic group," "promote resentment toward a race or class of people," and "advocate ethnic solidarity." See Weiner, "Arizona Bans Ethnic Studies—Update" and "Fox News Defends Arizona Ethnic Studies Ban."

from speaking for myself—what does that mean?—to thinking that I can control everything that *I* will be taken to mean.

The implications of these matters are taken up in the chapters that follow as I attend to the critical and institutional complexities that have shaped identity's academic sojourn. By focusing on the political animations of various academic fields and the institutional contexts that attend them, each chapter explores a specific object relation in order to consider how it shapes a field's political pursuits: in Women's Studies, gender; in Queer Studies, antinormativity; in Whiteness Studies, antiracist whiteness; in American Studies, internationalization; and in nearly all of the fields I write about, intersectionality. As readers will see, the object relations at stake in these discussions do not operate in any collective coherence to address or adjudicate the multiple registers in which identity functions as a coordinate of power, social formation, mode of interpellation, discourse of state and self-designation, political horizon, analytic concept, interpretative practice, field of study, or institutional emblem of difference. This list is incomplete, but such incompletion is easily harnessed to the point I wish to make, which is that "identity knowledges" are so mired in ongoing social and institutional relations that their analytical capacities are inseparable from the projections, attachments, and affects that propel them. For this reason, *Object Lessons* emphasizes those affects—anxiety, love, fear, and faith—that accompany, whether acknowledged or not, the political desire that attends both our relationship to our objects and analytics *and* our relationship to that relationship as well. Let's not pretend then that objects of study matter only because of what we want from them, or that what we want from them is adequate to the ways in which they inhabit and transform how we grasp the world. The issue at stake is more simple, if confounding: What am *I* without them? In its various explorations of identity knowledges, *Object Lessons* takes shape as both an answer—"nothing"—and a proposition: that the work ongoing on is as fantastic and incalculable as the belief we generate from it.

Getting Here

Each of the chapters to follow began as an individual performance bound to its own occasion, whether as a conference talk, keynote lecture, or invited essay. Their deeper ecology—what I think of as the psychic life of this book—arises from their relationship to relationships of various kinds, academic and non: between my own identity investments and the objects of study that reflect and extend them; between geopolitical histories and the local worlds of family, region, and nation that named and claimed me; between habits of learning formally passed on to me and the ones I was lucky enough to cultivate from people and places I found on my own. Disciplinarily, the forthcoming conversations evolved from the study of literature and the humanities more generally, and from cultural studies and critical theory most specifically. They primarily involve Feminist, African American, Queer, and U.S. Studies, along with the interconnections and non-coincidences in which these fields and their objects of study and critical analytics have diverged. My personal attachments to these fields have many origins, but I am most eager to cite a string of vibrant English teachers in public schools in Miami, Florida, where the work of daily life was bound to the complex negotiations that attend identity's cultural sojourn.[9] It was in one of those schools, Horace Mann Junior High, that I had my first mature inkling of what white skin privilege meant and when and how it could be deployed or not in the shifting allegiances of the schoolyard, as black, Cuban, and white kids learned lessons the classroom could never adequately teach. Surely this is neither the only nor best reason to account for the fact that the first piece of *Object Lessons* to be drafted was about the academic emergence of Whiteness Studies as a project of antiracist knowledge production. But it would be a major misunderstanding of the force of identity to dismiss it as inconsequential altogether. People drawn to identity knowledges have often been forced—by circumstance, history, pride, anger, or the sheer arrogance of those around them—to attend to what seems so massively obvious: that, to cite Eve Kosofsky Sedgwick's stunningly sparse first axiom in *The Epistemology of the Closet*: "People are different from one another."[10]

9. My thanks especially to Mrs. Williams in second grade, who set me on this path by making me a "T.O.T." (Teacher of Tomorrow); Mrs. Grant in seventh grade, who taught me a serious love of the well-diagrammed sentence; and Mrs. Kranick in ninth grade, who made sure I understood the difference between reading and interpretation.

10. "It is astonishing how few respectable conceptual tools we have for dealing with this self-evident fact," writes Sedgwick at the outset of the book that would for many years stand as the origin of queer theory, until scholars began to claim Judith Butler's *Gender Trouble: Feminism and the Subversion of Identity*, published the same year (1990), as a foundational contribution to the emergence of the field. Sedgwick's book, like Butler's, did

That junior high school was also the place in which other kinds of identity knowledges took vernacular shape, as when my best friends refused to vote for me for class president because I was a girl, or when Louisiana Fuller held my hand and the exhilaration and fear of it prompted my mother to explain the sad plight of "homosexuals" and why we should pity but not hate them. To say that identity studies would arrive much later to provide analytic purchase on the social emergencies created around these passages in and out of identities—the calling forth into a girldom quite different from the one I had known, no less than the specter of the kind of person my mother was sure I would not become—is to recognize why students continue to describe themselves as transformed or transfixed by fields that offer counternarratives of self and social possession. Identity studies work as sites of social, political, and intellectual engagement because they emphasize the needs they exist to represent, making treasures out of the insights, analyses, and theories that have been crafted to describe and ameliorate the general incapacity for difference to register on the scale of social value.

But what happens if the need is too great for the theory to sufficiently feed it, or if the object that represents the need becomes diminished by the worldly limits in which it is forced to live? What happens when what you once loved no longer satisfies your belief that it can give you what you want? These questions are what led me from the study of whiteness to that of *gender* and the standing ovation it has received in the last decade as the critical means to rejuvenate the optimism once signified by *women* in the field inaugurated in that name. This optimism is fascinating to me not because I discount its authenticity or want to argue with its future-generating authority, but because of the political belief it sustains in critical practice as an agency of social change.

Other chapters were first drafted under the influence of different affects and affiliations. "Critical Kinship" began as an exploration of the methodological difficulties of interdisciplinary research—a focus that had its own

---

not use the term "queer theory," but its pursuit of antihomophobic inquiry and its cascading performance as well as theorization of the difference between identity and identification are hallmarks of what would be narrated retrospectively as the origin of the field. My discussion of the impact of the discourse of normativity in the final chapter of this book offers one gloss on how Butler's work has traveled from its primary engagement with feminism to become a founding queer theoretical text. See Sedgwick, *Epistemology of the Closet*, 22.

experiential basis when I took part as the sole humanist in an interinstitutional project on race and nature.[11] Resisting suggestions by colleagues that ethnographic method would rescue my analysis from the tourist sensibility they found in its travels through an incongruent archive (from legal cases to popular film to feminist analyses of reproductive technology), I wrote instead about method as an idiom of intimacy while trying to account for the intertwined logics of race and gender that served methodologically as both my map and compass. This framework allowed me to reflect on the antiparadigmatic work of humanistic scholarship, along with its devotion to "dead" texts, living political contexts, and representation as the privileged venue for considerations of culture. "Refusing Identification" was initially drafted for a Fulbright visit to New Zealand where I wanted to deliver a keynote that could track the ways in which the internationalizing project of American Studies in the United States was incommensurate with the circulation and sign of "America" as it traveled across different university systems, political economies, regional histories, and social formations around the world. "Telling Time" was written as an invited response to Ian Halley's "Queer Theory by Men" and used his primary combatants, feminism and queer theory, to detail the critical dilemmas that ensue when social movement discourses and academic itineraries are critically converged. The final chapter of this book, "The Vertigo of Critique," began as a contribution to conversations about gender, sexuality, and heteronormativity and was first delivered in Norway, which helped to bring home to me the specificity of the U.S. university as both the context and the limit of my understanding of identity formation and academic knowledge politics in general.[12] It was later revamped for inclusion

11. For the most comprehensive discussion of the history of interdisciplinarity in the U.S. university, see Klein, *Interdisciplinarity* and *Crossing Boundaries.*

12. In making a point about the U.S. university, I am not necessarily consolidating it into a homogeneous entity, though the scale in which I seek to mark it is more transnational than domestic in scope. I readily agree that the U.S. university is deeply hierarchical in structure, that the class system that mediates its practices of hailing students to its very different doors is the effect of social organizations and governmental rationalities that it reiterates and reflects, even when it purports to be the agency of their transformation. But class differences within the U.S. university constitute, in part, its institutional form in a global context, adjudicating divisions of knowledge, skill, and labor, and managing certain kinds of state and economic interests across boundaries that dissolve or solidify in ways we cannot always predict.

in a Blackwell volume aimed at assessing the state of Queer Studies, where it became more fully engaged with the ways that *gender* has achieved critical priority in a field purportedly devoted to *sex*.[13]

All of these critical forays have been substantially revised for inclusion here, but none was rewritten to generate a line of thought that it did not at least insinuate. Properly speaking, then, *Object Lessons* is not a collection of previously published essays but an assemblage of critical conversations shaped and reshaped by both my belated monographic intentions and the wishes of readers who engaged the challenge of helping me sort through its separate and collectivized forms. These readers have been differently arrayed across the fields that concern me, being specialists in some, initiates in others. All have had a personal, institutional, or intellectual commitment to identity as the means for apprehending the relationship, broadly speaking, between human beings and their social worlds. Few have needed to be convinced that identity is irreducible to a single politics or that its most crucial questions arrive after agendas have been made. While other academic projects might stage identity debates to intervene in the critical practices of their home disciplines, *Object Lessons* hopes to recruit and sustain readers who share an interest in using identity to travel toward the affects, political horizons, and critical limits of the fields of study that have been established in its name. On behalf of these readers, my purpose is twofold: to inhabit identity's aspirations in the critical trajectories, discursive practices, and methodological priorities that it has so profoundly inspired, while exploring how various fields reach or exact a limit, become disciplinary instead of interventionist, and mimic radicality instead of teaching us how to become radically undone. Let me emphasize that this itinerary is not a response to what right-leaning cultural warriors have tagged disparagingly as "political correctness," nor is it an argument against any of the straw dogs that would emerge if I gave them their turn. *Object Lessons* is motivated instead by the desire to exist somewhere—if not a social world, political movement, or institutional space, then at the very least a

---

13. In "'Oh, the Fun We'll Have,'" Heather Love argues that current attention to *gender* in Sexuality Studies arises from the emergence of trans criticism. But as I argue in the last chapter of this book, the field's founding gesture to disarticulate gender and sexuality has never been fulfilled, raising the possibility that *gender* has been its central object of study all along. Certainly the retrospective nomination of *Gender Trouble* as a foundational queer theoretical text offers evidence to support this suggestion.

textual environment, an argument, even a series of words—in which identity and its knowledges are encountered in ways just as surprising, unnerving, and conflicted as we are.

Yes, *we*. That towering inferno of universalism. That monstrous display of self-infatuation. That master stroke of white-woman-speech. Voices warn me away from the danger. Hit backspace. Rephrase. Take comfort in grammar's singularity. But how can I not want this tantalizing hallucination? Or more to the point, why must I ignore its pulsing heat when identity knowledges are nothing without the haunting specter and affective traction of *we*? If the protocols of critical speech have taught us to avoid the risk, it is just as true to say that identity knowledges rarely take political or critical aim without some measure of hope that *we* will struggle into existence—partial and contingent to be sure, but resonant and agential. In the taut space between the *we* that must be disciplined and the *we* that is desired, *I* presents itself as the desiring subject's safest bet. But how safe is any *I*—indeed, how safe am I?—when the descriptive content no less than the protocols in which I come to speech are bound to histories and scripts that are given credit for knowing me at the start? My strategy in the pages that follow is to inhabit the error, not to avoid it, and certainly not to take refuge in the small cave of the *I*, even as I mobilize it in order to help specify the tense and longed-for translations that mark the distance I am trying to travel from me to *you*—the preamble to whatever can be made to stand for *we*. I anticipate *your* resistance, but here's the truth: *I* am not legible to myself without it. In this state of constitutive dependency, where the contingencies of grammar refract the identitarian dilemmas on which identity knowledges are staked, *Object Lessons* engages not only how and why *we* has been so harshly condemned but the hope that our struggle with it reveals. What, after all, fuels the fierceness of our objection to *we*: the wish it reveals or the fact that the wish has yet to come true?

Field Work

Generally speaking, *Object Lessons* is organized around the assumption that identity studies are distinguished from other areas of contemporary knowledge in the U.S. university by their acknowledged attachment to the political. I say *acknowledged* because of the importance of situating this book in the territory between two connected but not identical claims: between the familiar observation in identity studies that there are political stakes to all knowledge production and my own insistence, borne from the investigations that have brought me here, that a critical perspective on the operation of the political within identity-based fields has not been sufficiently engaged. This last statement might strike you as counterintuitive if not downright contradictory, as I have already emphasized how profoundly identity knowledges identify themselves as practices of social justice. But deliberating on a field's political discourse is not the same thing as deliberating on the operations of the political that constitute it. The former entails examining a field's political rhetorics and the way these are staked to critical relationships of various kinds, including the constitution of the object and the methods that are made congruent with it. While *Object Lessons* is explicitly engaged in just these kinds of maneuvers, it does so as part of its larger task to unravel the meaning and critical implications of the operation of the political as it generates the affective force that constitutes the psychic life of a field or what Donald E. Pease calls in the context of American Studies the "field-Imaginary."[14] For Pease, the field imaginary denotes "the disciplinary unconscious"—that domain of critical interpellation through which practitioners learn to pursue particular objects, protocols, methods of study, and interpretative vocabularies as the means for expressing and inhabiting their belonging to the field.

How does one study a field imaginary? As Pease defines it, the field imaginary is only accessible from a critical position produced outside of it, as those within the field "can neither reflect upon its terms nor subject them to critical scrutiny."[15] From this perspective, *Object Lessons* cannot possibly proceed to read the field imaginary of identity knowledges because its author is too enmeshed in that which she seeks to decipher, too indebted to their critical ecologies, and far too attached to the ideas and histories that have called them forth to stand a chance of getting outside of them, no matter the fact—and indeed it is a fact—that she has experienced wave after wave of ambivalence at precisely those moments when identity's truth serums were being most liberally served. But Pease's account underestimates the implications of the psychoanalytic model he is wed to, in that there can be no outside perspective unencumbered by disciplinary obligations and field-forming injunctions of its own. While academic culture has

14. Pease, "New Americanists," 11.
15. Pease, "New Americanists," 12.

enshrined the rhetorical methods that allow scholars to claim an uncontaminated authority, it is hardly the case that anyone can travel very far without dragging more of herself along than she can possibly know. In other words, the scholar in pursuit of discerning a field's imaginary has unconscious disciplinary attachments too.

But the deeper problem in Pease's formulation comes from the opposite direction, as we are asked to imagine a subject so disciplined by a field imaginary (or by laws, governments, or the slaps that follow parental displeasure) as to be completely ignorant of any of the rules. Which subject is that? Not me and, I venture, not you. Run a red light, steal candy, kill a bird, refuse to wear a dress, change your pronoun, marry your brother, lie to customs, cheat, live on the streets. These are not equivalent cases, but their differing affective registers might work to graphically suggest that the fevered pitch of critical debates over agency in the ongoing volley between humanist and posthumanist theories of the subject have little heat if we take seriously the idea that it is precisely because we are inside of ideology, subjected to its work, that we can know anything about it.[16] All of this is meant to say that being shaped by the field imaginary one seeks to explicate is not grounds for critical dismissal. In this study, it is the life blood that makes it possible to inhabit the affective contours and critical conundrums of U.S. identity knowledges today.

It is, then, from within a field that one is most instructed on how best to abide by its rules, as no practitioner becomes legitimate to herself or to others without acquiring fluency in the skills a field offers, including how to recognize and read the objects of study prioritized by it. These skills amount to more than technical training in the citational forms, critical traditions, and major figures that accompany field narration; they are also lessons in the value forms and belief structures that accompany critical practice, where visionary and belligerent critics can be found, and moral judgments (whether admitted or not) accompany nearly everything we touch, from critical rubrics, research topics, and objects of study to methods

16. This acknowledgment would seriously undercut current faith in critical practice as the means for discerning the political operations of what others cannot see. Much more will be said throughout *Object Lessons* about how the rhetoric of the political circulates in academic culture in ways that commodify politics for professional advancement.

and arguments as well.[17] Critical predilections do change of course—what was once a field's most prohibited object of study (masculinity for Women's Studies, say, or whiteness for Ethnic Studies) can become central to its itinerary. These transformations are not simply about the latest academic fashion, no matter the fact that commodification is always a decisive factor in shaping the publication value of politically oriented academic work. The pursuit of the new is also crucial to the ongoing work of field formation, as it enables practitioners to engage, revise, and extend a field's critical and political significance by compulsively debating it. Don't be distracted by the anxious tones of critical dissension or the high drama that ensues in field encounters with university administrations or toxic legislatures or, more benignly, by the rush to embrace the latest critical thing (once it was postmodernism and cultural studies, now it is globalization and species-ism). Such exercises do not undermine the field imaginary so much as generate and sustain it by providing the occasion to defend the critical authority it hones.

Threats to the existence of the field are formative, then, even constitutive of the field imaginary, serving as the means for evoking and evincing the political value it simultaneously produces and proclaims. This is as true of the field imaginary of American Studies in its current post-national formation as it is of those academic knowledge domains coordinated around minoritized identity. All find their critical authority at odds with their public influence—and all take their abjection in the public political

---

17. I use the word *moral* as a provocation toward considering how political desire is bound to evaluations and optimisms that collate in various ways around *the good*. Sometimes this "good" can be pointedly set against the moral order of dominant formulations as when it is politically good to be a bad subject, or when bad social subjects become good objects of study (as in the case of sex workers for pro-sex feminism or pedophiles for Queer Studies). But most often it operates as the implicit position occupied by the left critic herself.

In her compelling discussion of celebratory accounts of racial hybridity, Sandra K. Soto offers an example of the critical production of "good subjects" that I am highlighting here: "What the key terms used to mark racialized difference as inherently transgressive have in common is their indelible dependence on what can only be a fantasy of a normative center inhabited by homogenous, static, racially pure, stagnant, uninteresting, and simple sovereign subjects. The celebration of hybridity not only helps reify the fantasy of the sovereign subject but also threatens to transmute marginality itself into a form of authenticity." See Soto, *Reading Chican@ Like a Queer*, 3–4.

sphere as evidence of their political value. One expects nothing less of a discourse aimed at left political intervention, of course, but what are the implications *within* the field of such a relationship between critical authority and political value? Or, more to the point, what does it mean that practitioners are taught to read, generate, and evaluate critical practice according to the status of the field's discourse outside the material locus of its production—that is, outside the accumulation of professional capital that attends the reproduction of critical hegemonies within the field? What kinds of affective and analytic expectations and, yes, regulations are thus required to ensure safe passage between the field's self-defining hegemonies and the modes of critical world building it attaches to them? And what can the field *not* afford to know in order to guarantee its reproduction in the disciplinary terms on which its commitment to the political turns?

These are the kinds of questions that generate my ongoing attention to the field imaginary of identity knowledges, as they foreground the crucial difference between a field's discourse of the political and the operations of the political that constitute it. By considering these questions as distinctly disciplinary ones, I am not aiming for a broad condemnation of the seeming reduction of identity's radical potential to academic institutionalization nor am I lamenting the fact that professionalization circulates particular critical discourses as political ones in a capital-generating nexus of critical authority and prestige. Social movements, as far as I am concerned, are no less disciplinary than academic fields of study, just differently so. Each of the chapters of *Object Lessons* thus seeks to explore some of the ways—startling, optimistic, angry, and belligerent—in which identity knowledges perform their hope that critical practice will be commensurate with both the political desire that incites it and the world it describes and seeks to transform. If in the process we are prone to considering ourselves outside of disciplinarity altogether, it is not because we are unaware of the rules. On the contrary, we find them comforting and alluring. This, then, is the consequence of the labor that *field work* performs, as practitioners find relief in the belief that the value of critical practice is its political value and that the political agency the field generates is ultimately the critic's own.

Analytic Detachments

It is surprising to find myself traveling so intensely with the language of psychoanalysis in this book, as I would characterize the genesis of my own intellectual formation as collated around discourses that sought distance from the seemingly overdetermined domains that psychoanalysis has traced: the personal, intimate, familial, domestic, experiential, fantastical, imaginary, and purportedly unreal. My earliest introduction into identity forms of analysis in both African American and Women's Studies were drawn from materialist genealogies, with ideology critique a prime focus as it was introduced to me through cultural studies in the early 1980s. Of course, psychoanalysis was everywhere—especially in feminist film theory and in the trans-Atlantic migrations of French feminism—but I see now that I was particularly deaf to its genealogical specificity. Today, I suppose it is true to say, I remain deaf to psychoanalysis still, in the sense that the conversations in this book remain disengaged from many of the debates that have long concerned scholars whose primary interpretative attachments lie there.[18] At no point in the chapters that follow do I review, argue, or align myself with specific psychoanalytic authorities, whether Sigmund Freud, Melanie Klein, Jacques Lacan, Jean Laplanche, or Frantz Fanon; I stake next to nothing on sorting through the different traditions of psychoanalytic thought that are at the heart of contemporary psychoanalytic controversies in those academic domains (the humanities and interpretative social sciences) that are most resonant for identity knowledges today.[19]

18. For those interested in a study that traces the object through psychoanalytic theory with great rigor, see McCallum, *Object Lessons*. When I first encountered McCallum's *Object Lessons*, I had just submitted an essay to *Signs* for publication under the same main title. There are great overlaps in our mutual interest in desire, belief, and knowledge, but the itineraries of our critical endeavors are decidedly different. I hope Erin will forgive me for persisting with the title, and that my readers will see in her book the debt of influence that I continue to owe.

19. The amount of scholarship that does this work is impossible to cite in even a sufficiently representative way, but important projects that are pertinent for the conversations in *Object Lessons* include: Abel et al., *Female Subjects in Black and White*; Dean and Lane, *Homosexuality and Psychoanalysis*; Khanna, *Dark Continents*; Lane, *The Psychoanalysis of Race*; Fuss, *Identification Papers*; Gallop, *The Daughter's Seduction*; Britzman, *Lost Subjects, Contested Objects*; and Spillers, "'All the Things You Could Be by Now.'"

How, then, does a book emerge to claim no primary theoretical investment in psychoanalysis that nonetheless cultivates whatever self-identity might be said to describe it by focusing on the antimaterial ephemera that psychoanalysis so lovingly engages: affects, impulses, and wishes, along with the critical force of desire? How can I return, repeatedly, to the language of objects, identifications, and attachments without imagining myself in debt or duty to psychoanalysis, and why is it that I would choose to defend myself—here and now—against the expectation that, for credibility's sake, I should plot my travels carefully, giving my reader a clear indication of how I move from the founding texts and theoretical precepts of psychoanalysis to the conversations about the identity knowledges collected here? Indeed, why would I invite what I know to be a strategy of academic intellectual dismissal by refusing to authorize *Object Lessons* according to the habits of critical authority that currently invest academic discourses with the power to speak—power cultivated by arming ourselves with an interpretative practice that we offer as more capable, productive, and enabling than any other? You recognize the motion: "only X analytic" will provide the nuance, perspective, explanation, or solution that *this* inquiry needs; "only Z authority" will lead us out of the critical morass that registers the poverty of now.

The conversations staged in this book move in different ways across these issues of authority and interpretative practice, but without amassing critical determination for signature theories or signature theorists. To be sure, no mode of thinking that is accessible to me is far afield from the transformations in humanistic inquiry that mark the history of my construction as an academic subject, dateline the late 1970s and 1980s, in the province of the United States. These transformations, as is now well known, pushed to the foreground problems of representation, language, and discourse, which also engendered new kinds of struggles over conceptions of power, human agency, and the possibility of social change. In the long view, my academic sojourn was framed by the dimorphic genealogies of Marx and Freud, whose competition for authority occupied a great deal of the language of the U.S. Left, especially feminist, in the decades of academic training that formed me. While it might be true to say that, like most U.S. scholars of my generation, I turned to Foucault as a way not simply to split but to overcome the difference, I am more infatuated today with what happens in proximity to critical theory's ambitions than in the detail that is generated in debt or obligation to any specific figure or strand of it. This is not to say that the ensuing chapters share no theoretical project, but it does explain why I have not used my introduction to map the theoretical debates and legacies of the critical vernacular that I use. To put this another way, let me simply say—because I have been asked this before—that I offer no overarching theory of desire from which I have derived my use of the phrase *political desire*, nor do I delineate a specific theoretical understanding of what psychic processes are engaged and performed by attachment and investment. For me, their importance is not conceptual, at least not in the way that theoretical discourses live and die according to the value conferred on the concepts derived from them.

As antithetical as it is to the generation of critical authority, let alone to the cultivation of expertise, this book resists the magnificent lure of anchoring its inquiries in the epistemological privileges accorded to distinct theoretical traditions and a genealogical excavation of their central terms. My use of *object relations* is not, then, a theoretical commitment to a distinct body of psychoanalytic thought, but a reflection of my interest in the simplest idea the phrase helps to deliver: namely, that objects of study are as fully enmeshed in fantasy, projection, and desire as those that inhabit the more familiar itinerary of intimate life, such as sex, lover, parent, sibling, friend.[20] By object, I mean to designate targets of study that reflect a seemingly material existence in the world (as in people, goods, laws, books, or films) and those that do not reveal such materiality in any immediately graspable way (as in discourse, ideology, history, personhood, the unconscious, and desire itself). By relation, I mean the constitutive dependence of one thing on another, such that no critical practice can be considered the consequence of its own singular agencies. In this loose conceptual framework, I view the very attempt *to know* as an intimate relation, crafted within and from the sociality and materiality of a world we inherit; and I take the proposition that *knowing is a means to do justice* as an attempt to transform that intimacy into reinventing the world. The foremost stakes of

20. The two most important figures in object relations theory are widely regarded as Melanie Klein and D. W. Winnicott. See Klein, *The Collected Writings of Melanie Klein*, Vols. 1–4; Winnicott, *Playing and Reality* and *The Child, the Family, and the Outside World*; Winnicott with Khan, *Holding and Interpretation*; and Winnicott et al., *Babies and Their Mothers*. Recent engagements with object relations include Phillips, *Winnicott*, "Winnicott's Hamlet," and *On Kissing, Tickling, and Being Bored*; and Sedgwick, "Melanie Klein and the Difference Affect Makes."

this project are to be found here, in the interpretative interplay between social life, critical practice, and political commitment. My title, *Object Lessons*, is meant to capture the force of this pedagogical point—that identity knowledges are bound to much more than what we use them to know—in order to license attention to the impulses that keep us enthralled to them.

Still, something must be said about psychoanalysis itself, especially given the fact that it has no established relation to identity knowledges per se. Indeed, some of the fields that concern me have been decidedly torn about the utility of psychoanalysis, while others have little formal relationship to it at all. Contemporary U.S. academic feminism was born in the 1960s in its longing to reject Freud, which was countered in passion only by its concurrent hope for reconfiguring Marx, and is sustained today by its use, transformation, and ambivalence toward both. American Studies, in its interdisciplinary leanings toward history and literature, spent most of the twentieth century trying to amass archives it could call its own, only to have them undone in the post–Cold War era by critiques launched from identity and postcolonial domains. Psychoanalysis has mattered to some key figures in the New Americanist iteration of the field, but not often, though the current cultivation of affect as a frame for thinking about political feeling in the unfolding of empire bears a psychoanalytic genealogy that is sometimes named.[21] Queer Studies has perhaps been marked more decisively by an affirmative relation to psychoanalysis than other domains of identity studies, which is of course a development with much queer irony given the long-standing historical antipathy in lesbian and gay communities and in the early formation of LGBT Studies to medical psychiatry's pathologizing account of homosexuality and transgender identifications. But in the critical emergence of queer theory as a project that simultaneously disarticulated acts from identities and imagined political affiliation in practices aimed at contesting heteronormativity's unconscious force, psychoanalysis joined ideology critique to effect a fascinating recalculation of various productivities, including most pointedly desire, representation, embodiment, sex, labor, and kinship. Current efforts to

21. There is now a lengthy archive on affect. See especially Ahmed, *The Cultural Politics of Emotion* and "Collective Feelings"; Berlant, "The Subject of True Feelings"; Hemmings, "Invoking Affect"; Sedgwick, *Touching Feeling*; Hardt, "Affective Labor"; Giardini, "Public Affects"; Clough, "Affect and Control"; and Clough with Halley, *The Affective Turn*.

situate the study of sexuality transnationally and as a means to rethink race both within and against the earliest configuration of the queer theoretical enterprise are varied in their investments in psychoanalysis, with one signature essay making explicit its rejection of psychoanalysis while other scholarly projects, often elaborated under the trope of racial melancholia, move quite distinctly in the opposite direction.[22]

What is collated under the sign of psychoanalysis is inconsistent across the disciplines. Humanistic scholarship is far more interested in psychoanalysis as a genealogy of interpretative practice originating in Freud than is work in the social sciences, where psychology is itself a fully formed discipline whose analytical priorities favor other traditions of clinical practice, most prominently those focused on behavior and cognition. To a great extent and for reasons that go well beyond my brief explanation, it is humanistic inquiry that keeps alive the interpretative legacy of Freud and his heirs by engaging psychoanalysis as a specific historical and theoretical discourse. The disciplinary divisions described here—humanistic psychoanalysis on one hand and social scientific psychology on the other— have made it difficult for interdisciplinary traffic, as the two frameworks harbor vastly different understandings of subjectivity, psyche, affect, the individual, and the social. Recently, Antonio Viego has traced the path of these disciplinary divisions as they have shaped conceptions of racialization and racialized subjectivity in Ethnic Studies. Crafted as a protest against the rejection not just of psychoanalysis but of Lacanian psychoanalysis, Viego's book, *Dead Subjects*, takes aim at the long-standing dominance of ego psychology in the twentieth century and its repeated assimilation (often in the guise of antiracism) of racialized subjects to a fully socialized and idealized "conscious" subjectivity, a subject divided not within herself but against a social world whose exclusion she must seek to

---

22. In "Global Identities," Inderpal Grewal and Caren Kaplan write, "We want to argue that the study of sexuality in a transnational frame must be detached from psychoanalysis as a primary method in order to resist the universalization of the Western body as sexual difference. Psychoanalysis is a powerful interpretive tool, but it has become a form of biomedicine and cannot be utilized in ignorance of its own power structures" (667–68). Other scholarship that considers the transnational formation of sexuality routes much of its inquiry through a rethinking of both psychoanalysis and the psychic. See especially Eng and Kazanjian, "Introduction: Mourning Remains"; Eng and Han, "A Dialogue on Racial Melancholia"; and Muñoz, *Disidentifications*.

master.[23] Beginning his study by reading documents on the treatment of mental illness in African Americans in the nineteenth century, in which doctors were surprised to "discover" that these patients had (literal) dreams, Viego elaborates a much longer story about the complexity of conceptualizing racialized subjects as fully human—which in Lacanian terms means as subjects formed in language, shaped by unconscious life. For him, it is the disavowal of the workings of the unconscious and of language that continues today to condemn racialized subjects to the not-yet or almost human.

Readers of *Dead Subjects* will be surprised and some, no doubt, will be irritated by the reclamation of Lacan for race and ethnic studies, given how little Lacan set his gaze directly on the issue of racialization.[24] But for those immune to the lure of siding for or against Lacan, Viego's challenge to the epistemic equations made within the field imaginary of identity knowledges is as timely as it is courageous, as he asks practitioners to forgo the pleasure of desiring a subject who can fully know, not just herself but the conditions of her own and the world's making. While I carry no brief for Lacan, I think it possible to say that Viego and I share a commitment to

23. See Viego, *Dead Subjects*. For a general sense of the different disciplinary dispensations shaping *race* as an analytic in Latino Studies, see Darder and Torres, "Mapping Latino Studies"; Lugones and Price, "The Inseparability of Race, Class, and Gender in Latino Studies"; and Viego, "The Unconscious of Latino/a Studies."

24. The critical challenge of *Dead Subjects* lies precisely in Viego's appropriation of a theory that fails to attend to racialization to theorize race. In doing so he challenges a certain expectation in identity knowledges that inattention to racialization is a tacit subordination of race, if not the condition on which white supremacy is founded and forwarded. But the double bind for contemporary critics is that the signifying value of race is overdetermined simultaneously by hypervisibility and invisibility—by both presence and absence. Hence work on "race" that aligns it solely with the racialized subject always risks reproducing the elision between race and racialized bodies that inaugurates the analytic pursuit of race, while work that eschews either the racialized subject or the direct address to race risks being read as a continued investment in white universalism. In the process, as I discuss in chapter 3, the minoritized racial subject keeps returning in critical practices as the figure required to signify antiracist political commitments. Toni Morrison's *Playing in the Dark* evokes some of the complexity at stake here in its demonstration of the ways in which canonical U.S. literature reflects a discourse of racialization precisely through the absence of one, while that absence is figured as the haunting specter of an "Africanist presence." For a genealogical account of the dynamic of visibility in U.S. discourses of embodiment, see my *American Anatomies*.

interrupting projects that not only fantasize the subject's liberation into autonomy and coherent self-production but imagine the possibility of doing so as the singular goal of interpretative practice as a whole. Perhaps this is why I am drawn to psychoanalysis as an idiom for considering the relational practices of knowledge production, because in the very form of its practice lies a commitment I share not to the analyst's expert ability to discover the "truth" of the subject or to shore up the subject's "own" truth but to the relational encounter itself, without which there is little that interests me. If this relationality is structurally artificial—manufactured as it is by enormous expense—the practice it proposes nonetheless insists that that there can be no self-production without others. (From this perspective, it is truly strange to consider the repeated critique that psychoanalysis is fundamentally a privatizing, individualist, and antisocial form.) Indeed, what compels me toward psychoanalysis is the relational practice that generates it. This means, paradoxically, that what is most important for me is not its interpretative acumen or analytical validity but its "inspiration," as Leo Bersani has put it, "for modes of exchange that can only take place outside of psychoanalysis."[25] *Outside of psychoanalysis* is the space of all kinds of complex, rewarding, and unnerving encounters, including those that have no overt traffic with psychoanalysis as such. In the chapters of this book, it is the inspiration of psychoanalysis that I most consistently follow as I read identity knowledges in relational terms, repeatedly sacrificing psychoanalysis per se "for the sake," in Bersani's words, "of its most invaluable lesson."[26]

My hope is that readers will follow me there, insinuating themselves into the relationships that *Object Lessons* describes, analyzes, and performs without feeling deprived that there is no systematic rendering of the scholarly content, theoretical scope, or national practice of U.S. identity knowledges waiting for them at the end. What I offer instead is a series of critical encounters, a kind of stage setting or, better yet, scene making: with a variety of identity objects of study (women, whiteness, "America," sex), analytic practices (gender, race, intersectionality, the queer theoretic), and fields of study (American Studies, Whiteness Studies, Women's Studies, Queer Studies, Ethnic Studies), along with considerable attention to the

25. Bersani and Phillips, "The It in the I," 4.
26. Bersani and Phillips, "The It in the I," 4.

emergent aspirations of the transnational, international, and global that might be said to characterize the humanities and interpretative social sciences in the new century as a whole. In doing so, I hope that readers will become interested in the resonances as much as the contradictions that arise between what I say and what they want, such that the object lessons that attend this project multiply not only from your identificatory refusals but from the investments and insistences that make you feel most secure. The conversations in each of the following chapters are offered in this context, as a provocation to be sure, but also as a constitutive recognition: these words have no meaning without you.

Inhabitations

How, then, does one study a field imaginary? Where is it to be found? On what critical terrain can it be convincingly deciphered? These questions are not easily answered, which is why the best approach comes in offering a deeper description of what is at stake in reading *Object Lessons* as a whole. The book begins with "Doing Justice with Objects (Or, the 'Progress' of Gender)," which uses the battle between *women* and *gender* as the keyword for naming feminist field domains in order to explore the congested terrain of representation that identity fields so often configure.[27] By reconstructing

27. Other identity-based fields have not been quite as riven as Women's—and now Gender—Studies by the crisis of their self-nomination, though there has been considerable debate across all of the fields that concern me about their primary object of study and its status in generating the research agendas of field domains. In American Studies, the debate has collated around the audacity of using "American" as a signifier for North America alone and especially for the United States (see especially Radway, "'What's in a Name?'"). In African American Studies, scholars have taken up the transnational turn through the primary critical rubric of diaspora, paying attention to the uneven development of the study of the African diaspora across the institutional fields that comprise it. Tina Campt and Deborah Thomas's ongoing project on "diasporic hegemonies" attends to the overlapping intellectual agendas of African American, Afro-Caribbean, African, and Black European Studies. In their introduction to a special issue of *Feminist Review* on the topic, they describe how "the dominance of US-based cultural and intellectual discourses on diasporic relations, origin stories, and authenticity narratives can privilege paradigms that stress community solidarity at the expense of analytic attention to key differences within and among populations that might be understood as diasporic" (3). See Campt and Thomas, "Editorial: Gendering Diaspora." See also Hartman, *Lose Your*

a genealogy of the process through which *women* and *gender* have lost their mutual referentiality, I am interested in the "progress" now attributed to the differences they stand for, such that *gender* is taken to bear none of the faults that have accrued to *women*. In this story of disappointing love objects and optimistic new ones, it becomes possible to discern certain core beliefs that structure the field imaginary, including two of the most powerful ones: first, that justice is best served by stitching field domain and object of analysis into representational coherence and, second, that the critical utility of an object of study is born in its commensurability with the political desire invested in it. My chapter takes shape around the supposition that commensurability is an impossibility, in part because political desire is always excessive—excessive to the conditions, imaginations, and objects that are used to represent it. Hence I structure the chapter around the simple prediction that *gender*, like *women*, will come to fail. What category will replace it? I end by deliberating on one likely heir, *women of color*, and the challenge the transnational now presents to scholars hoping to sustain their belief in the political capacity of an analytic investment. By explicating the convergentist and realist representational demands that attend the field imaginary of Women's Studies, "Doing Justice" examines the field-generating belief that an object of study materializes both the worldly referent it is used to name and the political desire that wields it for change.

In the second chapter, I approach the justice-object relation by thinking more directly about time, as a progress narrative is nothing if not a temporal emplotment. It is one of modernity's surest ways of convincing its subjects that the future can be grasped with conscious intention.[28] This is

---

Mother. In counterpoint, a major conference in 2004 at the University of Illinois, Beyond a Boundary: Area, Ethnic/Race and Gender Studies and the "New" Global Imperative, highlighted the concern that U.S. Ethnic Studies was losing both institutional support and intellectual priority in the shift from national to transnational and global frameworks.

28. Even in those venues of identity studies most absorbed in antihumanist traditions, it is difficult to pretend that the future's security is not the resonant goal—Lee Edelman's *No Future* being the stunning objection that might be said to confirm the rule. See Edelman's various attempts to demonstrate why queer critique should refuse a politics of progression: *No Future*, "Antagonism, Negativity, and the Subject of Queer Theory," and "Ever After." Other takes on the question of the future include: Ahmed, *The Promise of Happiness*, especially 160–61; Halberstam, "The Anti-social Turn in Queer

not to say that critical practices devoted to the future's transformation are merely complicit with modernity, as if there is some space from which we can think beyond the historical embeddedness that such an accusation disdainfully glosses. *Object Lessons* expends no energy on such "exposure," pursuing instead the claim that there is no objective outside from which to assess what we can know. In "Telling Time (When Feminism and Queer Theory Diverge)," I take up the question—to be developed across the chapters of the book—of what it means to say that all our thinking and speaking comes from *within* by considering the different temporalities within which identity knowledges speak, not simply to the disciplines but to one another and to the public sphere in which their claims to do justice are routinely aimed. My main concern is to differentiate social movements from the institutionalized projects founded in their names in order to appreciate their incommensurabilities as political projects, social phenomena, interpellative forms, and historical entities. The chapter is organized as a response to Ian Halley's polemical argument that in order to have a pro-sex, shame-affirmative queer theoretic, critics must "take a break from feminism"—that is, refuse the convergentist thinking that would insist that every analysis of sexuality serves as a cogent analysis of gender as well. By siding with Ian's call for divergence, I explicate the nonequivalence between his two key opponents—feminism and queer theory—in order to consider how divergence is not simply central to the process of institutionalization but definitive, indeed constitutive, of it. The pedagogical force of this point refracts across *Object Lessons* in numerous ways, as convergence is a primary syntax in the field imaginary of identity knowledges, underlying both the demand that an object of study be commensurate with the political desire that calls it forth and the attendant assumption that critical practice is an act of justice. By considering divergence as foundational to the migration of identity from its orientations in social movements to its generation of academic knowledge forms, I trace the multiple transformations in identity's critical and affective operations that accompany its academic sojourn. In the end, I argue that Halley does not take divergence far enough, which would require situating the contestations between feminism and queer theory in their different temporalities and affects from the start.

Studies"; and Muñoz, "Thinking beyond Antirelationality and Antiutopianism in Queer Critique" and *Cruising Utopia*.

Read together, the first two chapters offer a meditation on the work of identification as central to identity's academic knowledge production. In the opening chapter on the progress of *gender*, identification is the disciplinary force that weds field domain and object of study into representational coherence, with justice being the effect of methods and interpretative practices that conform to the field imaginary's primary disciplinary demand. This is a convergentist project, in which the political commitment that generates the field imaginary is demonstrated by pursuing coherence, synchronicity, inclusion, and equivalence between the objects, analytics, and methods it institutionally arrays. In the second chapter, identification works not through an affective or rhetorical convergence of social movement with academic knowledge production but on the grounds of attachments that live on this side of institutionalization where posthumanist critiques of representation and agency have generative authority in the anti-integrationist field imaginary of queer theory. This project is aimed at privileging asynchronicity, nonequivalence, incommensurability, and irreducible difference in order to wed critical practice to the political aspirations that attend it. In each of these cases, which speak to the disjunctive temporalities at work within identity knowledge domains, the field imaginary is staked to identificatory grounds, as good and bad objects abound to navigate the relationship between critical practice and social justice. While Ian resists identifying with feminism's convergentist agenda, his queer theoretic invests nonetheless in the field imaginary's golden rule: that objects and analytics of study can be made to deliver everything we want from them.

But what about the function of disidentification in generating identification's allure? After all, *gender*'s critical promise is secured by mobilizing disidentifications with *women* just as the demand to take a break from feminism serves as precondition for igniting the queer theoretic's political ambition. The third and fourth chapters of *Object Lessons* plumb this aspect of identity's object relations by considering the structure and affect of refusing identification with the figure that founds the field, as in Whiteness Studies and American Studies. In both cases, the field domain is oversaturated by the geopolitical power of its primary object of study, requiring various kinds of critical strategies to answer the call for justice. In "The Political Conscious (Whiteness Studies and the Paradox of Particularity)," I explore the optimistic claim that making whiteness an object of study undermines the disembodied universalism on which white supremacy in

Western modernity depends. Through various readings of white particularity in critical and popular discourses alike, the chapter argues against the assumption that white supremacy operates through universalism alone in order to make sense of the elasticity of white power as a transforming historical form. One of my main points here is that white disaffiliation from white supremacy in its segregationist formation *is* the hegemonic configuration of white supremacy in the post–Civil Rights multiculturalist era—a point that Whiteness Studies must subordinate in order to establish disidentification as the strategic mechanism of white antiracism. Such disidentification banks enormously on the status of white self-consciousness and hence on consciousness itself as an antiracist political instrument. But the idealism that Whiteness Studies bestows on knowing and on a fully conscious subject reiterates the constitution of the humanist subject whose white particularity is submerged by the universalizing dictates of white privilege that travel under the guise of rational man. The "paradox" in the chapter's title has to do, then, with the problem of making consciousness the centerpiece of a project aimed at undoing the very subject whose privileged consciousness is the universalized condition of whiteness under Western epistemological rule. The massive hope invested in a white subject who can produce the right kind of agency to bring down his own political overordination is surely inspiring, but it hardly predicts a future in which white-on-white preoccupations are deferred.

As many readers know, Whiteness Studies faltered quite quickly on the contradictory entanglements of its own political aspirations, as seeking to dismantle the power that an object of study holds in the world by refusing identification with it is no easy feat, especially when a field bears the name of the entity it seeks to oppose and the power the object holds clearly exceeds one's critical identification with it. Add to this the sheer fact that dismantling the iconic status of a critical object is a far cry from dismantling the geopolitical power the object stands for, and one can see how genuinely vexed is the deconstructivist move to attend with rigor to the master term. It might even be harder than trying to collate power for an object of study that is routinely subordinated in the regimes of everyday life since the very act of paying attention to it confers value. In chapter 4, "Refusing Identification (Americanist Pursuits of Global Noncomplicity)," I consider these issues in the context of American Studies where the current critical demand to internationalize the field is bent toward securing a perspective uncontaminated not only by the global authority the object wields but by the critical priorities that dominate its practice in the United States. Djelal Kadir calls these practices "American American Studies," which I contextualize less disparagingly as the New American Studies, whose investments in disentangling critical practice from imperial complicities have already been traced through my explication of the concept of a field imaginary above. By exploring how internationalization tropes the discourse of the "outside" that is central to New American Studies, my chapter argues that internationalist proclamations participate in the same field imaginary that their identificatory refusals otherwise condemn. This argument is not made in order to relish the grand ah-ha, as if learning how to expose someone else's implication in what they protest is an inoculation against revealing my own. I'm more interested in the critical force of the charge and the assurance it routinely delivers that critics are not only in control of their object attachments but that what we say about them is the surest truth of what they mean. The point here is that objects of study are bound to multiple relationships, such that the conscious attempt to refuse an identification is in no way a guarantee that one can, let alone that one has done so.

In the fifth chapter, "Critical Kinship (Universal Aspirations and Intersectional Judgements)," I move the conversation about the ideal of noncomplicity and the critic's avowedly conscious intentions to the terrain of intersectional investments in order to consider one of the major lessons the project of this book has taught me: that objects can resist what we try to make of them. The chapter focuses initially on a fascinating case involving a fertility clinic mistake and the two couples—one black, one white—who seek legal custody of the same child. The juridical setting of the story is germane to the itinerary of the chapter, as it is the link between this case and the centrality of "the case study" in intersectional theory that allows me to plot the juridical imaginary that intersectionality relies upon and the consequences of this for feminist commitments to the study of race and gender. Crenshaw's inaugural work on intersectionality was chiefly concerned with employment discrimination and violence against black women, whose "intersectional identity as both women *and* of color" engendered their dual marginalization "within both" feminist and antiracist discourses.[29] In recent years, intersectionality has been given a life of its

29. Crenshaw, "Mapping the Margins," 1244.

own, becoming an imperative to attend evenly and adequately to identity's composite whole: race, ethnicity, gender, sexuality, class, nation, religion, and increasingly age and ability. Such an insistence builds on Crenshaw's own concern for political and legal amelioration and seeks to forge not only analytic bridges but convergences between the political projects engaged by identity politics and the academic domains they name.

The case that I bring to the conversation features a white woman who gives birth to a black child whose embryo was not her own. While feminist scholarship has routinely sided with the birth mother in disputes arising from reproductive technologies, often by claiming it as an antiracist position, my discussion situates the case in the historical context of white racial theft of black reproduction, where it is hardly an easy decision to privilege gestational labor—but just as difficult, I contend, not to do so when one considers the way that prioritizing genetics risks reinscribing essentialist understandings of both race and kinship. By reflecting on the way race and gender are incoherently arrayed in the case, such that adjudicating the dispute renders the analysis of its complexity woefully incomplete, the chapter approaches intersectional analysis more as a political aspiration than a methodological resolution to the multiplicities of identity that incite it. In doing so, I track the incommensurabilities that accompany its travels from, first, the specific province of law and, second, the particularity of black women's occlusion in U.S. discourses on race and gender.[30] "Critical Kinship"

30. The 2009 National Women's Studies Association conference call for papers foregrounds a familiar narrative about intersectionality as the composite figure for yoking method, theory, and politics:

> A multiracial feminist approach to gender equity and liberation necessarily begins at the intersection ... of systems of domination. Intersectionality accounts for simultaneous privilege and oppression and refuses any hierarchy of oppressions or of identity. Intersectional feminist politics are coalitional and focus on a collective approach to freedom. In the United States, what we now call an "intersectional" model of feminist analysis and politics has a long trajectory: a complex genealogy of intersectionality as concept and practice can be traced among women of color feminisms in particular. Yet, has W[omen's] S[tudies] changed enough? Is there still a tendency toward gender universals? Are there still claims that intersectionality isn't viable or that one can't "do it all" or "account for everything" without being incoherent? Whose notions of coherence and incoherence hold sway in the field of WS? (www.nwsaconference.org/cms/sites/default/files/NWSA_CFP2009.pdf)

thus mediates on the conundrum that the fertility clinic's mistake raises for intersectional inquiries, adding a third category to the important work done by Eve Sedgwick on paranoid and reparative readings: paradigmatic.[31] For it is in the context of its own attachment to paradigmatic reading that intersectional analysis stages its commitment to justice—as if the imbrications of race and gender actually conform to juridical logic, such that knowing which side to take in one case can serve as the precedent for knowing which side to take in every case. In thinking about the problems generated by paradigmatic reading, this chapter explores not only the cost to feminist theory and to the complexity of "black women's experience" of rendering social life through the instrumental reasoning of juridical form, but the security that this relationship to the object of study affords through the guarantee that it promises to deliver: that the object of study, once named, will always be the same. Interpellated now into the field imaginary on intersectionality's own terms, "black women's experience" is interestingly disciplined by the normative account that has come to describe it— disciplined, that is, in order to be made legible for political amelioration by the reading that intersectionality performs.

Such an inquiry into the disciplinary force of political commitment is foregrounded throughout *Object Lessons* by a studied attention to the field imaginary and its distribution of knowing subjects and their variously coveted, condemned, or refused objects of study. In the final chapter, "The Vertigo of Critique: Rethinking Heteronormativity," I continue this dis-

---

By associating hegemonic feminism with resistance to intersectionality, the conference call reiterates the belief that intersectionality always works in favor of the complexity and political interests of women of color. This is a disciplinary operation: it consigns women of color to a distinct critical position from which they can claim speech in the field while expending no worry over its own generic representation of them. In these terms, one could not be both a woman of color and a critic of intersectional "coherence." Chapter 5 explores in greater detail the paradigmatic reading protocols forwarded by intersectional imperatives.

31. See Sedgwick, "Paranoid Reading and Reparative Reading." It was not until late in the process of finishing this book that I returned to this amazing essay. While I remembered reading it, I had no idea how much it had influenced me. *Object Lessons* follows Sedgwick's call for a reparative reading practice by trying to overcome the paranoid impulse to ward off pain by projecting it everywhere in favor of cultivating—perhaps even beholding—other relations to objects. As is often the case, the force of a lesson can live a long time before we recognize it.

cussion by considering the way that the shape of a question produces the answer it seeks and what happens to critique when the authority of the question is undone. The chapter began as an abstract for a conference presentation on queer cultural investments in gender transitivity. My original intention was to track how *sex* as the defining object of study for queer scholarship had been eclipsed by the proliferation of *gender* in order to contribute a queer theoretical approach to the conference focus on heternormativity. In the context of "Doing Justice with Objects," this was the story of *gender*'s ascendency from the other direction, where it was amassing enormous authority to reconfigure queer cultural and theoretical agendas—a story that the focus on its sojourn through feminist contexts tended to elide. But as I pursued the topic, I grew increasingly distracted by my own founding assumptions. What after all was "queer culture" and why did I assume that a commitment to gender's transitivity belonged to queer culture alone? Or more to the point, why was I so willing to repeat the belief that *to be against* heteronormativity was *to be for* gender's transitivity, as if the heteronormative could have no investment in gender's transitivity as well? Where did this equation between gender transitivity and antinormativity come from? Was it a historicist reading of gender, a de-biologizing one, or a political one? Or was the equation the consequence of a political commitment that mistook the questions it posed as a materialist reading of the social formation as a whole? These matters made it impossible to write the talk I had promised, propelling me instead into considering this: that the gesture of citing one's queer disidentification with normativity was itself a disciplinary norm, the very position from which practitioners could assume that their critical practice was unquestionably queer.

In a certain sense, "The Vertigo of Critique" is the affective center of *Object Lessons*, if not one of its key starting points, as each chapter grapples in one way or another with the core assumption that critique has taught me: that critical practice is a political counter to normalizing agencies of every kind.[32] Whether in the mode of dialectical materialism, deconstruction,

32. The concept of critique travels in multiple critical traditions, being deployed variously as an epistemology, rhetorical form, or mode of politics. In *Object Lessons*, I am less interested in parsing these distinctions than in exploring the affective and rhetorical work that critique performs as the reigning critical discourse of political commitment in the humanities and interpretative social sciences. On the critical history of critique, see Michel Foucault, "What Is Critique?"; Michael Hardt, "The Militancy of Theory"; Talal

feminist standpoint, critical race, or queer reading, critique has been alluring because of the promise it makes, which is that through the routes and rhetorics of knowledge production we can travel the distance from speculation to truth, from desire to political comprehension, from wanting a different social world to having the faith that we can make it so. To be sure, critique can also be repetitious and exhausting, self-congratulatory and self-absorbed, but the narcissism it cultivates is nothing if not thrilling. Even when cloaked in skepticism, it allows us to proceed as if we are right.[33] How can I not want everything that it aims to make true? The book in your hands is a meditation on this question. It both reflects and refracts the history of my own reliance on the practices and procedures of critique and the various ways in which the authority it offers has come to unsettle me. As readers will see, I now worry over its repetitions and prohibitions, find myself estranged by its pace, and am unnerved by what it chooses not to question, know, or love. Most of all, I long to linger in the spaces of what it insists is done. *Object Lessons* is not an argument against critique as much as an encounter with its excessive reach. It records my growing interest in questioning left political desire for critical practice to rescue us from . . . well . . . nearly everything, including the very complexity of identity as it moves incongruently and unevenly across analytic, social, psychic, affective, and historical terrains. It seems strange to say this, but critique has come to haunt me because it promises to deliver too much.

Asad, et al., *Is Critique Secular?*; and Judith Butler, "What Is Critique?" and "Non-Thinking in the Name of the Normative."

33. For those of us raised on postmodern understandings of the contingency of knowledge and truth, it is hard to argue with the growing assessment that the skeptical stance of *knowing that we cannot know* is itself a positive investment in knowing nonetheless. My sense is that the so-called postmodern turn has not so much diluted the force of knowledge's explanatory function as marked a shift in the language in which the operations of the social are conceived—I am thinking especially of the shift away from the overtly scientized language of "systems of oppression" toward the now ubiquitous and systematic postulation of "norms" and "normativities" that characterizes so much of academic left critique. Indeed, there is no dearth of evidence—as all of the chapters here demonstrate in one way or another—to support the contention that even in its postmodern posture, academic left critique continues to engage knowledge as the agency of its political function and to prioritize theory as the domain of proper political knowledge aimed at social change. This last point is one explored in depth by Kirstie McClure in her important but too often ignored essay, "The Issue of Foundations."

Object Lessons is not, then, a critique. It is not even a critique of critique.

It is not an intervention. I am not trying to make us conscious of critical habits so that we can change them.

It is not an argument against other arguments, nor a dismissal of what others have said or done.

It is not a new theory. It offers no new objects or analytics of study.

It is an inhabitation of the world-making stakes of identity knowledges and the field imaginary that sutures us to them—a performance, in other words, of the risk and reward, the amnesia and optimism, and the fear and pleasure sustained by living with and within them.

ONE

....

Doing Justice with Objects

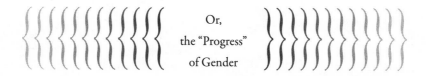

Or,
the "Progress"
of Gender

In the beginning, the most familiar version of the story goes, identity entered U.S. institutions of higher education as a palpable value for democratic life, inaugurating new practices of public access and accountability, and cultivating both new objects of study and the interdisciplinary fields that would be singularly devoted to them. In identity's most heroic scene, usually set in the late 1970s, the hierarchies of wealth, sex, and color were tacitly exposed as students and scholars sought to close the gap between the state and its citizens, institutions and the communities they were said to serve, and democracy and the incipient violences of capitalism. In time, identity's institutional and intellectual capacities were sorely blunted; diversity diverted its political attentions toward student services and development; multiculturalism upended differences by making them all seem the same; and the transatlantic critique of the subject challenged its sovereign investments. To be sure, this quick glimpse of identity's position in the political economy of the always receding historical present underestimates the complexity of its historical sojourn and the very intense battles in the United States in the past century over its public, private, and academic utility alike—just as it fails to account for the fact that what is often referred to as "identity politics" was rarely recognized as such by those who have been given credit for inaugurating it. But the sweep of the story has a point, less about the actual substance of historical change or our ability to track it than about the affect that might symptomatically register it in the present. So much of what matters to me about identity knowledges emerges here, in the felt discordance between the political possibility that identity represents and the fear of what it has become, which is to say the discordance between what we have invested in it and how it might live in the world on terms not wholly—sometimes not even approximately—our own.

Elsewhere I will pay attention to the issue that hovers in the background, where political optimism is rocked by its encounter with the contingency of historical transformation, underscoring the extent to which the materials available for identity knowledges to think with and through—concepts, languages, disciplines, rhetorics, social practices, and cultural forms—have no fixed political essence, which means that they are not immune to becoming something other than what we want from them. For now, however, I want simply to set the stage for the various inquiries in this book by considering the shape, force, and consequences of the political commitment that underwrites identity's academic sojourn and serves as the distinguishing disciplinary characteristic of the various fields collated in its name. My primary example in this chapter is Women's Studies and the political commitment that institutionalizes its disciplinary formation, thereby determining its object and analytic dispositions, methodological priorities, rhetorical forms, and the field-forming narratives that accompany and frame them—all in a complex and at times anxiety-ridden calculus that confers (or withholds) critical authority and belonging in the field. To talk about identity knowledges as disciplinary formations is to find oneself immediately violating their first and most insistent rule, which takes their inaugurating commitment to justice as the means to overcome the distance, if not the distinction, between social movements and the institutionalized domains of study that seek to politically nurture them. Under this rule, the institutionalized object of study is the political referent it stands for, which is why identity knowledges so often seek to explicate their referent's historical and social itineraries in order to practice doing justice to and for them. My aim in *Object Lessons* is not to challenge this disciplinarity or to reorient the critical apparatus that sustains it, but to explore the ways in which its political promises are engaged and performed. Indeed, my point throughout is that such disciplinarity is absolutely alluring, as the political agency it confers on objects and analytics of study forwards the deeply satisfying belief that critical practice is the terrain of political resolution itself.

In this chapter, I consider these issues by following the discourse of justice that attends one identity object of study—*women*—whose well-rehearsed failure to remain conceptually coherent and universally referential for *all* women within the field domain of Women's Studies has inaugurated a turn toward a host of new investments organized increasingly under the sign of *gender*. While many academic feminists of my generation remember when *gender* was a synonym for women, the term has come to collate much of what the category of *women* is said to exclude: from men, masculinity, and queer sexualities to trans and intersex identities and analysis.[1] Hence, one now encounters *gender* as a means both to

---

1. Let me highlight what I take to be the most important critical and historical conditions on which the intelligibility of *gender* as an increasingly capacious term might be said to rest. The first is theoretical, as *gender*'s proliferating referentiality has been aided by deconstructive approaches to the regulatory regime of sex, sexuality, and gender. No text is more famous on this score than Judith Butler's *Gender Trouble: Feminism and the Subversion of Identity*, which argued that while the idea of a male or female body served as gender's seemingly neutral sexed referent, it could only do so as a consequence of the ideological structure of sexual difference that gender names. Hence, "sex itself is a gendered category," Butler wrote, thereby defining "sex" not as gender's necessary precondition, but as one of gender's most powerful effects (7). Second is the disciplinary disposition that underwrites and follows this theoretical turn, as the revolution that Butler now represents reveals an increasing tension within U.S. academic feminist discourses over the value of interpretative and empirical knowledges. While the social sciences have long been invested in antiessentialist understandings of gender—so much so that any credit accorded the humanities as the origin of social constructionist theory is simply an error in the history of knowledge—their deepest interest has been tied to explicating social formation. With the growing domination of the humanities, social constructionist theory has largely been transformed into a postepistemological project focusing primarily on subject constitution. Implicit in the progress narrative that grants *gender* a range of new significations, then, is its migration from social scientific understandings of antiessentialism to its analytic expansion in postmodern genealogies of humanistic thought.

The third and fourth conditions reverse the relations of expansion and resignification that underwrite the two delineated above by cordoning off arenas of interrogation that could otherwise be said to undermine *gender*'s proliferating purview. I will gloss

describe the constraints of heteropatriarchal social formation and to figure subversion, disidentification, and dissidence in identity attachments and everyday life. It operates as a coordinate for approaching the complexities of social subordination (classic intersectionality) and as an analytic for unraveling a wide range of discursive, economic, and geopolitical processes. It functions as well to denote emergent identities and is implicated in, if not central to, the practices and politics of contemporary social movements of various kinds. In serving as a referent for a range of objects of study and analytic practices, as well as the subjects that might be said to mirror them, *gender* performs the optimistic hope that a relation of compatibility, if not

---

these as the biological and the posthuman, respectively. In the case of the former, one might remember that the academic publishing industry positively exploded in the 1990s with "body studies," and yet while the body was everywhere, its biology, which I take from Elizabeth A. Wilson as conceptually separate from human agency or conscious discernment, was theoretically mute. In the recent return to considerations of the body that reject theories of the discursive, it is not at all clear that *gender* will be a significant term (see especially Wilson, "Gut Feminism"). In much the same way, it is difficult to assess how far *gender*'s analytic capacities can be stretched in conversations that collate a broad range of post-humanist questions, including speciesism, animal ethics, and environmental studies. To be sure, all of these arenas are impacted by gender and most have been studied within familiar feminist frameworks. But a thoroughgoing critique will undoubtedly raise challenging questions, the most pressing of which concerns humanism's colonization of the province and practice of both politics and knowledge production within Women's and Gender Studies as we have known them.

Finally, it seems to me that *gender*'s proliferating capacity to house divergent projects has been conditioned by the itineraries through which identity knowledges have traversed the U.S. university, making it important to say that the story I am here tracking is not a universalizing one. In Eastern Europe, for instance, the rise of Gender Studies, funded by the postsocialist state or by Western foundations, heralds a much different political imaginary for the field than its deployment in a liberal democracy keen on memorializing its own history of political dissent as part of the exceptionalist discourse of U.S. empire. Indeed, a different discussion would be in order to understand the legibility of both *gender* and Gender Studies in other world regions, one that would plot how and when *gender* might mute the politicization of discourses on women, how and when it might signal state power instead of indigenous feminist desires, and on what geopolitical and economic terms it might become an area of study at all. The fifth condition, then, is simply that the progress of *gender* under examination in this chapter has no global itinerary and it is necessary to resist any impulse to give it one.

consistency, between critical practice and field domain can (finally) be won. My subtitle, "The 'Progress' of Gender," is meant to foreground the temporal and aspirational aspects of these far-reaching field transformations and to focus attention on the transferential idealism that underwrites *gender*'s refashioning as politically progressive precisely where *women* is not—as a means for achieving representational inclusion, historical precision, subjective complexity, social reparation, and theoretical sophistication. Such transferential practices promise to move the field toward critical coherence and political completion, now in the turn from *women* to *gender* and soon, no doubt, from *gender* to whatever will come to signify the ways in which it will have failed. Intersectionality perhaps? Or *women of color* or transnational feminism? (I'll take up the inevitability of the afterlife of *gender* at this chapter's end.) Above all, it is this practice of transference that interests me, as it makes legible the ways in which the disciplinary apparatus of Women's Studies stages its political desire as a representational practice, using its object and analytic relations as the institutionalized means for performing the commitment to justice that incites it.

Gender is not alone, of course, in being the occasion for object transference, nor is it the only category that collates optimism in identity-oriented fields today. Think here of *queer* in relation to Gay and Lesbian Studies, or *trans* in relation to queer, or *diaspora* in relation to both Ethnic and Queer Studies. Or consider how other terms—interdisciplinarity say— are routinely heralded as figures of political no less than critical progress. But while *gender* is not exceptional, its wide-reaching agency in field transformation in Women's Studies makes it an important case study for examining the imperative to do justice that has structured U.S. academic identity domains from their institutional beginnings. Indeed, no other term has so extensively revised the self-identity of an identity-based field, remapping what is taken to be its critical mission and the meaning of the concepts that attend it. At numerous institutions, *gender* now stands as the singular figure evoking the field domain, as in Gender Studies (Indiana University) or Critical Gender Studies (University of California–San Diego). At other institutions, it figures cohabitation, as in Gender and Women's Studies (Berkeley), Women and Gender Studies (UC-Davis), and Women's and Gender Studies (Rutgers University). At still others, it instigates a trilogy, as in Women, Gender, and Sexuality Studies (Trinity College) or Women's, Gender, and Sexuality Studies

(Colby College).[2] All of these configurations mark a decisive difference between terms that were once decisively converged, making the progress of *gender* the means to reflect not simply on the analytic divergences that have animated *gender*'s development as both a category of analysis and an object of study in the past three decades but on the political investments that have propelled the resignifying project altogether—investments that enable the field's name to serve as the privileged arena for staging and resolving anxieties over its political coherence.

The path my conversation traces is this one: I begin by looking closely at *gender* as a progress narrative in order to discern the practices of transference that underwrite its portability across a range of differently situated critical projects. By foregrounding the work of transference, I explore the field imaginary in which *gender* has emerged as the privileged supplement, if not the collectivizing sign, for political attachment in the afterlife of *women*.[3] My project is not to hold onto *women* or to revel in its loss, but to

2. The landscape of the name change is quickly evolving, but at the point of this book's publication, one could find the following configurations. *Women and Gender Studies*: Bates College, Grand Valley State University, Sweet Briar College, and University of Virginia; *Women's and Gender Studies*: Amherst College, Bucknell University, Carleton College, Dartmouth College, DePaul University, Eckerd College, Furman University, Kenyon College, Louisiana State University, MIT, North Carolina State University, Sonoma State University, Rutgers University, and University of Texas; *Gender and Women's Studies*: Connecticut College, Scripps College, University of California–Berkeley, and University of Illinois–Chicago; *Women's, Gender, and Sexuality Studies*: American University, Colby College, Miami University, Macalester College, and Yale University; *Women, Gender, and Sexuality Studies*: Harvard University, Johns Hopkins University, Rice University, and Trinity College; *Gender Studies*: Austin College, University of Chicago, Eastern Oregon University, Indiana University, Lawrence University, Lewis and Clark University, Mount Union College, Missouri State University, College of St. Benedict, College of California, University of Arkansas, University of Notre Dame, University of Utah, Valparaiso University, Wabash College, and Whitman College; *Gender and Sexuality Studies*: Brown University, Bryn Mawr College, Haverford College, Princeton University, and New York University; *Women's Studies/Gender Studies*: Occidental College and Pennsylvania State University–Erie; *Feminist Studies*: Southwestern University, Stanford University, and University of California–Santa Cruz; and *Comparative Women's Studies*: Spelman College.

3. To be sure, no tracking of the critical history of *gender* can possibly be complete, given its different meanings in various disciplinary and theoretical traditions. My

meditate on the implications of believing the story that the progress of *gender* imparts: not simply that *women* is an analytically singular, insular category of analysis, but that its exclusivity can be corrected by addition or substitution, such that *gender* will be capable of giving us everything that *women* does not. To what understanding of the category of *women* does this idealization of *gender* commit us? And why is U.S. academic feminism so deeply in need of believing that an object or analytic, configured properly, will be adequate to all the wishes that are invested in it? To put these questions on the critical terrain that governs *Object Lessons* as a whole: What disciplinary apparatus generates this pursuit of a representative sign to organize the many intellectual projects and critical genealogies about bodies, identities, sexuality, gender, race, and ethnic, national, and economic difference that have come to exist within the institutional domain first named Women's Studies? What critical practices and object itineraries underwrite the demand for representation, inclusion, accuracy, or identity congruence in the figure of the field's primary name? And what will we do when *gender* can no longer sustain our investment in its ability to resolve the problems that it both collates and names? These questions and the conversations they generate in the following pages are animated by my contention that objects and analytic categories are always incommensurate with the political desire invested in them, which is not an argument against objects, analytics, or the practices of identity knowledges that seek to do justice with and through them. It is rather an engagement with the disciplinary shape and force of the field imaginary that conditions and compels the disciplinary subjects *we* have become. In the end, then, this chapter is less about *gender* and its critical capacities per se than an engagement with the fascinating conundrum of political desire that generates our disciplinary commitment to doing justice with, to, and through our objects of

---

argument here is circumscribed by the rhetorical structure of the chapter I have penned, which organizes its interrogation of the progress narrative around one highly visible example, Leora Auslander's essay, "Do Women's + Feminist + Men's + Lesbian and Gay + Queer Studies = Gender Studies?" which appeared in the provocatively titled special issue of *differences* called "Women's Studies on the Edge." Other narratives about *gender*'s emergence into field-naming priority will likely have different features, but it is rare today to find one devoid of the imprint of progress. All further page notations to this essay are indicated in the text.

study and the analytics we develop to discern them. This conundrum, it seems to me, is as pleasing as it is vexed, which is why a deliberation on the promises that sustain it is well overdue.

I. Transferential Idealism

In "Women's Studies on the Edge," a special issue of *differences* published in 1999, Leora Auslander opens the volume by thinking about the composite intellectual projects that coalesce under the framework of *gender*.[4] Her essay "Do Women's + Feminist + Men's + Lesbian and Gay + Queer Studies = Gender Studies?" offers an affirmative answer to the central question its title poses, finding in the move from Women's to Gender Studies an intellectual expansion, such that "the study of masculinity, feminist gender studies, and gay, lesbian, and queer studies each have an equal voice" (25). Positioned as the volume's optimistic answer to the dystopic diagnosis in one of the concluding essays, Wendy Brown's controversial "The Impossibility of Women's Studies," Auslander's keynote offers assurance that the edge can become an intellectually cutting and politically capacious one

---

4. While the "Women's Studies on the Edge" volume was published as *differences* 9.3 (Fall 1997), it did not appear until 1999 because of press delays, which is why it occupies an especially prominent place in millennial conversations about the future of the field. Thinkers as diverse as Susan Gubar, Lynne Segal, Martha Nussbaum, Naomi Schor, Joan Wallach Scott, Ellen Messer-Davidow, and Wendy Brown all took part in this conversation. While many scholars expressed concern over the theoretic turn in academic feminism, where poststructuralism was seen as driving scholarship away from practical politics, a few (such as Brown and Scott) found failure in the circumscription of thought that an instrumentalizing understanding of politics entailed. I have read the former group as "apocalyptic" narrators who worried that feminism's future was threatened, if not already at an untimely end. The latter scholars resisted the apocalyptic formulation by refusing the demand for historical continuity. For Brown, this meant postulating the end of Women's Studies as a degree-granting entity. For Scott, it meant a willingness to inhabit the "edge" where there was no uniform way to apprehend the political past nor to guarantee the field's ability to generate a knowable feminist future. See Messer-Davidow, *Disciplining Feminism*; Schor, *Bad Objects*, ix–xvi; Brown, "The Impossibility of Women's Studies"; Gubar, "What Ails Feminist Criticism?"; Nussbaum, "The Professor of Parody"; Scott, "Introduction," to *Women's Studies on the Edge*, i–iv; Wiegman, "Feminism's Apocalyptic Futures" and "The Possibility of Women's Studies."

when *gender* reconfigures the priority of *women*. To a certain extent, the question that Auslander's essay posed was not in 1999 a contentious one, at least not in the sense that scholars would have debated whether the terms it collated represented the terrain claimed by Gender Studies or not. Indeed, while new analytic terrains were rapidly emerging at the time the essay appeared—trans and intersex being the most obvious ones—the proposition that *gender* was the functional category for designating a wide array of object and analytic investments was increasingly routine. The more pressing issue had to do with what this meant for the future of the field, in terms of both its political identity and the intellectual priorities that would be cultivated to sustain it. For some scholars, such as Shirley Yee and Mary Evans, the nomination of Gender Studies was an incorporation of women that could likely engender their displacement; certainly, in Yee's terms, it could function to marginalize feminist methods and interpretative practices and to erase the hard-won visibility of both scholars of color and scholarship on women of color.[5] As Yee writes in her own contribution to "Women's Studies on the Edge," "Scholarship that has interrogated 'women' has enabled scholars to see the category as a window for examining interlocking systems of power and inequality as well as giving voice to historically marginalized groups."[6] While gender for Yee is analytically important, the turn to it as the means to rename the field threatens to undermine the ways in which "The 'Women' in Women's Studies," to quote her essay's title, collates a history of struggle over differences among women.

The story Auslander tells is not bound, however, to the dilemma of the 1990s over the name change, in part because the Center for Gender Studies at the University of Chicago never supplanted a Women's Studies program. Indeed, in 1995 when the center was founded there were no identity studies programs at the university at all, though faculty had been teaching courses and organizing workshops on identity objects and analytics for a

---

5. Yee, "The 'Women' in Women's Studies"; and Evans, "The Problem of Gender for Women's Studies."

6. Yee, "The 'Women' in Women's Studies," 54. Interestingly, Yee's treatment of the question was not included in the book version of *Women's Studies on the Edge*, ed. Joan Wallach Scott. Several new essays, however, were added to the collection, including Gayle Salamon, "Transfeminism and the Future of Gender," and Saba Mahmood, "Feminism, Democracy, and Empire," thereby foregrounding transgender and transnational analytics as emergent political priorities for the field.

decade. Auslander's essay is thus a rather odd contribution, as even she notes, to a special issue on the future of Women's Studies. And yet her essay's project of narrativizing the center's institutional history and intellectual rationale displays important aspects of the transferential idealism that proliferated throughout the 1990s, such that a term once used synonymously with *women* could emerge not simply as distinct from it, but as capable of signifying for many scholars a collaborative destination for the future of the field. How did *gender* accumulate this kind of capital, and what effect did its accumulation have on the various objects and analytics that it came to collectively represent? The grammar of Auslander's title is instructive. By situating *women* at the farthest distance from *gender*, the title secures gender's power by allocating it the space of being after: after the "fact" of *women*'s categorical failure, after differences among women riveted the field, after the public political crisis of feminism, after the field's contentious battle over men, after the identity attachments of Gay and Lesbian Studies, after the deconstructive invocations of queer. In being both destination and summation, *gender* could simultaneously (miraculously) signify and exceed each of its constituent parts. Its utility was thus borne in what we might call its critical transitivity, which is indicated by Auslander in the mathematical formula she adopts, such that *gender* travels through and accumulates multiple analytic and object domains— women, feminist, men, lesbian and gay, and queer. In large part, her essay is organized to detail the converging and diverging routes by which *gender* emerged to claim oversight and priority, the hope it carried with it, and the worry its progress raised along the way.

First the hope.

As Auslander tells it, the emergence of the Center for Gender Studies at the University of Chicago was effected as a collaboration between scholars long invested in Women's Studies and those working within Gay and Lesbian Studies. For reasons both intellectual and institutional, the center's founders rejected the idea of developing

> two programs, one in women's studies and one in gay and lesbian studies—because it seemed regressive to us. Separate programs would make joint work more difficult, endorse a return to an identity-based research and teaching model, and would leave no room for the study of gender differentiation or of masculinity in terms other than those provided by women's or gay and lesbian studies. (3)

The representation of Women's and Gay and Lesbian Studies as exclusive and literal-minded identity projects serves here as the necessary precondition for *gender*'s progress, transmuting the institutional challenge of how best to engage the multiple constituencies interested in the study of gender and sexuality into a matter of equal representation collated by the field name. The capacity given to *gender* to manage such institutional work has been central to its proliferation. I've heard numerous anecdotal tales that link departmental name changes to the presence of gay men on the faculty. "Once we hired John, it didn't make sense to be called Women's Studies anymore." The institutional history Auslander recounts is not, then, unique:

> Most of the men actively engaged . . . in the creation of the Center had been involved in gay politics and saw their work in relation to that practice. They did not all identify as feminists, nor did they necessarily see feminist theory as central to their work. In parallel, many of the women committed to work on gender were not particularly committed to gay and lesbian politics and had never seriously engaged lesbian and gay theory. (9)

In the intellectual figure and in the institutional practice of Gender Studies, each of these projects—Women's Studies and Gay and Lesbian Studies—could be expanded, drawing scholars and students with multiple intellectual and political investments to the activities of the center. In this moment of her narrative, then, *gender* has the positive institutional function of arraying a constituency whose political attachments are varied and incommensurate in their particulars, but "parallel" in their reproduction of identity investments as the foundation of critical practice. More important perhaps, the accumulative logic holds forth the promise of ongoing expansion, such that the emergence of new gender or sexuality discourses, objects of study, or identitarian figures can be accommodated by the field. Accumulation, then, begets an institutional domain that fulfills the political demand for representation and inclusion.

For Auslander, the intellectual gain in the move to gender for Women's Studies scholars arises from its ability to confer respect and attention to issues subordinated by the "women's studies paradigm," which, as she tells it, was chiefly centered on "documenting women's experiences and discovering their past actions" in contexts that "emphasized women's difference from men" (6). Its dissolution is presented as the consequence of four developments. The first and most famous was the demise of universal woman wrought by critical attention to hierarchies of race, sexuality, and class:

> Whether in the very marked class differences among women that any close study of the women's suffrage movement immediately brought to the surface, or in the radically different lives lived by white and black women in the antebellum United States, or in the contrasting experiences of European women and their colonized subjects, taking "women" unmodified as the unit of analysis came to seem increasingly unworkable. (6–7)

The second development entailed retheorizing gender as a "relational system," one that required not just a description of women's variously subordinated social positioning, but in its most rigorous form a critical account of how "women" came to be produced by the very gendered systems feminism used to represent them—and used them to represent (7). Joan W. Scott's radical revision and challenge to feminism's stake in an essentialized account not simply of women but of gender—evinced by "Gender—A Useful Category of Historical Analysis" (1986)—keynotes this theoretical development.[7] The third challenge to the Women's Studies paradigm was identitarian, arising from "the fact that men qua men came to be perceived as a legitimate and important subject of research for feminist scholars" (7). And finally, in the midst of these different developments was the rise of critical theory and with it the analytical force of poststructuralism, which catapulted humanistic inquiry into antideterminist understandings of both the subject and social life.[8] As Auslander tells it, then, the hope for Women's Studies was that *gender* could organize the consequences of the

7. See Scott, "Gender—A Useful Category of Analysis."

8. Auslander provides no gloss of the "autonomous developments in the fields of literary studies and philosophy—generally referred to by the rather too inclusive and thus too vague terms of poststructuralism and deconstruction," thus leaving open the question of how *women* was disarrayed on grounds distinct from the critique of its exclusionary universalisms. For more comprehensive discussions of the challenge to both feminism and women wrought by poststructuralism, see Weedon, *Feminist Practice and Poststructuralist Theory*; Alcoff, "Cultural Feminism versus Poststructuralism"; Scott, "Deconstructing Equality-versus-Difference"; Phelan, "Feminist Theory, Poststructuralism, and Performance"; Fuss, *Essentially Speaking*; and Butler and Scott, *Feminists Theorize the Political*.

dismantling of the field's founding paradigm by bringing issues of sexuality, sexual desire, and sexual orientation into critical contact with the study of women's differences, gender as a relational system, masculinity, and emergent theoretical explorations of language, subjectivity, and power.

If the critique of the Women's Studies paradigm arrives at the doorstep of Sexuality Studies as the projection of a field-defining transformation, the itinerary that Gay and Lesbian Studies must travel is less about reciprocity with Women's Studies than about carrying them both toward a future arrival into Queer Studies. Indeed, for Auslander, gender in the Women's Studies paradigm was "inadequate for the gender studies model we [were] developing, which seeks to *integrate fully* studies of sexuality and of gender" (emphasis added, 9). Integration is made possible in part by the theoretical work that *queer* brings to the table, as it reroutes identitarian logics and reconfigures the conception and practice of politics. " 'Queerness' was coined as a term that allowed people to avoid categorization by sexual practice, made the case for the voluntarism of identity, and underscored, by its appropriation of a pejorative term, its contestation of social norms" (11). As such, queer becomes the analytic analog to the model of gender being sought: "Queer is like gender in that it melds rather than separates analysis of men and women; it is like gender in that it emphasizes questioning of seemingly fixed identities; it is like gender in that it preserves the domain of gay and lesbian studies while creating a new way of thinking about sexual formations and particularly about processes of differentiation" (11).

The hope here is that by bringing Queer Studies into critical conversation with Women's Studies through Gay and Lesbian Studies as a collaborative institutional project, scholars working in each of these domains will "learn from each other. Thinking about sexuality, gender, gay and lesbian rights, queerness, and feminism will be mutually enriching" (12). Most important, "the strength of this *inclusive* model of gender studies" is that it puts pressure on scholars to attend to issues marginalized by prevailing paradigms (emphasis added, 23). For "those who tend to think primarily about the social construction of *gender*," it means keeping "*sexuality* in their field of vision. It obliges those who work primarily on gay male studies and/or masculinity to keep questions of gender and feminism in mind. It obliges those whose engagement is primarily with lesbian studies to think about continuities and disjunctures along lines of gender and sexuality" (23). In other words, it secures the collaboration between practitioners by establishing a category to generate affiliations between and among objects of study and the political projects that accrue to them, thereby integrating the field by giving it a name that can function as a term of resonant inclusion, one in which "the study of masculinity, feminist gender studies, and gay, lesbian, and queer studies each have an equal voice" (25).

Now her worries.

Auslander articulates several concerns about the present and future of Gender Studies, including its potential distance from contemporary feminist politics; its inability to achieve the field's long-standing demand for a comprehensive interdisciplinarity; and its continued subordination of race as a category of analysis, which raises the specter of, in her words, "gender studies as white" (23). In their own ways, each of these worries has been cited as part of the failure of Women's Studies, but Auslander does not note the continuity, arguing instead that *gender* can address the "pitfalls of the women's studies programs created during the 1970s" (3). As she says in her conclusion, "whatever its difficulties, gender studies is the most powerful model of research we have. . . . My faith in [it] is not merely an abstract faith—the paradigm has enabled both individual and collective projects that would have been impossible without it" (23).

But how does one leap over the incongruencies and elisions that *gender* is already known to mark in order to trumpet its generative and integrative potential nonetheless? That is, how does one assert *gender*'s ability to travel more coherently and inclusively into the political, institutional, and intellectual terrain where *women* has failed while also acknowledging that *gender* might reach its own critical and institutional limit by muting, in its representational power, the field's commitment to long-standing feminist social issues; to race as a crucial axis for the interpretation of culture, identity, and power; and to the possibility of disciplinary crossings with the natural and physical sciences? Or perhaps I should ask the question this way: How much faith does it take to invest in *gender* against the limitations of *women* even after identifying the ways in which *gender* fails as a fully integrative, critically mobile, and politically capacious framework? One answer is to say that it takes about as much faith as it did (and does) to invest in the political aspiration that accompanied *women*. Another is to say that *faith in the object relation* is as much a disciplinary effect as a disciplinary command, which is why the progress Auslander seeks is not generated by *gender* no matter *gender*'s powerful role in representing and evoking it. This is not to argue with Auslander's smaller assertion that at her institution *gender* enabled collaborations impossible without it. But it is to orient this discussion toward the interior life of the progress narrative and the relations of misrecognition and denial to which it commits identity knowledges: misrecognition of the fact that the propulsion of progress produces the very failure that incites its optimistic turn to new objects and analytics, and denial that the utopic consecration of any set of privileged attachments will generate ever-newer elisions, thereby postponing the arrival into completion that progress heralds and demands. From this perspective, the progress narrative of gender tells us little about *gender*'s inherent critical capacities—and more than we might be willing to know about how thoroughly steeped is the field in the affective relays in which the object is taken as the means and mechanism for materializing the political desire that sustains critical authority. To explicate this, I want to look briefly at Auslander's discussion of *race* since it figures in her narrative as the progress of *gender*'s most persistent threat.

At Auslander's institution, the Center for Gender Studies was established alongside a Center for Race, Politics, and Culture. The two centers have collaborated on a number of projects and share physical space, but their autonomy remains important, Auslander writes, for both institutional and intellectual reasons. Indeed, she devotes a long section of her essay to answering the question, "Why did we not create a center for the study of difference or 'otherness'?" by specifying how *gender* and *race* must be understood to diverge while gender and sexuality cannot. The first argument collates around the historical whiteness of her university setting, where "the study of race is . . . still more fragile than that of gender studies (although not than the study of sexuality)" and centers have a proven record of serving as a vehicle for "the integration of people of color" (21, 22). Hence their utility as an antiracist institutional form requires that the Center for Race, Politics, and Culture remain distinct. The second argument concerns the analytic dispensations of gender and race, especially in their differing relationships to the biological sciences and psychoanalysis. "[W]hat we now understand as racial difference," she writes, "is easily mutable and erasable through interracial reproduction," while "the vast majority of the world's population is still sexually embodied as male or female"; hence "it is clear that the biological sciences will not help us to understand differentiation by race" (21). The case of psychoanalysis is similar, in that "conceptions of gender roles and sexual desire are established early in life and . . . are powerful enough that all students engaged in gender studies must have familiarity with them. . . . There are no parallel arguments for the establishment of conceptions of race with the very first months and years of life" (21). Hence, "The central importance of psychoanalysis and psychology to the study of sexuality offers another, very different, intellectual reason for separating the two centers" (21). But why assume that the need for the autonomous existence of the Center for Race, Politics, and Culture means that the Center for Gender Studies must understand its intellectual mission as the integrated study of gender and sexuality alone—or what Auslander calls at one point "gender/sexuality"—especially as that particular merger has been under pressure since queer theory began its own institutional sojourn? After all, institutional arguments are neither indicative nor predictive of the intellectual pressures that might be brought to bear on feminist and sexuality studies scholars to make *race* an analytic priority—and to do so in a way that does not contribute to the university's reduction of it to diversity management.

To be sure, there are other strange elisions and associations at work in this part of Auslander's argument, but trying to unravel the incoherence of her arguments for the critical autonomy of race is not finally my point. Rather, I want to foreground the defensive moves that shore up her progress narrative, as it is clear that race is the essay's structuring contradiction While the language in which it appears elicits a haunting suspicion—when does autonomy give way to equality-in-separation?—the symptomatic reading would take the essay's refusal to figure race within the province of the psychoanalytic as the psychic condition on which *gender*'s progress is pursued. In this regard, race is no mere afterthought but the very excess or remainder of the anxiety that the turn away from the founding paradigm of *women* can neither allay nor undo, no matter the intensity of the transferential investment. Indeed, the essay's attempts to address the "danger of reinforcing a model that figures . . . gender studies as white" echoes the long-standing critique that now lives within *women*, thereby presenting evidence that threatens to undermine faith in *gender* while professing faith in it nonetheless (22–23). "There are no immediate and obvious answers to this problem," Auslander writes. "Merging gender and race centers into one center for the study of 'otherness' is not a good idea. Cooperation and openness clearly is" (23).

Against the figure of a conflated and unspecified "otherness," Auslander justifies the priority of *gender* as the referential sign of the field on the grounds of institutional form, almost as if the essay had its origin in the competition over the allocation of resources, the political economy of diversity, and the organization of expertise and authority—in short, those aspects of the university that mark it as a political institution and simultaneously shape and condition how projects emerge, if they do so at all. And yet, the essay never situates the priority claimed for *gender* as a matter of institutional strategy; it is not even clear whether or not the prospect of a Center for the Study of Difference was a real one. Instead, *gender*'s now characteristic proliferations stand as evidence of the field's ability to transcend the compromise of its founding paradigm, and in this the institutional form cultivated in the negotiation of the university as a political institution is made wholly congruent with the critical integrity of the field. By using the institutionalization of *gender*'s priority as proof that both analytic and political progress have been made, *gender* thus circulates as the newly authentic and authenticating sign of the future of the field.

While the propulsion of the progress narrative is bound to the euphoria of its promised transcendence, its internal structure is contradictory in the extreme. Let me highlight four crucial aspects: failure, dependence, incorporation, and disavowal. *Failure*: while the progress narrative is dedicated to a future in which the political transformation it heralds will be complete, the optimism it generates is conditioned by the failure it routinely cites. In these terms, it is not *gender* that enables the field to surpass the incapacities of *women*, but *women*'s failure that enables *gender* to perform the transference that gives critical no less than political force to the progress narrative. *Dependence*: in the propulsion to overcome what has failed, the progress narrative is both formally and affectively dependent on the objects and attachments it promises to leave behind, which makes that which is overcome absolutely essential to its functioning—the very engine of the faith that attends and sustains it. This means that *gender*'s critical and political value is not only dependent on *women* but that there can be no narrative of progress without it. *Incorporation*: in the interplay between failure and dependence, the progress narrative cultivates optimism through the transferential relationships it hones, thereby offering the field the possibility of a future that infinitely includes. In this promise, lost belief can be restored, failure overcome, and new investments represented, all by turning critical attention from one object, analytic practice, cultural form, or critical motion to another. To read the progress narrative in this way, as a transferential practice, means acknowledging the fantasy of abundance, newness, and resignification that makes it such a powerful tool in the regeneration of the political desire that founds the field. *Disavowal*: And yet, as Auslander's essay so clearly depicts, the promise of the transferential investment in *gender* is conditioned on disavowing any similarity between it and the category of *women* it corrects, incorporates, and ultimately supersedes. This disavowal is collated, as I discussed above, around the critical figure of *race*, which serves as Auslander's most resonant exception to the incorporative logic on which *gender*'s progress is based. But this does not mean that *race* is categorically disavowed by the progress narrative. My point is rather that the anxious attention to race in Auslander's essay indicates how profoundly the *similarity* between *women* and *gender* must be refused for the progress narrative to do its work.[9]

What would it mean if we resisted the disciplinary imperative to "move on"? This is the question that generates my turn in the following section to

---

9. At stake in this discussion of race is a certain resistance to identity-based protocols of interpretation that compel practitioners to take every instance in which an object or analytic is subordinated as indicative of its universal subordination, thereby fusing its critical operation with the left political narrative in which subordination and repression serve as the key terms for historicizing identity as a structure of inequality. For by privileging "presence," identity knowledges often ascribe the critical investment in race to the foregrounded presence of a minoritized identity object of study—he or she who must be seen and heard for the analytic capacity of race to be registered. While this demand for presence may reproduce the critical no less than political authority at stake in identity knowledges, it exerts a disciplinary force on the very objects it seeks to liberate, making them produce legibility, visibility, and presence as the primary political idiom in which social justice can be thought. Under the sway of this idiom, it becomes difficult to discern the ways in which oversaturation and hypervisibility operate as modes of discrimination, re-marking subjects and objects precisely along the lines of their social differentiation while casting their political subjectivity from within that position alone.

Civil Rights struggle is a telling example of this conundrum. While it is often regarded as an identitarian project engaged in giving visibility and voice to those excluded by white masculine universalisms, some of its most potent political criticisms have been aimed at the hypervisibility through which the racialized and gendered subject has been reduced to specular embodiment. From this perspective, the seemingly liberal demand for inclusion into rights-bearing citizenship must also be read as a demand to be destigmatized in representational forms, which would entail the right to escape from both referentiality and particularity altogether. While scholarship in identity knowledges may grapple in nuanced ways with visibility, my larger interest concerns the consequences of a disciplinary apparatus that relies on presence to produce evidence of the commitment to justice.

what the narrative of *gender*'s progress is most bent on eclipsing: the complicated entanglements of *women*. My point in tracking back to life before *gender*'s analytic departure is not meant to restore the field to representational monogamy, or to chastise Auslander for finding so little critical heat in it. I take it as a matter of course—though one routinely ignored—that critical practice is indebted to the urgencies of its own time and location, which means that where and how one enters a discussion will help to determine the shape of the terrain one understands herself to be in. (This is perhaps at the heart of every problem now flagged as generational.) There is no critical history that can account for the entirety of the past it offers to explain, nor one that can produce satisfaction for all those invested in it, no matter how insistent we are in reading every act of criticism in precisely this way. Reading well requires more than self-defensive inhalation. As for the writing: Too much will always have changed by the time you get to the end of what you think you want to say, unless you have the rare ability to withstand being changed by what you do or think. These and other delays—most pointedly the publication process—will make it difficult to discern, if we come to focus on it at all, the *now* and *then* that any narrative account of the past as a relation to the present entails. Hence, my interest in what is performed by Auslander's equation is not intended as a dismissal of her investment nor as a means to "correct" her narrative. One hears in her essay the need to figure out how to organize disparate scholarly and political trajectories into critical coherence, and to do so in ways that have institutional viability as well as pedagogical reach. What conditions my inquiry here is something else. Call it a wish that our objects and analytics of study might survive even our most impassioned use of them.

II. *What Was* Women?

It is fascinating to consider the historical security that the progress narrative of gender now imparts, situating as it does the category of *women* as the inaugural moment for the field, not a vehicle for traveling very far. Indeed, academic feminism in the United States as a whole has largely abandoned attempts to solve the crisis of the category of *women*, remaining confident instead that its critical deconstruction, no less than its longstanding activist critique, advances a more compelling future than any that seeks to wrench *women* from its familiar complicity with universaliz-

ing norms. One catches a glimpse of this in the finality by which Auslander can declare the failure of "the women's studies paradigm." But she is
not alone. Every undergraduate and graduate student in Women's and
Gender Studies that I have known in the past twenty years takes it as a
matter of fact that *women* is the scene of exclusion, if not a real or symbolic
figure of political and epistemological violence, even as they are preparing
to dedicate themselves to academic, activist, and professional careers that
collate women as a central concern. So convinced are we now of the category of *women*'s inability to remain conceptually coherent and politically
progressive that pointing toward it as a contemporary form of political
belief risks being allied with those bourgeois feminist discourses still
awaiting their own intersectional, poststructuralist, and postnationalist
self-critique. Still, it is worth saying that the story of how *women* came to
travel as a referent of both political privilege and critical impossibility is
indeed a story, and hence it is embedded in historical and critical processes
irreducible to the reigning consensus concerning the category of *women*'s
purported intrinsic incapacities. That consensus, let's be clear, says more
about the power that the *narrative of incapacity* now holds than it does
about how *women*'s dissolution evolved, and it is striking how much
attention to contestations within and between poststructuralist theory
(or its "foreign" predecessor "French feminism") and identity-oriented
discourses of difference (racial, sexual, national, and economic) we have
forfeited in the process. Indeed, as Clare Hemmings has explored, the
repeated and at times nearly unconscious reproduction of the consensus
narrative about academic feminism's past functions to consolidate and
order its constituent parts, packaging the at times chaotic diversity of its
critical and political activities into set pieces: lesbian feminism, black
feminism, poststructuralist feminism, postcolonial feminism, queer
theory.[10] In a certain sense, then, the unification of a history no longer in
need of detailed explication serves as a kind of resolution, as *women* is
made to yield something, in its categorical failure, that academic feminism can finally agree on.

Auslander's title glosses the problem and poses the resolution in what I
have explicated as a mathematical formula, positioning *women* as far from

10. See Hemmings, "Telling Feminist Stories."

gender as grammar can perform. The distance traveled between the two is made possible, as I have noted, by consolidation, as each category's contribution to gender's compounded interest requires that it be legible as a discrete entity of its own. From this perspective, *gender*'s formulaic progression is contingent on a calculated stasis, which raises issues about how, precisely, to calibrate the boundaries that separate some objects and analytics from others. Where, for instance, does *women* end and *feminist* begin? Or how do we discern the dividing lines between *lesbian/gay* and *queer*? Or conversely, what generates the sense, written in Auslander and elsewhere, that *women* and *men* are so categorically complete that no one would need to figure the means of giving them a distinct affiliation or differentiation? History or culture do the work embedded in the essay's progression, yielding a stage in this economy of equivalences for the study of men. But Auslander's narrative says very little about that entity in the middle, let alone how it acquired its transitional position. We do know that the study of men came to exist, as she tells it, "in parallel to other expansions of our purview," and that it registered "the fact that men qua men came to be perceived as a legitimate and important subject for research for feminist scholars" (7). But when Auslander gives us her essay's only explication of the kinds of research that mattered, she both leaps over the debates that accompanied them and massively narrows their conceptual reach:

> [W]e came to see, for example, that if we wanted to analyze men's hostility to sharing workplaces with women, we needed to study how they understood their place as men. . . . Likewise . . . the massive death rates of young black men in America's inner cities surely required . . . comprehending how manliness is being defined in those social sites. . . . Analyzing the dynamics behind Robert Bly's men's movement or the Million Man March requires consideration of the construction of masculinity. Adequate explanations of how men come to understand their gender and sexuality are crucial *even* if one's primary preoccupation is women. Given the relational nature of gender, and the centrality of processes of differentiation to its making, ignorance of one gender produces ignorance of the other. (emphasis added, 7)

In this, Auslander figures the turn to men and masculinity as the consequence of feminism's self-defining critical agency, such that the dissolution of its seemingly exclusive focus on *women* had its origin in the need to overcome partiality and "ignorance"—a mode of progressive perfection in which feminism expands its analytic worldview.

For Auslander, then, the progress of *gender* makes it possible to take for granted, in the name of feminism, what was in no way an easy or unidirectional transition for Women's Studies as a field. In retrospect, of course, it is difficult *not* to read the turn to masculinity as a signature move of U.S. academic feminism in the late 1980s when the seemingly natural relationship between men, masculinity, and the social order of male supremacy was critically de-essentialized from a variety of inter/disciplinary and political perspectives. Scholarship on the history of manhood and the social construction of masculinity appeared, along with studies of the men's movement, dissident masculinities, masculinity and theory, and the relationship of men to feminism.[11] Some of this work took its departure from conversations about race and racial hierarchy, following the theoretical imperative of what is now glossed as women of color critique, which cast doubt on universalist representations of male supremacy and women's commonly structured oppression.[12] Others took their cue from cultural

11. On histories of manhood and masculinity as a social construction, see Carrigan et al., "Toward a New Sociology of Masculinity"; Brod, *The Making of Masculinities*; Kaufman, *Beyond Patriarchy*; Kimmel, *Changing Men*; Chapman and Rutherford, *Male Order*; Leverenz, *Manhood and the American Renaissance*; Newfield, "The Politics of Male Suffering"; Gilmore, *Mankind in the Making*; Kaufman and Messner, *Men's Lives*; Hearn, *Men in the Public Eye*; Rotundo, *American Manhood*; Herdt, *Guardians of the Flutes Volume 1*; Berger et al., *Constructing Masculinity*; Nelson, *National Manhood*; and Hine and Jenkins, *A Question of Manhood*. On the men's movement, see Hagan, *Women Respond to the Men's Movement*; Kimmel and Kaufman, "The New Men's Movement"; Messner, *Politics of Masculinities*; and Clatterbaugh, *Contemporary Perspectives on Masculinity*. On dissident masculinities, see Segal, *Slow Motion*; Penley, *Male Trouble*; Edwards, *Erotics and Politics*; and Cornwall and Lindisfarne, *Dislocating Masculinity*. On masculinity and social theory, see Leverenz, "The Politics of Emerson's Man-Making Words"; Hearn, *The Gender of Oppression*; Hearn and Morgan, *Men, Masculinities, and Social Theory*; Di Stefano, *Configurations of Masculinity*; and Seidler, *Unreasonable Men*. On the relationship of men to feminism, see Jardine and Smith, *Men in Feminism*; Boone and Cadden, *Engendering Men*; Modleski, *Feminism Without Women*; Digby, *Men Doing Feminism*; and Murphy, *Feminism and Masculinities*.

12. One of the most important expressions of how an examination of the social position of women of color requires disassembling *men* as a monolithic category was the

studies and sought to decipher the cultural representation of diverse masculinities, the male body as spectacle, and generic conventions of masculine representation.[13] Still other scholarship reflected on the relationship between sexuality and gender, isolating the history of male homosocial bonds or interrupting the consolidation of masculinity with biogenetic male bodies altogether by considering practices of identification in butch-femme and drag cultures.[14] Across the spectrum, the category of *men* was simultaneously de-universalized and differentiated from within by way of race, class, and sexuality (more so than nation, region, or religion), and a new critical vocabulary emerged to elaborate social constructionist understandings of the historical consolidation of masculinity and maleness,

---

Combahee River Collective's "A Black Feminist Statement." Founded in 1974, the collective's 1977 statement emphasized the importance of the political relationship between black women and men: "Although we are feminists and lesbians, we feel solidarity with progressive Black men and do not advocate the fractionalization that white women who are separatists demand. Our situation as Black people necessitates that we have solidarity around the fact of race. . . . We struggle together with Black men against racism, while we also struggle with Black men about sexism" (16). As other black feminists—bell hooks, Michele Wallace, Audre Lorde, and Angela Davis—added their critical analysis of the complexity of social power arrangements to the feminist theoretical archive, the study of men and masculinity emerged for many scholars as part of an antiracist project to rethink "patriarchy" as an uneven and differentiated form of social power and organization. See especially Combahee River Collective, "A Black Feminist Statement"; hooks, "Men: Comrades in Struggle"; Lorde, "Man Child"; and Wallace, *Black Macho*.

13. On the cultural representation of diverse masculinities, see Edelman, "Redeeming the Phallus"; Blount and Cunningham, *Representing Black Men*; Robinson, *Marked Men*; and Eng, *Racial Castration*. On the male body, see Neale, "Masculinity as Spectacle"; Silverman, *Male Subjectivity at the Margins*; Lehman, *Running Scared*; Thomas, *Male Matters*; Tuana et al., *Revealing Male Bodies*; and Bordo, "Reading the Male Body" and *The Male Body*. On genre conventions and masculine representation, see Cohan and Hark, *Screening the Male*; Jeffords, *Hard Bodies*; and Cohan, *Masked Men*.

14. On the homosocial bond, see Sedgwick, *Between Men*; Jeffords, *The Remasculinization of America*; Mercer, "Imaging the Black Man's Sex"; Yingling, "How the Eye Is Caste"; Segal, *Slow Motion*; and my own *American Anatomies*. The genealogy of masculinity without men begins with Gayle Rubin's "Of Catamites and Kings" and is followed by a proliferating archive that engages gender transitivity and embodiments in a range of configurations. See especially Halberstam, *Female Masculinity*; Stryker and Whittle, *The Transgender Studies Reader*; and Salamon, *Assuming a Body*.

which opened the way to considerations of masculinity as a discourse of identification and gender formation "without men."

While all this attention to men and masculinity represented an expansion of feminist research agendas, as Auslander asserts, it required a reduction of *women* as the universal referent for feminist inquiry, which created enormous anxiety for a field founded on the belief that its relation to its object of study was a reparative project not simply on behalf of women but in the service of women's emancipation. In ways that continue to strike feminist scholars as deeply ironic, the turn to men and masculinity threatened to reiterate the social effect of gender norms by rendering the study of women decidedly particular, which is to say incapable of exceeding its patriarchal signification as the locus of specificity, embodiment, and sexual difference—no matter the fact that much of the intention in masculinity studies was to unravel the false universalism that shaped the categories of both *man* and *men*. The paradox on offer here, to trope Joan W. Scott, was a profound indication of just how much the investment in *women* had come to set itself against.[15] For *women*'s political function operated as a symbolic refusal of the category's sociohistorical subordination, such that the value it accrued for the field was contingent on the distance it could travel from the very subordination it referenced in order to repeal. In being the figure for both what gender hierarchy condemned the majority of humans to *and* the aspiration toward a political counterforce, *women* was the scene of enormous political and psychic work. Indeed, it was overburdened by the political aspirations that attended it from the start—not just in terms of the universalism it sought to grasp on behalf of women's political agency, but in the complex entanglements it collated in its critical relation to gender. Hence on the one hand, academic feminism had to explain the historical legibility of women as a discernible category of persons by explicating women's position from within the very organization of gender that feminist analysis hoped to undo. Here, talking about gender was in some strong sense talking *against it*, which explains why so much academic feminist theory, like the movement discourses that inspired it, imagined women's liberation as the end of gender—as a sexually egalitarian genderless society. At the same time, feminist analysis sought to disarticulate the political meaning of *women* from dominant formulations of gender, which entailed

15. See Scott, *Only Paradoxes to Offer.*

moving the field in a different direction altogether. Hence the other hand: academic feminism forwarded *women* as a political unity in order to overcome the prescriptive discriminations and violences of gender. The critical authority, political capacity, and in some cases ontological priority of women was precisely what *this* deployment of gender was used to yield.

To say that the critical dispensations between *women* and *gender* were incommensurate is thus to mark the double moves that gender represented, as scholars deployed it to diagnose the structure of social division that produced women as one of its effects and *redeployed* it to evoke a constituency armed with the means to ameliorate the historical and cultural consequences of women's constitution as such. In this, *gender* instantiated the category of women, defined its mode of production, offered the critical leverage for interpreting it, and figured the possibility of imagining a political agency that could function both against and beyond it. And by professing that it did this all in the name of women, at times by consigning the study of gender to women alone, feminist analysis wed *gender* to *women* in its efforts to inhabit the calculus of justice that governed the field. No wonder, then, that the idea of wagering the meaning and utility of gender as a referent for the study of men would set off more than a few alarms. At least initially, it risked nearly everything that the field imaginary relied upon—which is to say it risked jettisoning not only the organization and function of critical practice but the distribution of value that underwrote it as a whole. I think of this organization in tripartite terms, as the relationship between referent, description, and critique. The referent establishes the identity of the object of study as a distinct value; description discerns the object's legibility in a range of relations (historical, experiential, discursive, social structural, economic, etc.); and critique calculates the consequences of the analytic relations that ensue as a means and a measure of inhabiting the field's self-defining goal: doing justice. Critique is thus the rhetorical means to cultivate the promise of social effectivity, as it is under its tutelage that the political stakes of descriptive practices (not the descriptions themselves) are deciphered, judged, rejected, and refined—approached, that is, not in terms of objectifying accuracy but as acts of justice in themselves. Through the interior workings of critical practice, then, the political aspirations attached to objects and their analytic discernments are read in relation to their real-world projections, and the relation to the object of study becomes both symbolically and materially weighted *as* indicative of the relation to the entity the object has come to represent. It is in the context of this *critical realism* that narratives of the field's past and its future are written and revised, which is to say that it is from its presumptions that the shift from *women* to *gender* is performed as a practice of political progress. I will have more to say in the next section about the disciplinarity that critical realism installs over the object of study, especially in its relation to the social world it both represents and comes to stand in for. For now, however, I want simply to foreground the point that the critical relation between *women* and *gender* was far more complex and contradictory than the progress narrative of gender would lead us to believe—for all of the reasons I explain below.

As we all know, the most pervasive and damning critique that now attends the narrative of the failure of the founding paradigm—indeed the very critique that founds the paradigm as quintessentially failed—is its occlusion of differences among women. This occlusion tends to be narrated in one of two ways, though like Auslander, many scholars, condense the move to difference by casting poststructuralist deconstructions of the category of *women* as critically coincident with race and sexuality-based critiques of the category's universalist deployments in feminist discourses of all kinds, including academic ones. The distinctions lost in this narrative convergence abound: between social differences and *différance*; between the political contexts of U.S. identity discourses and French intellectual and political culture; and between critical theory and identity knowledges as they have unevenly collaborated and collided in both discursive and institutional sites.[16] As a consequence, Auslander's consensus story of the failure of the Women's Studies paradigm moves with very little citational sweat to its celebrated conclusion: that in its early reliance on

16. While these conflations have often been noted, there is as yet no transnational intellectual history that parses the cultural contexts, disciplinary priorities, and geopolitical migrations that might help us understand the multiple ways in which the impasses of *women* have been discerned. It is especially important to situate the work of the French feminists in the political and intellectual contents that structured their maneuvers and to track the temporal displacements that ensued as important work—think Luce Irigaray here—took nearly a decade to reach the U.S. English-speaking feminist audience. These issues are related to a long-standing problem, first indexed to me by Caren Kaplan, of the exceptionalist narrativizing that U.S. academic feminism performs about itself, making social movement its primary historical referent without registering the various non-U.S. intellectual traditions and political contexts that have shaped it.

women, scholarship in the field "tended to assume," as Auslander puts it, "that differences among women—of race, class, religion, sexual orientation, age—were less salient than their common sex" (6). On the face of it, this conclusion presents itself as a move toward justice, righting the wrong of the faulty universalism that *women* is said to engender by acknowledging that "women of color and lesbians argued that the experience of being white or black, straight or lesbian, were far from identical and perhaps not even analogous" (6). At the same time, this act of justice revamps the narrative of academic feminism as a tale of redemption: first for the field, which can now properly locate racism and heterosexism in the past, such that the present is figured as a scene of progress that opens to a future healed of repetition, contradiction, and complicity; and second for the very women—straight, white, middle-class, Western, and most often quintessentially American—whose hegemony was under assault by the critique launched against *their universalizing use* of *women*.

The slender distinction that emerges above between a critique of the category and a critique of the use of the category is crucial to understanding the role that *women* now plays in the pedagogy of progress that generates the narrative future of the field. Auslander's language is especially instructive here, as it reflects a pervasive habit across the study of women, gender, and sexuality to consign the agency of *women*'s failure to the category itself. The crisis, after all, is called the crisis of *the category* of women. She writes, "As research was done on the past and present of women's lives, as attempts were made to theorize women's domination, as scholars expanded their reach across the globe, it became clear that the category of 'woman,' or even of 'women' in the plural, obscured important differences" (6). The category obscured—not that the use of the category obscured . . . or that the critical apparatus at hand was no match for addressing the densities of the historical situations in which *women* became legible as a social entity in the first place . . . or that the disparate forms of minoritization that attended *women*'s global status as a subordinated majority overpowered the universalizing and retrospectively arrogant hope to speak to and for all women . . . or that the pedagogical insistence of the field on the transformative ground of the personal was unprepared for the institutionalization of racial and sexual norms that would quickly and radically narrow the composition of the audience it addressed . . . or that the very social movement that was said to inaugurate the field would bring with it a field imaginary that was temporally and geopolitically bound, along with a political vocabulary that had already universalized the conditions of its present into increasingly pat formulations of left agendas for social change. Not then that the difficulties encountered were a consequence of the complexities—critical, methodological, historical, geopolitical, linguistic, ideational—of deciphering the entity that the field had committed itself to, such that the very credibility of the field was staked to a calculus of justice as the measure of its success or failure. I am not saying that no one noted or understood these formidable and mind-numbing problems; they certainly and repeatedly did. But in the shorthand that Auslander and others now use—and yes, I have used it too—the field narrative takes a shortcut to the future, condemning the category in order to keep open the possibility that critical practice can be free from the historical and social weight that attends it and that a relation of justice can (still) be achieved. This, on its own, is an amazing transference, essentializing the category, not just what it refers to. The rhetorical force of "the category obscured" thus displaces a range of critical difficulties onto the faulty complicity of the category itself. In this, the progress narrative's turn against the referential sign of *women* can offer the field a phantasmatic leap beyond what the category's failure is thought to mean: feminist complicity with racism, heterosexism, universalism, and exclusion.

What happens in this context to the challenges made by "women of color and lesbians"? Or more to the point, from what political desire and critical location is their critique of the category of *women* made? After all, in no story of the field's history that I have ever encountered is their critique taken as a remaking of the founding paradigm. Instead, it is made to function as evidence of the seemingly essentialized nature of *women*'s catastrophic categorical failure. Such categorical essentialism, if you will, tends to situate critiques by "women of color and lesbians" as ends in themselves and not as powerful critical investments in the possibility of making *women* adequate to the political aspiration that the founding paradigm ascribed to it—that it could in fact operate as a resonant framework for political identification and action. In the grip of the progress narrative, critiques "by women of color and lesbians" actually work *to preserve* the founding paradigm as the exclusive domain of privileged women. After all, on what interpretative terms can we read such critiques as a matter of disidentification alone, as if the massive effort by women of color and lesbians to change the representational dispensation of *women* was expended with no interest in changing the calculus of who was and who was not included in it? Is it really possible that the critique of *women*'s exclusion was not marshaled as a political struggle over inclusion, which is to say as a battle precisely by women of color and lesbians to be included in the referential scope and historical purview of the field's exploration and idealization of *women*? The idea that only those who came to be privileged by the exclusionary effects of *women* had an investment in *women* as a political unity seems willfully ludicrous, enabling as it does a totalizing misrecognition of what such critiques were intended to do: to fulfill the aspiration of *women* as a political unity.[17] I want to emphasize this last phrase, "political unity,"

17. My narrative of the identity-difference axis of twentieth-century feminist thought is devoted to countering the now-normative assumption that early second-wave feminism was indifferent to race, class, sexuality, or nationality—an assumption that disturbingly casts both women of color and lesbians as belated arrivals to feminist critical practice and movement, as I discuss here. Actual examination of documents from the 1960s and 1970s demonstrates that issues of race and sexuality, especially, were given more than incidental discussion, and many of us trained in the first undergraduate generation of Women's Studies were schooled in the political analyses offered by Barbara Smith, Audre Lorde, and other black lesbian feminists. This is not a defense against the charges that feminism or Women's Studies were white centric or overtly racist, heterosexist, or homophobic; rather it is an argument against writing the early and vibrant discussion of race and sexuality out of the history of the founding of Women's Studies. It is also to argue for critical attention to the way that the most exclusionary work continues to be given priority in narratives concerning the field's past, thereby confirming the very story being told instead of prioritizing the contestations from the outset over *women*'s political signification and critical utility.

The U.S. archive on black women in early feminist analysis is extensive. I highlight here significant work from the late 1960s to around 1985, which covers the time frame in which the vast majority of programs and departments in the United States were founded and the professional apparatus institutionalized. See Beale, "Double Jeopardy"; Murray, "The Liberation of Black Women"; Ladner, *Tomorrow's Tomorrow*; King, "The Politics of Sexual Stereotypes"; Walker, *In Search of Our Mothers' Gardens*; Smith, "Doing Research on Black Women"; Russell, "Black-Eyed Blues Connections"; Lewis, "A Response to Inequality"; Dandridge, "On Novels by Black American Women"; Bell et al., *Sturdy Black Bridges*; Bethel and Smith, "The Black Woman's Issue"; Dill, "The Dialectics of Black Womanhood"; Rodgers-Rose, *The Black Woman*; Cross et al., "Face-to-Face, Day-to-Day, Racism CR"; Carver, "Building Coalitions Between Women's Studies and Black Studies"; Brinson, "Teaching Black Women's Heritage"; Smith, "Racism and Women's Studies"; Hull, "Researching Alice Dunbar-Nelson"; Tate, "Nella Larsen's *Passing*"; Hull et al., *All the Women Are White*; Davis, *Women, Race and Class*; hooks, *Ain't I a Woman*; Steady, *The Black Woman Cross-Culturally*; Gilkes, "From Slavery to Social

in order to put pressure on our understanding of the political intensity and density of the universalizing gestures that underwrote *women*, which disappear when the critique of the category of women and the critique of the deployment of the category are wholly converged.

An important case to consider in this context is the tradition of standpoint theory, which sought to construct an antiessentialist understanding of the epistemological and political grounds for feminism's deployment of *women*.[18] Scholars thus purposely, at times rigorously, resisted the idea that *women*'s political unity could ever be assumed in advance, approaching it instead as a political achievement. In this regard, *women* represented a historical emergence, not a natural unity, and its political capacity was contingent to varying degrees on the analytic force derived from feminism itself. Nancy Hartsock followed Marx's formulation of the proletariat to develop this line of inquiry, crafting the everyday labor of women as a realm of political activity that could constitute what she called the feminist standpoint.[19] Catherine MacKinnon took women to be the consequence of patriarchal gender to such an extent that feminism was the sole means by which any interpretative vantage on them could be achieved.[20] Patricia Hill Collins's now-definitive work situated the experience of black women as the standpoint that would be rendered theoretically important by black feminist intellectual work.[21] To be sure, there was scholarship that trafficked in essentialist and mythological formulations of women, and even the work I have cited was not without "error" in its attempt to sustain social constructionist understandings of women's experience as the ground for emancipatory analysis. The point I am making is this: that to the extent that the progress narrative of *gender* situates the critique of the

---

Welfare"; Dill, "Race, Class, and Gender"; Tate, *Black Women Writers at Work*; Giddings, *When and Where I Enter*; Jones, *Labor of Love, Labor of Sorrow*; Higginbotham, "Race and Class Barriers to Black Women's College Attendance"; and White, *Ar'n't I a Woman?*

18. On the standpoint tradition, see Harding, *The Standpoint Reader*, which collects all the key work in the field, including that of Dorothy Smith, Nancy Hartsock, and Patricia Hill Collins. See also Haraway, "A Manifesto for Cyborgs" and "Situated Knowledges"; Hennessy, "Women's Lives/Feminist Knowledge"; Bar On, "Marginality and Epistemic Privilege"; and Weeks, *Constituting Feminist Subjects*.

19. See Hartsock, "The Feminist Standpoint."

20. See especially MacKinnon, "Feminism, Marxism, Method, and the State."

21. See Collins, "The Social Construction of Black Feminist Thought."

category of *women* as outside the struggle to produce and evince the political agency of *women*, it has not only misunderstood the founding paradigm but consecrated its self-defining political superiority precisely by doing so. One need only look at the closing exhortation in Hortense Spillers's 1983 essay, "Interstices: A Small Drama of Words," to see how the critique of universalist deployments of *women* is made on behalf of the aspirations of the founding paradigm, not outside it or as a means to bring its use to an end:

> In putting afoot a new woman, we delight in remembering that half the world is female. We are challenged, though, when we recall that more than half the globe's female half is yellow, brown, black, and red. I do not mean to suggest that "white" . . . is an addendum, but, rather, only an angle on a thematic vision whose agents . . . have the radical chance . . . to help orchestrate the dialectics of a world-wide new-woman. As I see it, the goal is . . . a global restoration and dispersal of power.[22]

All of this is to say, then, that the political purchase of the consensus narrative that renders women's differences the end of the category of *women* is designed to cleanse the present of political complicity and sustain the field's self-defining emancipatory capacity. The conceptual leaps

---

22. Spillers, "Interstices," 96. Spillers's essay is remarkable for its elegant and incisive commitment to women as a plurality, not a pre-given unity, and to the possibility of feminism as a language for recalibrating the symbolic arrangements of power in which women's differences are staked to power:

> We hope to show in time how African-American women's peculiar American encounter, in the specific symbolic formation we mean, differs in both degree and kind from Anglo-American women's. We should not be at all surprised that difference among women is the case, but I am suggesting that in order to anticipate a more definitive social criticism, feminist thinkers, whom African-American women must confront in greater numbers on the issues, must begin to take on the dialectical challenge of determining *in the discourse* the actual realities of American women in their pluralistic ways of being. By "actual," I do not intend to mean, or even deny, some superior truth about life outside books, but, rather, to say that feminist discourse can risk greater truth by examining its profoundest symbolic assumptions, by inquiring into the herstory of American women with a sharpened integrity of thought and feeling. . . . By doing so, I believe that we understand more completely the seductive means of power at whatever point it involves women. (80)

involved here are extensive and costly, as we are led to believe that every commitment to *women* as the horizon of the field can only be interpreted as an investment in the category's universalizing effects. Hence, as Auslander puts it, scholarship conducted under the sign of *women* "assume[d]"—and now we have a new universal to counter an old one—"that differences among women . . . were less salient than their common sex" (6). But to seek to discern the commonality of "common sex" is not necessarily to believe that differences were or are less salient. On the contrary, it may be precisely because of the saliency of differences that one seeks to produce with great political passion a discourse and organizational program of "common sex." To cast the investment in the founding paradigm this way is not to deny the racist or homophobic effects of *women*'s deployment, but it is to question: (1) the now sedimented equation between the aspiration to wield *women* as a political unity and racism and homophobia, and (2) the consequential assumption that the flight from the category of *women* is the necessary political resolution to racism and homophobia. I take neither of these assumptions as unquestionably true, wanting instead to explore when *women*'s deployment was/is a political aspiration to overcome differences (as in Spillers) and when it is a refusal to grant those differences their analytic or political due. This is necessary for a variety of reasons, not the least of which is to account in far more nuanced ways for the complexity of racism in the history of the field and the institutions and culture in which it is embedded. For the generic logic of unmarked universalism is not the only means by which white hegemony is secured, as I discuss at length in chapter·4. It can arrive cloaked in the discourse of diversity, multiculturalism, or difference itself and even feature as its author the racialized or sexualized subject who is now rather ruthlessly bound to appearing only in that role. In these contexts, both critical and cultural, the left political aspiration for difference to lead to the resolution of inequality and hierarchy is transformed from a political strategy into a struggle over what identity and difference will mean in the unfolding complexity of historical change itself.

In other words, if the use of *women* yielded too much sameness at the price of obscuring differences within identity, the turn to center differences has brought with it its own problems, not the least of which, for academic feminism, is a rather impoverished equation that to talk about differences is to be against, even outside of, universalism and its exclusivist effects. Indeed, the now routine condemnation of the exclusivist occlusions of *women* functions to reassure the field that attending to differences is the means to craft a critical project and analytic perspective that does not exclude. But the political desire to transcend exclusion *is* a universalist desire—different to be sure from the metaphysical inscriptions arising from U.S. feminism's historical convergence with Western humanism, but nonetheless committed to the prospect of a conceptual practice that can overcome partiality and particularity to endlessly include. This is the promise and, I would add, the irresolvable contradiction of the discourse of intersectionality, which is steeped in a rhetorical rejection of universalism through its critique of singular axes of identity and power, but consecrated by a universalist desire to found a wholly comprehensive, nonexclusive articulation of the workings of power. While much more will be said in a later chapter about intersectionality, the point I want to emphasize is that identity and difference are not opposed to one another. Their relation is not analogous to the terms by which universalism is set against particularity and difference, or the way inclusion is taken as the opposite of exclusion. While there is enormous comfort in the belief that any critical practice that eventuates in harming those it was once used to protect was politically complicit all along, it is important to stress how profoundly identity has been made and remade by the cultural and political struggles to which it has been put, which makes it just as important to say that attending to differences is no inoculation against political complicity either—in part because nothing is. As my brief tour through the conservative deployments of difference has hoped to suggest, the consequences of our political tactics, including the use of critical practice as a political tactic, is not ours to control. To a certain extent, *Object Lessons* can be read as a long meditation on the ways in which the field imaginary of identity knowledges situates us to be genuinely surprised every time we (re)discover not only this fact but the one that it leads to, which is that there is no secure place from which to claim alterity to what is now thought of as the normative production of the political in the contemporary world. No secure place: not an attachment to identity or difference; not a new critical category; not a new political strategy; not even critique.

So what exactly does this interruption of the progress narrative of *gender* teach us? Is it that we need greater vigilance in refusing its demanding grip, which would allow us to inhabit the complexity of *women* less as a gendered identity than as a political aspiration, one in which the analogies between investments in *women* and *gender* could be sufficiently revealed so as to be enthusiastically explored? Is the aim of this entire discussion about pleading the rather simple case that what people now want from *gender*, others wanted from *women* too, which might be taken to mean that we should agree to stop producing such transferential investments and rethink the field and its political imaginary in their entirety? After all, there is no way to read this chapter without surmising that I have an investment in saying something about what *women* was in a voice that does not repeat *gender*'s castigating account of it, which could be an argument for turning the past into something other than the province of dead knowledge on which the privilege of the present's progressive relation to the future so routinely depends. Still, I'd like to insist that the answer to these questions is no—no, the lesson in interrupting the progress narrative is not about exposing the transferential hallucinations of *gender* or revealing *women*'s political complexity or forging a new field-inhabiting subjectivity. It is not about cleaning up the "mistakes" we might have made in trying to move on in order to move on more cleanly, or imagining that we can control or determine the activities of transference, as if the animations and indeterminacies of political desire are resolutely different from other kinds of desire. Nor am I saying that the narrative of *women* that now concedes the field's analytic future to *gender* is wrong, as if the resolution of the disciplinary dependence on progress is simply to insist on rendering the past more historically complex. Interrupting the progress narrative is not the same thing as undoing it. The lesson to be gleaned from this discussion of the progress narrative is about understanding what practitioners face in trying to get out from under its skin.

III. *Critical Realism: A Disciplinary Primer*

Modes of knowledge production have long been a site of intense contestation in feminist analysis, as the problem of explicating *women*'s complex historical emergence meets up with the political desire to find something in excess of social determination to remake as a tool for both envisioning and enacting change. One can read the arc of feminist theory as it passes through genealogies of Marxism and psychoanalysis as a compelling and at times deeply confounding deliberation on the political import of analytic beginnings. The crude underbelly of our now sophisticated formulations requires some measure of choice between the capacities of theories aimed at understanding the structure of material life and those that want critical purchase on the complexity of the human as a subject formed within it. While the decision to prioritize one or the other is often taken as a cogent representation of the scholar's political worldview, these choices are not merely "the" choices but mark out interpretive intelligibilities that attend the organization of knowledge that academic feminism simultaneously inherits and continues to negotiate. We are all familiar with the way that the priorities of the social or the human subject have lived in discretely defined disciplinary domains called the social sciences and the humanities. In the past thirty years, the traffic between these domains has been increasingly intense and prolific, with no small credit due to the rising pitch of interdisciplinarity. Once a figure for the radical potential of transgressing "the discipline" of the traditional disciplines, interdisciplinarity is now a key word in the university's own discourse of self-invention and direction, sharing space with the international and global in ways that make its earlier idiom of diversity and community seem incredibly provincial, which is to say domestically quaint. In many U.S. universities today, interdisciplinarity is indexed to the social value of knowledge, bent toward solving difficult contemporary problems (air pollution, say, or global poverty) and aimed at conservative legislatures and critics of higher education who find no satisfaction in the Cold War language of the Enlightened citizen as the goal of publicly funded mass education. No matter the importance of many of the problems that interdisciplinarity is now used to address, it has been wed to the university's self-rationalizing instrumental discourse, which many onlookers take as a symptom not simply of the U.S. university's global decline but of its rapid reformation by the logics of privatization that undergird neoliberalism on a global scale.[23]

As is well known, academic feminism consecrated its self-identity and authority on a formidable critique of the order of the disciplines, first by insisting that the study of Enlightened Western man as the index of the human was both a methodological and an interpretative error and, second, by forwarding the idea that in the disciplinary allocation of objects and analytics of study, the disciplines were themselves complicit with the reproduction of the rationalities of Western modernity and the masculinism,

23. For scholarship that points toward the kind of argument I cite here, see Aronowitz, *The Knowledge Factory*; Giroux and Myrsiades, *Beyond the Corporate University*; Newfield, *Unmaking the Public University*; Slaughter and Rhoades, *Academic Capitalism and the New Economy*; and Washburn, *University Inc.*

race supremacy, and exploitative coloniality on which it was and continues to be based. While we now take "the personal as the political" as the field's most resonant political motto, it was the implicit admonition—"you cannot change what you do not understand"—that underwrote the imperative to critical practice on the whole and helped to define interdisciplinarity as the means for transcending the fragmentation, insularity, and partiality that disciplinary perspectives were taken to perpetuate. Unlike the administrative discourse that attends interdisciplinarity today, it was once used by academic feminism in distinctly political terms: as the resolution of contemporary inequalities and hierarchy. In this way, academic feminism figured knowledge as a mode of both production and social reproduction, one profoundly implicated in women's systematic subordination across the range of their differences no less than in the identificatory entrapments of psychic life. Beneath the various debates that now comprise the intellectual history of academic feminism, then, lies a resolute, indeed unwavering commitment to knowledge production as the scene of political struggle, one that wagers the relationship between *what* and *how* we know as crucial to knowing what *to do*.[24] And it is here, in the propulsion that moves from critique to transformation, that we can see not only the progress narrative in its incipient formulation but the force of interdisciplinarity as the imagined means to institutionalize feminist resistance to the normalizing agencies of the traditional disciplines. As Sabine Hark speculates, "Interdisciplinarity is not only one of the founding and key defining elements of feminist knowledge projects" but "can almost certainly

24. This relation can be seen in nearly every document written by the National Women's Studies Association. In its 2008 national consensus report (Reynolds et al., *A National Census of Women's and Gender Studies Programs in U.S. Institutions of Higher Education*), the field is narrated thus:

> [G]iven its origins in the women's movement, women's studies was from its beginnings activist in its orientation, as much committed to transforming women's roles in the world as simply to understanding such roles. Its goal was not "disinterested" academic inquiry, but was clearly focused upon ending of oppression against women and challenging traditional paradigms.
>
> Indeed, women's studies' relationship to the women's movement was crucial in establishing and developing the field. The women's movement helped pressure colleges and universities to establish women's studies programs and helped establish the study of women as a worthy endeavor. (3–4)

be found in virtually every mission statement or [Women's Studies] program description . . . anywhere in the world [today]."[25]

Regardless of the ways in which interdisciplinarity has become a broader institutional goal, now routinely cast in depoliticizing terms, there remains a studied emphasis on disciplinary transcendence as vital to the intellectual mission of Women's and indeed Gender Studies as a whole.[26] In a much-cited 1998 essay published in a special issue of *Feminist Studies* on the future of the field, Judith Allen and Sally Kitch pose their inquiry as a question: "Disciplined by Disciplines? The Need for an *Interdisciplinary* Research Mission in Women's Studies." For Allen and Kitch, the field's founding imperative toward interdisciplinarity has been best achieved in the realm of instruction, where classroom pedagogies and curricular formation reflect the "synepistemic cooperation" that transcends the multidisciplinarity that is so often mistaken as interdisciplinarity.[27] In their terms, genuine interdisciplinarity is evidenced by "the *integration* of disciplines to create a new epistemology; to rebuild the prevailing structure of knowledge; and to create new organizing concepts, methodologies, or skills" (276). By surveying the scholarship presented in well-known feminist anthologies and journals, Allen and Kitch find that in the domain of research the field is far too beholden, as their title indicates, to the method-

25. Hark, "Magical Sign," 20.

26. The archive in Women's Studies about interdisciplinarity and the politics of the disciplines is extensive. See especially Howe, "Breaking the Disciplines"; Spender, *Men's Studies Modified*; Boxer, "For and about Women," *When Women Ask the Questions*, and "Unruly Knowledge"; Bowles and Klein, *Theories of Women's Studies*; Craine et al., *Crossing Boundaries*; Gunew, *Feminist Knowledge as Critique and Construct* and "Feminist Cultural Literacy"; Hartman and Messer-Davidow, *(En)Gendering Knowledge*; Elam, *Feminism and Deconstruction* and "Taking Account of Women's Studies"; Stacey, "Disloyal to the Disciplines"; Martin, "Success and Its Failures"; Pryse, "Trans/Feminist Methodology"; Romero, "Disciplining the Feminist Bodies of Knowledge"; Zimmerman, "Women's Studies, NWSA, and the Future of the (Inter)Discipline"; Blee, "Contending with Disciplinarity"; and Buker, "Is Women's Studies a Disciplinary or an Interdisciplinary Field of Inquiry?" Many of these conversations draw on the foundational work on interdisciplinarity of Julie Thompson Klein. See her major book, *Interdisciplinarity*, and "Blurring, Cracking, and Crossing." See also Parker et al., *Interdisciplinarity and Social Justice*.

27. Allen and Kitch, "Disciplined by the Disciplines?" 277, 283. Further page notations are indicated in the text.

ological priorities, critical vocabularies, forms of evidence, practices of argument, and cultures of professional identity characteristic of the traditional disciplines, which limits the scope of feminist inquiry. They take this situation as especially unnerving in the context of the growth of Women's Studies doctoral programs, whose intellectual rigor requires, as they put it, "full interdisciplinarity," as "the lives, conditions, productivity, and future of women cannot be fully contemplated within the confines of traditionally conceived disciplines; indeed, some of the most important questions cannot even be raised within those parameters" (275, 282).[28] Notably, their use of *women* is repeatedly emphasized as an international and cross-cultural marker, such that "the intellectual mission" of the field requires "a discipline-transcendent command of the full array of knowledges that have shaped conventional understandings of women, gender, and sexuality in an international and cross-cultural frame" (278).[29] The scope of the project, then, is global in multiple senses, as future Women's Studies scholars must be prepared to overcome the disciplinary divisions that characterize the modern university, along with the nationalist biases and monocultural frameworks that have limited the reach of feminist research in the past. In this way, the integration that is sought comes vested with

28. In the same issue, Susan Stanford Friedman takes the opposite position, arguing against the establishment of the doctorate in the field precisely because interdisciplinarity as the goal can underprepare students for the rigors of research. See her "(Inter)disciplinarity and the Question for the Women's Studies Ph.D."

29. Another frequently cited essay on interdisciplinarity is Marjorie Pryse's "Critical Interdisciplinarity, Women's Studies, and Cross-Cultural Insight," which similarly weds postdisciplinary diversity to women's differences. In its terms, critical interdisciplinarity is "guided by analysis of the intersections of race, class, gender, sexuality, and the structures and policies of nation-states in women's lives" and, when taken up by feminist scholars as a "postcolonial strategy" "can undermine the disciplinary boundaries established by an administrative organization"—in this case the organization of the disciplines, which Pryse reads as akin to nation-states (6). The metaphoric leaps and consolidations of intersectional, interdisciplinary, and postcoloniality produce a fascinating, if confounding, call for a distinctly feminist methodology, one that hopes to use interdisciplinarity "to produce cross-cultural insight" as "an actively anti-racist, anti-classist, anti-homophobic, and anti-imperialist form of feminist thinking" (2). In seeking to guarantee in advance the political productivity of interdisciplinarity as a form of intersectional analysis, Pryse performs the primary syntax of the field imaginary by leveling distinctions between object, referent, analytic, method, and political aim—in short, the mode of interpretative practice that I call critical realism.

universalizing desire, as the goal of transcending both disciplinary and sociohistorical-cultural differences is conditioned by a vision of feminist knowledge that excludes nothing.

What interests me about Allen and Kitch's essay is less their studied faith in interdisciplinarity or anyone's ability to know when it is fully achieved than the route by which they stage their argument for its import to the field. For it is here that we begin to see the operations and consequences of what I have been referring to as the field's own disciplinarity. They write:

> The desirability of interdisciplinary approaches . . . becomes obvious when we consider key problems arising throughout feminist theory and policy debates. . . . [V]iolence furnishes one indicative example. The recent United Nations Fourth World Conference on Women in Beijing showed unanimous transnational and cross-cultural agreement that violence against women was an urgent international emergency. (278)

Scholarship in the disciplines on the topic, however, "has been uneven," so much so that any of the disciplines that routinely study violence—history, sociology, law, psychology, and literature—fail to reveal "the broad and enduring nature of the problem" (278, 279). In looking at the limits of history, the authors note that scholars must "study violence through . . . court records; coroner's proceedings, newspapers, police blotters, or annual statistics; or else through personal records, such as diaries, letters, and reminiscences. By definition, reliance on such sources limits inquiry to occasions when violence was discovered, reported, prosecuted, or admitted" (279). Similarly, the predilections of literary study might provide important analyses of "the symbolic and discursive aspects of gendered violence"— precisely of the kind, they stress, that are excluded from the disciplinary apparatus of law—but literary scholarship in general is "so exclusively textual that nondiscursive material realities leading to or resulting from violence typically slip out of analytical range" (280). In the end, then, the authors confirm "that only an interdisciplinary approach to violence reveals its most urgent dimensions," and in doing so they provide evidence for their conclusion that "*endogenous* academic interdisciplinarity is thus a response to *exogenous* social interdisciplinarity" (279, 282). In this, the work of feminist scholarship—indeed the research mission of the field altogether—is married to the political urgencies of the present, such that what brings academic knowledge production into existence on distinctly feminist terms is a contemporary social world that requires explication to achieve radical transformation. "When disciplinarity is the only institutional framework . . . progress is made one discipline at a time," they write (286). Not so, then, with interdisciplinarity, which promises to move the field forward cogently as a whole.

But to be against the disciplines is not to be outside of disciplinarity altogether, as no academic project emerges into institutional legibility as a distinct field of inquiry without establishing normative and self-legislating critical definitions—or what James Chandler describes as "styles of thought."[30] In naming the burgeoning array of interdisciplinary fields that now comprise the U.S. university "shadow disciplines," Chandler is careful to link disciplinarity to more than content or method, seeing it as "something more permanent and less procedural, something perhaps more definable in terms of professional attachment, a sense of belonging."[31] In addition, "for a set of intellectual practices to count as a discipline there must be some sort of institutional framework in which whatever regularity they impose can be mediated and effected," but such a framework need not be a department, as a "disciplinary system can evolve beyond the structure" that has most often "administer[ed] it."[32] The kind of disciplinarity that might be said to accrue to both disciplines and interdisciplinary programs is a consequence of what I would call the work of field formation, which requires a reproductive apparatus that can generate and sustain the critical rationalities, objects of study, and modes of inquiry that enable a field to both claim and perpetuate its identity as a self-legitimating academic authority. Here, the routine distinction between traditional disciplines and interdisciplinary fields of study gives way to an understanding of disciplinarity as the ongoing and extensive process by which a field is institutionally formalized and critically governed. In this context, the disciplinarity of Women's and Gender Studies proceeds precisely from its formalization of the political as the value that differentiates it from traditional fields of study, which delivers the scholars who speak in its name into a disciplinary conscription of a distinct kind. While we might find this conscription profoundly productive, if not inherently progressive, the political demand that governs the field establishes a disciplinary calculus of justice

30. Chandler, "Introduction," 732.
31. Chandler, "Introduction," 737, 733.
32. Chandler, "Introduction," 734.

through which critical practice is both judged and judged to matter. Within this calculus, enormous attention is paid to objects and analytics of study as the referential sign of the field's political intentions, which is why I say that the value of the object or analytic of study arises from the disciplinarity that attends it, making it both the invested emblem of political attachment and the hoped-for vehicle for enacting social change.

The disciplinarity at work here accounts not only for how the relationship between *women* and *gender* has amassed so much field-forming value, but why Allen and Kitch turn to violence as the exemplary case to cultivate allegiance to interdisciplinarity. To be sure, one hesitates to interrupt the conversation that Allen and Kitch stage to cite the disciplinarity that attends it given the urgency of violence against women as a long-standing feminist issue. But violence is no random or neutral choice, especially in an essay intent on marshaling support for departmentalization as the best institutional form to foster the field's autonomy. Like all practitioners, Allen and Kitch know the critical and symbolic value that accrues to violence—it has an obvious link to social movement, which is emphasized by referencing its status as a consensus item at the UN World Conference on Women; it cultivates the idea of a commitment to women's differences, in that violence against women is cited as "a major priority among delegates who could agree on little else"; it registers the political relation between Women's Studies and feminism by prioritizing action-oriented research; and it signals the field's commitment to addressing and ameliorating inequality (278). The value of the figure of violence is matched only by the claim that accompanies it in which an endogamous social demand becomes the impulse and rationale for critical practice on the whole.

In all of these ways, violence lives up to the political desire invested in the field as a project of social transformation, serving as an unambiguous object of study for the necessary work of justice. And in this, its use reflects and defines the unacknowledged—and unacknowledgable—disciplinarity of the field. *Unacknowledged:* because progress is dependent on it— dependent, that is, on a relation to the political that casts critical practice as the counter to normalizing agencies of every kind, including those that might be said to constitute the academic feminist and her objects and analytics of study as historical entities as well. *Unacknowledgable:* because the power this disciplinarity wields is antithetical to the belief in political transformation that generates it, which is why the pursuit of critical authority and institutional power are routinely performed through the discourse of political progress to begin with. Unacknowledgable, then, because the sheer force of the field's authenticating discipline undermines any overt embrace of the forms of power it enables practitioners to seek.

Through the example of violence as a quintessentially just object, then, Allen and Kitch offer what many scholars have taken as a compelling argument for departmentalization, forwarding interdisciplinarity as a political tool for disrupting not only the disciplinary organization of knowledge but that organization's repeated marginalization of the urgencies that attend a comprehensive study of women, gender, and sexuality.[33] "Problem focused and innovation oriented rather than discipline bound, interdisciplinary research," they write, "can yield new findings, theories, or methods otherwise inaccessible via disciplinary or even multidisciplinary paths" (277). Here as elsewhere the definitional freedom given to interdisciplinarity functions as the mechanism and form for fulfilling the field's founding political mission, which in the context of their overall argument is exacted in terms of institutional form.[34] "[B]ecoming a department," they write, "is the most direct way . . . to affect the structures of knowledge, build the basis for innovative interdisciplinary work, and promote the hiring of a representative and diverse faculty—including women of color—who will produce the institutional changes women's studies was designed to effect" (291). Nothing less is at stake than "the future of the field" (281).

33. Allen and Kitch are not alone in this instrumentalization of interdisciplinarity. As Hark rightly notes, while the "language of interdisciplinarity . . . provided feminists foremost with a means to articulate their ideas, to make room for their knowledge within the academe, and to differentiate and distinguish their project from already established disciplines," it has been a "vehicle for institutionalization"—which is to say a strategy for securing and sustaining institutional power and authority ("Magical Sign," 22).

34. This progress proceeds by understanding interdisciplinarity as wholly opposed to both the disciplines and the university as a political institution. Hence, no attention is paid to the ways in which interdisciplinarity is so conceptually and methodologically dependent on the traditional disciplines for definition that any act of breaking away from them risks its own conceptual erasure. To consider this issue from a different direction, we might say that in opposing the disciplines, interdisciplinarity plays a crucial role in reproducing them by repeatedly affirming the discreteness of their identities and the force of their institutional authority. The other major problem with positing interdisciplinarity as political progress in relation to the disciplines is the fantasy that it is somehow free from being implicated in the logic of the market that grips the university as a whole.

It is in this context of field-generating futurity that I want to fore-ground how the progress narratives of gender and interdisciplinarity are linked by way of the disciplinarity that shapes the field imaginary as a whole. Each narrative features a similar tale of constraint, partiality, and exclusion that gives way to inclusion, expansion, and powerful self-affirming critical authority: *gender* overcomes the impasses of *women*; interdisciplinarity transcends the occlusions of the disciplines. In each narrative, the field is saved from failure and the agencies that affect the rescue are fig-ured as intellectual advances, made possible in part by their ability to marshal the discourse of the new, which is disarticulated from commodi-fication by gesturing toward larger institutional ideals of crossover audi-ences (gender), innovation and invention (interdisciplinarity), and social relevance (both). Moreover, while each argument is collated around insti-tutional resources, neither depicts its drive toward institutionalization as strategic—that is, as a negotiation of the political economy of the univer-sity and its own complicated management of the incongruencies between resources, expertise, social diversity, and public political culture. To be sure, no program or department in identity studies has come into being without formulating strategic maneuvers, but what is striking is how these maneuvers are rarely represented as political calculations bound to the institutional contexts in which the argument for them takes place. In-stead, the negotiation of institutional resources is regularly cast as a cru-cial advance toward the fulfillment of the field's political aspirations, which means that the progress narrative does more than simply shape the discourse of institutionalization. It is, as I have been arguing, a central feature of the disciplinary operations of the field.[35] Indeed, I would go so

35. Under the auspices of the progress narrative, then, all forms of institutionaliza-tion are cast in terms of political progress—and this is the case no matter how often scholars worry that institutionalization depoliticizes the academic feminist project as a whole. That worry, let's be clear, is hardly ever expressed as a way to interrupt the disci-plinary regime within which institutional form, object of study, field domain, and criti-cal practice are made to converge; more often it proceeds as a demand for renewing the convergences, leaving the logic at stake alone. For instance, when Messer-Davidow mar-shals her critique of institutionalization in *Disciplining Feminism* by focusing on the ways in which academic professionalization and poststructuralist theory have under-mined the field's political commitments, she is not making a plea that academic efforts on behalf of feminism leave the institution altogether. On the contrary, the argument of the book is bent toward changing academic feminism's course such that the insurrec-

far as to say that the progress narrative is now the hegemonic critical practice that confirms not only the practitioner's identity as a legitimate member of the field but the structure of value by which all critical, institutional, pedagogical, methodological, and theoretical developments have come to be apprehended and judged. When Allen and Kitch, like Auslander, take up the progress narrative, they are inhabiting the rhetorical and affective idioms in which field authority is disciplinarily defined and secured.

Women's Studies, of course, is not alone in constructing a disciplinary apparatus contingent on the political demand that inaugurated its existence as a field of study. Every knowledge project that takes itself as pursuing a field formation commensurate with its political needs is bound up in generating a disciplinary apparatus that can produce, protect, and sustain the field imaginary's primary investment in it. If I sound critical, it is not because I am seeking a field imaginary free of disciplinarity or, conversely, because I want an institutional project free from politics; there is no such thing as either. But I am trying to emphasize how the progress narrative that is intrinsic to identity knowledges operates as a cover story for the very disciplinarity that it incites and performs—first on the objects and analytics of study that it commits itself to and, second, on the practitioners who

---

tionary ideals of the founding generation can be restored and the field can function "again" as a potent force of social and institutional intervention. In marshaling its lament against academic feminism's contemporary institutionalization as the means to (re)secure the field's political aspirations, *Disciplining Feminism* does more than endorse the disciplinarity I am tracking here: it *wields* it not only by equating political commitment with the perspective that motivates it, but by reiterating the belief that justice proceeds from the calculated convergence of critical practice, political action, utopic aspiration, and institutionalization. As might by now be clear, the disciplinary structure of the field is coincident with its political imaginary, which means that feminism is not disciplined by the university, as Messer-Davidow and others have claimed, but that feminism is the origin and agency of the disciplinary apparatus that has come to structure, govern, and define the discursive operations of the field, including those that deploy *gender* as the means to maintain faith in progress. These relations constitute the primary syntax of the field, which I have been calling the field imaginary. Such disciplinarity is simultaneously the effect and enactment of the complex exchange between the investment in political transformation and the institutionalized demand for its materialization, which is to say in the hoped-for convergence between the political desire that attends critical practice and its world-building manifestations.

earn their field credibility by reproducing the assumptions, convergences, and affective relations that it begets. In the discussions that I have been following, it is the disciplinary reproduction of the political demand to do justice that not only situates interdisciplinarity as the progressive emblem of the field's transgression of disciplinary norms, if not of disciplinarity altogether, but that also crafts *gender* as the projected fulfillment of those aspirations for coherence once cogently represented by *women*. By naming this structure *critical realism* I mean to foreground the imperative toward materialization that underwrites it, as critical practice becomes the means and measure of the field's capacity to represent itself as a practice of justice. How many times, after all, have we read or written that *this* critical practice (always the one we are engaged in) is no mere intellectual exercise but a transformative critique that can expose, resist, or undo the normativities, violences, and injustices within which and against which we speak?[36] It is not that I want to discard the familiar claim that *how* we conceptualize a problem matters—and matters deeply—but I am interested in the possibility that it may matter differently than the ways in which the disciplinary inclinations of critical realism would lead us to claim. Explanation or explication may not inaugurate resolution, though the belief that it will, along with the belief that the belief itself is outside the normative practices of cultural production, is one of the most powerful effects of the disciplinarity inaugurated by academic feminism that I am discerning here. Through this belief, the transferential relation that underwrites the movement of identity projects from the terrain of struggles over institutionalized exclusions to academic inquiries is materialized in the object relation, enabling critical practice to serve as the referential link to the exogamy of the social world that is taken to inaugurate, necessitate, justify, inhabit, and determine the shape and value of its activities. Here, critical practice

36. It has become a cliché to describe one's scholarly work in the language of resistance, so much so that the term, once ubiquitous, is rarely used today. And yet, while critical theory's rise to authority in feminist scholarship has inaugurated a substantively different scholarly idiom, its current emphasis on critique as a world transforming agency is consistent with the way that "resistance" first traveled as the primary figure of political value. In its inaugural and poststructuralist idioms, then, feminist scholarship remains enthralled to a disciplinary apparatus that figures critical practice as a form of political agency—and often, ironically, as the only political agency within reach.

is both the figure of justice and the agency through which it can be achieved.

This is just one way of saying that the transferential relations that underwrite the progress narrative are contingent on a set of conflations between the dispositions and deployments of critical practice on the one hand and the complexities and political emergencies of social life on the other. These conflations arise not from analytical mistakes, no matter how decisively the pedagogy of critical realism that enacts them would teach us otherwise, such that the work of correcting an analysis (or its object of study or its analytic) becomes the locus of political resolution. The point of my discussion is not to seek to dispense with critical realism or simply to expose its routines and ruses. I have been more interested in understanding the disciplinarity that founds it and in reading this disciplinarity as both a consequence and figure of the political aspirations that underlie and over-determine the field's self-legitimating narratives, interpretative reflexes, theoretical itineraries, object priorities, and modes of address—in short the critical rationalities through which it reproduces itself and confers authority on the practitioners who seek to speak in its name. That such authority is both the outcome and measure of practices of governance borne in the political desire to escape governmentality and the rule of institutional law altogether is not an indictment of academic projects that stand in historical, ideological, and narrative relation to social movements and that craft, in their honor, a commitment to doing justice. It is not an indictment because the point here is not about exposing disciplinarity in order to overcome it. As I have been stressing, it is about making the dilemmas that accompany the demand for commensurability as compelling as the political promise the demand now holds. In other words, this chapter seeks to take the power of our disciplinary belief in critical practice as seriously as we do.

IV. And When Gender Fails . . .

If the language of the political I have been using throughout this chapter turns repeatedly to the generic figures of justice and social transformation, this should not be read as evidence that I lack opinions about what would constitute their contemporary realization. Nor is it a reflection of the paucity of agendas that reside within the identity field of study that has chiefly organized this chapter's concerns. My task has been to explore the disciplinary force and affective power of the commitment to political commitment by paying attention to the political as a generic discourse and to the hegemony of the belief that underlies it.[37] The terms I have used to do this—political desire, field imaginary, field formation, progress narrative, and critical realism—have been aimed at deciphering the conundrums that ensue when the political aspiration to enact justice is a field's self-authorizing disciplinary identity and definitive disciplinary rule. Readers who contend that this itinerary abandons real politics will be missing my point even as they inadvertently confirm it, as one of the primary effects of the disciplinarity that I am tracking here is the demand it exacts on practitioners to deliver just such an accusation: that in the absence of the performance of a decisive political claim there can be no political commitments at all—or only bad ones.[38] It is the interpellative force of this accusation and the

37. It is difficult to find scholarship that does not stake its operations on something other than a claim for the political consequences of its endeavors, and even more difficult to encounter work that does not conform to the rhetorical formula that such disciplinarity begets, which routinely affirms one's own attachments by describing the errors and incapacities that characterize the critical analyses offered by others. Hence we read arguments that claim that only a return to materialist analysis can counter the ludic predilections of contemporary capitalism, or that only the itineraries of poststructuralist theory can rescue us from liberal humanism's arrogant individualism, or that only intersectional analysis can reveal the complexity of subjectivity, or that only an emphasis on embodied knowledge can unravel the epistemological exclusions of minoritized abjection, or that only a rejection of identity's self-centered humanism can attend to contemporary environmental emergencies, or that only a global theory of globalization has a chance of undermining the violence it engenders, or that only a commitment to collective transnational action can outrun the reaches of neoliberalism and its reorganization of economic and everyday life. Instead of offering specific examples for each of these rhetorical invocations, I hope that their familiarity will be sufficient for the larger point I use them to make. Still, if examples are needed, see any of my earlier publications.

38. I am well aware that the itinerary of this chapter will raise the question for readers about whether or not I am too quickly or easily dismissing the urgency of women's differences by challenging the critique of the category on which attention to that urgency has come to rest. Am I inadvertently producing an alibi for academic feminism's exclusions by focusing on the analytic and psychic dispensations that live in a field imaginary profoundly indebted to the disciplinarity that underwrites it? Can I refuse to rehearse the critique of the category of *women* and still be taken as committed to difference? Or is *that* critique the only political calculus in which a commitment to difference can be

shame that it both covets and induces that is central to the field's ongoing subject construction. Over time, the threat of the accusation can be so fully ingested that the critic responds to it without it ever being spoken, providing her own political rationales and agenda-setting conclusions as the means to cultivate legitimacy and authority as a practitioner in the field. Such authority, let's be clear, is as intoxicating as it is rewarding, and not just on the grounds of critical capital alone. The ingestion of the disciplinary structure has enormous psychic benefits precisely because of the promise it both makes and helps us hold dear, which is that our relationship to objects and analytics of study, along with critical practice as a whole, can be made commensurate with the political commitments we take them to bear. Hence the field-securing necessity of the very pedagogical lesson this chapter has been tracking, where *categories*, not critical agencies, are said to fail, and new objects and analytics become the valued terrain for sustaining the progress that underwrites the field imaginary's political dispensation to begin with.

The problem at the heart of the progress narrative of *gender* is not, then, about gender per se nor the belief that *gender* is now used to defend: that the justice-achieving future we want lives in critical practice, if only its generative relations and epistemological priorities can be properly conceived. Instead, my point has been that the progress narrative is a symptom of the disciplinary apparatus that requires it, which is calculated to overcome the anxiety that not only incites but endlessly nags it—the anxiety raised by the suspicion that what needs to be changed may be beyond our control. To acknowledge this anxiety is not to say that critical practice has no political implications, or that nothing can be done in the face of the emergency of the present, or that the desire for agency of any kind is fantastical in the most negative sense. But it is to suggest that the disciplinary structure is as compensatory as it is ideational, in part because the temporality of historical transformation it must inhabit is both unwieldy and unpredictable. Think here of the differences in historical weight, affect,

convincingly evinced? To put this most starkly, does my inability to muster passionate belief in the ongoing investment in critical practice as a resolution to contemporary urgencies indicate a failure of political commitment altogether? These questions arise from the disciplinary force of the commitment to justice that *Object Lessons* seeks to track, which is precisely why I am interested in the object relation as central to academic feminism's critical practice of political belief.

and transformative appeal between community activisms; revolutionary movements; state-based reform; and organized political participation— and then place each of these alongside the threats of recuperation; the evisceration of democratic political forms; and the reduction of citizen sovereignty. These and other forms of transformation and interruption stand in stark contrast to the profound belief that disciplinarity engenders: that knowing will lead to knowing what to do. Linda Zerilli, among others, has challenged the idea that the domain of knowledge can be so prioritized, demonstrating how some of the most profound social normativities are inhabited not where knowledge practices explicate the nuances of their operations but in the reflexes, habits, and the ongoing discernments that feminist critics often quite succinctly understand but cannot undo.[39] Her example concerns the gap between our own rather pointed critical knowing of the socially constructed nature of sex and gender *and* the feminist critic's inhabitations of everyday life in which the categories of men and women are experienced in all their fictional realness. But there are a host of other examples to bear out the point that while ignorance can be a form of privilege, its opposite—critical thinking and the knowing it promises to lead us to—may not finally be able to settle the relation between political aspiration and the agency it hopes to cultivate and command.

The void at the heart of the language of "the political," "social change," and "justice" is an effect not of indecision or imprecision, then, but of the complex temporality that structures the field imaginary: where on the one hand the disciplinary commitment to the political is borne in the historical configuration of the present while being bound, on the other hand, to the scene of the future in which the projection of the materialization of justice is forced to live. In this temporal glitch between the inadequate but overwhelming present and the necessity of a future that will evince change, the field imaginary performs and projects, as well as deflects, the anxiety of agency that underwrites it. The familiar debate glossed as theory versus practice is one inflection of the anxiety being highlighted here. While often called a divide, the theory/practice formulation is a dependent relation, more circular than divisional as each "side" repeatedly stresses the incapacities of agency invested in the other. So, for instance, practice is the realist check on theory and its passionate forays into modes of thinking

39. See Zerilli, "Doing Without Knowing."

and analysis that love to hone what is more abstract than concrete, more ideational than real, more symptomatic than apparent while theory presses against the insistence for instrumentalized knowledge and destinations of critical thought that can materialize, with expediency, the political desire that motivates it—all this even as the language of theory comes steeped in its own idiom of instrumental function whenever it wagers itself as an analogue for politics as a whole. To take up one side or other of the divide is to reiterate the hopeful belief that agency lives somewhere close by and that with just the right instrument—call it a strategy, an object of study, or an analytic—we can intentionally grasp it.

In parsing the theory/practice divide in this way, I am trying to foreground the power of the disciplinary rule that displaces the stakes of the debate by eliding the anxiety of agency that underlies it with the agential projections of critical practice—and further to make clear that the conundrums of disciplinarity and the ideational animations of critique cannot be settled by a rhetorical insistence on critical itineraries alone, whether linked to theory or practice or wrapped in the language of community, public knowledge, policy, or action-oriented research. This is because the theory/practice divide is a symptom of the anxiety of agency it evokes and cites, not an acknowledgment of, let alone an engagement with, it. While the repetition of the debate can certainly buttress the hope that what matters is *which* itinerary of critical practice we choose, it also relieves the field from arriving into the dilemma of its and our own limited agency, a limit that is not new but recurrent and part of both the complexity and difficulty of demanding to *know* how to use knowledge to exact justice from the contemporary world. This is not to say that the compensatory resolutions of the disciplinary pedagogies we learn are false or even that they are insufficient, but rather that there is more at stake than we have dared to think about the disciplinarity through which the object investments of critical practice are now performed. In the opening foray that this chapter delivers into *Object Lessons* as a whole, the problem that I am naming is simply this: that being made by the world we seek to change is always at odds with the disciplinary demand to make critical practice the means and the measure of our capacity to do so.

In the context of this chapter's specific attentions, my argument has been woven together by the idea that the consensus narrative about *women*'s categorical crisis says more about the field imaginary's function to allay anxieties over agency than it does about the ongoing contradictions of a global majority category whose inhabitants inhabit the world on highly differentiated minoritarian terms. Hence, as I have argued from the outset, *gender* is not exceptional as a term invested with the hope for the future's completion. Other analytic terms and identity categories similarly circulate, depending on the context and critical vision that underlie and mobilize the aspirations attached to them. But no term, it seems to me, shares a more complex or contradictory kinship to *women* than *women of color*, that category that has come to specify the occlusions of race, wealth, and empire so resonant in the narrative of categorical crisis. The significance of this latter complexity is only now emerging into critical visibility, making its way into Women's and Gender Studies in increasingly fraught debates over the priority accorded to transnational and postcolonial feminist analysis. While these debates are still less apparent in publication venues than in scenes of institutional life (such as conferences, national organizations, and departmental cultures), their lines of stress collate around the relationship between the study and status of race in the United States and its formation across various global sites, such that significant differences in political perspective and critical agenda can resonate within the framework *women of color*.[40] The characteristics of these differing perspectives are not uniform, but one important aspect of them arises from interpreting the transnational as the means by which the priority long sought for addressing the political situation of U.S. women of color—often powerfully figured as African American women—has been subordinated, with the added effect that "transnational feminism" operates in the discourse of academic hiring as a referent for non-U.S., non–Anglo American scholars. From this perspective, Women's and Gender Studies departments can now produce "diversity" in their ranks and curricular practices without having to address the early historical critique of the Women's Studies paradigm offered by the centrality of U.S. black feminism to universal *women*. To be sure, many feminist scholars take the transnational as a signifier for the analysis of race that reconfigures and challenges the practice of nation-based knowledge organization without discounting the significance of national struggle as one important route of political change. And there are many important projects that seek precisely to work across

40. See Holloway, "'Cruel Enough to Stop the Blood'"; Moallem, "'Women of Color in the U.S.'"; and Soto, "Where in the Transnational World Are U.S. Women of Color."

geopolitical and disciplinary boundaries to consider the uneven and differential routes by which the history of race and racial formation might be collectively, though not uniformly, understood.[41]

My point here is not to adjudicate the debate but to demonstrate how emerging contestations over the transnational have implications for the category *women of color* and its political and analytic capacities to figure the historical, geopolitical, and experiential differences that comprise it, which speaks to the compelling problem of categorical coherence and field-forming progress on the whole.[42] Or to follow the deconstructive itineraries offered by Rey Chow, we might say that supplemental terms that do the work of disarticulating universalisms bear within them their own supplemental renegotiation, making the future they work to evoke the scene for their own potential categorical transformation.[43] There is always difference in identity—even when the specification of an identity has been deployed to mark its difference from a dominant or dominating term. How this difference becomes politically or critically useful is historically complex, mediated in this case by the turn in U.S. educational institutions to global initiatives and by renewed emphases in Women's and Gender Studies on internationalizing its research and teaching agendas. My sense, then, is that while the most famous story in Women's Studies is about the crisis of the category of *women* and the progress entailed in taking distance from its failed promise of inclusion, there can be no ultimate categorical security, no representational cohesion, no object or analytic fulfillment— not even in the antiuniversalizing rubrics that have most productively

---

41. See especially Weinbaum et al., *The Modern Girl Around the World*.

42. Rachel Lee has written in a different vein about *women of color* in the field imaginary of Women's Studies, identifying how the category has been figured in contradictory temporalities, as both a late arrival and the future's completion. Her discussion stresses the importance of comparativity across race and ethnic analytics as a way to displace binary narrative logics that reiterate the centrality of white hegemony in order to condemn it, and that homogenize the multiple and divergent histories of U.S. racialization. She argues instead for exploring the differences, in history, identification, and political practice between minoritized racial and ethnic groups. While her focus is on the United States, more recent conversations about comparative racialization seek to address multiple institutional and geopolitics locations, including area knowledges; both itineraries have contributed to my thinking here. See Lee, "Notes from the (Non)Field"; and Shih, "Comparative Racialization."

43. See Chow, "When Whiteness Feminizes. . . ."

marked *women*'s differentiation and that lead to other investments and the progress narratives they incite. This is because, as I argue in more detail in the next chapter, divergence is itself a significant feature of institutional-ization, which repeatedly works to confound and undermine the converg-ing aspirations that animate identity knowledges to do justice by linking radically disparate scales of experience and analysis at once: from the indi-vidual and affective to the collective, social structural, economic, and geopolitical. This means that there is no escape from categorical crisis in identity knowledges, even if there are periods of reprieve, when the turn from one vexed scene of complex failure—to use the language of the progress narrative—finds aspirational optimism in the massively desired possibility of new or newly collectivizing terms. While I understand the poli-tical hope at the heart of this transferential desire, I anticipate the disap-pointment that inevitably follows when categories become overwritten by their incapacity to deliver the future they are used to wield. This is not to undermine the aspiration that promotes and invests in the transferential relation but to mark its powerful affective force.

All of this is to suggest that we are now in the midst of emerging diver-gences within the global majoritarian category, *women of color*, which finds its political formation increasingly articulated across geopolitical terrains that force *race* into different critical alignments to discern its competing uses, territorialities, temporalities, national frames of reference, and iden-tity formations. No one, I suspect, will call it a categorical crisis, at least no time soon, but the tensions that are increasingly articulated in and around transnational feminism already bear the mark of familiar stresses about who speaks for whom and which women have the authority to define and determine the frames of solidarity that generate the aspiration toward the political legibility and coherency of the group. While I can anticipate a host of objections to the analogy that underlines my discussion here, I nonetheless think that the story of *women* that we now tell will be re-peated, under different historical and cultural conditions, and in ways not wholly consistent with it, by the very categories, terms, and rubrics— whether political or critical—that have named, underscored, and sought to counter *women*'s faulty political utility. For me, this means that the turn away from *women*, repeated each time we repeat the crisis narrative in nearly ritualistic fashion, is a way to sustain *women*'s aspiration without having to engage with its most exacting and difficult lesson. That lesson is not the one that academic feminism has come to rely on, which imagines specification and particularity as the progressive route beyond *women's* universalist pretensions where it is possible to secure the field's representational authority, critical coherence, and political utility at once. To approach these issues from a different direction, we might say that the problem is not that *women* is always or essentially or inherently exclusionary, or that its deployment indicates a commitment to privileging the privileged by rendering differences obscure. The problem is more pervasive and daunting than that. Conceptual rubrics, like identitarian ones, are riven by the incommensurability between what they stand for and what—and who— comprises them. No aspect of these object relations is more critically important than another, but the conditions under which the category operates in critical practice and those it seeks to decipher, represent, and remake are not analytically, psychically, or socially the same.

I harbor no impossible wish to do battle with a field imaginary, certainly not one as powerful as that which governs Women's and Gender Studies in the United States today—and definitely not one that is the animating force of my own intellectual allegiances, the very mode and method through which my political desires have been addressed and expressed. Nor in meditating on *women of color* as a term am I interested in undermining the optimism that has long attended its resonant, urgent, and politically necessary demand. My purpose is not to expose or condemn the desire we invest in objects and analytics, but to pay attention to that desire, to the way it shapes the field's disciplinary form and generates both its and our critical capacities in order to learn something about the conundrum that accompanies a disciplinary apparatus that promises to make critical practice an agency for doing justice. This means acknowledging that practices of transference can be enormously satisfying, in that the movement from one object of study or analytic to one another is a powerful means for managing inadequacy and loss. Hence, I have argued that the contemporary lure of *gender* is about far more than castigating *women*, precisely because *gender* is invested with the promise to sustain the relationship to the world that *women* once stood for. In this, it reanimates the promise that the field imaginary holds forth to render a vision of the world adequate to the political desire that engages us in it. While this vision often lives most vibrantly in negative formation, as a deep refusal of identification with what *is*, the creative mastery that is alive in identity knowledges generates the belief in a future (and future-oriented) affirmative formulation, which is why I read the political desire of feminist academic production through its projections and idealizations, and in its ongoing translation of critical practice as a defining signature of its progressively invested political subjectivity.

We might say, then, that the transferential work that *gender* performs is achieved in the aspiration attached to it, not because it has demonstrated the capacity to explain, revise, and settle everything that scholars have used or want to use it to do. This is no alibi for the way that categories of identity or analysis really can disappoint us, but it does help to make the point that the categorical imperative that drives critical practice belongs not to it alone, but is the effect—indeed the demand—of the field imaginary that shapes not simply critical practice but the field as a whole. How else can we account for the ways in which our objects of study and analytic categories have come to be burdened with so much work? And why are we so willing to trust that the failure of a category to deliver what we want is always its fault? In the overarching concerns of *Object Lessons*, then, the significance of tracking the progress of *gender* lies less in the content of its formulations or the prized precision through which it has come to signify a host of critical attachments than in the transferential work that it performs to sustain our belief in the future-transforming capacities of critical practice in the aftermath of the impasses of *women*. In offering both an object and an analytic that can take up where *women* faltered, *gender* renews faith in the field's ability to know how to travel the distance from political aspiration to believing that such aspirations can come true. If, in the end, *gender* reaches the limit of its ability to sustain this most passionate, most important disciplinary belief, let's remember what has been forgotten about *women*: it never had the chance of surviving what we wanted from it either.

....

TWO

Telling Time

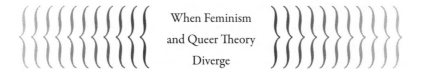

When Feminism
and Queer Theory
Diverge

A progress narrative is, quite obviously, a temporal formation, but in the framework of *Object Lessons* it is also a wish—to get past the beginning, to make good use of time, to know where one is going. If we read its operations only to condemn the false promises it makes, we risk overlooking the power the wish holds by ceding the whole terrain of politics and agency to materiality (and our ability to discern it) alone. My point in following the progress of *gender* in the last chapter was not to lament or chastise its capture of the field imaginary of Women's and now Gender Studies, even as I sought to interrupt its propulsion in order to pay attention to what the turn to *gender* was a turn away from. I wanted instead to inhabit the utopic force of the wish and to witness the ways that it shapes the political rhetorics, institutional aspirations, critical affects, and object relations in which identity knowledges produce and reflect their commitment to doing justice. In doing so, I sought to highlight the paradox that underlies identity knowledges as a whole: that the priority of the political that so defiantly characterizes them serves as their most insistent, most demanding disciplinary rule. There is, I contend, no escape from this predicament in which the institutionalization of identity as an object and analytic of study is bound to reproducing the very hope that inspires it as the disciplinary idiom for legible, no less than legitimate, belonging to the field. While the signifier of the political changes both within and across identity domains, the resonant investment in political commitment as the disciplinary syntax is not simply consistent, but constitutive. The lessons to be learned here arise not from trying to outrun disciplinarity or institutionalization, but from engaging the spell that the disciplinary apparatus casts, which entails ongoing attention to the ways in which critical practice serves as the animating scene of political desire in identity-oriented fields.

To that end, this chapter seeks to attend to institutionalization more fully and formally by considering how the itineraries of social movements collated around identity rubrics and the academic fields they provoke diverge, in political idiom, historical form, and affective force. While the predominant discussion of institutionalization typically laments this divergence—often condemning institutionalization for evacuating identity and its minoritized knowledges of their radical political effects— I begin these inquiries by presupposing that every political struggle in whatever idiom or venue is always profoundly, indeed inextricably, double valenced, being simultaneously an agent and a target of change. There is no agency that comes into being on its own or that acts autonomously, no agency that has the power to remain intact, to not be shaped and remade, resignified, even undone by its worldly sojourn. This is why it seems so strange to me when scholars expend enormous energy to critique such phenomena as homonormativity and queer liberalism without exploring how struggles to undo any form of phobic exclusion can never be made immune either to the desire for accessing traditional forms and formulas of normative U.S. life or to reinterpretation, if not reinvention, by the conservative forces that cede political ground to minoritized existence in the process.[1] While I might share the sense that becoming a legible state subject on the terrain of one's identity-based subjection is always dicey, I hold no belief that the critical project of saying so tells us as much as we need to know about the complicated historical itineraries in which political struggles over identity have been and continue to be remade. "Transformation" as

---

1. On homonormativity, see especially Duggan, "The New Homonormativity"; and Puar, "Mapping U.S. Homonormativities."

the goal of left/progressive politics—whether insurgent, radical, avant-garde, or left-of-center mainstream—cannot be determined or acknowledged solely on the grounds of one's own attachments, unless we find it convincing that an accusatory discourse of incipient complicity has traction in compelling people to want the political future that we do.[2] The central issue for thinking about political struggle is not, then, located in the determinacies of what changes and what seemingly remains the same but in grasping the challenge of the fact that nothing is static or, from a different direction, that transformation is all there is. From this perspective, continuity is the effect of change, not its subordination or eradication, and being other than what it once was is the persistent, not exceptional, condition of everything engaged by identity knowledges. These are all simple enough observations, cliché even, but that doesn't mean they are easy to remember when critical practice is bound to a disciplinary apparatus that reproduces the priority of its own authority as the means and the measure for doing politically transgressive work. Here, the failure of transformation to match the political idealizations nurtured by the field imaginary serves as the disciplinary point of departure, being both the engine of critical authority and the rhetorical form through which it draws its analytic force.[3]

2. I am confident that readers would not willingly consent to the belief that *doing* politics is about establishing your critical position in order to admonish those who do not share it for their lack of clarity, sophistication, theoretical rigor, political commitment, or critical insight. And yet, the rhetorical structure so routinely inhabited in what I am calling left identity critique takes its own passionate staging of the inner life of the political order—which can be defined in macropolitical terms, such as globalization and neoliberalism, as much as localizing and micropolitical ones—as an argument aimed not simply at the epistemologies that anchor domination but at the subjectivities historically cultivated in the process. Here the distinction between critiquing a discourse and critiquing the subjects made by it can quickly collapse in a textual environment in which the privileged model of political subjectivity is the critic's own.

3. Evidence for these metacritical ruminations lives most animatedly in the province of humanities-oriented work shaped by the critical genealogies of cultural studies, where political intimacy with the present takes priority, even in historically bent work, such that the rhetorical form of the argument proceeds through a calculated assessment of the relationship between the critic's objects of study and the hope of leftist political transformations. As I have emphasized, the criteria for the political is not uniform, but I have been struck in recent years by the resurgence of a familiar taxonomy in which "reformist"

My attention to the institutionalization of identity in this chapter seeks to counter the routines of shock that often accompany such discussions, where the sheer fact that identity's itinerary has not lived up to everything that has been projected onto it becomes the sole framework for understanding what academic institutionalization is. I will argue against the often heard postulation that institutionalization is always a political domestication by insisting on the necessary divergence of identity in its transit from social movement projects to academic ones, thus asking for more, not less, differentiation between the two—which means questioning all impulses and incitements to produce equivalencies between the critical registers, social scales, and psychic formations of identity across the diverse array of institutional sites and historical modalities in which it has lived.[4] In mak-

---

political projects are figured against more "radical" or "alternative" ones—with reformism serving as a code phrase for projects that seek transformation within the U.S. state apparatus, thereby participating in the violences of liberal democracy by buttressing its universalist debt to individualism and the autonomous agency it inscribes. What interests me throughout *Object Lessons* is not the extent to which the critique of reformism or any other figure of political constraint or failure is exacting, useful, or true, but what it means for critical practice to be so decisively relied upon as the means *for knowing this*, as if the procedures of analysis, methodological priorities, objects of study to which it turns to produce its own critical authority are not themselves bound to a fantasy of agency— one that is credited with the ability to intervene in both disciplinary orders of knowledge and social orders of governmentality through the sheer power of the critical claim to do so. I take my point to hold even in those cases where critics explicitly theorize political agency as the effect of contradiction (between say capitalism and democracy, or white supremacist and patriarchal formations), or that define alternativity as the excess or ghostly remains of political struggle, as the matter at stake is not the sophistication of the theoretical formulation but the investment it demonstrates in the agency of critical practice.

4. Many scholars have warned against the institutional domestication of identity knowledges. One of the most noteworthy is Judith Butler, who uses precisely this language when she reflects on the shared objects of study that link feminist and queer scholarly critique:

> I would insist that both feminist and queer studies need to move beyond . . . the institutional separatisms which work effectively to keep thought narrow, sectarian, and self-serving. The critique of the conservative force of institutionalization ought to be kept alive as a crucial mode of self-interrogation in the rush to acquire new legitimacy. . . . There is more to learn from upsetting such grounds, reversing the exclusions by which they are instated, and resisting the institutional domesti-

ing an argument for divergence, I am seeking to disorganize identity as it functions as a critical referent and political sign by bringing difference to identity as the key feature of its metacritical discernment. I thus hope to foreground the various ways that institutionalization transforms identity's political calculus and to provide a more nuanced critical anatomy of the translations and migrations through which an institutionalized academic object of study emerges into disciplinary form, both in its relation to and difference from the referent it names and from the social movement it is said to bear. My chapter's title, "Telling Time," is meant to situate this discussion in the conceptual register that best evokes the ongoing and irre-solvable difficulty of grasping historical praxis from our inadequate posi-tion within it. To learn to tell time is about deciphering the transformations produced by, with, and to identity as its moves into academic institutional form, becoming other to itself. From this perspective, identity and its po-litical value are just as contextually situated, socially imbricated, and his-torically dependent as we are. No doubt the ease of saying this provides little comfort in addressing the challenge of saying how.

In its immediate conjuncture, this chapter shares with "Doing Justice with Objects" a counterintuitive inclination to think of the political desire that animates identity knowledges as part of and not sheer resistance to the force of disciplinary rule. While the first chapter looked at how the narrative of *gender*'s progress works to sustain faith in a comprehensive, representative, and inclusive field, this chapter explores the fraught rela-tions attending queer theory elided by Leora Auslander's devoutly opti-mistic depiction. For some scholars, *gender* cannot possibly serve as the

---

cation of queer thinking. For normalizing the queer would be, after all, its sad finish. ("Against Proper Objects," 21)

Here, Butler arrays a number of now-familiar assumptions about critical practice that are at the heart of *Object Lessons*'s inquiries into the disciplinary formation of identity knowledges, including the notion that critique is the privileged means to counter "the conservative force of institutionalization," and that a reverence for the "antinormative" is essential to cultivating a less-complicit political imaginary for the work of academic fields. The paradox of course is that it is precisely this consolidation of the alternative perspective, put into play by self-interrogation and manifesting a position resistant not just to institutional norms but to becoming normative, that has become the characteris-tic description and reproductive mechanism not only of queer theory but of much schol-arship in identity domains today.

cover term and analytic framework for a queer theoretical approach to sexuality, being too bound to identity models on the one hand and too overly committed to feminism's tacit privileging of women on the other. From this point of view, which has deep genealogical roots in the work of such key thinkers as Gayle Rubin and Eve Kosofsky Sedgwick, the analytic distinction between gender and sexuality is fundamentally important for unpacking the density of sexuality as a set of practices and identifications that require a certain degree of critical no less than political autonomy. In the shorthand that might be said to govern such critical investments, gender is implicated in sexuality but sexuality is not explicable from within any of the various deployments of gender that found it as an analytic framework. In many field-forming narratives, it is precisely this distinction that is taken as the inaugural act of queer theory, the analytic precondition for its elaboration of a range of anti-identitarian critical and political commitments. In such contexts, the inclusive logic that allows *gender* to signify the study of sexuality can only be an impediment to queer theoretical aspirations, not their generation.[5] To pay attention to the object relations cultivated here, where the incommensurability and differentiation between gender and sexuality stand in striking contrast to the aspiration expressed elsewhere for *gender*'s accumulative agency is to parse the political desire attending identity knowledges from rather different affective and analytic directions. Disidentification no less than prohibition become pivotal features for a critical project that seeks to reject critical realism as the route for apprehending power, and that subsequently prioritizes the nonidentical, unassimilable, and anti-institutional as the means to rethink not only politics and identity but political subjectivity itself.[6] While sexuality is

5. Admittedly, Auslander's narrative of gender's progress is not organized around the nominative, queer theory; she uses the rubric *Queer Studies*, which I take to be more analytically aligned with the accumulative force of *gender* as an object and analytic of study than gender has ever been with queer theory. These distinctions are important not only for the conversation underway here, but for further meditations on queer theory in chapter 6.

6. The concept of disidentification has received a great deal of theoretical attention and is arrayed in multiple analytic directions across the work that comprises contemporary queer critique. In José Esteban Muñoz's *Disidentifications: Queers of Color and the Performance of Politics*, it is used to evoke the passage beyond the false choice between toxic forms of identification with normative performances of personhood and simple counteridentifications. Disidentification, he writes, "is a step further than cracking open

rendered congruent with gender in many contemporary critical discourses, what interests me is the insistence, born in the attachment to a queer theoretic, that explicitly seeks to turn the tables on what it means to do justice to or with one's object of study by steadfastly refusing identification, collaboration, or convergence between terms and terrains of analysis no less than the politics understood as endemic to them.

In its local detail, the chapter is forged as a response to an essay by Janet Halley, written under the signature of "Ian Halley" and published in the *Duke Journal of Gender, Law and Policy* in 2004.[7] A precursor to the provocative and spellbinding book, *Split Decisions: How and Why to Take a*

---

the code of the majority; it proceeds to use this code as raw material for representing a disempowered politics or positionality that has been rendered unthinkable by the dominant culture"; in this, disidentification is a crucial practice for generating "a queer lifeworld that is smokey, mysterious, and ultimately contestatory" (31, 34). My use of disidentification in this book tends to collate around the disciplinary apparatus of identity knowledges, which marshals it as a political value such that one is never more fully within the field imaginary than when she figures her analysis as coincident with a set of transformative political aims made resonant outside of it, whether through specific social subjects or the categories of analysis used to represent and discern them.

7. "Queer Theory by Men" began as the 2002 Brainerd Currie Memorial Lecture at the Duke University Law School under the title "A Map of Feminist and Queer Theories of Sexuality and Sexual Regulation." It set forth a reading in which sexual regulation was to feminism precisely what sexuality was to queer theory: the product of key political commitments and theoretical articulations which, especially in the former case, had profound and disturbing implications for the workings of law. When the *Duke Journal of Gender, Law, and Policy* organized a special issue to address it, invited respondents received a new draft titled, "A Map of American Feminist Legal Thought: Sexual-Subordination Feminism, Its Derivatives, and Its Contestants," which worked to foreground those implications by naming the form of feminist thought—"sexual subordination feminism"—that Halley wanted to take a break from. This was followed by an important reconfiguration in which the title emphasized the theoretical priority that sexual subordination feminism could not: "The Politics of Theoretical Indeterminacy: Deciding in the Splits Between Feminism(s), Gay Identity Politics, and Queer Theory." This version contained much of the argument that was printed in the volume, though it had not coalesced in the provocative finale: "Queer Theory by Men," signed by Ian Halley. That final version would come later and it would feature numerous additions, including nods to feminism's hybrid forms and nonminimalist political and theoretical meanderings. Still, Ian reinforced Janet's founding argument in his third footnote: "if you push hard enough, almost any currently available feminist text will eventually manifest its commitment to M > F" (8).

Break from Feminism, "Queer Theory by Men" seeks to develop a left critique that inhabits and extends the most radical potential of queer theory, which for Ian lies in its ability to pursue sexuality as an object of study apart from the political sensibilities and critical institutions established by feminism. As Ian writes, "we probably wouldn't *have* queer theory if there had not been the need for . . . pro-sex opposition to cultural feminist moralism and to male/female model regulatory ambitions."[8] In Ian's terms, feminism operates through an insistent critique of subordination, such that it is always in some definitive relation to "M>F," with F as "the disadvantaged or subordinated element" that must be defended (8). Hence, "feminism opposes the subordination of F. It frames itself as a justice or emancipatory project" (8). Queer theory, on the other hand, is a "complex array of projects" that rejects feminism's paradigmatic commitments in favor of "a rich brew of pro-gay, sex liberationist, gay-male, lesbian, bisexual, transgender, and sex-practice-based sex-radical, sex-positive, anti-male/female model, anti-cultural-feminist political engagements, some more postmodernizing than others, some feminist, others not" (13–14). Less a destination for organizing tension-laden object relations than the consequence of a collective set of political engagements with sexual alterity, queer theory as Ian defines it is a critical project that follows the itineraries of anti-identity, posthumanist thought. Its divergentist determinations—not male/female model, not cultural-feminist, not antigay, not not-sex-positive—situate it against the accumulationist progress of *gender* by refusing to compromise. In Ian's hands, queer theory has no intention of settling for inclusion.

My interest in "Queer Theory by Men" lies precisely here, where the critical dedication to *divergence* promises to fulfill queer theory's anti-identitarian commitments by refusing two kinds of convergentist demands. The first is object oriented and works, as we saw in chapter 1, as an insistence that projects collated around the same phenomena (in this case gender and sexuality) should be merged to yield a collective agenda, one that collates even as it differentiates the entities it includes. Ian rejects this by assuming, in the language of *Object Lessons*, that there is no uniform or

8. Ian Halley, "Queer Theory by Men," 50. Throughout this chapter, I honor the essay's gender performativity by citing its author as "Ian." All references to "Halley" are meant to signify Janet Halley, the author of the performance. Further page references appear in the text.

singular relation on which critical apprehension of the object can be based and further that the contestations that arise are not impasses to be negotiated but the terrain to be inhabited by politically engaged scholars. As he tells it, convergence means not only obliterating the historical and political specificity of the object but killing off the optimistic attachments that underlie left critique altogether. The second demand arises from the first and concerns what I think of as the ethical position that frames the political. As Ian depicts it, convergentism is a sensibility overwritten by a sentimental moralism, making it "terrible to have a theory of homosexuality that [is] not ultimately feminist, or a feminism that [does] not wholly encompass our theory of homosexuality" precisely because either reflects a narcissistic self-interest, raising the fear that to avow one's own political desires puts everyone else at risk (9). In such terms, to diverge is always to become a bad political subject. Ian argues against this way of thinking, attacking equivalence and commensurability as emblems of the good in favor of a conception of politics that foregrounds both the value and utility of divergence. Dedicated to its own desires, "Queer Theory by Men" crafts the analytic and political consequences of a queer theoretic diverged from feminism at every turn.

Ian's commitment to divergence is both necessary and convincing and will be important to more than this chapter's foray into identity knowledges and their object and analytic pursuits. But as might already be clear, the cost of his insistence is borne almost fully by feminism—or as Ian writes it "Feminism"—which becomes the mother of all convergentism, so adamantly conditioned by it that Ian can hone his love of divergence as if it belongs to the queer theoretic alone. But how can the legal hegemony of sexual subordination feminism be laid so neatly, indeed so completely at Feminism's feet? Did Feminism reduce herself to a singular subordinating definition or is there more to be said about her unwieldy transportation, even translation, not just through law but across the social spectrum, including the institution of the university and its organization into disciplines? This chapter responds to these questions through its own rather heated engagement with "Queer Theory by Men" by resituating the relationship between feminism and queer theory in the context of their most important epistemic distinctions, which means paying attention to what I think of as the discordant temporalities that will help explain the necessity of their divergence on different grounds. By discordant temporality, I mean something along the lines of what Hortense Spillers has described as the epistemic shift that political projects organized around identity undergo as they are transformed into academic domains of study.[9] After all, feminism and queer theory are not equivalent terms. The more obvious analogs would be *feminism and queer activism*, which name commensurate political practices. Or *Women's Studies and Gay and Lesbian Studies*, which name the institutional sites inaugurated by feminism and gay and lesbian movements. Or *Feminist Studies and Queer Studies*, which foreground the political intuitions and commitments of academic inquiries that form cross-disciplinary fields, often arriving into coherence as field and program names of their own. Or *feminist theory and queer theory*, which twin two terms resonate with political signification with the increasingly privileged province of theory as the critical currency of the contemporary humanities.[10] The point is not that Ian needs to change his inquiry to explore equivalent terms, but that attending to the relationship between his terms— feminism and queer theory—requires a different kind of attention, no less than a different elaboration of divergence.

To be sure, *this* is a far cry from Ian's arrival into "the astonishingly complex political, intellectual and theoretical array" that comprises his queer theoretic (13). It deploys divergence in the interests of telling time, which entails following the often incommensurate itineraries that identity

9. Spillers, "Women in/of the Academy." Specifically, Spillers identifies the threshold as that which transforms identity from its "pre-theoretical" deployment in social movement to its postinstitutionalized theoretical elaboration. While Spillers is careful to say that in the use of "pre-theoretical" she is not forging a hierarchy or progressivist teleology, I find this language too weighty in the context of theory's academic privilege. Hence I use *pre-institutional* and *internal critique* to register the different epistemic modes that have accompanied identity's itinerary in the U.S. university.

10. Ian's imprecise vocabulary is not his alone. The realm of identity knowledges is rife with these slippages, even in contexts in which the theoretical framework is so adamantly poststructuralist and so critical of identity fundamentalisms that one would otherwise predict a heightened interest in differentiating identity concepts, political rubrics, fields of study, and the analytic capacities and significations drawn by and for them. Such differentiations would require attention to how and when terms meld or fracture, making it difficult to move without explanation from, say, feminism to Feminist Studies to feminist theory or, alternatively, from queer to queer culture to queer scholar to queer theoretical critique, or from third world to African American to black to women of color to race. In various chapters, *Object Lessons* grapples with the impulse and implication of such critical convergences.

as a politics has taken, how it has entered various discursive and institutional contexts and been shaped and reshaped by the struggles it has found there. Legal institution. The University. Disciplines and their interdisciplinary kin. The whole incomprehensible kettle of psychic life. Sex, and whatever we think comprises it. While Ian takes divergence as a critical commitment we can choose to pursue, I will read it as the constitutive operation that underlies identity's historical sojourn altogether, which means that the difference he poses between feminism and queer theory will be cast by me as one of the most important effects of divergence itself. To that end, a good deal of this chapter will follow Spillers to discern distinctions among identity's activist deployments, state-based rhetorics, object formations, analytic practices, and its institutionalized, at times deeply anti-identitarian, theoretical elaborations—including the way that queer theory has recently been taken to task for its own identitarian ideals and occlusions. (Think transgender.[11]) I will have more to say shortly about the discordant temporalities that might help us sort out these relations, but for now I want to stress that the point in making these discernments is not to justify the academic nor to render activist impulses minor to theory's thrills. I'm not even trying to know the world better, in that quintessentially Enlightened move that gives conscious life ultimate agency in historical change. Nor am I seeking optimism in unknowability, as that stance can be used to inoculate us against the full implications of the indeterminacies that cement us *here*. My aim is to consider inhabiting change

11. The critical archive on transgender is extensive and assumes its own taxonomic inquiries into the animating distinctions between transgender, transsex, intersex, and queer. See, e.g., Valentine, "We're 'Not about Gender'"; Jagose and Kulick, "Thinking Sex/Thinking Gender"; Stryker and Whittle, *The Transgender Studies Reader*; More and Whittle, *Reclaiming Genders*; and C. Jacob Hale's bibliography, "Introducing Transgender Studies into the Undergraduate Philosophy Curriculum." Signature texts in the transgender archive include: Stone, "The Empire Strikes Back"; Feinberg, *Transgender Liberation*; Stryker, "My Words to Victor Frankenstein above the Village of Chamounix"; Bornstein, *Gender Outlaw*; Prosser, *Second Skins*; Chase, "Hermaphrodites with Attitude" and "Affronting Reason"; Hale, "Consuming the Living, Dis(re)membering the Dead in the Butch/FTM Borderlands"; Namaste, *Invisible Lives*; and Nestle et al., *GenderQueer*. For discussions of the relationship between trans scholarship and Feminist Studies, see Heyes, "Reading Transgender, Rethinking Women's Studies"; Hausman, "Recent Transgender Theory"; and Salamon, "Transfeminism and the Future of Gender."

without disavowing either the power of our once-powerful attachments or what those attachments tell us about where and who we have been.

To follow the itinerary I delineate above will necessitate some studied attention to the way that "Queer Theory by Men" tries to have its cake and eat it too. For while Ian offers a compelling commitment to some of the most profound and to my mind productive anti-identitarian impulses of queer theory, he ends up enacting his rebellion against feminism in a performative grammar of identitarian attachment to the belligerent textual bodies of variously embodied men.[12] This, of course, is the kind of critical move that can hurt, not because the turn to men is, well, to *men*, but because there is already so very little in the queer theoretical archive that would allow us to arrive anywhere else—and I want the queer theoretic to do some work on behalf of the analytic mobilities of that seemingly defunct figure, "the lesbian," who has been reduced, unsexed, domesticated, uglied, and abjected by forces too numerous to list, including those of feminism and queer theory.[13] If I forge an attachment to her in the pages

12. One of my favorite moments in Foucault's work is his response to purported sexual differences between lesbians and gay men. Interviewer: "lesbians seem in the main to want from other women what one finds in stable heterosexual relationships: support, affection, long-term commitment, and so on." Foucault: "All I can do is explode with laughter. . . . [T]he distinction offered doesn't seem to be convincing, in terms of what I observe in the behavior of lesbian women" ("Sexual Choice, Sexual Act," 156).

13. This is not quite the same issue that Biddy Martin discussed in 1992 when she took up the relationship between gender and sexuality in early queer theoretical work, but it comes interestingly close. In Martin's terms, the problem of the queer theoretic was its investment in masculinity as a privileged figure of mobility against the fixity and stasis of the overmarked feminine. In reading the work of Sedgwick and Butler—*Epistemology of the Closet* and *Gender Trouble* specifically—Martin argued, "Too often, anti-determinist accounts that challenge feminist norms depend on the visible difference represented by cross-gender identifications to represent the mobility and differentiation that 'the feminine' or 'the femme' supposedly cannot." Martin was concerned with figuring out what feminist and queer theories might jointly "complicate and put into motion," and so her analysis focused on the complicated discourse of femme and butch, in which sexuality is fully staked to gender difference but not in M > F terms (94). In many ways, Martin's analysis was prescient, not only because of that decade's proliferation of masculinities and the cultural shift of transsexual discourses from MTF to FTM, but the way that "gay men" would increasingly serve as a referent for alternative psychic economies and practices of sexuality and desire, a point she noted even then (104). Most certainly, Martin was correct when she diagnosed that the "analytic and political separation

that follow by taking "Janet" as the lesbian's symptomatic displacement, it is not because I wish to impose on Halley an identificatory truth that she may not share. But it is to mark the spot where Ian's argument for a queer theoretic, forwarded in performative garb as "Queer Theory by Men" and manifested by what I take to be the authority of "his" signature, sends me into a performative frenzy of my own, leading me to the potentially false hope that I might be able to use divergence to extract some space for the lesbian to claim her own affections for a sex-affirmative, shame-affirmative, irrational, anti-identitarian, anti-male-female, and antiessentialist queer theoretic.[14] In this effort, I chastise Ian for not taking his commitment to

---

of gender and sexuality [that] has been the rallying cry of a great deal of queer theory . . . has too often proceeded . . . by way of . . . reductionist accounts of the varieties of feminist approaches to just one feminism" (72–73). In this, she saw how governance feminism was playing a role by providing the rule against which the queer theoretic's divergence could turn. And yet, in reading the stasis accorded to feminism and femininity in the queer theoretic, Martin's topography of gender has undergone extensive revision. While masculinity continues to be the scene for various kinds of mobile identifications, gender is not consigned, as Martin argued, to the "indicatively female body" but operates as a profoundly transitive signifier, one that can evoke a spectrum of gender identities that have no *predictable* relation (but *always* some relation, whether of abjection, incorporation, or something else) to the female feminine, cast as either heterosexual or femme. It is this reformulation that I use here to challenge the reduction of gender to minimalist Feminism's terms. See Martin, "Sexualities Without Genders and Other Queer Utopias."

14. My interest, let me be clear, is not to discover what Janet really meant when she conceded her signature to Ian. We're all too weary from the inquisitors of truth to keep probing that initial editorial dilemma: is "Ian" Janet's new pre- or post-op name, or "merely" a performance meant to mark a difference between gendered bodies and critical authorities? Can one write a response if the context is indeterminate, if we do not know if "Ian" is parody or truth? And would Janet's claim to Ian's identitarian realness cancel the performative gesture of the signature altogether? Or is the performance the means by which Ian's claim to realness is made real? Of course, for anyone who has followed the progress of *gender*, it is no deep surprise to encounter an escape from the constraints of feminism's *women* as a route through *men* (regardless of how in this very process, the substance of the category of *men* itself has been changed). One could even say that Ian's own signatory use of FTM drag brings the performative stakes of gender as a theater of animated desires and political possibilities to another level, making us pay attention to the ways that queer critique, like all critique, *assembles* its investments, produces and uses its objects, and cultivates its own criteria of value and evaluation—all as a way of forging a critical practice staked to a world we might politically want. The dependencies

divergence far enough, which entails paying attention to the incommensurate itineraries of *feminism*, a social movement, and *queer theory*, an academic mode of critique—and hence to the vastly different temporalities, affective formations, and institutional relations that characterize their historical and political nonconvergence. It also means recognizing that the legal codification of sexual subordination feminism is a divergentist operation, as the feminism produced in law and Feminism are not the same. None of this comes close to the project Ian set for himself, which makes my use of his work an example of the critical procedures that I track throughout this book, where the constitution of an object of study works repeatedly as a scene for the unfolding of political desires that find their articulation in relation to the figures, languages, and arguments offered by others. In its performance of the work of object relations, then, this chapter engages Ian's political desires by setting his wishes both within and against my own. If Janet had not invented him, I would have had to.

On Ian's Terms

"Queer Theory by Men" intends to provoke. It seeks to demonstrate why "it would be good for left pro-sex intellectual and political work, including feminist work of this kind, if people doing it could occasionally Take a Break from Feminism" (7).[15] To that end, the essay is organized in four parts. The first provides a "minimalist definition of [U.S.] feminism"; the second offers a genealogy of "feminism, gay-identity politics and queer theory"; the third locates the analytic capacities of the queer theoretic through a close reading of two texts by men; and the fourth analyzes a legal case, *Twyman v. Twyman*, to explore the critical legal consequences of the discussion (7). Given the essay's central provocation, the stakes of Ian's definition of feminism are high, and he knows it. Here's an important passage from the first section:

----

that this entails are not easy to decipher let alone escape or undo, which underlies one of the core arguments of this book.

15. Notably, the lecture version of the essay was far more polemical in its rhetorical formulation than the published version by Ian, which tempers many of Janet Halley's first claims with temporal mediations, as in the case cited here where the break from feminism is figured as an occasional one. Influenced by my first encounters with the argument, I'm convinced that Ian's hesitations are rhetorical not argumentative concessions.

First, to be feminism, a position must make a distinction between M and F. Different feminisms do this differently: some see men and women, some see male and female, some see masculine and feminine. . . . However a particular feminism manages [this] . . . it is not "a feminism" unless it turns in some central or core way on a distinction between M and F.

Second, to be a feminism . . . a position must posit some kind of subordination as between M and F, in which F is the disadvantaged or subordinated element. At this point feminism is descriptive and not normative: M>F.

And third (here is the normative turn), feminism opposes the subordination of F. It frames itself as a justice or emancipatory project. As between M and F, and possibly because M>F, feminism carries a brief for F. (8)

Beyond these attributes, Ian discusses feminisms that concern themselves "with powers that operate not across the M/F distinction, but along the many distinctions that we refer to when we speak of 'class,' 'race,' and 'empire'" (9). These are "'hybrid' feminisms, because they set out to examine (at least) two incommensurate modalities of power at once" (9). For Ian, feminism's core attribute is sexual subordination, which is routinely accompanied by a moral economy and is often aversive, in his terms, to liberationist conceptions of sex. Hence, queer theory answers the urgent political and critical need to oppose "cultural feminist moralism" and the "male/female model" that frames it (50).

The bulk of "Queer Theory by Men" argues for the "divergence" of the study of sexuality from sexual subordination, rejecting the familiar demand to converge gender and sexuality into a single political or institutional agenda. To explicate this necessary refusal, Ian begins by examining the work of Catherine A. MacKinnon, whose formulation of the male/female model "has become the paradigmatic understanding of sexuality in sexual-subordination feminism in the United States" (10). But MacKinnon's perspective was not always such a problem. Her early work offered a theory of sexuality that was decidedly radical in its anti-identitarian commitments, as when she insisted, as Ian puts it, that "[m]ale dominance and female subordination did not merely *rank* the genders: they *produced* them" (10). This argument made any claim to "women's point of view" untenable because that viewpoint was "already constituted *as its subordination*" (10). Ian sees great potential for feminism in MacKinnon's insight that "desire and . . . knowledge are inhabited throughout by the epistemology of this power structure" because it brings into view the sheer difficulty of accounting for women in rigorous historical terms (10). But the Later MacKinnon breaks ranks with the early work and begins to show signs of affiliation with what is now called cultural feminism. This MacKinnon seeks regulatory redress in the courts on behalf of women who suffer the effects of sexual subordination, which means that she has shifted her investments toward claiming an epistemological privilege for women's experience. MacKinnon's later work thus relies on the analytic capacity of feminism to craft a legal project that reflects the experiential authority of women *as women*. Sexual harassment law, antirape legislation, domestic violence resolution and protection: The feminist ambition at work in these projects seeks to defend women against male sexuality, which becomes "a vast social problem" (12). Ian's insistence on taking a break from feminism in order to develop a queer theoretic arises here, where the Later MacKinnon conceives of women-as-men's-victims and offers a theory of sexuality that mirrors a social theory of subordination (12).

Following his discussion of MacKinnon, Ian turns to other left progressive projects—gay identity politics, pro-sex feminism, and postmodernism—in order to more fully establish the historical forces, analytic frameworks, and modes of disidentification that generate the divergent intellectual and political ambitions of queer theory. Four points of his narrative are especially important, as they provide the complex genealogy of queer theory that governs his essay. (1) In contrast to familiar analogies that link gay liberation to black Civil Rights, Ian sees the gay movement's presentation as "a *subordinated-sexuality movement*" as troping feminism by figuring gay people as a distinct social group in need of justice and revaluation. This establishes the queer theoretic as a departure not only from feminism but from identitarian gay politics. (2) By reading the genocidal challenge of AIDS as undermining gay sexual liberationist impulses, Ian historicizes the political and intellectual split that shapes the opposition between pro-gay marriage centrism and antinormative queer world building in the United States today. This split has been central to the elaboration of the queer theoretic and is encoded in one of the most important distinctions it hones between subordination projects and "shame affirmative" ones (12). (3) In critiquing the moralism of sexual subordination feminism, Ian emphasizes that it produced its own political backlash within feminism (now called the sex wars), which resulted in scores of pro-sex, avant-garde feminists denouncing their political alliance with feminism. Many of the projects they took up as a result were cast overtly as queer, thereby situating a radical critique of feminism within the queer theoretic. (4) In his final move, Ian signals how the arrival of postmodernism to U.S. intellectual circles offered new formulations of subjectivity and power, challenging the logics of identity and subordination that had been so foundational to the study of gender and sexuality. These formulations provided a set of new politically inflected intellectual commitments to underwrite queer theoretical initiatives. Through these discontinuous plot lines, Ian forwards a capacious definition of the queer theoretic, which he finds wherever "identity *and* subordination *and* morality come under left critique" (13).

With the genealogies of feminism and queer theory in place, the essay opens into its longest and most crucial section on queer theory by men in order to depict how far the queer theoretical can travel with feminism before needing to take a break from it. Here, Ian focuses on "male authors who insist on their sexual interests": Leo Bersani in "Is the Rectum a Grave?" and Duncan Kennedy in "Sexual Abuse, Sexy Dressing, and the Eroticization of Domination" (14).[16] In Bersani's canonical essay, Ian finds a strange alliance with MacKinnon, since it is through MacKinnon's understanding of male sexual desire as an expression of misogyny that Bersani reads, in both gay male culture and its homophobic counterpart, a "misogynist association of gay male anal receptivity with female sexual subordination" (15). Rather than reject this association, Bersani accepts, "as a *pro-gay male description* . . . the proposition that '[t]o be penetrated is to abdicate power'" (15). He thus "offers us a classic example of the 'perverse' in queer argumentation" by agreeing with MacKinnon "that phallocentrism is a social calamity," but on queerer grounds: "because it blocks *men's* access to the 'humiliation of the self' *enjoyed* by women" (17). While Ian loves this queer reversal, the queer theoretic requires much more than this to accomplish the break from feminism that he seeks. Three other aspects of Bersani's essay are more effective in meeting the challenge. The

16. See Bersani, "Is the Rectum a Grave?"; and Kennedy, "Sexual Abuse, Sexy Dressing and the Eroticization of Domination."

first is the fact that Bersani's transvaluation of abjection carries no brief for F; it is politically linked to men, "and, even more to the point, [to] male/male sexual desire" (18). The second attends Bersani's focus on sexuality as the scene of dissolution, which is not indebted to the male/female model since "access to that abjection is a distinctive virtue of *sexuality generally*," just as the "will to dominate that introduces the self into its being" is neither sex specific nor dependent on a gendered understanding of the human subject (19). Hence, "[t]his formulation definitely Takes a Break from Feminism in the sense that it stakes sexuality to something *other than* M/F" (19). A final applause goes to Bersani's commitment to divergence, which is born in the insistence "that the form and value of power in sexual abjection are unique to it, nonhomologous to and analytically nontransferrable to other forms of power" (19). In short, "because sexual experience is *primordially* about the struggle of the self for mastery over the body and the world, it cannot *derive* its paradoxes of power from the social subordinations" (19). In these various ways, Bersani refuses to converge his theory of sexuality with a theory of the social, which goes a long way toward establishing the critical obligations and analytics that Ian finds necessary to the queer theoretic.

But Bersani does not take Ian there, in part because his essay remains enthralled to a politics of moral outrage. In order to demonstrate how best to overcome this affiliation with governance feminism, Ian turns to the work of Duncan Kennedy, a self-described heterosexual white middle-class male "who wants there to be women (on the street, in the media, at work) who can afford to be erotically thrilling *to him*" (29). As a critical legal theorist, Kennedy is interested in "how to regulate sexual abuse . . . to maximize women's safe . . . engagement in sexy dressing, sexually meaningful play, and sex with men" (29). Kennedy's agenda has infuriated feminists, and he was the target of a now-classic feminist critique in critical legal studies.[17] But for Ian, Kennedy's refusal to accede to feminist moralism puts him on the side of a queer theoretic; his work is queer "*because* of its embrace of male heterosexual erotic interests," which diverge both from "feminist strictures" and from "homo- and bi-supremacy" (29). Like Bersani, Kennedy works through MacKinnon's theory of sexuality, while departing from it in three significant ways. First, Kennedy does not conceive

17. See West, "Deconstructing the CLS-FEM Split."

of law as an arena of guaranteed political outcomes, given that regulation is "embedded in noisy enforcement systems" (30). Hence, laws always miss their targets, at least some of the time; they always abuse those whose interests they seek to redress, at least some of the time. Second, for Kennedy, the social relationships that law seeks to regulate are not produced in law but are played out in "*the shadow of the law*," such that people make incalculable "bargains" about their interests, risks, and immunities (31). This means that contrary to feminist investments, one can never know in advance the content or contours of "women's interests" or "men's interests." Hence, women's safety from sexual harm could be aligned with some men's heterosexual erotic interests—that is, "if women knew it was safer to be sexy *to them*" (32). And finally, Kennedy challenges the image of eroticized domination found in feminism as so massively "rationalized" that its "'totalitarian gender system seems paranoid'" (quoted in Ian Halley 33). Following postmodernist theories of the subject, he is interested in gender's regulatory failure and in the performative interruptions that demonstrate, against the stability of the M/F model, a far more fractured and labile formation, one in which the feminist legal demand to know is profoundly unsettled. For Ian, it is Kennedy's arrival at uncertainty that offers the most invaluable queer theoretic purchase: "'The truth' and 'the real' are not the ground upon which we can base our cost/benefit assessments, but *effects* in a sexual semiosis that is pervasively riven with paradox and knowable only through the murky epistemes of desire and politics" (38). Still, as with Bersani, Ian laments that Kennedy doesn't make his break from feminism complete. This would mean asking "whether the erotic/power dynamics between 'men' and 'women' arise *outside* gender *tout court*" in order to undercut the M/F model altogether (37).

In both essays, then, Ian finds the break from feminism to be less decisive than he wants, as each "avoids some of its own analytic consequences by Cutting Feminism Some Slack" (38). To demonstrate how to fulfill his own queer theoretical aspirations, Ian devotes the last section of "Queer Theory by Men" to a reading of the legal documents pertaining to the dissolution of the 1969 marriage of Sheila and William Twyman. The case study is riveting in its details. As Ian describes it, "Sheila filed for divorce in 1985, and not long thereafter amended her claim to include a tort action" against William for "intentionally and cruelly" imposing "deviate sexual acts" on her (39). The court granted the divorce and awarded Sheila $15,000 in damages for emotional distress; William appealed. Court documents offer various details of the couple's history, but the general narrative goes like this: Early in the relationship, William introduced bondage into the couple's sex life. At first Sheila consented, but later she refused on the grounds that she had been raped before the marriage. Several years later, Sheila found out that William was in therapy; William confessed to an affair and said that it was the consequence of Sheila's refusal to have S/M sex. The Twymans then entered couple's counseling and Sheila consented again to bondage activities, but in the end felt too humiliated by them to continue; indeed, she reported that these activities reengaged the trauma of her prior rape. In their last sexual encounter, Sheila was "injured to the point of bleeding" (40). As Ian reads it, the justices understood William to be a knowing subject whose insistence on S/M to save the marriage put Sheila's emotional well-being at risk (39). Their reading, Ian contends, was shaped by sexual subordination feminism and was not just bad for William but "bad for women," as it taught Sheila to experience herself "as utterly powerless, utterly broken," and to live within her suffering in order to exact justice (44, 45–46). Feminism, Ian writes, "might be partly responsible not only for her power, but also for the terrible suffering that grounds it" (46).[18]

18. In reading the appeals documents, Ian focuses less on the story of the Twymans' marriage than on the justices' discernments of it, and ultimately on their acquiescence to the picture Sheila paints of herself as William's victim. For Ian, this acquiescence is written through and through by sexual subordination feminism. To counter it, he asks, "can feminism accommodate a completely reversed image of the Twymans' marriage?" The answer begins to sketch how a queer theoretic would approach the case. I quote at length:

> Imagine it: the utter pathos of William, begging for sex he can't get from his wife, guiltily sneaking off to have it with another woman, whipped through round after round of psychotherapy to figure out why he is such a pervert and finally submitted to the public humiliation of testifying about his hopeless intimacies and suffering a published opinion deciding that his marital conduct is very likely outrageous, beyond all possible bounds of decency, atrocious, and utterly intolerable in a civilized society. As against that, imagine: the astonishing powers of Sheila, laying down the moral law of the couple's sex life, pursuing William like a Fury for breaking it and extracting not only a fault based divorce, but possibly also money damages specifically premised on her alliance with the state against him. . . . Can feminism acknowledge that women emerge from the court's decision

A queer theoretic, on the other hand, would expel "the presumption, silently carried along in all the opinions of the court, that Sheila Twyman has a meaningful moral claim that William's conduct was wrong," and it would require a refusal to grant the "'trauma of having been raped'" to every sexual act as if the act and not the organization of knowledge and power in which Sheila deployed her history was what was at stake (47). But more than this, the queer theoretic, no longer beholden to M>F, would be able to ascertain "the intense, and formally almost identical, sexual pathos of Shiela [sic] and William. Both are committed to the idea that they have deep, inner, injured sexual selves beyond which they cannot move one micron and which they must enact with near-fatal completeness" (47). In Foucauldian terms, William is "a classic subject of the psychiatrization of perversions"; Sheila the classic subject of "rape trauma" (47). And what of the regulatory regime that operates to produce them? Ian names "marital monogamy," which offers deep scripts for inhabiting power's force relations, for monitoring behavior, and for generating sexual revenge (48). Beyond this, Ian interprets the court case—which lasted eight years—as itself "a paroxysm of intimacy, a sustained crescendo of erotic interrelatedness," one that continued the social elaboration of the monogamy rule by trafficking in its violation (48). Through his analysis of the Twyman case, Ian takes a break from feminism to forge a reading "without a victim and a victimizer, without dominance and submission, without M/F—but *with* power" (48). In doing so, he seeks to demonstrate how the queer theoretic renders sexuality as complex as the psychic and social semiosis in which it exists.

---

with new bargaining power in marriage and a new role as enforcers of marital property? And can feminism see how costly this "bargaining endowment" might be *to women*, who can tap into it only if they find the sex in question painful and humiliating? Can feminism read the case as male subordination and female domination—and *still* as bad for women? (43–44)

"Very possibly," Ian writes, but that would require cutting feminism too much slack (44). Instead, Ian affirms that "Sheila Twyman is no ally of mine"; she is "no weakling, but rather . . . a formidable enemy who will pursue her goals with fierce drive"; and "*feminism* might be partly responsible not only for her power, but also for the terrible suffering that grounds it" (46).

This, then, is the core argument for "Taking a Break from Feminism": that governance feminism reiterates women's subordination to men as its narrative priority and legal strategy, making it the default position for ascertaining and elaborating gender in/equality, which blinds critics to the necessary project of accounting for *the complexities of subordination as power.* While the importance of questioning these effects is certain, I confess to a case of vertigo when following Ian's taxonomic leaps from sexual subordination feminism to Feminism, and from Feminism to Late MacKinnonite projects of legal reform. It is for this reason that I read Ian as offering "weak divergence," because the Feminism he promises to suspend for the queer theoretic to do its exacting work is so impervious to what might challenge it, so captured by normative time, and so ensconced in legal scale that it has no capacity to register the ways in which feminism has diverged repeatedly from itself, proliferated in contradiction across academic, social, institutional, national, and political domains, and recognized, even when repeating, its own contradictions and complicities. Even Ian's move to recognize "hybrid feminisms" confirms the authority of the taxonomic rule he initially establishes, reserving "feminism" for a monotheistic commitment to the mathematical formulation $M > F$. Resolutely convergentist as he defines it, Feminism is truly a mess. She is bent on exacting her share of monumental history, which keeps her enthralled to the state; she is driven by a masochism she can never avow and hence she incessantly makes injury the narrative she repeatedly repeats (woman is always victim, sex is forever trauma, sexuality and social inequality converge); she refutes the unconscious; she judges; she always calls the police.

Ian's queer theory, on the other hand, is gloriously maximalist. It gets to live everywhere, inhabiting "the intersections of postmodernism, gay male politics, pro-sex leftism, and so on," while "suspend[ing] feminism" (14). In this, queer theory gets to *think* without subordination to feminism's instrumentalizing legal demand and to do so in a mode divorced from an address to the state and to state ameliorations as the only legitimate horizon of the political; it can explore without shame the sexual importance of shaming affect, which allows it not only to have theoretic purchase in domains quite distinct from the legal, but to imagine personhood as nonidentical, self-contradictory, and only partially described, initiated, and inhabited by the visible workings of social power; it can locate, as an ethics, its own desire for a new sexual imaginary while deploying its theoretic grammar not as a new truth but as a highly contingent and speculative critical practice of freedom; its speculative freedoms can be apprehended without universalist insistence, by which I mean that Ian's divergentist queer theory never risks trying to represent everyone, nor does its refusal to do so threaten to jettison his critical act from left political thought altogether. This deployment of queer theory allows it to occupy differing and nonsyncretic times; roam across various epistemic, affective, and theoretical domains without ever being reduced to any single one of them; and remain in awe of (but unintimidated by) what it doesn't know—all while refusing to give in to insecurity or fear that it has opened itself up to way too much. In this, it diverges from minimalist Feminism at every turn, while being divergentist in its own cultural and critical itineraries.

No wonder Ian finds queer theory so irresistible. Me too. And who wouldn't? But what do we do with the fact that many queer theorists regularly break the rules of avant-garde dis-order and marshal queer theory for a host of convergentist desires of their own, not simply as evidenced in the well-known collapse into "gay and lesbian," but in the way it gets bent toward self-knowability and a host of guarantees for political change and evolved futures?[19] Can the heat of the culturalist bent in contemporary theory, where affirmation is the other side of subordination and representational practices become the locus of creative resistance, really be laid so formally and so completely at Feminism's feet, as if the "queer" is not also generated and mobilized in celebration not so much of sexual subordination per se but of subalternity itself? Or more crucially, doesn't queer theory have its own storehouse of *goodness*, including the goodness it finds by arming its "bad" subjects with the radical potential of critical and cultural perversity? My sense is that the "maximalist" interpretation of queer theory that Ian offers works by privileging its *aspiration* toward affirming "*practices/performativity/mobility,*" which requires subordinating all attention to the ways in which queer theory has failed to practice its commitment to "*disaffirming identities/essence/stability*" as such (51). Indeed,

19. I eschew the demand to name names as the proper method for providing evidence, as the point here is to foreground what *Object Lessons* takes as one of its inaugurating conditions: that it is impossible not to traffic in the reproduction of identity from within the auspices of identity knowledges, no matter how resolutely one may be moved by their traditions of anti-identity critique.

Ian acknowledges as much, albeit in the appendix, by specifying that the anti-identity commitments of queer theory are contradicted *in practice*, as "queer theoretic work ... often affirms [sexual orientation and gender identities] descriptively, strategically and even *normatively*" (emphasis added, 52).[20] By glossing over the fact that the theoretical impulses of queer theory are never completely disarticulated from the kinds of identitarian attachments or minimalist functionalism that it sets out to critique, Ian seems convinced that the queer theoretic bears none of the contradictions attending feminism. Or to put this another way, we might say that in Ian's hands, the queer theoretic loses none of its conceptual reach when its instantiations falter, while Feminism comes to a screeching minimalist halt precisely because her instantiations do.

To summarize, the problems I am identifying here are twofold. Most obviously, there's the rather overdetermined matter of Feminism's minimization. Subordinated first to a taxonomic rule, Feminism is blamed for the very subordination Ian's definition condemns her to. Then there's the way that Janet's exodus leaves the domain of anti-identitarian critical thought about sexuality to the identitarian insistence of "Queer Theory *by Men*." Why exact the rule of gender when one rushes to reject it every time it is pronounced on feminism's terms? I would prefer to differentiate entrapment in U.S. feminism's legal discourse of woman from entrapment by "woman," which would enable us to critique governance projects without conceding the entire meaning of either woman or the analytic of gender to the terms of governance feminism's M>F rule. In the process, we could register the fact that the governance project secured by feminism in law is not equivalent to feminism in its traversal of either public culture or the academy, and neither of these are congruent with those feminist theoretics that have arisen to marshal their own internal critique, challenging either the liberal subject or her pursuit of rights-bearing citizenship in a history of nation formation in which "liberated" women help sustain imperialist superiority.[21] The divergences

20. In an interesting rhetorical move, Ian casts the disparity between aspiration and practice as part of the "queer appetite for paradox"; hence queer work "will be *more interested*, descriptively and normatively, in practices than identities, in performativity than essences, and in mobility than stabilities" (emphasis added, 51, 52).

21. I hope that subsequent critical attention to "Queer Theory by Men" will address more fully the questions I raise here about the institutionalization of feminism in law.

among feminisms, between feminism as a political movement and its various institutionalizations, and between feminism and queer theory are worth fighting for. Paying attention to them enables a commitment to divergence but without subordinating the theoretic we want to a version of feminism we can only reject. If there are differences between feminism and the subjects who act or speak in its name—as we must insist there are—these differences need something other than the language of one-way power. Feminism, even U.S. feminism, is not so monolithic, so mono causal, so strict in its self-articulation, so unforgiving, so definitively solid that we are uniformly subordinated to its disciplinary will, unless of course we begin and end with just such a description of it. But why do so, especially when feminist theoretics lurk everywhere to refuse to concede feminism to such minimalist rehearsals? If Ian wants to argue for taking a break from feminism, that's fine, but can't we do it for a better reason than insisting that Feminism won't let us think or that we cannot speak against it and be heard? *That* is simply a way of trying to win an argument without really having one or worse, a way of being resentful for a subordination we have effectively committed ourselves to. Minimalist Feminism, after all, has been minimalized.

Suffice it to say that we have now entered the dicey terrain of affect where left critical disappointment lives as the living consequence of the psychic weight of the transferences that bind our theoretical and political attachments. Many of my own critical inquiries in the last decade have been attuned to this very issue, as I have been tracking the range of despair that might be said to turn U.S. academic feminism "against itself."[22] Throughout this work, I have been developing an argument that Ian would surely find appealing in its counterintuitive force: that contemporary U.S. feminism is not adequate to the knowledge project of Gender or Women's Studies, which means that I have been refusing to consign the itinerary of the interdisciplinary project feminism inaugurated to any public political

---

One could begin by looking at the work of Mary Joe Frug, the sexy dresser to whom Duncan Kennedy dedicated his essay, given how her book breaks ranks with MacKinnonite reform to open up an antihumanist legal project for feminism. See her *Postmodern Legal Feminism*.

22. Five essays comprise this project: "What Ails Feminist Criticism"; "Feminism, Institutionalism, and the Idiom of Failure"; "Feminism's Apocalyptic Futures"; "Academic Feminism Against Itself"; and "Feminism's Broken English."

manifestation of it. My goal has been to argue instead for the importance of differentiating among feminism's various and incommensurable deployments—as social movement, political theory, historical force, epistemological perspective, psychic attachment, intellectual tradition, and methodological entity—and to do so in a context that considers the discordant temporalities that mark feminism's own transit through the social domains and institutions that both shape and sustain our current understanding of and relation to it. I have also been interested in how feminism's academic sojourn has been shaped by the emergence of theory as both a genre of critical writing and a privileged political idiom in the disciplinary protocols of the humanities and interpretative social sciences. This has drawn me into considering the route through which the political claim arrived into critical legibility as a form of academic left expertise.[23] As you can see, these issues relate rather directly to the concerns I have raised here about Ian's incomplete attention to divergence and provide the context for turning our attention more directly to the discordant temporalities of feminism and queer theory.

23. This issue is especially important for engaging with the complex but irreducible relationship between identity's function and form across the terrain of the social (including the legal system) and its animation of various domains of academic inquiry. How, in the course of forty years, could a claim for the political utility of knowledge production become so decisive a feature of the humanities and interpretative social sciences that graduate training would come to be conducted, as it now is, through a tacit assumption that such inquiry *is* political, thereby displacing long standing debates about if and how and when the study of culture, language, literature, art, history, and human experience could be considered political at all? The hegemony of the political claim is of course a story of significant proportion, with genealogies that reach from the transatlantic migration of critical theory and its explosive encounter with the political culture and intellectual discourses of U.S. academic institutions to the history of the disciplines themselves and the dissolution of the Cold War split that nourished a division between the study of social formation and that of national cultural expression. For my purposes, the politicization of the human sciences in the name of left critical inquiry is absolutely central to the academic itinerary of identity. This is certainly the case with the queer theoretical approach to sexuality, which took shape largely in departments of English in the early 1990s in the context of wide ranging disciplinary conversations about canon formation, elite and mass cultural objects of study, anti-humanist conceptions of the subject, post-identity regimes of knowledge, and the methodological ends of various empiricisms. See especially Sedgwick, "Gender Studies."

Time Travel

How, then, do we read the discordant temporalities of feminism and queer theory? Let's begin by reasserting, as I did at the outset, that feminism and queer theory are not analogous entities, and let's agree that in historical terms, feminism preceded queer theory. It acquired its political resonance as what I would call a *preinstitutional* discourse, by which I mean that it found its most powerful and evocative political grammar outside of—because it was poised against—the dominant institutional practices of U.S. life (law, government, education, even the norms of everyday intimacies). Queer theory, unlike feminism, is not the inaugurating political discourse for an academic movement but a powerful critique of the ways in which identity, as political project and academic domain, came to be situated in both public politics and the U.S. university. While feminism articulates the utopian horizon of the movement's academic institutional intervention to study women as a feminist political practice, queer theory departs from the identity project that most centrally bore it, Gay and Lesbian Studies, to question the constitution of homosexual identity as the primary means for advancing a critical understanding of sexuality. This does not mean, as Eve Kosofsky Sedgwick articulated years ago, that queer theory can be inhabited without a powerful antihomophobic commitment that encompasses a critical gaze toward gay and lesbian issues.[24] But the refusal to suture queer theory to the identitarian ground of Gay and Lesbian Studies marks its genesis as a critical departure from within academic organizations of knowledge and hence as a mode of *internal critique*. The animating political and critical force of queer theory—its divergentism—thus requires the prior arrival, if you will, of sexual identity as an arena of inquiry onto the academic scene.

For various reasons, the divergentist operations represented by internal critique are going to occupy me for more than a few pages, which delays our arrival into the ecstatic animations of the kind of queer theoretic which both Ian and I seek. This postponement is not an icy deferral, no matter how utterly unsexy is a conversation about institutionalization and internal critique. But there's been altogether too little consideration of the academic itinerary of identity in the terms that Spillers offers us, which compel attention to the ways in which social movement "becomes a different kind of

24. See especially Sedgwick, *Tendencies*, 1–20.

movement" and identity is drawn into both a different and a different *kind* of struggle as it has become a familiar if contentious feature of the U.S. university in the past forty years. Of course, there are numerous narratives—some I have already discussed—that seek to emphasize continuities between the project of institutional intervention launched by social movements and the various analytics that have been developed to deepen identity's academic inquiry. In analyzing two of them in chapter 1—the progress narratives of gender and interdisciplinarity respectively—I was not seeking to undermine the sense, articulated throughout identity knowledges, that identity's inaugurating imperative included both a demand for democratic access and an epistemological charge aimed at the universalist pretensions at the heart of the monoculture of Western humanism's knowledge order. Indeed, it was through the explicit formulation that bodies embodied knowledge and hence that different bodies would engender new knowledges that identity projects linked issues of access to the inaugurating imperative to decolonize the mind, which would not only liberate subordinated knowledges, but defetishize scientific expertise and restore to the province of history and culture various groups denied entry to official national narration. By twinning the demand for whole new categories of persons to be taken seriously as bearers of history, makers of culture, and social actors with a methodological insistence that the human object of study had a right to be studied by those very subjects who identitarily constituted it, identity projects crafted what I call their *inaugural value form*: a confederacy between subject and object, knower and the object to be known.[25] If, in the context of Spillers's argument, we need to consider the ways in which this value form has undergone critique and revision from within the very fields established to lay claim to it, the point, as readers already know, is not to cast identity's academic itinerary as the deformation of progress. It is instead to understand the ways in which the inaugural value form and the broader discourse of access and inclusion that accompanied it have diverged, in large part because they address different mechanisms of institutional reproduction and are part of overlapping but not identical domains of the institution's operations. Still, it is important to say that the aim of the inaugural value form, to give knowledge to those subordinated by dominant

25. Standpoint theory is perhaps the most developed example in feminism of the inaugural value form. For an overview of this critical tradition, see Hekman, "Truth and Method."

regimes of knowledge, pushed forward important questions about the relationship between knowledge and identity formations, and hence about the utility of subjective accounts of world making for those subjects rendered as indelibly mute objects by epistemologies of Western modernity.

Ian's point, of course, is that as a practice of legal argument, the value of the inaugural form is based on paradigmatic submission, which has a decidedly disciplinary effect on the very subjects its intervention seeks to represent. This is at the core of what he finds most troubling about feminism. For by claiming an epistemological priority for women, feminism has had not only to assume its own ability to know the constituency of women on whose behalf it speaks, but to constitute that constituency as interchangeable with itself. Feminism thus knows because of what women already know, and women already know because they are women who know. To be sure, feminism's academic itinerary has been shaped perhaps more so than any other identity knowledge by the problems that arise from this insistence, especially given its own long-standing inability to account for why some women become feminists while so many others do not. But its now-routine insistence, in the various institutional contexts in which it has been heard, on seeking freedom for women repeatedly consigns them to *having to be women*. I share Ian's suspicion of the governance projects that are authorized by this reduction, and I understand why such governance projects have sent Janet running from the room. But I lack confidence that the queer theoretic will rescue us from this mess. Sure, the overt turn to "men" enacts queer theory's challenge to the propriety of the inaugural value form by perversely using the prospect of men's self-interest as the means to travel beyond minimalist feminism's sexual (mis)conceptions and by divorcing the logics of textual embodiments from corporeal embodiments altogether. This allows for a rich interpretation of the struggle for domination that animates the marriage and long legal struggle of the Twymans, giving us a fabulously dense encounter with the specter of William as Sheila's victim—a specter repeated, it seems to me, in the prospect that we are all subordinated to governance feminism's subordination rule. And it foregrounds the queer theoretic's capacity to challenge state-based understandings of social change,[26] the equation of

26. See especially Brown, *States of Injury* and "Suffering the Paradoxes of Rights"; Butler, *Excitable Speech*; and Reddy, "Asian Diasporas, Neoliberalism, and Family" and "Time for Rights?"

legal redress with international justice,[27] the perpetuation of normativity and normative sexual cultures,[28] and the liberal utility of identity to make equivalent everything from political perspective to complex psychic life.[29] In thus dismantling both the epistemological assumptions of identity's inaugural value form and the political guarantee that the subject/object relation was made to offer, the queer theoretic Ian mobilizes refuses to play a supporting role in the decisively constraining and altogether outrageous recuperation of the political aspirations of what identity might be said to have once stood for.

Still, there's a long way to go from reveling in queer theory's possibilities to exacting its theoretic purchase, especially given the untimely interruption of everything we cannot control, including our unruly selves and the world's haunting ability to resurrect, against our best intentions, *its version* of itself. So let's not assume—to make the *first* of several points—that as a form of internal critique, queer theory bears a truth that identity's inaugural form does not, no matter how much evidence can be marshaled to undermine belief in the epistemological alignment of minoritized bodies with progressive knowledges that was the hallmark of identity's institutional incursion. And, *second*, let's not take the manipulation of identity's inaugural value form in the past three decades as an effect of an original error, as if the value form was riven from the beginning by an incarcerating logic. Ergo: because identity logics have been mobilized in the service of more governance, more empire, more war, more impoverishment, we now "know" that they were designed for failure from the get-go. Queer theory's effectiveness in figuring divergence from feminism or any of identity's agendas of institutional incursion does not close the book on the adequacy of identity politics or its inaugural value form, nor does it liberate us from the problematic of identity altogether. What we might learn here arises from something far more interesting than our ability to generate a narra-

27. See Patton, "Stealth Bombers of Desire"; Miller, "Sexual but Not Reproductive" and "Gay Enough"; and Franke, "Putting Sex to Work."

28. See Delany, *Times Square Red, Times Square Blue*; Harper, *Private Affairs*; Muñoz, "The Future in the Present"; Berlant and Warner, "Sex in Public"; Warner, *The Trouble with Normal*; and Ferguson, *Aberrations in Black*.

29. For four different understandings of the problem of identitarian reductionism and psychic life, see Dean, *Beyond Sexuality*; Reid-Pharr, *Black Gay Man*; Soto, *Reading Chican@ Like a Queer*; and Viego, *Dead Subjects*.

tive of progressive critical or theoretical correctness, given how profoundly the changing contexts that mark identity's travels and transform the terms and meanings of its modes of address also transform our relationship to it. The threshold, then, might best be conceived as an encounter with two sets of consequences: first with the doubly minoritizing strategies of "diversity" that reduce movement aims and agendas to minimalist terms in university cultures that have vigorously fought back; and second with the course of identity's epistemic travels in disciplinary orders of knowledge, where the critique of exclusion is followed by claims of origination as identity is arrayed into discrete objects and analytics of inquiry, into methodological protocols, and ultimately into self-affirming fields of study, often described as interdisciplines. In this latter context, Spillers's discussion situates divergence as a necessary, even inescapable, operation of academic institutionalization. In more declarative terms, we could say that divergence is the action of identity's emergence within a disciplinary register, the mechanism of its field formation and ongoing elaboration and, more specifically, the force that underlies the institutional history and political relation between feminism and queer theory to begin with. Thus reflecting the threshold moment, queer theory is an effect of identity's transformation from a discourse of political change to an object of study, from social movement to field formation, from animating politic to critical practice.

But queer theory is not the engine of that transformation. Rather, the presence, indeed growing legitimacy, of any discourse of internal critique demonstrates that the threshold has already been crossed. In other words, internal critique is not an origin; it is a divergence from one. This, then, is the *third* point of these ruminations: that queer theory is not the agency of sexuality's transformation from one kind of movement to another; it is the effect of that transformation. This does not mean that internal critique can never be used to define and constitute its own origin—surely the mobilization of queer theory as the inaugurating critical practice for a new field of study, often called Queer Studies (or LGBTQ or even more simply Sexuality Studies), demonstrates the ways in which scholars consolidate modes of internal critique into the chief currency of academic legitimization. But I want to steer clear of insinuating that it is the anti-identitarian theoretic that converts social movement into another kind of movement, since part of what propels divergence—to get to my *fourth* point—is not the context of its negation, disidentification, or practice of differentiation, but the sheer activity of it. These animations are absolutely central to the work of identity in its historical and psychic manifestations, where the convergence into some form of sameness is the necessary move to generate difference. Woman is not man is not white is not heterosexual is not Western is not wealthy is not . . . all of which necessitates the consolidation of woman, man, white, heterosexual, Western, and so on, into knowable taxonomic markers. While there is now a long-standing lament in some quarters of the Left about the seeming "fragmentation" that identity politics has generated around its key hegemonized figures—Women, Ethnic/Racial Subject, Worker, and (later) Sexual Minority—the academic project of identity knowledges in the U.S. university is absolutely contingent on developing, exploring, and elaborating such differentiations. The dissolution of the priority of one into the optimistic investment in another is the action of disciplinary regeneration itself, as the previous chapter on the "progress" of *gender* tried to suggest.

From women to gender, then, or from gay to queer, African American to Black Diaspora, American Studies to Transnational American Studies, women to women of color, queer to transgender, U.S. Indian to Native American to First Nation . . . each differentiation, each distinction, each animating disidentification performs the central feature of disciplinary production: the inexhaustibility of the field's self-perpetuating identity. Fields of study perform inexhaustibility continuously, in processes of divergence that remake objects of study, shift theoretical commitments, forge new methodologies, transform canons, elaborate archives, define new analytics, change names—all as the means of producing the *not-that* that legitimates its continuation and restores some kind of faith in the ability of critical practice to travel the distance from various impoverishments that reveal, as I put it before, the constraints of still being *here*. In the specific case under discussion, we can say, then, that when queer theory defines itself as not-feminism (or as not-gay-and-lesbian), it enacts a claim for its own discernible identity, a claim that will inevitably be challenged for the boundaries it thereby enacts. The struggle over definitional control is determining, with the historical cacophony of feminism reduced to a taxonomic rule. In these contexts, who can be surprised that queer theory has been rendered rule bound and exclusivist by the divergentist operations of bisexual, transgender, and critical race theory?[30] And who will be

30. On *bisexuality* and queer theory, see Hemmings, *Bisexual Spaces: A Geography of Sexuality and Gender*; Angelides, *A History of Bisexuality*; and Hall and Pramaggiore, *Representing Bisexualities*; on *transgender* and queer theory, see Stryker, "Transgender

surprised when the taxonomic determinations of each of these discourses are taken up, such that their legibilities as not-queer theory or, more precisely, as not-white, not-gay-supremacist, or not-sexuality-centered queer theory reveal the defining limits that will be said to have undermined their critical emergence as well? These are the ongoing, incessant operations of divergence that function less to perfect the project in the political terms wielded by the discourse of internal critique than to generate value and futurity for the field and confer authority on the subjects thereby legitimated to speak within it. We've seen this before, but one doesn't need to call such divergences progress, no matter how manifestly useful that narrative has been. The point here is simply that the agency critics seek for critical practice positively comes alive when field-forming transformations can be embraced as both necessary and true.

My *fifth* point, then, is my most contentious one: that the political claims that frame the discursive maneuvers of internal critique are not the biggest stakes in this game. In fact, they work to reproduce a number of significant misrecognitions, which repeatedly converge the politics of knowledge in the university and its culture of critical authority with the animations of political contestations across the multiple domains of contemporary life. So, for instance, when queer theory is accused of being ludic, of reinscribing the neoliberal subject that is taken as characteristic of global capital, critical practice is converged entirely into the operations of political economy, with the consequence that the critique of critical practice is taken both as commensurate with and *as* a critique of global capital, with no small refusal to attend to the cultural capital garnered in the name of the political in the process. Or conversely, when Ian stakes his investment in a queer theoretic divergent from minimalist feminism's formulation in U.S. law, he defines the "rich brew of pro-gay, sex liberationist, gay-male, lesbian, bisexual, transgender, and sex-practice-based sex-radical, sex-positive, anti-male/female model, anti-cultural-feminist political engagements, some more postmodernizing than others" as "queer theory," as if the aim and content of critical theory is the prevailing sign and equivalent gestation of left projects organized around gender and sexuality wherever they go (9).

Studies" and "Transgender History, Homonormativity, and Disciplinarity"; and on race and queer theory, see Arondekar, "Border/Line Sex"; Johnson, "'Quare' Studies, or (Almost) Everything I Know about Queer Studies I Learned from My Grandmother"; Barnard, *Queer Race*; and Ford, "What's Queer about Race?"

Hence, the very ways in which the critical apparatus is a privileged mode of production in the university, partaking as it does in the equally privileged discourse of the political that founds contemporary identity critique, is effectively, even if unconsciously, denied. What we get instead is fantastic and indeed fantastical: a dissimulation of the institutional struggles over disciplinary expertise, critical authority, and the finer points of interpretive practice in favor of queer theory's divergence from feminism as the engine of its own collectivizing ideal. To get polemical about it, I would say that the queer theoretic's refusal of identification with feminism underscores the political convergences that engender Ian's maximized account of the analytic formation of the "queer." Even those who want "a firm understanding of queer as a political metaphor without a fixed referent" are exacting referential indeterminacy at a steep price. How firm will this grip be? Who will wield it? And what calculus of the "political" will determine both the value and the authority of this claim to queer critical expertise?[31]

As readers already know, my point is not that fields of study and the theoretics they cultivate have no business attending to their political implications. Rather, our inattention to the transformation of identity from one kind of movement to another has displaced rather than fine-tuned the vocabulary of both politics and politicality within the analytic practices and critical discourses of identity knowledges. The problem is not that familiar canard that "if everything is political then nothing is." Nor is it that "if everything is equally political, then our gestures toward the political are meaningless." It is that the transit of the political claim from one kind of struggle to another transforms the meaning and work of both the political and the claim for it. Eva Cherniavsky assures us that this problem is not our fault; it is a symptom of a wider crisis of the political in contemporary U.S. culture, one that is played out at fever pitch in the humanities and interpretative social sciences where contestations over the Western meaning of the human, "his" cultural inheritance, and "his" imaginative life are being brokered by increasingly instrumentalist dictums, including the instrumentality of identity itself.[32] This means that our desire for a queer theoretic or even a hybrid feminism or any of the current reconfigurations

31. I hope that David L. Eng, Judith Halberstam, and José Esteban Muñoz will allow me this small use of them to make my contentious point. See their "Introduction: What's Queer about Queer Studies Now?" 1.

32. Cherniavsky, "Neocitizenship and Critique."

of identity's critical locutions cannot be formulated as antithetical to the inaugural struggle over identity. For Cherniavsky, the crisis of the political lives in the intellectual left in the way that it (we) consistently figure our critique as a kind of rapture, the place where we are no longer bogged down by the animations of history, where our subjectivities are not thick with the contradictions we discern everywhere else. Behold, a future made possible by the critical work of now. The problem, then, is not what we cling to, but the way we convince ourselves that we don't.[33] This is why Cherniavsky would insist, even when I want to think the contrary, that the alternative political imaginary inaugurated by identity is sustained by our critique of it, and why she would point out, even when I don't want to hear it, that beneath the antifoundationalist rhetoric, identity critique is routinely staked on the representational value of our embodiment nonetheless. Halley parodies the performance of it, while investing in it: "Queer Theory *by Men*," signed *Ian* Halley. And so do I, using the critical capital evinced by that first editorial invitation to address Ian as the means to cultivate the political imaginary for the lesbian that I want. While we can't fix our desire (and who would want to), we can follow its effects on the disciplinary apparatus, which means considering how (and this is my *sixth* point) the political imaginary generated by queer critique becomes a disciplinizing agency, not simply because the critical authority we have amassed to proclaim our investments in *not-identity* arises from our institutional location as experts in identity knowledges, but because the claim for being political in the process that everywhere underwrites left identity critique *is* the most heavily invested sign of our professionalization in identity domains. You can't get to Yale without it, which means, Dorothy, we are really *not* in Kansas anymore.

So where does all this leave us? Smack in the middle of the concerns of *Object Lessons* and its pursuit of the powerfully affective, complex, incommensurate, and nonequivalent relations that beget and frustrate identity knowledges. Those invested in the idea that identity knowledges extend and sustain the social movements that brought them into being will be disappointed by my repeated assertion that the sojourn in the university has transformed both the value and meaning of identity *and* the kind of struggle that now exists over its epistemic authority. They will want the

33. See Brown, "Resisting Left Melancholy."

modes and methods of academic inquiry to work harder to return these fields to their activist conceptions, such that the study of identity can consecrate the authority of the dispossessed in the vaulted halls and classrooms of an institution built on the delineation, historically speaking, of multiple embodied exclusions. For those who view formal inclusion as the beginning of a different struggle, the decolonization of knowledge evoked by the inaugural value form will travel without angst away from the subject-object compact to live in various disciplinary discourses and to contest in numerous ways the historical negotiations of identity's political horizons. But the idea that the now-privileged method of this travel—critique—can be read as evidence of an intensely passionate investment in academic cultures of expertise and in the disciplinary modes of value and recognition that govern academic knowledge production might sting. As will the idea that our expertise, embodied in the representational value of our embodiment, is inseparable from the very instrumentalization of identity we critique. And yet, the judgment I register here and elsewhere is not over embodiment or professionalization per se, nor do I think that anyone ever lives in utter congruence with the discernments that she uses her time to study and explicate. The issue here is about the disavowal that underwrites the way the political claim is deployed, not just as proof of progressive intention but as resistance and risk—even as it functions as the required, indeed rote, gesture that demonstrates intellectual belonging to a field. If all this is taken as a means to paint me as dismissing theory, queer or not, I can only hope you will keep reading. Nothing here says that the transformation of identity from one kind of struggle to another makes the one we are now in insignificant or insufficiently political, but it does foreground the problem of discerning how precisely it is political in the disciplinary contexts in which such claims are made. My *seventh* point is that internal critique is not the same thing as nor a substitute for the identity-based claim, and that their divergence is neither a bad nor a good thing. It is part of what we might study in the institutional transformation of identity's knowledge project from social movement to an academic object of study and field domain in the university, the very cleavage that might begin to teach us something else.

To be sure, much more could be said about how twentieth-century U.S. social movements were overwritten by juridical conceptions of subjects and politics, which would allow me to elaborate more fully my earlier point about how Ian converges feminism into the shape of its transit through the institution of law. But I've been most interested in extraditing queer theory from the maximalist itinerary ascribed to it and in demonstrating, more through echo than comparison or analogy, how the crisis of complicity overwrites identity knowledges in both their affirmative and antihumanist traditions. Hence, I have located queer theory as a mode of internal critique generated by reformulations in the humanities and interpretative social sciences, which have been profoundly affected in the last forty years by new conceptions of language, representation, meaning, and subjectivity—conceptions often arising in the aftermath of social revolt but with no causal determined relation to it. And identity's inaugural form? She's still doing her important institutional work, which means the threshold is and will continue to be crossed. This is because internal critique does not kill the political authority that identity-based claims make on a social field, which includes the university, nor *is it immune to them*.[34] The *final* point, then, is simply this: There is no definitive authority that

34. This is clear from the itinerary of transgender. While the category has been mobilized in the last fifteen years as a framework for political action around an emergent sphere of person articulation, it has also operated as a form of internal critique in numerous fields, including Women's Studies, where it has and continues to challenge biological foundations for sexed identity; Gay and Lesbian Studies, where it rebels against the deployment of gender as scrutable on the terrain of sexuality alone; and Queer Studies, where it has even insisted on affirming gender normativity and intransitivity without giving up on its claim to queer. The simultaneity of identitarian affirmation with internal critique demonstrates that identity studies are not just sites of critical engagement with the social formation but productive features of it, which means that they are not simply extensions or responses to a political engine that exists outside the university, but powerful agencies in the ongoing elaboration of identity and identitarian claims. The institutional embeddedness of identity studies does political work on behalf of the inaugural form they have come to critique by providing resonant disciplinary discourses for new identity projects to be imagined, explored, and archived within and against them. The battle that can and has ensued over who owns the identity form and the analytic that both represents and diverges from it—those who retain the privileges of birth sex and those who do not—has been intense and demonstrates how contested the traffic at the threshold can be. At the same time, the example of transgender reveals how the divergentist work I have been tracking does not (has not, will not) remain internal to internal critique's analytic operations. This, no matter how much hand-wringing can accompany the academic institutionalization of identity as the seeming end of social movement and "real politics," or how much scorn can attend the haunting return of identity's inaugural form as the death knell of the productive possibilities of an anti-identitarian theoretic altogether.

the inaugural form or internal critique wield over one another. One does not cancel the other. To diverge is not to undo nor is it simply to oppose. And neither is singularly progressive—or not—on their own. More crucially perhaps, the political dispensation that accompanies each cannot be settled, either in advance or retrospectively, either by wish or proclamation.

In this, it becomes possible to begin to imagine that the desire I expressed at the outset—for a queer theoretic that collates something for or from the lesbian—is not necessarily a retrograde, essentialist, or fundamentalist repetition of a convergentist investment in *women* animated by the M>F distinction. It is not necessarily a nostalgic grasp at a now-degraded material form, one that minimalist feminism has completely captured and which the queer theoretic is right to leave behind, since on the terms Ian poses it, it will only continue to wrench epistemic authority from embodiment in order to match wits with the institutions of the state, no matter the fact that the hard fight wagered against the violences of governance will turn out to be bound to governance nonetheless. It is not necessarily any of these things because the claim to identify with a figure, no less than the category that is said to represent it, is at least as divergentist in its own historical travels as the identificatory refusal that counters it—and just as incomplete. It is this possibility that grappling with identity's epistemic and institutional discordancies can lead us to: that the political desire that mobilizes each sits in a different relation not only to the critical practices they invite and the ideations of the social world that encompass, frame, and regenerate them, but to the heavily weighted forms of critical embodiment that both do and don't travel coherently across them. This makes the seeming struggle between the authority of experience to name its own critical condition and the authority of a theoretic to unravel identity's epistemic double bind absolutely confounding, as the value of one never completely cancels out the value or authority of the other. All of this is to say that there is more going on in Janet's departure than a refusal to identify with sexual subordination feminism—beginning with the critical authority she confers on Ian before she goes.

Getting What I Want

Let's return to my opening deliberation on the way that Ian's queer theoretic requires for its startling, delicious, divergentist appeal a mode of critical investment drawn from identifications with men. My supposition has been that this identification is a performative alliance that seeks distance from Feminism's M>F fundamentalism by seeking distance from proximity to F and the pedagogy of victimization that ensnares her. In this reading, any identificatory attachment to the lesbian bears too much M>F intimacy, thereby threatening the queer theoretic's capacity to do sexy and divergent work. But surely lesbians have cultivated the kind of pleasures that the queer theoretic seeks—self-annihilation, eroticized domination and subordination, and a host of sex-positive identifications—and in ways expressly intended *not* to give woman's sexuality over wholly to governance feminism's version of her. While "Kitty" MacKinnon doesn't want the pro-sex, antipornography, S and M girls and bois and their perversely anticoupled and coupled perversities to interrupt her discourse of gender and subordination, there is no reason for us to exile them too. Think Joan Nestle, Amber Hollibaugh, Susie Bright, Gayle Rubin, Pat Califia. Remember Barnard 1983: Pleasure and Danger.[35] If the queer theoretic has not registered any of this, we need a better explanation than to give in to the self-perpetuating myth that liberal feminism and its stern arm of governance made everything so.[36] Nor is it adequate to say that all this sex-positive work has no analytic truck with the lesbian because people we once called lesbians don't want to be called that anymore. The disidentification with *that* lesbian—wearing her womonbornwomononly button and clad in that dowdy dress or crunchy androgyny or, worse, in that unshapely power suit that accompanies her kid-bearing SUV—is real, to be sure, but let's take our lessons from divergentism and try not to wield these contestations and contradictions as taxonomic emergencies requiring an immediate classificatory surgery. Better to understand them as part of the force that identity generates *within* community formations, where the historical particularities

35. For the feminist pro-sex lesbian archive, begin with Bright, *Sexwise* and *Susie Sexpert's Lesbian Sex World*; Califia, *Public Sex*; Duggan and Hunter, *Sex Wars*; Hollibaugh, *My Dangerous Desires*; Nestle, *A Restricted Country*; Kipnis, *Ecstasy Unlimited* and *Bound and Gagged*; and Vance, *Pleasure and Danger*.

36. After all, people get down for all kinds of subordination, but every bottom knows the importance of maintaining faith in the top's interest in her pleasure. If liberal feminism does not give a damn, there are others out there who do, and they do not call everything they do *not-feminism*. Sometimes people want to invent their transgression beyond the inversion of taxonomic rules. And sometimes what's hot is transgressing the rule of avant-garde transgression, including queer theory's own.

of identitarian attachments are routinely codified and resisted by the very subjects who use them to craft new world-making projects to house their persistent desires, of both the sexual and political kind. If the lesbian's early twentieth-century status as the quintessence of U.S. nonnormative gender is by the beginning of the twenty-first so radically reconfigured that she can represent gender neutrality, even conservativity, we are not in the midst of representational or ontological singularity but the work of divergence itself—a divergence, I want to emphasize, that exists within identity social formations, not just between them and the academic venues that they first authorized. Here, then, is an additional way we might try to think the importance of divergence to the queer theoretic, one that not only refuses to converge the lesbian with Feminism's minimalist definition of F or to concede the terrain of masculine identifications wholly to bio-men, but that reads the relationship between gender and sexuality on non-convergentist, nonanalogous, *and* nonoppositional terms from beginning to end.

Like all minoritized identity forms, the lesbian first coalesced into categorical coherence through epistemic and corporeal violence; she came to life as a species of person through those processes that reduced the human to populations, acts to identities, self-recognition to saturated discipline; she is part of a dense and shifting modern map of human relations, an "identity" produced by discourses of social abjection and politically reclaimed for the purposes of amelioration, which means that she has been used—wielded even—for wildly different political ambitions and critical aims, often in ways that make her unrecognizable across domains. In the different arenas in which we follow her, she is a figure whose power is powerfully divergent: being both the frame for identitarian commitments and for their refusals; for the fantasy of utter self-attachment and for profound, unassimilable disidentifications; and for relations that are not always discernible on the grounds of (dis)identification at all. She can be historically discontinuous, even with those versions most thought to be herself and even in those situations when the postulation of her transhistorical coherence is required for something new to enunciate itself—as when queer takes on the very identity destinations it otherwise disavows and both includes and reduces her, or when dykebois and genderqueers seek defiantly to be anything except her. These enunciations rely on making the lesbian solid enough to perform their own self-fashioning reclamations—indeed it is their proximity to and intimacy with her that makes their divergence from her possible. Divergence is working here, then, within the identity discourse that founds and transforms both subjective and community formations, remaking the discourses they reflect and circulate, which is why I say that raising the question of the lesbian in this context is not necessarily a fundamentalist feminist return to F at all, in part because the disaggregation of dimorphic sex from sexuality and gender has everything to do with the lesbian's historical sojourn. For while the mannish lesbian of sexological lore made gender inversion diagnostically knowable as she provided the clinical and analytic drag on the heteronormative conflation of sex and gender, the current erotic investment in the circulation and performative masculinities of bodies that span a spectrum from F to M unravel a host of systematic assumptions by demonstrating that there is a spectrum and not simply crossed or invertible identificatory positions. But more than this, the proliferation of masculinities that cannot be said to depart in any simple way from F or to arrive into the categorical certainty of biomen (precisely because they raise the stakes on what we understand F or M on their own to entail) demonstrates how *the desire for gender* has become one of the most powerful and interesting features of both U.S. queer culture and academic queer critique today.[37] It lies at the heart of the queer theoretic that I seek, where the question of gender returns not as antithetical to queer sexuality, but as an increasingly prominent language for it.[38] This is the issue that will concern me most fully when I take up the problem of heteronormativity as the centerpiece of queer critique in chapter 6.

All of this is to say that we do not need to render gender analytically secondary in order to articulate sexuality on grounds that don't retread

37. Well into the writing and rewriting of this chapter, I came across Sheila Jeffreys's essay, "Heterosexuality and the Desire for Gender." For Jeffreys, "The feminist project has always been the abolition of gender, not the reclaiming of it"; hence her essay takes open, unapologetic aim at transgender activists who "are not creating a 'third' but merely recreating the two genders of male supremacy" (90). My use of the phrase takes shape against the negative political value she attributes to it.

38. In *Female Masculinity*, Judith Halberstam developed the title concept in a frame of more or less coincidence with "masculinity without men." In the decade that followed her inquiries, a more decisive split would emerge between these two terms, as "without men" took on a destination irreducible to "female" in contemporary critical and cultural idioms.

male/female difference, precisely because we do not need to reduce gender to its dimorphic ascriptions. We can explore instead gender's erotic significations in a host of transitivities that are now revising U.S. queer cultural and critical discourses of sex, desire, and embodiment by reading such revisions as significant in a variety of divergentist ways. Certainly, there's something to be said for understanding butch-femme in its oldest historical formation in this way, and even more to be said about how the transitivity of gender—as embodiment, identification, and theoretic—is resolutely bound up in erotic life, part of the transgressions that enable desire itself. This would diverge entirely from minimalist Feminism's minimalist rules, and it would undermine Ian's strict insistence on an analytic split between gender and sexuality as the means for a queer theoretic to fully emerge. Gender in these terms is not against sexuality but also not in place of it, nor does it operate to settle all differences by accumulating within it every destination for thinking sex, gender, and sexuality. Lest anyone think that this is merely a theoretical strategy for a narcissistic reclamation of the lesbian, let me insist that gay men also need something other than *their* reduction to sex practices and counterdomesticities in the queer theoretic. This is not an argument for revising their sex into fantasies of domestic coupledom— the U.S. Supreme Court is taking care of that—but it is to say that the allocation of sexuality to masculine identifications and gender to minimalist Feminism is a rather rule-bound formula for delivering to the queer theoretic a sexual imaginary founded on its ability to transgress the rules.[39]

Still, readers might wonder if I have escaped the very thing that I have wanted Ian to resist by foregrounding the possibilities of gender's transitivity as the means to escape minimalist Feminism's grip. What after all *is* masculinity irreducible to the province of bio-men but evidence of my own excruciating entrapment in the fundamentalist scene of dimorphic sex-as-gender, no matter my definitional plea to the contrary? What is a bio-man but the projection of the two-sex system I am adamantly trying to oppose? Isn't all this trafficking in masculinity, gay male and everything else, just another way to dress feminism up (or down), to put woman off or shut her up before getting off on being so different, so much more hip than even that once-hip version of her, the lesbian? If the traffic in men as the dis-

39. On the pastoralization of sex in recent U.S. and international law, see Adler, "The Future of Sodomy" and "The Dignity of Sex."

course of sexual alterity means an escape from the private and domestic, aren't women tacitly condemned to suffocate in the essentialized domains of their homey reproductive function? The counter that I offer, which stresses certain affiliations with "Queer Theory by Men" while trying to get what I want too, goes this way. Yes, we can read the desire that animates the proliferation of masculinities without men or of an analytic investment in men as a reiterative performance of the gendered terms of the U.S. public sphere where an aversion to being either female or woman is the expression of broader structures of social constraint. *We certainly can*, and there will be many who would appreciate it. But pursuing such a reading means settling, as Ian so rightly discusses, for a theory of the social conscription of dimorphic sex *as* our theory of sexuality and desire, which assumes much too much: not just that a certain version of the social is the sexual but also, most profoundly, that masculinity without men is a psychic aversion to being woman that femininity is not. I'm not the first to think that feminism as a discourse about gender, power, and women is finally far more tied to disidentifications with the category that animates its political desire than with identification, and that its "psychic life" operates by a fundamental refusal to grapple with the possibility that in trying to speak in the name of woman it has sought to repair its own deep ambivalence about, even rejection of being "her." Please don't take me to be saying that within feminism there is a tradition of misogyny, even if you already know that I have been moved by just such an argument before.[40] Rather, because U.S. feminism's aversion, ambivalence, and rejection of female woman is precisely what its counterdiscourse of identification and love has sought to compensate for, I see feminism as constituted on and by its own self-annihilating principle. This is another sign of its deep divergentism, which is too often managed by disavowing the scary thread of this thought instead of engaging it on its most challenging terms: that disidentification with and distrust of woman does not belong to patriarchy alone. From this vantage point, "Taking a Break from Feminism" as a way to disidentify with women's subordination and with feminism's infatuation with it in the name of some other horizon of the political *is* a familiar tactic in feminism's itinerary, one that sets feminism both beside and against itself as an intrinsic feature of its historical sojourn.

40. See Gubar, "Feminist Misogyny."

Make no mistake then: I am not faulting Ian because his identifications collate around men, nor am I saying that being bound to what we seek to resist is a contradiction that the rigors of critical practice should or even can fix. I take such dependencies as axiomatic, not only in my pursuit of a queer theoretic that can fulfill my investments in the lesbian, but in *Object Lessons* as a whole. Axiomatic: that we are enthralled by what we resist; that the complexities of our attachments are not ours to consciously behold; that what we think we want rarely satisfies us in the end. The point of this chapter has been to follow Ian's lead by arriving somewhere other than where he wants to take us. My goals were multiple: to extract more analytic purchase out of his insistence on divergence by using it to read the processes of institutionalization that underwrite the necessary and to my mind irreducible estrangement of feminism from queer theory—without leaving gender to minimalist Feminism or feminism to a reductive minimalism, or giving all the critical thrills to internal critique as liberation from the complicities of identity's remaking in the aftermath of social movements. While I wanted to affirm the importance of Ian's resistance to a reading of the social conscription of dimorphic sex *as* a theory of sexuality and desire, I also wanted to resist excising gender from sexuality altogether, which is why I refused to take either gender or sexuality as devoid of divergences of their own. By offering a divergentist account of lesbian sex practices and antireproductive cultures, I hoped to travel the distance between the subordination ethos coalescing around F to the mobile transgressions collating around men that Ian found so engaging, while also arguing for attention to feminism's own internal critiques, which have been deployed against its compensatory attempts at secure knowing and unambiguous love by investments that are deserving of much more than the name hybrid.

To be sure, there are other matters to be pursued in tracking the consequences of Ian's demand for divergence: toward a fuller account of masculinities without men, which would teach us about gender's rehabilitation as a grammar of queer sexuality and desire; toward transitive embodiments, which continue to reveal the incongruities of social M>F; and toward a queer theoretic that can attend to the animating possibilities of the desire for gender itself. But these will have to wait—at least until the last chapter of *Object Lessons*. Suffice it to say that I would have loved to make more analytic luster out of Ian's delirium for self-shattering and to revel a bit myself in the pleasures to be had in the dissolution of subjectivity as the basis for theorizing no less than having sex.[41] I also wanted to spend more time honoring his impassioned insistence that the queer theoretic needs to jettison minimalist accounts of gender in the sphere of law, which would require some attention to the ways in which the juridical apparatus both captures and cultivates specific aspects of feminism's aspirations, redefining them in the process. This issue has been postponed until chapter 5. In all this, I hope I registered the fact that Ian's pursuit of a queer theoretic dedicated to sexual practices and nonidentitarian psychic elaborations was bound to the very object relations that have compelled my own critical obsessions. If he staked his political desire as a form of resistance, refusing identification with MacKinnon and her hegemonic feminism as a legal rule, I was moved to try to fulfill mine by *not* turning to identificatory refusals, even when Ian's identifications and mine diverged and even when such divergences caused me enormous concern. Such a rhetorical performance was hard to do, in part because everything I have learned about critical authority urges me to travel in the opposite direction, toward demonstrating not simply why someone else's analytic itineraries and worldbuilding aspirations are inadequate but how they are wrong.

41. I also wanted to consider Bersani's work further, especially because he has now retreated from his earlier infatuation with masochism in "Is the Rectum a Grave?" In "Sociality and Sexuality," he writes of his own work:

> Much of this now seems to me a rather facile, even irresponsible celebration of "self-defeat." Masochism is not a viable alternative to mastery, either practically or theoretically. The defeat of the self belongs to the same relational system, the same relational imagination, as the self's exercise of power; it is merely the transgressive version of that exercise. Masochism consents to, indeed embraces that theft of being which mastery would remedy by obliterating otherness through a fantasmatic invasion of difference. (648)

In no sense is Bersani discounting the importance of critical attention to self-defeat, but he does mean to emphasize that "to privilege [it] in the relational field is to reduce that entire field to libidinal relationality" (648). His analysis allows us to understand how countermoves tend not to escape the systems they challenge but to confirm their very logics, if only from a different angle or analytic side. The attachment to the refusal can be what is most thrilling. Hence, no matter how compelling the masochistic pleasure in self-shattering, it is not a new alternative to the pastoralizing discourse of sex but that which the pastoralizing discourse animates by being so aggressively set against it. We've seen this theoretical double bind before, beginning with the minimalist definition of feminism that Ian offers.

And what about Janet? Isn't this long and attentive embrace of Ian part of a strategy calculated to entice her to return? After all, I have spent an enormous amount of time trying to separate feminism from governance feminism in order for queer theory to attend to its own desire for gender without the threat of gender-as-subordination taking up all the room. I have theorized the institutional process through which the theoretic emerges to reflect and refract the identity discourses that both found and confound it, not just to reconvene the possibility that feminist theory might actually have something useful to say in its own anticonvergentist itineraries, but to begin to imagine a queer theoretic that won't banish the lesbian simply because cultural feminism once made some very unsexy claims on and for her. I have done all this to perform a queer theoretic that can be charmed by how far those "hybrid" feminisms have gone in revising the academic domain first named by feminism—all as a way to implicitly demonstrate that Janet's reasons for leaving are not the only way to render the relationship between feminism and queer theory. Still, I'm certain that none of this will be as inviting as what I intend. Whatever governs Janet's attachment to feminism by setting her so powerfully against it is not going to let go in the face of my critical wishes, no matter the fact that everything I have been able to say about feminism and queer theory is indebted to her. This is one of the things that I have learned about critical practice as the scene of transferential relations: My dependencies on others may help me get what I want but they won't settle the differences that stand between us. Like it or not, under the auspices of identity knowledges, what we share the most begins and ends in divergence.

THREE

The Political Conscious

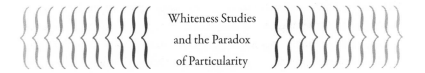 Whiteness Studies
and the Paradox
of Particularity

To say that the object relations tracked in the preceding chapters work through vastly different affective registers is only to impart the obvious. Progress narratives are generically optimistic and the one that takes *gender* as its guide is no different. Its faith in the future is so fantastically calibrated that every delay makes the grand march forward more glorious. The queer theoretic, in contrast, looks as if it were born in flames, ignited by resisting everything that tries to cozy up to it. In this, it has a perverse relation to the demand to do justice that I have defined as an animating feature of identity knowledges as a whole, as its goal is to keep the world of state-oriented struggle at arm's length. Its stake is antiregulatory to the extreme, which means that it resists the entire culture of the political that conditions the turn to state amelioration and begs for both recognition and representation to begin with. How feminist projects have come to reside in *that* culture, doing the kind of work that Ian's queer theoretic so chillingly protests, has a lot to do with the difficulty of exacting historical agency solely on the terms of one's own political choosing. Ian's clear recognition of this conundrum—that feminism got more (often by settling for less) than it wanted—produces the declarative *no* that echoes across the space that divides his political desire from governance agendas and that makes him not simply hesitate before asking the law for judgment but assume that justice will always require the refusal to do so. It is this that gives his queer theoretic so much hope as it promises to shield critical practice from the incursion of unforeseen harms. In their contrasting relations, the progress narrative of *gender* offers a transferential practice to avert loss in a transcendent narrative of accumulative futurity while the queer theoretic generates its critical capacity by taking aim at a set of historical consequences that hindsight gives it the agency to outrun.

Beneath the affective contrasts that most acutely differentiate them, then, the first two chapters are forays into the critical tactics of keeping and telling time. Their collective work for the broader strokes of *Object Lessons* lies not in making judgments about their temporal strategies, or the different political desires they amass around institutionalization, or the pleasures and dangers of governance. Ultimately I'm not even focused on the widely different dispositions my interlocutors grant to *gender*'s analytic capacity or the critical destiny of what they designate as queer, as the core of what interests me arises less in the particulars of what scholars want their objects and analytics to do than in the agency that we take to reside in them as an implicit assent to disciplinary rule. By foregrounding the interpretative struggle over a distinct confederation of terms—women, gender, sexuality, sex—the first two chapters hoped to show how identity knowledges were both reliant on and vexed by the identificatory relays that founded their minoritized forms. The middle chapters of this book turn in the opposite direction, toward majoritarian identity formations and their academic institutionalization. In both Whiteness Studies and American Studies—the two cases that concern me—practitioners are instructed into disciplinary practice through overt and self-conscious articulations of the field as a political project aimed at unmasking, critiquing, and even destroying the object of study that names them. If identity knowledges are more typically understood as crafting epistemic authority for their minoritized objects of study—women, queers, racially subordinated ethnics, and the minor forms of citizen that collate around each—critical practice is here oriented toward undoing the epistemological and geopolitical privileges that accrue to the object's overdetermined worldly value.

But how does one refuse an identification, especially if an identity attachment is not necessarily consciously held or if the advantage conferred on it operates regardless of the subject's consent? As I will detail in the pages to follow, an inordinate amount of critical force is attributed to the productivities of *conscious* political intentions: the antiracist white subject that Whiteness Studies seeks to cultivate is the consequence of a deliberate refusal of white skin privilege; the anti-imperial, postnationalist subject in American Studies marks the field's deliberately self-conscious encounter with an object of study whose power it promises to undo. By calling this chapter "The Political Conscious," I foreground the emphasis on conscious political subjects that attends identity projects that take aim at majoritarian objects of study. My first pursuit is Whiteness Studies and the conundrum of its disciplinary emphasis on white self-reflection, autocritique, and political consciousness as the means to achieve social justice.[1]

Whiteness Studies, some of us remember, emerged in the 1990s with the hope of differentiating, in the name of antiracism, the relationships among bodies, identities, and subjectivities that have constituted the universalist privilege of white racial formation in modernity. From the outset, it was greeted with skepticism. Did whiteness need *more* attention; did white people really need to devote more time to studying themselves? For many feminist scholars the anxieties it raised recalled the turn toward the study of masculinity that had marked the end of the 1980s, but the critical difficulties that faced it were far more challenging, in part because the goal of masculinity studies had never been calibrated to the destruction of masculinity altogether. Indeed, the force of discerning the difference between men and masculinity had been crucial to opening the door to female masculinity and to forms of masculinity incongruent with the biogenetic determinations that had accompanied the earliest feminist depictions of patriarchal sex. Whiteness Studies, on the other hand, arrived fully clothed in abolitionist rhetoric. Its promise was to destroy not only white supremacy but white identity and identification, if not the white race itself. While its commitment to social construction was apparent in its consensus that whiteness was not a biological category, the field's primary discourses struggled to bridge the gap between the social production of the meaning of whiteness and the privileges that repeatedly accrued to the corporeal embodiments of white skin. Its methodological resolution fell to the

1. The title is a play on Fredric Jameson's influential *The Political Unconscious: Narrative as a Socially Symbolic Act*, which offered a field-changing pedagogy for reorienting the relationship between politics and textuality for generations of humanities scholars.

agency of an antiracist white subject, one whose political commitments could be made distinct from white supremacy and refunctioned as cross-race and cross-class struggle through both the refusal and redirection of identification.[2] The contradictions that arise here underlie what George Lipsitz has aptly called "the impossibility of the anti-racist subject," which points to the difficulty of any critical enterprise that hopes to undo the multiple effects of dominant identity formations by projecting an increasingly empowered self-knowing subject.[3] How such critical agency can be differentiated from the narcissism of white subjectivity that underwrites Western humanist traditions is a major issue, along with the prospect that white antiracism is itself a symptomatic feature of white self- and social mastery, not its political or epistemological displacement. For these reasons, it certainly is no surprise that a decade or so into the new century, Whiteness Studies has all but disappeared. To be sure, scholars continue to study whiteness. David Roediger for one has published three new books in this century and has revised his field-setting work, *The Wages of Whiteness*. And many new titles across the disciplines have appeared that demonstrate the ongoing utility of making whiteness an object of inquiry.[4] But

2. While it is not possible to write the queer theoretic as a genealogical influence on Whiteness Studies, it is important to register the collision of social constructionist and deconstructivist maneuvers that orient both fields, whereby identity's historical emphasis on embodiment as the source and alibi of meaning is jettisoned in favor of identifications that have no essential direction or target, no matter how much the work of normative culture proceeds as if identification and identity are congruent. In queer theory, it is Eve Kosofsky Sedgwick's work that is most influential in this regard; for her, queer identifications have no uniform, determined, or knowable relation to identity recognitions or embodied acts. The theoretical apparatus of Whiteness Studies was similarly inclined, but the field imaginary held what I have called a critical realist understanding of the political; hence when all was said and done, identifications needed to be represented by acts of white antiracism, wholly legible as forms of political transgression in a wider sphere of politics. The distinctions I am noting here are complex but are no doubt linked to the disciplinary differences that underwrite work in each domain, with literary and cultural studies having primary influence in queer theory and history in Whiteness Studies.

3. In private correspondence, August 18, 1997. My thanks to George Lipsitz for his thoughtful and thorough consideration of the issues raised in this chapter.

4. See Roediger, *Colored White*, *Working Toward Whiteness*, *The Wages of Whiteness* (rev. and exp. ed.), and *How Race Survived U.S. History*. Other important texts in the new century include Doane and Bonilla-Silva, *White Out*; Hartigan, *Odd Tribes*; Hill,

Whiteness Studies as an autonomous field, listed on curricula vitae and supported by its own institutional initiatives, conferences, and publishing venues, has lost most of its critical appeal.[5]

This chapter proceeds by trying to inhabit the temporal cleavage that marks my conversation so far—between what was once the present urgency of the 1990s, signified by the resonant formulation, "Whiteness Studies is . . . ," and the now possible retrospection, "Whiteness Studies was . . ." I begin by telling the story about the emergence of whiteness as an injured identity in the aftermath of Civil Rights reform in order to sketch the three major premises about whiteness that shape my general itinerary and generate my broadest contention that whiteness is neither monolithic nor historically stable, but produced and (re)configured in complex relation to both the political projects and critical discourses attending racialized resistance and the mutations and transformations that accompany the proliferating historical meanings, structures, practices, and psychologies of white racial power itself. I then consider the broader cultural context of the 1990s in which Whiteness Studies emerged as an institutionalized academic project before reading, in detail, the popular "fable" of whiteness that stands at the center of that decade: *Forrest Gump*, the film that one month before the Oklahoma City bombing garnered six Academy Awards, including Best Picture. As the sixth highest-earning film in the 1990s, *Forrest Gump* was more than a box office success; it was a masterpiece of white racial regeneration performed to the tune of liberal antiracism. The heroicism it offered was profoundly antimuscular, even as its narrative was driven by—indeed obsessed with—the violence of the memory archive of twentieth-century racial struggle. Set in the South at a bus stop, with a protagonist whose great-great-grandfather was the founder of the Klan

After Whiteness; Pugliese, "Race as Category Crisis"; and Ware and Back, *Out of Whiteness*. For recent assessment of the field, see Kolchin, "Whiteness Studies"; Leonardo, "The Souls of White Folk"; Doane, "Rethinking Whiteness Studies"; McCarthy, "Contradictions of Power and Identity"; Riggs, "Why Whiteness Studies"; Hartman, "The Rise and Fall of Whiteness Studies"; and McWhorter, "Where Do White People Come From?"

5. In 2011, only Australia had a national organization devoted to Whiteness Studies as a formal institutional entity, called the Australian Critical Race and Whiteness Studies Association, which sponsored a journal of the same name. See the association's Web site, www.acrawsa.org.au/index.html.

and whose mother lives in a run-down plantation, the film follows Gump on a national sojourn, processing familiar images of racial trauma and social dissent—integration, Black Power, Vietnam, and the murder of national leaders. But Gump, born with a curved spine and "subnormal" intelligence, is never fully present to the scenes that engulf him, which arms him with the film's antiepistemological punch line: "I may not be a smart man, but I know how to love."[6] Knowing how to love is the film's pedagogical answer to the dilemma it confronts—the fact not only that the origins of white identity are bound to a history of white racial violence, but that the present cannot be conceived apart from it. This means that Gump is always in the location of a particularized whiteness. And yet, since love trumps knowledge and sentiment is valued over interpretation and meaning, the disposition of the white subject that emerges, now disaffiliated from the inheritances of white supremacy, is a simultaneously private and "unconscious" one.

The route by which the film deprives its antiracist white subject of critical agency is fascinating, if utterly infuriating, especially given the way it both tropes and shifts the terms by which the antiracism of Whiteness Studies sought to work. This is not to establish an analogy between *Forrest Gump* and Whiteness Studies; far from it. But I am interested in several tense and contradictory convergences—the way, for instance, each figures the antiracist subject through narrative practices that emphasize a "discursive" blackness and that hold cross-racial bonding as a means for disarticulating the white subject from white supremacist power—always in terms of male subjects and almost always in language dedicated to the resignification of the nation. While one depicts consciousness as the form of the white subject's antiracist resolution, the other finds succor in love as a

6. This point is even more salient when one compares the film version to the novel from which it was adapted, the 1986 *Forrest Gump* by Winston Groom. The novel features a far less innocent Gump—he smokes pot, cusses, and is promiscuous. Jenny does not die, and Gump's friend Bubba is a white (not a black) southerner. In addition, the film produces the monumentalist history that its main character fails repeatedly to register, while in the novel Gump's activities are not profoundly historical: he is a pro wrestler, a member of a rock band, etc. On the adaptation from the novel, see Lavery, "'No Box of Chocolates': The Adaptation of Forrest Gump." For an analysis of the historical memory refused by the film, see especially Burgoyne, *Film Nation*, 104–22; and Nadel, *Flatlining on the Field of Dreams*, 205–10.

panacea for not having to know the meaning of the history that makes him, and both sustain their visions on tropes of mobility to de-universalize white power and interrupt its conflation with white skin. If, for Whiteness Studies, consciousness and critical agency mark the difference between *Forrest Gump*'s fantasy of postracism and its own, *Forrest Gump* helps make legible the unconscious of Whiteness Studies, whose desire to be fully conscious enables it to misrecognize its own relation to contemporary racial formation. The goal, then, is to discern not simply what *Forrest Gump* hopes to forget but what the hyperconsciousness of Whiteness Studies could not let itself know. Call this, if you will, an analysis of the compulsion to form a disciplinary endeavor called Whiteness Studies in the first place. In the final section, I return to the present tense of my retrospection, catching up to the future that is nothing like what Whiteness Studies had hoped.

The Tale of Two Museums

In Laurens, South Carolina, John Howard operates a store front in the old Echo Theater, which is located, as they say, just a stone's throw from the county courthouse in the center part of town. "The World's Only Klan Museum" blares the marquee. Inside, there are robes and books, Confederate flags, pocket knives, "White Power" sweatshirts, even T-shirts declaring, "It's a White Thing. You Wouldn't Understand."[7] In 1996, when the local authorities denied Howard a business license to sell souvenirs in the Redneck Shop, he took his case to court.[8] His counsel was Suzanne Coe,

7. The Redneck Shop remains in operation. See Howard's Web site: www.myspace.com/theredneckshop. In 2006, the shop served as the conference venue for the World Klan Congress. See John Sugg's report, "Inside the Secret World of White Supremacy."

8. I have drawn my information about the original controversy from media sources. See Bragg, "In a South Carolina Town"; and April E. Moorefield's extensive local coverage: "New Klan 'Museum' Gets Chilly Reception," "Citizens Call for a Cautious Protest of Redneck Shop in Laurens County," "Ribbons Aim to Promote Racial Unity," "Ralliers Say Hate Belongs in Past," "Help Close Redneck Shop, Jesse Jackson Urges Reno," "Reno to Review Request for Redneck Shop Probe," "Laurens Police Arrest Suspect in Front of Store," "Attorney: Man Charged in Redneck Shop Damage Not Malicious," "Beasley Called Too Quiet on Racism," "Redneck Shop Rally Slated to Be Just One of Many," "City Would Deny Redneck Shop License," "Redneck Shop Reopens in Laurens Without Business License, Sues City," "Laurens Gives New License to Controversial

the Civil Rights lawyer who challenged the sex segregation policies at the all-male military academy, the Citadel, in 1993.[9] While public discussion focused on the controversial nature of the Redneck Shop's business, the legal matter, according to Coe, was the shop's First Amendment right to exist: "the Constitution," she told reporters, "is bigger than any of us."[10] In Alabama, the Birmingham Civil Rights Institute is located across from the Sixteenth Street Baptist Church, site of multiple bombings in the 1960s, including the now-famous one that killed four black girls. Inside the museum are replicas and remnants from the period of official segregation: public bathrooms marked "white" and "colored," pieces of a yellow school bus, a segregated street scene. In the gift shop, patrons can purchase African American history books, posters, postcards, and T-shirts emblazoned with the image of Dr. Martin Luther King. For Howard, as for his Civil Rights lawyer, the existence of the Alabama museum—and the legal protections

---

Redneck Shop," "Walk to Statehouse to Protest Redneck Shop"; and with James T. Hammond, "Suspect in Attack on Redneck Shop Decries Hate, Apathy."

See also Landrum, "Jesse Jackson, Ministers Discuss the Redneck Shop"; Hammond, "Legislators Want Stiffer Penalties for Hate Crimes"; Maudlin, "Residents Rally Against Redneck Shop"; Thomas-Lynn, "Redneck Shop Operator Opens Klan Museum"; Perry, "Klan Plans to Recruit in Laurens"; and Hakim, "Redneck Shop Sticker Upsets Church-goers" and "Church Rally Defies Klan."

9. Shannon Faulkner was admitted to the prestigious all-male military college, the Citadel, in 1993 with an application that withheld information about her sex. When the college administration discovered that she was female, they rescinded admittance. Faulkner sued and a U.S. district judge in South Carolina ruled against the Citadel, on the grounds that single-sex education at publicly funded institutions was unconstitutional. The Citadel appealed, but lost its efforts to keep Faulkner out of the cadet corps when no comparable military education program for women in the state could be established to admit her. In August 1995, the Citadel requested that the U.S. Supreme Court hear its appeal; Chief Justice William Rehnquist and Anthony Scalia denied the review. Days later, Faulkner began what was to be a short sojourn as a cadet. She was admitted to the infirmary with five other cadets in the afternoon of the first day with heat exhaustion. At the end of the week she announced that she was leaving the Citadel because of emotional distress and harassment. Celebrations by the male cadets, including chants, "We're all male here," were widely reported. See Catherine S. Manegold's early coverage of the case, "The Citadel's Lone Wolf: Shannon Faulkner," and her later book, *In Glory's Shadow*. See also Bennett-Haigney, "New Fronts in the Citadel Battle."

10. See Moorefield, "Laurens Gives New License."

that enabled it and other such projects to come into being—establish the legitimacy of, if not the legal precedent for, the Klan Museum, guaranteeing Howard's right, in his terms, to display pride in being white.

So many of the characteristics of U.S. racial discourse in the 1990s are exhibited in John Howard's story. Most notably, it figures the national project of dismantling state sanctioned segregation as a new regime of governmental suppression by mobilizing the language of Civil Rights to *protect*— not protest—the public production of white supremacist identity. Like other cases that evoke the specter of "reverse discrimination," Howard's lawsuit turns the tables on the history of race in the slave-holding South, ascribing to whiteness the minoritized, racially traumatized position from which to reclaim forms of racial expression once sanctioned, even celebrated, by the social and legal practices of segregation.[11] In the language of critical theory, we might say that in asking the apparatus of the state to adjudicate his "minority" injury, Howard *lays claim to the particular* as the means to secure access to the abstractly disembodied ledger of rights that are understood as fundamental to the universal promise of U.S. democratic citizenship—a citizenship whose national sojourn has entailed both overt and covert investments in whiteness as its embodied norm.[12] Rather than functioning to undo the universality of citizenship as whiteness, then, particularity is here a decisive part of the circuitry of white power, the paradoxical means to inhabit the state structure of universal entitlements while vociferously claiming a distinctly racialized whiteness that stands counter to the universality that would otherwise disguise it. In this, particularity routes Howard through whiteness as a universal power while supporting and sustaining his identifications as a minoritized subject whose racial identity is repeatedly cast as under both local and state threat.

11. In Howard's words, "I'm sorry there has been such a problem concerning the city. But it is a clear violation of my civil rights, and I'm sure the federal judge will get it cleared up quickly. I hope no one else will have to go through what I've been through." Quoted in Moorefield, "Redneck Shop Reopens." The city pleaded no contest to the suit (filed in the Eighth Judicial Circuit in Laurens County, South Carolina), which claimed that Howard's due process, equal protection, and First Amendment rights had been violated by the city council. A business license was issued to the Redneck Shop in November 1996.

12. On citizenship, abstraction, and the promise of the universal, see especially Warner, "The Mass Public and the Mass Subject."

Since the case has been settled in Howard's favor, can he still preserve his injury?[13] This might seem like an odd question, but I ask it in order to advance three premises about the study of whiteness that govern my discussion here. The *first* is historical: that the distinctiveness of southern white supremacist identity since the Civil War hinges on a repeated appeal to the minoritized, injured "nature" of whiteness.[14] To be injured—by the economic transformations of Emancipation, by the perceived loss of all-white social spaces, by the seeming dissolution of whiteness as the condition of citizen subjectivity—provides the basis of white supremacist collective self-fashioning, which has and continues to function by producing the threat of its own extinction as the justification and motivation for both legal and extralegal responses and retaliations.[15] As one of Howard's sup-

13. The story doesn't end with the resolution of the business license, but has a number of fascinating turns. Early in his quest for a business license, Howard sold the Echo Theater to his Klan protégé, Michael Burden, for reasons that aren't completely clear. Burden and his family lived in an apartment in the theater building in exchange for his collaboration in running the shop. When relations between Burden and Howard turned sour in early 1996, the Burden family found itself homeless until the pastor of the black Baptist church, David Kennedy, stepped in. Kennedy, the key community activist organizing against the shop's existence, provided short-term housing for the family and helped Burden fulfill his desire to apologize publicly for his role in supporting the Redneck Shop. While Burden eventually transferred his ownership of the theater to the New Beginning Baptist Church, the deed specified that John Howard had a lifetime guarantee to run the Redneck Shop rent-free in the building. To this day, the Redneck Shop is housed in a building owned by New Beginning Baptist Church. In 2008, the church filed a lawsuit against Howard who, it claimed, had sought to undermine its ownership of the property by illegally seeking to transfer the property to other Klan members. On the Burden aspect of the story, see Bragg, "Converted by Love, a Former Klansman Finds Ally at Black Church"; and Moorefield, "Change of Heart Closes Redneck Shop," "Redneck Shop Hits Roadblock," and "Man Sorry for His Role in Redneck Shop." For the 2008 controversy, see Connor, "Black Church Seeks Control of 'Klan Museum.'"

14. In the period of nineteenth-century Reconstruction, the ranks of white supremacy swelled from the shared belief in the ascendancy of a new privileged blackness and with it white injury. See Ayers, *Vengeance and Justice*, especially "The Crisis of the New South," 223–65; Gilmore, *Gender and Jim Crow*, 77–89, 94–99; and Smith, *Managing White Supremacy*.

15. Jessie Daniels's *White Lies* provides an analysis of the documents of contemporary white supremacist organizations, exploring in particular the language of "victimization." See especially pp. 35–43. Her later book furthers this investigation by analyzing

porters attested, "[The shop] should have never been closed down to start with. This is part of my past. My great-grandfather fought for the Confederacy. The United States stands for people's rights. . . . I don't think our heritage should be put in a back room."[16] The discourse of injury, then, is not new to white identity production, no matter how complexly situated it is in the rise of multiculturalism that many critics take to be the source of the second reconstruction's reconstruction.[17]

The *second* premise is theoretical: to the extent that critical race theorists have assumed that the power of whiteness arises from its appropriation of the universal and that the universal is opposed to and hence devoid of the particular, we have failed to interpret the tension between particularity and universality that characterizes not simply the legal discourse of race (where early documents enfranchise the "white person"), but the changing contours of white power and privilege in the last three centuries. Apartheid structures, both slavery and Jim Crow segregation, indeed universalized whiteness through the entitlements of the citizen-subject, but they simultaneously mobilized a vast social geometry of white particularity, as the declarative warning "For Whites Only" ominously suggested. While Civil Rights reform was successful in ending legal segregation, we

---

white supremacist organization and expression in the first decade of the twenty-first century. See Daniels, *Cyber Racism*. See also Ridgeway, *Blood in the Face*; Dobratz and Shanks-Miele, *The White Separatist Movement in the United States*; Bonilla-Silva, *White Supremacy and Racism in the Post-Civil Rights Era*; and Swain and Nieli, *Contemporary Voices of White Nationalism in America*. For an important recent discussion of the historical specificities of white supremacy as a nation-founding project in the nineteenth century, see McCurry, *Confederate Reckoning*.

16. Quoted in Moorefield, "Redneck Shop Reopens."

17. The Civil Rights movement is often called the Second Reconstruction, thus generating continuity between the abolition of slavery and the end of official legal segregation. For many critics, the rise of "separate but equal" practices in the aftermath of nineteenth-century Reconstruction evinced a reconstruction of Reconstruction as new practices of white supremacy emerged in the codification of "separate but equal." Similarly, the period following the Civil Rights era, cast in the official language of integration via multiculturalism, is viewed as a recuperative project, managed most triumphantly by the Reagan administration and completed in the era of Bush-Clinton—thus generating the notion of the reconstruction of the Second Reconstruction. See especially Marable, *Race, Reform, and Rebellion*; and Kousser, *Colorblind Injustice*. On the general left critique of multiculturalism, see Gordon and Newfield, *Mapping Multiculturalism*; and Willett, *Theorizing Multiculturalism*.

witnessed at the end of the twentieth century the growing legalization of powerful new strategies that refunctioned the particular as the vehicle for extending the universal reach of whiteness.[18] How do we account for the fact that John Howard's Redneck Shop has been taken by whites as a distasteful attempt to resurrect white racial supremacy while other endeavors (such as anti–affirmative action legislation) have been enthusiastically received, even as they too function to promote and protect the property investments of whiteness? The answer to this question, which entails an analysis of the ways in which white power has and continues to reconstruct itself in the context of segregation's official demise, leads to my final two premises. But first, I need to tell you more about John Howard's story.

In Laurens, a multiracial town of about 10,000, Howard was not a popular man. Everyone wanted him and his Redneck Shop out. This was a town with a violent history. "For decades," *New York Times* reporter Rick Bragg writes in covering the story, "a piece of rotted rope dangled from a railroad trestle, just outside this little town, a reminder of the last lynching in Laurens County. It was back in 1913, but people still talk of the black man wrongly accused of rape, and the white mob that hanged him."[19] The

18. Think, for instance, of California's 1996 state ballot initiative, Proposition 209, which essentially abolished affirmative action programs in state institutions in California. Funded by the California Civil Rights Initiative Campaign and led by University of California Regent Ward Connerly, 209 inaugurated a slate of similar attempts to amend state constitutions across the United States. By 2008, Michigan, Washington, and Nebraska had joined California with amendments outlawing race-based considerations in public institutions. Colorado voted down a proposed amendment, while Arizona affirmed a referendum in 2010. In 2009, Connerly's American Civil Rights Institute began organizing the movement for a state constitutional amendment in Missouri. See Americans for a Fair Chance, "Anti-Affirmative Action Threats in the States."

19. Bragg, "In a South Carolina Town." For a much fuller history, see Baker, "Under the Rope." As Baker so pertinently notes, many of the central actors in the struggle over the Redneck Shop are heirs of the region's long history of racial violence. David Kennedy, pastor of the New Beginnings Baptist Church which now owns the Echo Theater, is the great-nephew of Richard Puckett, who is regularly remembered as the victim hanged in 1913 by the lynch rope only recently torn down; it is his lynching that is featured in souvenir photos at the Redneck Shop. Ed McDaniel, a Laurens County councilman and source of media information during the initial Redneck Shop controversy, is also a descendant of a lynched man. Of the twenty-three informants that Baker interviewed for his study, all knew of the history of lynching in Laurens, though members of

lynch rope was not removed until 1986 when the trestle was destroyed, which means that at the time the Klan Museum opened, little more than a decade had gone by without a public reminder of violent white supremacy. It also means that no one was compelled, in the course of seventy-three years, to take the lynch rope down. And yet, the resurrection of white supremacy's public display in the downtown Klan Museum was met with an outpouring of white as well as black alarm. One way to read the difference in white response is through the politics of social space: the museum was located in the center part of town, in the most public of public spaces, while the lynch rope hung outside of town, along the road to and from Laurens's historically black section. The lynch rope thus signified the panoptic power of whiteness—always present but never fully visible. The Klan Museum, on the other hand, embodied whiteness in an open public display, marking its presence and visibility and thereby fixing it in an implicit narrative of both local and national violence. For whites, protesting the museum meant challenging the particularizing pact between segregationist ideologies and white embodied identity, which entailed constructing a new temporality for whiteness by casting Howard and his legacy project as profoundly dated and anachronistic. (I will have more to say about the place of memory in the discourse of contemporary whiteness shortly.) It also meant not just participating in but actively forging a counterwhiteness whose primary characteristic was its disaffiliation from John Howard and the white supremacist practices he defined and defended.[20]

It is this disaffiliation that might be thought of as the pedagogical lesson for whites of Civil Rights reform, where the transformation from segregation to integration reconstructed not only the materiality of black life

---

the black community were far more informed about the life details of the murdered men than were their white counterparts. Still, the local narrative that identified Puckett as the last lynching victim in Laurens was historically inaccurate; Baker reveals that Joe Stewart was lynched in 1920 and Norris Dandy in 1933. Unlike these later ones, however, Puckett's lynching was well documented in local and regional papers, which Baker ascribes to the spectacle nature of the event: according to newspaper sources, the lynch mob was over 2,000 strong, which was 40 percent of the county population in 1913.

20. At the height of the controversy, James Bryan, state senator from Laurens County, pointed out how stricken were local whites by the specter of Howard's racism. "I have had more complaints about the place from white people than from black residents. It's an embarrassment and does not reflect what Laurens County is all about." Quoted in Moorefield and Hammond, "Suspect in Attack."

in the United States, but the national imaginary of race and race discourse within which white identity since the 1960s has been anxiously forged.[21] Integration, no matter how failed in its utopian projections of a nation beyond race division, nonetheless powerfully suspended the acceptability of white supremacy's public display, so much so that the hegemonic formation of white identity in the postsegregationist era has come to be understood as taking shape in the rhetorical, if not always political, register of disaffiliation from white supremacist practices and discourses. The effect of this transformation in the public discourse of white identity formation has been double edged: while it mobilized the residents of Laurens, as elsewhere, to disaffiliate from Howard and the Klan, it also raised segregation and the Klan as referents for white supremacy in toto, which is why many white Americans at the end of the twentieth century could join efforts to undo Civil Rights reform without recognizing their activities or opinions as participation in what must now be taken as a widespread social and ideological reconfiguration of white identity, its power, and the mechanisms of its privilege. Think here of white suburban flight and the proliferation of gated communities, the privatization of institutions of higher learning and the growth of the prison industry, the English-only movement and the resurrection of states' rights, bans on public welfare for immigrants and pro-capital international trade agreements. Against these practices, Howard's Klan and its spawn began to be taken in the 1990s as the purveyors of U.S. white supremacy in total, which is just one of the many ways that the reconstruction of Civil Rights Reconstruction has been accomplished. Or to put this another way, seldom had U.S. whiteness been so widely represented as attuned to discourses of race and power, while so aggressively solidifying its advantage.

The split generated in the national white subject—between disaffiliation from white supremacist practices and disavowal of the structural

21. The familiar historical taxonomy of slavery-segregation-and-integration is perhaps best understood as a legal description of an official national position, which in and of itself tells us little about how other levels of government negotiated their relation to federal policy, let alone how individuals and communities came to inhabit the political imaginaries evoked and produced by such transformations. And yet, the depiction of the present that the taxonomy produces—of one distinctly different from the national agenda of slavery and segregation—has had a powerful social effect, underwriting much of the national political struggle I seek to attend to here.

reformation of white power and white investments in it—is central to my *third* premise: that the referential elision between segregation and white supremacy effected in the post–Civil Rights era foreclosed the elaboration of a coherent public discourse about the meaning and structure of contemporary white power. Indeed, the representational consolidation of segregation with white supremacy has functioned since the 1980s to dispute the claim that white supremacy *has a contemporary structure* and in this, the absence of official segregation has come to stand as historical "evidence" that institutionalized race inequality has ended. For Howard Winant, the contradictions at work here underlie what he calls "white racial dualism," a term meant to capture the "anxiety and conflict" that has accompanied the rise of white racial self-consciousness in the postsegregation era, such that whites "now experience a division in their racial identities."[22] While white people, as he writes, "inherit the legacy of white supremacy, from which they continue to benefit," they are also "subject to the moral and political challenges posed to that inheritance by the partial but real successes of the black movement. . . . As a result, white identities have been displaced and refigured: They are now contradictory, as well as confused and anxiety-ridden, to an unprecedented extent."[23] In seeking to understand the consequences of the loss of the unity between white identity and the white supremacist state, Winant tracks "the crisis of *whiteness*" as it is revealed in five post–Civil Rights racial projects: the far right, new right, neoconservative, (neo)liberal, and new abolitionist.[24] Only the far right project retains a wholly biologist explanation of race that overtly identifies with supremacist practices and discourses. All other projects, no matter how fundamentally neoracist or self-consciously postracist, frame themselves

22. Winant, "Behind Blue Eyes," 3.

23. Winant, "Behind Blue Eyes," 4.

24. Winant, "Behind Blue Eyes," 5–6. The term "racial project" has a very specific theoretical usage in Winant's work, drawing as it does on his groundbreaking collaboration with Michael Omi in *Racial Formation in the United States*. The term was developed more fully in the 1994 revised edition: "*A racial project is simultaneously an interpretation, representation, or explanation of racial dynamics, and an effort to reorganize and redistribute resources along particular racial lines.* Racial projects connect what race *means* in a particular discursive practice and the ways in which both social structures and everyday experiences are racially *organized*, based upon that meaning" (Omi and Winant, *Racial Formation in the United States*, 2nd ed., 56).

within the official national discourse of integrationist equality and thus work rhetorically to relocate understandings of race from biology to other primarily cultural grounds, except in the case of the far left project, abolitionism, which seeks to disaffiliate from whiteness in total through transracial political organizing, cross-racial identification, and postracist critique.[25] This means not only that white supremacist discourses as such have been decentered from the national lexicon, but that disaffiliation from such discourses *on both the left and the right* has been a defining feature of white political and cultural representation since the 1980s.

While Winant's analysis emphasizes the differences in political strategies that comprise and express the contradictions of white racial dualism, I

25. As he understands it, the new right emerged most forcefully in the "Reagan revolution" with a coded racial discourse that simultaneously denied its implicit address to whites and dismissed all claims to racial inequality as phantoms of populations that had been coddled by the state. The neoconservative project lacked the political base of the Republican Party but shared Reaganism's antistatism. While the new right appealed to white injury, the neoconservatives emphasized color-blind universalism, critiquing all forms of "race thinking" as being out of step with the new world of equality. Taken together, all the racial projects that emanate from the right seek "to preserve white identity from the particularity, the difference, which the 1960s movement challenge assigned to it" ("Behind Blue Eyes," 12).

To the left, Winant describes the neoliberal and abolitionist projects. The former seeks to limit white advantage while the latter intends to destroy it. The neoliberal project is best exemplified by the political strategy that delivered Clinton to the White House in 1992, which favored universalist appeals to national unity by undermining affirmative action (epitomized by the much-scorned "racial quota") and trumpeting "work for welfare" programs. Omi and Winant read the "New Democrat" movement as "centrist," emphasizing "moderate redistribution and cultural universalism" while "deliberately try[ing] to avoid racial themes" (*Racial Formation*, 2nd ed., 147). The ensuing (pseudo-) emphasis on class was taken by many as a vehicle for addressing structural racism without risking the descent into discord that discussions of race provoked. The neoliberal project thus worked "by ignoring race" at the level of public utterance, which allowed white voters angered by identity politics and the affective impact of Civil Rights protest to view the Democratic Party as directly addressing them (148). In subsequent discussions, Winant would drop the "neo" to name this project "liberal." See *The New Politics of Race*, especially 50–68.

The far left project of new abolitionism gets its name from the academic-activist work that emphasizes " 'the invention of whiteness' as a pivotal development in the rise of U.S. capitalism" (Winant, "Behind Blue Eyes," 10). As we will see, it is this project that generates some of the most important scholarship in Whiteness Studies in the 1990s.

have been drawn since the beginning of my inquiries to the liberalizing demand that all white racial projects inherit in the aftermath of Civil Rights reform—a demand that white identity be differentiated in discourse and image from white racist self-fashionings. This demand is as central to the abolitionist project as it is to the far right one, in the sense that neither can construct its project without charting its difference from the normative authority of the now-prototypical national "nonracist" white subject. The abolitionist project rejects the whole range of culturalist responses from both the right and center left in order to situate its own self-consciously antiracist politics against reformist accommodations and postracial recuperations. The far right sees itself at war with the representationally nonracist state, whose illegitimacy is the consequence of a belief in both natural hierarchy and the white race's providential claim to America. Both ends of the spectrum, along with those projects that emerge in the wide-ranging political practices of the middle terrain, are formed by what I call the hegemony of liberal whiteness. This term is not meant to map directly onto the racial projects defined by Winant or to indicate a coherent set of narrative maneuvers or political effects. I use it instead to register *the subject disposition and affective character* of whiteness in the popular cultural sphere, that domain of commodified identity production within which the post–Civil Rights meaning of race was (and is) nationally narrated and globally disseminated. As the governing ethos of the popular, liberal whiteness is best conceived not as a project, not even as a distinct phenomena, but as *the* cultural condition of the 1990s, that decisive decade that witnessed a proliferation of discourses devoted in various ways to denying, disrupting, interpreting, or reconfiguring but always engaging the problematic of whiteness that Winant cites as characteristic of postsegregation.[26]

26. In my 1999 version of this chapter published in *boundary 2*, I used the term "liberal whiteness" to evoke the familiar narrative practice in U.S. popular culture in the 1990s that sought to resituate whiteness by emphasizing sentimental affect, cross-racial feeling, and white innocence. In this revision, I am using the term differently in order to make a much larger claim about the liberal imperative that underwrites postsegregation, generating the range of white racial projects that Winant describes, from sentimental whiteness to neoconservative reclamations of white power to neofascist backlash. Liberal whiteness, then, refers to the way that all white racial representation in the decade is configured in relation not to state-authored white supremacy but to its representational suppression, itself a consequence of the transformation of the white supremacist state wrought by the legal end of segregation.

That was the decade, remember, after the "fall" of communism when the United States assumed its single superpower status under the guidance of the first "black" president (Bill Clinton), who put the finishing touches on the end of welfare, invaded Haiti without congressional approval, engaged in an undeclared war against Yugoslavia, signed the North American Free Trade Agreement, passed the military's Don't Ask, Don't Tell policy, entrusted the ministers of finance capital with major offices in the Treasury, and lied to a grand jury about a blow job.[27] Initiatives flourished to ban bilingual education, limit public spending on immigrants, police the border, and turn back affirmative action legislation—all as the "wigger" phenomenon took hold of the white middle class and rap was solidified as a global musical form. This was the decade of the Rodney King police beating and "the L.A. Riots"—the name now given to the rebellion that ensued when four white officers were acquitted of all charges in 1992. It was the decade of the resurgence of the white militia movement, which yielded the 1995 Oklahoma City bombings, the deadliest act of domestic terrorism in U.S. history.[28] And of course it was the decade of the round-the-clock media spectacle of O.J. Simpson's capture, trial, and release. It was also the period in which conservative media outlets were consolidated at the national level (by mid-decade,

---

See Wiegman, "Whiteness Studies." What interests me is how *all* discourses in the 1990s had to operate within this new terrain, including, as this chapter explores, the emergent field of Whiteness Studies.

27. In the midst of the 24/7 media engorgement of the Bill Clinton–Monica Lewinsky "scandal," Toni Morrison wrote, "African-American men seemed to understand [the attack on Clinton] right away. Years ago, in the middle of the Whitewater investigation, one heard the first murmurs: white skin notwithstanding, this is our first black President. . . . After all, Clinton displays almost every trope of blackness: single-parent household, born poor, working-class, saxophone-playing, McDonald's-and-junk-food-loving boy from Arkansas. And when virtually all the African-American Clinton appointees began, one by one, to disappear, when the President's body, his privacy, his unpoliced sexuality became the focus of the persecution, when he was metaphorically seized and bodysearched, who could gainsay these black men who knew whereof they spoke?" See Morrison, "Comment."

28. In 2006, the Southern Law Poverty Center reported that the U.S. military had relaxed standards since 9/11 that were aimed at thwarting the white militia movement's use of military training to their own ends, finding in one of its studies that "large numbers of neo-Nazi skinheads and other white supremacists were joining the armed forces to acquire combat training and access to weapons and explosives." See "SPLC Urges Congress to Investigate Extremism in the Military."

Fox Broadcasting had gone mainstream), thereby changing the tone and focus of public debate—so much so that the phrase "angry white men" was turned from critique to applause in the right-wing media's trumpeting of the social ills of the post-'60s. Conservative radio host Rush Limbaugh's popularity took not one, but two of his books to the top ranking on the *New York Times* best sellers list. Neoconservatism and the religious right converged on many domestic and foreign policy issues, setting up the Republican party's strategy of change under the banner of "compassionate conservatism" at the very end of the decade. Along the way, the battles over political correctness, the Western canon, and multiculturalism—like homosexuality, choice, and AIDS prevention—were frequent and vicious, and helped sweep the Republicans to congressional victories in 1994, which inaugurated Newt Gingrich's tenure as the speaker of the House.[29]

29. The film industry made billions parsing the conflicted terrain of whiteness, almost always in masculine form, with narratives troping angry white men (*Falling Down*, 1993) and their fears of racial annihilation (*The White Man's Burden*, 1995) alongside sentimentalizing depictions of white male injury (*Philadelphia*, 1993) and revisionist histories that located white innocence from within (*Forrest Gump*, 1994). Heroicism in the face of racist violence was figured as white and male (*Dances with Wolves*, 1990; *The Bodyguard*, 1992; *The Last of the Mohicans*, 1992; *Lone Star*, 1996; *A Time to Kill*, 1996); transracial solidarity and cooperation saved the nation (*Independence Day*, 1996); and white people were healed by blackness (*Grand Canyon*, 1991; *Six Degrees of Separation*, 1993; *Basketball Diaries*, 1995; *Pleasantville*, 1998). The genre of "stupid" white masculinity got off the ground, taking the edge off of failure and displacement (*Beverly Hills Ninja*, 1997; *Dumb and Dumber*, 1994), and the cross-racial buddy film reproduced its already enormous celebrity (*Another 48 Hours*, 1990; *White Men Can't Jump*, 1992; *Unforgiven*, 1992; *Lethal Weapon III*, 1992; *Die Hard with a Vengeance*, 1995; *Men in Black*, 1997; *Lethal Weapon IV*, 1998). Girl flicks had some national presence, with Whoopi Goldberg leading an interracial trio in the popular *Boys on the Side* (1995) or figuring, quite literally, as Demi Moore's white male lover in the much-discussed homoerotic scene in *Ghost* (1990). The number of films that held tight to the script that national U.S. life is all-white are too numerous to list, but they serve an important role in understanding popular culture as representing, not reconciling, the national psychic life of whiteness. Just as important are films that position white power as the condition but not the content or affect of social life, especially as depicted in the films that comprised the new black cinema of the decade, including those made by Spike Lee (*Jungle Fever*, 1991; *Malcolm X*, 1992), John Singleton (*Boyz n the Hood*, 1992), Albert Hughes (*Menace II Society*, 1993), Matty Rich (*Straight out of Brooklyn*, 1991), and Earnest R. Dickerson (*Juice*, 1992).

To be sure, this overview engenders its own historical and representational poverty, as such overviews always do. And, given my chapter's topic, it reproduces the very self-centeredness of whiteness that I have set out to track.[30] But how does one study the social productions and historical transformations of both white power and identity without replicating the priority that repeatedly produces and configures it? Or more to the point, through what critical practice does justice emerge when one constitutes an object of study as the means not simply to undermine but to destroy the political and historical power it wields? These are the questions that have haunted the academic field of Whiteness Studies since it emerged in the 1990s as a distinct enterprise devoted to explicating the problematic of whiteness in all of its vexed dimensions. Strictly speaking, of course, white identity had been studied before, as numerous scholars noted by citing Ethnic Studies in general or the black intellectual tradition that proceeded from W. E. B. DuBois to James Baldwin, Frantz Fanon, and Toni Morrison in particular.[31] But the academic press had not found the study of whiteness quite so interesting, nor had publishers gone out of their way, as they did throughout the 1990s, to secure books on the topic. Some scholars working on whiteness resisted the blatant commodification that cashed in on the currency of white identity narratives in popular culture, and many worried about the narcissistic gratifications of a political project that paradoxically centered whiteness in order to dismantle it. In 1997, Richard Dyer, a major contributor to the project of deconstructing whiteness, would write, "my blood runs cold at the thought that talking about white-

30. Both Karla Holloway and Radhika Mohanram have pointed to the contradictions that emerge in my discussion. For Holloway, the key issue is about the replication of white masculine centrality that arises from my attempt to chart such centrality as a consequence of the disciplinary apparatus of Whiteness Studies, while Mohanram notes the absence of the voices and perspectives of people of color in my discussion. See Holloway, "'Cruel Enough to Stop the Blood'"; and Mohanram, *Imperial White*.

31. Early feminist work has often been omitted from the citational histories that are intended to predate the enthusiastic production of the study of whiteness as a new field, such as *Yours in Struggle* by Elly Bulkin, Minnie Bruce Pratt, and Barbara Smith, which compellingly addressed white racial formation in relation to black and Jewish identities and political identifications. These repressions, as we will see, have had the effect of reconvening white masculinity as the generic subject of Whiteness Studies, even as the political aim of the field makes claims to abolish that subject's historical authority and centrality.

ness could lead to the development of something called 'White Studies.'"[32] Dyer's comments were too late, of course, as Whiteness Studies was by then seemingly secure, armed with a distinguished and rapidly increasing archive, and readied for the future with a slate of planned conferences, special sessions, edited collections, and journal issues devoted to it. Indeed, by the end of the century, whatever questions had emerged (and there were many) about the political meaning of a field called Whiteness Studies, there was so much citational power underwriting and reproducing it that its existence as something new was hard to dispute.

And there *was* something new about it: never before had the study of whiteness been declared its own field.[33] In this, Whiteness Studies figured a set of startling claims, first, that white scholars had an ethical duty to attend to their own racial identity; second, that the project of doing so constituted an autonomous academic field; and third, that this field *by definition* was engaged in antiracist work. The ethical imperative emerged from a set of deconstructive principles that sought not only to reverse the analytic gaze by making whiteness visible as a particular racial embodiment, but to expose invisibility as both the material condition and the epistemological logic of white universality, which had long been thought to be a cornerstone of white supremacy. Given the hypervisibility of the racially marked subject whose difference was always a form of embodied particularity, the

32. Dyer, *White*, 10.

33. For declarations of the field's arrival, see McMillen, "Lifting the Veil from Whiteness"; Stowe, "Uncolored People"; Bonnett, "'White Studies'"; Hill, "What Was (the White) Race?"; and Talbot, "Getting Credit for Being White."
By the end of the 1990s, the archive of Whiteness Studies was extensive. Frequent citations included Allen, *The Invention of the White Race*; Babb, *Whiteness Visible*; Cuomo and Hall, *Whiteness*; Delgado and Stefancic, *Critical White Studies*; Fine et al., *Off White*; Fishkin, "Interrogating 'Whiteness' Complicating 'Blackness'"; Frankenberg, *White Women, Race Matters*, and *Displacing Whiteness*; Hale, *Making Whiteness*; Hill, *Whiteness*; Ignatiev, *How the Irish Became White*; Ignatiev and Garvey, *Race Traitor*; Jacobson, *Whiteness of a Different Color*; Kincheloe et al., *White Reign*; Lipsitz, *The Possessive Investment in Whiteness*; López, *White by Law*; Lott, *Love and Theft* and "White Like Me"; Nakayama and Martin, *Whiteness*; Nelson, *National Manhood*; Newman, *White Women's Rights*; Pfeil, *White Guys*; Roediger, *Towards the Abolition of Whiteness*; Saxton, *The Rise and Fall of the White Republic*; Segrest, *Memoir of a Race Traitor*; Ware, *Beyond the Pale*; Wray and Newitz, *White Trash*; Young, *White Mythologies*; and Yúdice, "Neither Impugning nor Disavowing Whiteness Does a Viable Politics Make."

project of marking whiteness was heralded as a political subversion of white power and privilege from within, by yielding social subjects who both knew they were white and hence knew what their whiteness as a form of power continued to mean. At the heart of these maneuvers, however, lay a stunning contradiction, one that Dyer grappled with in his influential study of cinematic whiteness. As he wrote, "white people—not there as a category and everywhere as a fact—are difficult, if not impossible, to analyse *qua* white. The subject seems to fall apart in your hands as soon as you begin."[34] Indeed, in his terms, whiteness was so invisible as a racial form that white representation was repeatedly fractured into either individualism or varieties of regional and ethnic specificity such that its racial form continued to be obscured. "Any instance of white representation is always immediately something more specific—*Brief Encounter* is not about white people, it is about English middle-class people; *The Godfather* is not about white people, it is about Italian-American people; but *The Color Purple* is about black people, before it is about poor, southern U.S. people."[35] In reading infinite specificity as the vehicle by which white universality was both secured and protected, Dyer sought to evoke what I called earlier *particularity*—that is, the particularity of whiteness as a distinctly racialized cultural identity, biogenetic fiction, political form, and historical inheritance. Countering the twin invisibilities of infinite specificity and abstract universality, then, particularity was the valued analytic procedure for marking whiteness—serving as the means to contain its disappearance into heterogeneity and disembodied abstraction simultaneously.

Dyer worked on film, of course, which meant that much of his theoretical apparatus took the question of visibility as a formal one. Hence he considered such aspects of the cinematic apparatus as lighting, where the ideology of white beauty was literally produced. He also devoted a chapter to the aesthetic investment in the beauty of the dead white body and to the muscularity of white masculinity as an embodied spectacle in contemporary film. His work was about reading the particularity of whiteness as a distinctly visual form. But in the three dominant trajectories of scholarship that defined the distinct project of Whiteness Studies, the key register was the historical, not the cinematic: the race traitor school (which advo-

34. Dyer, "White," 46.
35. Dyer, "White," 46.

cated the abolition of whiteness by mapping a history of white disaffiliation from race privilege), the "white trash" school (which analyzed the
historical "racialization" of the permanent poor in order to demonstrate
the otherness of whiteness within), and the class solidarity school (which
rethought the history of working-class struggle as preamble to forging new
cross-racial alliances). Key to all three trajectories was Roediger's groundbreaking 1991 study of the creation of the white working class in the nineteenth century, *The Wages of Whiteness*, which rehearsed the history of the
"whitening" of Irish immigrants as a kind of paradigmatic case for understanding whiteness as a social construction. For the Irish immigrant,
whiteness was a compensatory "wage" that worked to disrupt black-Irish
or Chinese-Irish identifications in the context of industrial exploitation,
thereby pitting race against class identifications in ways that have haunted
working-class struggle for two centuries. While Roediger's project is quite
specifically a rearticulation of class struggle as an antiracist project, his
historical account of white racial formation was central to the political
horizon of Whiteness Studies, since it enabled contemporary white people
to imagine a political (as opposed to biological or cultural) identity beyond
the conflation of power and privilege with white skin. As James Baldwin
put it long ago, in a line that became a banner for Whiteness Studies as a
field, "As long as you think you are white, there's no hope for you."[36] Or, as
Roediger would gloss, "James Baldwin's point that Europeans arrived in
the U.S. and became white—'by deciding they were white' powerfully di-
rects our attention to the fact that white ethnics ... by and large chose
whiteness, and even struggled to be recognized as white."[37]

Whiteness Studies thus hoped to bring *consciousness* and *knowledge* to
bear on the historical problem of white racial supremacy and, in this, it was
a social constructionist project that sought to counter the massive problem
of white racial ambivalence that structured the public sphere. But to the
extent that its antiracist agenda was drawn repeatedly to a white subject
now hyperconscious of itself, Whiteness Studies was founded on an inescapable contradiction: its project to particularize whiteness was indebted
to the very structure of the universal that particularization sought to undo.
This was the case because particularization required an emphasis on the

36. See Baldwin, *The Price of the Ticket*.
37. Roediger, *Towards the Abolition of Whiteness*, 185.

body and on reconstituting the linkage between embodiment and identity that universalism had so powerfully disavowed for the white subject. To particularize was to refuse the universal's disembodied effect. And yet the destination of the dominant theoretical trajectories in Whiteness Studies were never toward the white body but away from it, and away from it in such a way that consciousness emerged as the methodological fix to the white body's universal authority—the very means to forge an antiracist white subject. One *saw* whiteness by *knowing* what whiteness had come to mean. But how did one come to know? And in what ways did such knowing challenge the universal authority of whiteness, especially given the fact that for everyone except the white subject, whiteness was never "invisible" to begin with? Or to put this another way, how was the fantasy of mastering the meaning of the body by subordinating it to conscious intentions *not* a replication of certain aspects of the universal power of whiteness, which had long produced a seemingly self-authorized subject able to determine the meaning of his subjectivity in the world? My answers to these questions take us into the heart of the "paradox of particularity" that titles my inquiry here.

Back to the Future

At the Civil Rights Institute in Birmingham, Alabama, visitors begin their tour by taking a seat on one of the narrow white benches that fill a darkened room behind the admissions booth. As the lights fade, an entire wall comes to life with documentary footage narrating the history of the state and its long and bloody battle to desegregate. A city founded during Reconstruction, Birmingham played a key role in the Civil Rights struggle by organizing one of the most successful uses of consumer power to grieve forms of inequality sanctioned by the state in U.S. history.[38] The Birmingham bus boycott drew widespread media attention as African American residents turned to other means, most notably walking, to navigate their city. The Civil Rights Institute thematizes this mass resistance by installing its visitor in a space organized around issues and images of mobility. When the documentary ends and the lights return, the movie screen rises dramatically to reveal the space of the museum on the other side. Every visi-

---

38. For a historical analysis of black resistance to public transportation segregation in Birmingham during World War II, see Kelley, "Contested Terrain."

tor to the museum must walk through the screen, so to speak, into rooms and corridors that contain artifacts of the material culture of segregation and the fight to undo it. At nearly every turn, there are more screens—a mock 1960s storefront where boxy televisions broadcast images of encounters between Freedom Fighters and the police; a video wall where multiple contemporary televisions juxtapose racist commercials, political interviews, and the speeches of Martin Luther King Jr. In a grand gesture where history and the present meet, the visitor is positioned in front of a picture window that looks out onto the Sixteenth Street Baptist Church across the street.

Forrest Gump, as I noted earlier, is set at a bus stop, and one of its main technological innovations is its clever insertion of the protagonist into nationally recognizable television scenes. In the most famous instance, Gump becomes a participant in George Wallace's failed attempt to block black entrance to the University of Alabama following the court order to desegregate. Positioned initially as a member of the crowd, Gump symbolically joins the students when he retrieves one of their dropped books. In this movement from witness to role player, Gump is strategically disaffiliated from the racist whiteness that Wallace so viciously represents, but the violence and anger of that historical moment are flattened by the innocence of Gump's unknowing gesture. In the spatializing logic of segregation, Gump is here a race traitor. He crosses the line of racial demarcation, disengaging from a white racial social body to join the black students, but the innocence of his action crucially depoliticizes the civic publicity of the whole scene. It is this kind of race traitor-ing that most characterizes the film, as Gump's movement in personal moral terms not only displaces the necessity of conscious identifications as precursors to public political action but consigns the entire realm of the "historical" to television, which installs a consumptive spectator as the ultimate witness—and postracist subject—of political change itself.

In its extraction of Gump from the legacy of southern segregationist identity, the film, we might say, de-essentializes the relationship among white skin, white privilege, and white racism, answering (or so it seems) the clarion call of contemporary theory to render race a social construction. But *Forrest Gump* establishes its investment in a nonessentialist whiteness by shifting the signification of segregation from emblem of black oppression and white material privilege to a form of white injury. This shift enables segregation to serve not only as the historical form of white particularity that must be disavowed, but also as the means for crafting a liberalized whiteness that is now, rhetorically speaking, kin to blackness. The film's preoccupation with mobility as the means to resignify segregation is apparent from the outset, where the narrative tellingly appoints a black woman to serve as the bus stop audience for the childhood portion of Gump's tale.[39] Without recognition of the meaning of her words, "my feet hurt," Gump remembers his first pair of shoes, or I should say he remembers through *his desire for* the woman's shoes his own personal history of mobility as a series of restrictions. The first was physical, as Gump was forced to wear leg braces to correct his curvature of the spine; the second was social, as Gump endured ridicule and exclusion because of his physical and mental disabilities. If the analogy between segregationist racialization and Gump's restricted mobility, ostracism, and physical "difference" isn't clear, the narrative locates the scene of Gump's social exclusion on a school bus where his classmates eagerly refuse him a seat. (Later in the film, he will again be refused a seat on a bus by his fellow inductees in the army.) These scenes perform two functions: they rewrite segregation as a discourse of injury no longer specific to black bodies, which installs whiteness as injury, and they define that injury as private, motivated not by a social system but by the prejudices and moral lacks of individuals who seem simply not to know better. That Gump can "know better" without ever knowing is of course the deep irony of the film. From this position, he gets to explain, "I may not be a smart man, but I know how to love."

If *Forrest Gump* is a sentimental white rendition of the history of segregationist apartheid, and if the film can be said to be a walk through the archive of popular national memory, its project does not end with white occupation of injury. That would be a version of John Howard's story.

39. As the red, white, and blue buses intermittently obstruct the camera's view of the bus stop, Gump's narrative advances from his early childhood through his college career, his tour in Vietnam, his various business adventures that render him a millionaire, and back to the film's final resting place, the heterosexual reproductive domestic sphere. Each person who listens to Gump is keyed by race and gender to the significant events of his narrative: the black woman gets the story of Gump's physical and mental difference, the discriminatory treatment handed him, and his final transcendence of the leg braces; the white women each hear portions of the romance narrative, which culminates in Gump's marriage to Jenny; and the white male listens to the episodes of war and economic accumulation. Notable here are the absence of the black male as audience as well as the schematic representation of race as a singularly black/white affair.

Forrest Gump has a more pedagogical mission: to demonstrate that difference and injury, even intellectual deficiency, are not impediments to the patriotic anthem of the American way of life. The plot thus advances through scenes in which Gump gains mobility, thereby exchanging injury and embodiment for liberation and transcendence. As a kid being chased by his classmates, he magically breaks free of his leg braces; as a teenager being harassed by boys in a truck with a Confederate flag license plate, he flees across a college football field, which results in a scholarship and All-American athletic career. In Vietnam, his ability to run saves his life and the lives of others, and in the film's oddest and longest segment devoted to mobility, Gump spends three years running from shore to shore, redrawing the boundaries of the nation's geographic identity and demonstrating that no region (no state, no neighborhood, no city street) is off limits or out of reach. All of this mobility critically recasts the segregationist history of the bus stop, even though that too must be left behind. In the final segments of the film, Gump discovers that he doesn't need the bus to get where he is going, as he is only blocks away from his destination where marriage, the domestic scenario and, miraculously, a completed paternity ("Little Forrest") await. He can easily walk there.

In his exodus from the bus stop and its symbolic evocation of national struggle and racial strife, Gump is extracted from the public political domain in favor of an insulated, privatized, and domestic realm. The mobility of his identifications and his symbolic minoritization thus function as preambles to a retreat from the iconic publicity of the nation—a retreat that emphasizes the emergence in the 1990s of what Lauren Berlant named the "intimate public sphere."[40] As she wrote in 1997, in a study that took *Forrest Gump* as symptomatic of a long and pervasive cultural reformation: "the intimate public sphere . . . renders citizenship as a condition of social membership produced by personal acts and values, especially acts originating and directed toward the family sphere."[41] With personhood no longer valued "as something directed toward public life," notions of the public

40. Berlant, *The Queen of America Goes to Washington City*, 5.

41. For Berlant's reading of *Forrest Gump*, see *The Queen of America Goes to Washington City*, 180–85 and 216–18. For additional analyses, see Byers, "History Re-membered"; Wang, "'A Struggle of Contending Stories'"; and Boyle, "New Man, Old Brutalisms?" For other angles of analysis, see Radstone, "Screening Trauma"; and Scott, "'Like a Box of Chocolates.'"

good become recognizable only from within the anatomized spaces of "simultaneously lived private worlds"—worlds, we might say, that meet at the bus stop but whose deepest meanings and political import are found elsewhere.[42] As this description makes clear, the intimate public sphere does not displace the national but resignifies it in privatized, even local terms, thereby casting feeling ("I know how to love") as the framework within which national life is performed and preserved. In the process, as Berlant writes, the family is repeatedly, often overtly, imaged and idealized as white, thus underscoring the implicit racial agenda of this new public intimacy. In the case of *Forrest Gump*, it gives to the protagonist's incessant movement a final resting place: in the last scene, outside his ancestral home on an Alabama country road, the white father helps his now motherless but perfectly intelligent son onto a school bus where, the film promises, Little Forrest will never be denied a seat. This resolution, in which sentimentalized white paternity ensures the survival of the nation-as-family, is predicated on Gump's celebrated failure to cognitively or narratively register the events he witnesses—predicated, that is, on Gump's native inability to forge anything but the most narcissistic and personalized of identifications, first with the mother who bore him and later with the child who doubles him. The film's commitment to a protagonist unable to read the historical archive he is moving through demonstrates the prevailing assumption of the Reagan years whereby, as Berlant puts it, "[the normal American] sees her/his identity as something sustained in private, personal, intimate relations; in contrast, only the abjected, degraded *lower* citizens of the United States will see themselves as sustained by public, coalitional, non-kin affiliations."[43]

The shift to the private and familial carries a certain risk, however, for a film whose protagonist is a southerner, an Alabaman, and the named descendant of the founder of the Ku Klux Klan. Under these conditions, too much familial intimacy risks sustaining a white identity that the film is sentimentally invested in undoing: the identity, that is, of the overtly racist American—the white southerner. As I have already suggested, a postsegregationist liberal imperative is characterized by a disaffiliation of whiteness from self-avowing forms of white superiority and identification. For this

42. Berlant, *The Queen of America Goes to Washington City*, 5.
43. Berlant, *The Queen of America Goes to Washington City*, 185.

reason, the first flashback narrative of the film, told to the black female witness, features Gump's Confederate hero ancestor, Nathan Bedford Forrest. A man born in poverty who grew rich as a slave trader and planter, *this* Forrest garnered fame during the Civil War as a brilliant, unconventional battle tactician who incited his men to massacre surrendering black troops at Ft. Pillow. (To this day, statues commemorate him in Tennessee and Alabama, and a state park in Memphis is named after him.) But in the film's memory archive, Nathan Bedford Forrest is ludicrous, not powerful or vicious; in Gump's mind, he would "dress up in . . . robes and . . . bed sheets and act like . . . ghosts or spooks or something." Gump's mother chose to name her son Forrest to remind him, in her words, that "sometimes people do things that just don't make no sense." The film's parable of naming functions as a pedagogy of counterwhiteness, disarticulating Gump from his genealogical inheritance by refusing its historical meaning. As if to emphasize the point, the patronymic, Forrest, lives in Gump's first name, and the repetition throughout the film of the line, "My name is Forrest, Forrest Gump," reminds the viewer repeatedly of the foundational displacement: from last name to first, from civil war to sentimental love, from the law of the father to the mother's moral lesson. In the narratives of national resolution offered by *Forrest Gump*, the descendant of the founder of the Klan can emerge at the end of the twentieth century shorn of his damaged patriarchal inheritance, which is to say that the intimacy of familial, personal relations has now been successfully separated from the past in order to construct a new postracist future, one structured by sentimental paternity, cross-racial friendship, discursive blackness, and white masculine (upward) mobility. In settling the problematic of whiteness to privilege white rebirth, innocence, and love, white power is strategically disarticulated from any inherent relation—historically, ideologically, politically—to white skin.[44] Or to put it another way, we can say that the film's de-essentializing project makes Gump's whiteness irrelevant to the very history in which it draws its political meaning.

44. This point is explicitly reinforced in the film through Gump's parodic commentary on the white bed sheets worn by members of the Klan. As the figure of white skin, the bed sheets can be cast off by Klan descendants, which means that the materialization of privilege symbolized by and invested in white skin has no necessary historical lineage. My thanks to Eva Cherniavsky for suggesting this reading of white skin.

The sentimental whiteness formed from these narrative displacements offers a subtle but telling commentary on one of the most volatile issues of the 1990s, affirmative action. In "Whiteness as Property," Cheryl Harris draws on the work of Ronald Fiscus to distinguish between two kinds of legal justice projects. The first, corrective justice, seeks "compensation for discrete and 'finished' harm done to minority group members or their ancestors," while the second, distributive justice, "is the claim an individual or group has to the positions or advantages or benefits they would have been awarded under fair conditions."[45] According to Harris, the goals of affirmative action—to address the harms done by institutionalized systems of racial disadvantage and oppression—are undermined when corrective justice sets the terms of discussion, interpretation, and legal redress. This is because harm is made addressable solely in individualized terms such that legal judgment becomes attentive above all to localizable agency and a discretely bounded event—that is, to a subject intending and producing harm for identifiably harmed subjects in a specific act or set of actions. In this way, the structural conditions in which white racial advantage are institutionally performed and perpetuated are rendered difficult to discern, as they can lack the individual agents and specified events necessary to constitute evidence. This is the context in which white discourses of refused responsibility circulate, as in the following familiar tropes: "My people didn't own slaves," "That was last century, not this one," "We were always poor," "I am not a racist." Such claims are not denials of racial injustice per se, as they often emerge in discursive contexts that affirm black disadvantage while asserting white innocence in the face of implied responsibility for it. But corrective justice models also opened the way for counterclaims of racial injury and fueled the backlash in the 1990s against affirmative action as itself a form of racism, making whiteness an identity in need of protection. This is the logic that underlies the 1978 "reverse discrimination" decision in the famous *Bakke* case, which inaugurated the idea of quotas as discriminatory to whites, even as it affirmed the constitutionality of affirmative action programs in general. By the 1990s, however, affirmative action in toto was under assault, as evidenced in the *Hopwood v. Texas* decision (1996) and in various state initiatives that functioned to

45. Fiscus, *The Constitutional Logic of Affirmative Action*, quoted in Harris, "Whiteness as Property," 1781.

reshape the language of equality to mean anti–affirmative action, as in California's Proposition 209 (1996), Washington's Initiative 200 (1998), and the One Florida Executive Order (1999).[46]

The complexity of the corrective/distributive justice divide and the forms of white injury that have emerged under the legal hegemony of the former are at work in the narrative practices of *Forrest Gump*, where the memory archive of racism and white violence is repeatedly on display— and repeatedly disarticulated from the distributive relation that the meaning of whiteness in the present would otherwise confer. Indeed, the film displays a passionate investment in defining the ends of two forms of race-based harm, slavery and segregation, in order to figure an antiracist white subject who has no more racial debts to pay. These investments are forged in multiple ways. Gump's mother, you might recall, supports her family by running a rooming house out of the old plantation that is the ancestral home in Greenbough, Alabama. This narrative act renders defunct the family's material advantage from the economics of slavery. Placed alongside the depiction of Nathan Bedford Forrest, now a silly, not dangerous, man, and performed at the symbolic scene of the bus stop, the dissolution of white material advantage makes Gump's eventual accumulation of wealth accidental, not intentional, which rewrites his whiteness as incidental and innocent, and thereby transforms the question of racial justice from the collective and national to the private and individual. This does not mean that Gump will have no racial debt to pay, but that his debt will not be historical—not about the ongoing economic or psychological privilege of whiteness as a material effect of slavery and segregation. Second, it will not be collective, not about a social identity enhanced and protected by the law as an economic investment. And third, it will be contextualized in relation to a state, which means that it will not infer that the state bears responsibility in matters of race and justice for correction or amends.

46. For a discussion of affirmative action in the midst of the backlash of the 1990s, see Morton, "Affirmative Action under Fire." For a copious account of the *Regents of the University of California v. Bakke*, see Ball, *The Bakke Case*. For additional left and center-left perspectives, see Ezosky, *Racism and Justice*; Curry, *The Affirmative Action Debate*; Leiter and Leiter, *Affirmative Action in Anti-Discrimination Law and Policy*; Wise, *Affirmative Action*; Post and Rogin, *Race and Representation*; Anderson, *The Pursuit of Fairness*; and Katznelson, *When Affirmative Action Was White*.

What, then, is Gump's debt? And why must there be a debt at all in a film so clearly devoted to the fantasy of postsegregationist white transcendence? To answer this question, we need to consider Gump's accumulation of wealth and to return, in time, to the issue of shoes, specifically the red and white Nike running shoes that serve as visual cues of the present tense of the film. Gump's accumulation of wealth has two primary forms: shrimp and computers. The shrimping business is borne of an interracial male confederation with Bubba, who gives Gump a seat in the film's second passage through the scene of the school bus along with knowledge about the shrimping business. When Bubba dies in the Vietnam War, Gump returns to the South and shrimp, only to make it big when a hurricane conveniently destroys every other boat but his in the black-owned industry. Gump's knowledge is quite literally African American knowledge, but the conversion of that "labor," if you will, into accumulation is effected through the laws of nature, not society. Any debt to be paid is thus a personal one arising from Gump's friendship with Bubba and not from the material advantages accorded to whiteness as an economic privilege. In this parable of the postsegregationist economics of black-white relations, the debt to be paid by Gump to Bubba's family—of half the profits of the shrimp business—is defined not by hierarchy or history, but as an honor to intimate male friendship. In separating Bubba's knowledge about the shrimping industry from his body and evacuating that body from the narrative scene, the film constructs Gump's antiracist liberal white subjectivity on a strategic denial: that identity, embodiment, and knowledge are historically linked.

Equally significant is the film's inability to imagine the black male as surviving the trauma of the racial history Gump will live through.[47] This is

47. The black male is the victim in the film of two different evacuations, both of which demonstrate the film's incapacity to imagine him as part of the present or the future. The first is his symbolic absence at the scene of the bus stop, the second his premature death. The latter he shares with the central white female character, Jenny, who dies from what the film never names but suggests is AIDS. Indeed, the film feminizes blackness by producing an analogy between both characters, as Bubba comes to occupy the place of Jenny in the second scene of exclusion and outsider bonding on the school bus. It is Jenny, after all, who allows Gump a place to sit on the bus in the earliest scene when all the white boys have denied him room; when this racialized site is plumbed a second time, Bubba occupies the narrative space initially held by Jenny. Their eventual deaths, as the deaths of the feminine and of the black male buddy, are crucial to Gump's simultaneous claim to and transcendence of injury, since they mark specific bodies as the bearers of

especially striking since the other form of debt that the film imagines for Gump is likewise borne of a male friendship and features Gump playing a role of compensation that has likewise been detached in the film from any kind of critique of the state. In his relationship with Lt. Dan, whose patriotic family has lost a son in every war since the Revolution, Gump both rescues and redeems the multiply injured white Vietnam veteran. This redemption is thematized through mobility as Lt. Dan, initially disabled by the loss of his legs in the war, comes finally to walk again with the aid of artificial limbs, thereby doubling the film's investment in mobility as the resignification of white masculinity. Importantly, the symbolic reconstruction of Lt. Dan's traumatized white male body is accompanied by his own heterosexual completion, which is demonstrated by the introduction of his fiancee, Susan, the only person of Asian descent in a film that devotes significant narrative time to the Vietnam War and its aftermath. And yet the film's commentary on the war is never able to reverberate beyond the sphere of intimate private relationships among U.S. men, as Susan evokes both a history and a racial discourse that the film has no mechanism or motive to speak, even as it requires her presence as both witness and accomplice to Lt. Dan's remasculinization.[48] Her insertion into the scene of heterosexual intimacy privatizes the national narrative of war in Southeast Asia, thereby displacing the economics of accumulation that have followed U.S. interventions in the region. By this, I am referring to the significance of Gump and Lt. Dan's investment in Apple Computers, an industry whose transnational circuits of production and distribution are indelibly linked to postwar capitalist expansion in Southeast Asia. If the Vietnam War cost Lt. Dan his legs, his economic mobility is nonetheless enabled by it, as is Gump's, and yet it is precisely this that the film's thematic focus on segregation, mobility, and the resurrection of a privatized U.S. nation occlude. In moving the sites of the accumulation of wealth from shrimping to computer investments, *Forrest Gump* depicts without commentary capital's contemporary mobility from local, regional forms of industry and their racialized histories to transnational practices of production and exchange.

---

national trauma—Jenny is tied to the antiwar and drug cultures of the '60s and '70s, while Bubba becomes the fallen emblem of a failed imperial war.

48. On the broader contexts of the remasculinization of the white Vietnam veteran, see Jeffords, *The Remasculinization of America*.

With these circuits in mind, let's return now to the opening scene of the film when a feather floats gently from the sky to land on Gump's red and white Nike running shoes. As the first material detail of the protagonist, Gump's running shoes are simultaneously his signature and personal trademark, the commodity linkage between embodiment and mobility that inaugurates his memory archive and serves in the end to demonstrate his transcendence not only of the trauma of history but of the social meaning of his own embodied identity. More than this, however, the Nike shoes "ground" Gump's magical movement in an unconscious relation to a commodity that itself became associated in the 1990s with the worst aspects of transnational modes of production. In the context of media revelations about Nike's exploitative working conditions in Southeast Asia, the corporation's commodity presence in *Forrest Gump* seems quite overtly engaged in a project of resignification. Through Gump, Nike can seek the reification of all material relations that is the effect of the protagonist's mode of narration, which means participating in the film's celebration of intimate affect as the means to resignify the national beyond the contestations between public citizens and the state. This celebration is demonstrated in two moves: first, in the way that the televisual archive that Gump moves through works to disavow the power of presidents and other state leaders, and hence to undermine not simply the authority but the value of contestation at the level of the state; and second, in the way the film endorses the shore-to-shore logic of nation as a geographical entity, manifested by Gump's seemingly motive-less three-year run across the United States.[49] With the state represented as the site of traumatic instability, loss of decorum, or simple comic incomprehensibility, the nation arises in illustrious geographical wholeness. Transporting Gump there, beyond the historical problematic of the bus stop, are his Nike running shoes. Their resignification as a private commodity relation fulfills Nike's own corporate fantasy of an innocent (that is to say nonexploitative) history.

In the figure of the shoes, then, lies the film's investment in the simultaneous transnational accumulation of capital in the aftermath of imperial

---

49. Gump's run, while denied an explanation in the film, begins the day after July 4—the day after Jenny has "run off" without explanation. In the final moves of the narrative, we will find out that it was their encounter on the fourth of July that created Little Forrest, thereby reinforcing the relation between white paternity and national futurity.

war and the reinvigoration of a national symbolic, rescued now through the individual's pedagogical identification with the commodity (and conversely, the commodity's identification of the individual). As Gump is marked quite literally first and foremost by the trademark, the trademark becomes the film's earliest mechanism for ascribing to Gump a particularizing identity. It is, importantly, an identity that situates him from the outset beyond the specific national contestations of the bus stop, beyond any recognition or reception of the embodied knowledge of the black woman's utterance, "my feet hurt." Gump's debt, after all, has been paid; compensatory justice, imaginable only at the individual level, has been achieved; all that remains is the telling of the tale. If, in the film's formula, that telling takes shape as a walk through the archive of segregation and black-white racial relations, Gump's innocence, which is to say his rescued whiteness, "stands" on his inexhaustible and dematerialized relation to the commodity.[50] As Gump declares about his coveted box of chocolates, "I could eat about a million and a half of these."

Whiteness Studies in Forrest Gump's America

Forrest Gump's celebration of the white race traitor who defies the logic of segregation and the history of southern racism in order to participate innocently in the new order of global capital is certainly a far cry from the ideals of Whiteness Studies, which seek a conscious agent of social change whose disaffiliation from white supremacy (in critical and social practice both) not only brings whiteness into critical view but threatens to destroy white power from within. And yet, even as the popular and the academic move toward decisively different political goals, they both begin their projects of rearticulating a postsegregationist white identity at the site of the historical. In *Forrest Gump*, this entails rendering the history of violent white power incomprehensible, if not comic—the Klan leader, remember, liked "to dress up in . . . robes and . . . bed sheets and act like . . . ghosts or spooks or something"—thereby refunctioning the present as the origin for a new America no longer held in grief or guilt to a violently unredeemable

---

50. For an understanding of the material investment in whiteness as a relation of inexhaustability to the commodity, see especially Cherniavsky, *Incorporations*, and for an exploration of whiteness as a process of simultaneous materialization and dematerialization, see McKee, *Producing American Races*.

past. To recall Winant, we might say that the film parses white racial dualism for a sentimental resolution of mutual injury, intimate affect, and cross-racial friendship—all as precursor, of course, to the renewal of white paternity and economic mobility in the emergent circuits of transnational capital. Resolution indeed! But the failure of the film's emphasis on particularity to undermine the reconstruction of whiteness is itself an important index of the difficulty of making particularity the paradigmatic means for dismantling white supremacy. This is not only because the film must first rescue Gump *from* particularity—that is, from the particularity of white supremacist segregationist identity, represented by his southern inheritances—before it can begin to redeem him and generate the non-meaning of his white skin. It is also because the project of reparticularizing him takes shape through the kind of mobile affinities that arise from the prerogatives of the universal in the first place. As I hope to explain, the universal must be understood not simply as the privilege of disembodiment, which underwrites hyperspecificity (à la Dyer), but as implicated in the de-essentialized subjectivity on which the mobility of antiracist identifications depends. One of the deepest complicities of *Forrest Gump* is how it stages its protagonist's intellectual deficiency as a defense against having to account for what his mobility means.

Whiteness Studies, in contrast, turns with urgency to the historical to serve as the critical construction site for constituting a postsegregationist antiracist white subject. In four regularly cited texts—Roediger's *The Wages of Whiteness* and *Towards the Abolition of Whiteness*, Theodore Allen's *The Invention of the White Race*, and Noel Ignatiev's *How the Irish Became White*—historians chart the effects of industrialization and with it wage labor on the racialization of ethnic immigrants in the nineteenth century. In doing so, they locate whiteness not in the epidermal "reality" of white skin, but in complex economic and political processes and practices. As W. E. B. DuBois diagnosed in *Black Reconstruction* (1935), whiteness emerged as the compensatory psychological and public "wage" that enabled various groups, especially the so-called black Irish, to negotiate a social status simultaneously distinct from and opposed to that of the slave or ex-slave.[51] For Roediger, who is the most widely cited scholar in the emergent archive of Whiteness Studies, this negotiation is a tragic failure of

51. See W. E. B. DuBois, *Black Reconstruction in America*.

insurgent class consciousness, since much of the force behind the discursive racialization of the Irish as black arose from their large occupation of unskilled and domestic labor. "[W]hiteness was a way in which white workers responded to a fear of dependency on wage labor and to the necessities of capitalist work discipline."[52] By paying close attention to the Irish's own struggle against the negative racialization that accompanied their lower-class status in the United States, Roediger demonstrates how "working class formation and the systematic development of a sense of whiteness went hand in hand for the US white working class," so much so, in fact, that the very meaning of "worker" would be implicitly understood as "white" by the end of the century (*Wages* 8). While some scholars disagree with Roediger's insistence that the Irish *pursued* white identity—Allen, for instance, says the Irish were "bamboozled" by the ruling class[53]—much of the work in Whiteness Studies depends for its political force on the disciplinary legacy of labor history put into play by Roediger. Taking conscious political action and the centrality of the subject as an agent and not simply an object of history, labor history, Roediger explains, "has consistently stressed the role of workers as creators of their own culture [and therefore] it is particularly well positioned to understand that white identity is not merely the product of elites or of discourses."[54] In other words, labor history offers the methodological imperative to read social subjects as the agents of the histories that make them.

In this retrieval of the historical as the site of human agency, labor history jump starts, we might say, the critical project of imagining an antiracist white subject in the present, for if whiteness is historically produced and if its production requires something more than the physical characteristic of skin color, then whiteness as a form of political identification, if not racial identity, can be undone. This stress on the active process of "unthinking" whiteness as a structure of power and privilege is certainly a compelling counter to the unconscious white subject celebrated in *Forrest Gump* and it offers, through the political project mapped by labor history, a means to refunction working-class struggle as cross-racial alliance. But once the theoretical precepts of labor history become installed as the governing disciplinary apparatus of Whiteness Studies—that is, once the

52. Roediger, *The Wages of Whiteness*, 13. All further citations are included in the text.
53. Allen, *The Invention of the White Race*, 199.
54. Roediger, *Towards the Abolition of Whiteness*, 75–76.

historical retrieval of agency and the story of prewhite ethnics who chose whiteness in the tense interplay between race and class come to define the possibility of the antiracist white subject—the field begins to generate a range of contradictory, at times disturbing, effects. The most critically important include: (1) an emphasis on agency that situates a white humanist subject at the center of social constructionist analysis; (2) the use of class as the transfer point between looking white and "being" white, which relies solely on notions of economic interest to figure the psychic implications of the white "wage"; and (3) the equation of economic disempowerment with minoritization and racialization. Each of these effects must be read further in the context of popular culture in the 1990s, where the problematic of whiteness is likewise shaped, as I have discussed, not only by the contradictory and tense interplay between the universal and the particular, but by a desire for an antiracist white subject who refutes the historical inheritances of white power. In both discursive locations, history serves to construct white mobility and comes to rescue contemporary whiteness from the transcendent universalism that has been understood as its most damaging mode of reproductive power.

To trace the critical effects I have delineated above, I want to turn to a brief passage at the end of Roediger's introductory comments in *Towards the Abolition of Whiteness*. Here, in an economist language of investment and divestiture, Roediger hopes to inspire working-class whites to give up the compensatory psychological and public wage of whiteness by forging class-based political identifications with people of color:

> we cannot *afford* to ignore the political implications [that] . . . whites are confessing their confusion about whether it is really *worth* the effort to be white. We need to say that it is not *worth* it and that many of us do not want to do it. Initiatives [should] . . . expos[e] how whiteness is used to make whites settle for hopelessness in politics and misery in everyday life. . . . Our opposition should focus on contrasting the *bankruptcy* of white politics with the possibilities of nonwhiteness. We should point out not just that whites and people of color often have common economic *interests* but that people of color currently act on those *interests* far more consistently . . . precisely because they are not burdened by whiteness.[55]

55. Roediger, *Towards the Abolition of Whiteness*, 16–17, emphasis added.

Casting whiteness as the burden that prevents working-class whites from identifying their fundamental material interests, Roediger differentiates identity from identification in order to redirect the "possessive investment in whiteness," as George Lipsitz calls it, toward political allegiances with those designated as nonwhite.[56] Such identificatory mobility is central to Roediger's social constructionist account of whiteness, countering what we might think of as the political and theoretical *immobility* of an essentialized subject. For when looking white and being white are collapsed, white identity becomes saturated with, if not wholly indistinguishable from, political identifications with white supremacy. To pry apart this essentialized relation, Roediger emphasizes the mobility of political identifications as forms of conscious animation and redirection. Working-class whites need to "cross over" there, to trade against the faulty essentialist confederacy between white power and white skin, in order to discover the class "interests" that are already theirs. In using class as the mechanism for this transportation, Roediger's critical model passes through the prewhite ethnic to a complex citing of cross-racial economic affinities to secure a future of post–white working-class struggle.

But the language Roediger uses undermines the political project he maps by revealing the unconscious relations on which white hyperconsciousness depends. Not only are whites "burdened" by a form of racial identity that leads to bankrupt politics and both "hopelessness" and "misery in everyday life," but they are also cut off from access to their real "interests" by the very whiteness that is otherwise thought to be a privilege. Here, the privilege of whiteness is an empty mirage, something that working-class white people have merely "settle[d] for." People of color, on the other hand, have settled for nothing, for in their nonwhiteness, they are bound by proximity to their real economic interests. It is significantly their racial and not their class identities—note the language, "people of color"—that enable them to "act on those interests far more consistently." As such, the split subjectivity that

56. See Lipsitz, "The Possessive Investment in Whiteness" for a discussion of how national policies in the twentieth century furthered the political agenda of white racial supremacy and material advantage. For instance, Federal Housing Administration programs funneled money toward white Americans in the suburbs instead of into multiethnic urban neighborhoods, thereby restructuring in more segregated ways the racialization of social space in the second half of the century. See also George Sanchez's useful response to Lipsitz in the same issue of *American Quarterly*, "Reading Reginald Denny."

underlies intersecting hierarchies of race and class is conceptually reserved for whites alone, and the strategy of mobile identification that Roediger heralds is the necessary adjudication of the difference—the "confusion"— that lives within. The dual relation that emerges, in which nonwhiteness functions rhetorically and schematically as the site of the real while white-ness signifies social and economic bankruptcy, establishes whiteness as an injured identity: injured, that is, by whiteness itself.

In the context of my conversation about the trope of mobility in *Forrest Gump*, the critical moves articulated here reverse the political investment but not the spatializing logic that accompanies the popularized race traitor-ing white subject in the postsegregationist era. It is the white subject who crosses the segregationist boundaries of both knowledge and political iden-tification while people of color remain politically identified with the social margins where the relation between race and class is figured as more inti-mately, one hesitates to say more essentially, interested. The fruit of the social constructionist enterprise is to be found, then, fully on the side of the antiracist white subject, the one that must be rescued from its racial "self" by marking the difference between identity and political identification. Roediger names this difference "nonwhiteness," and in so doing not only reconvenes the very elision of white with racist that he otherwise sets out to contest, but demonstrates how overwritten is the antiracist subject by the determinations of universal privilege itself—determinations that include the ability to command a complex theory of agency and subject construction for itself. This is not to charge Roediger with political complicity or theo-retical failure, but to begin to map the conundrum that Whiteness Studies finds itself in, as it pursues a knowing white subject that can write its political commitments against the burden that whiteness represents. Whether or not those otherwise consigned to the immobility that attends "nonwhiteness"— that is, "people of color"—will welcome or benefit from white identificatory mobility is a question that the archive of Whiteness Studies does not an-swer. What it offers instead is a rather powerful romance with the fantasy of life outside the "white corral," as Jonathan Scott calls it.[57] It is this ro-mance with "nonwhiteness" that shapes the political grammar of Whiteness Studies, generating various strategies to link antiracist white subjectivity to both the socially minor and minoritized.

57. Scott, "Inside the White Corral."

This is nowhere more apparent than in the activist quasi-academic journal *Race Traitor*, which urges its readers to "abolish the white race from within."[58] Troping the emphasis on conscious agency drawn from labor history and finding political sustenance in individual narratives of race traitoring, the various authors collected in *Race Traitor* posit white abolitionism as necessary to "solving the social problems of our age" (10). In the opening editorial to the Routledge volume that collects the first five issues of the journal, editors Noel Ignatiev and John Garvey describe the *Race Traitor* project: "The existence of the white race depends on the willingness of those assigned to it to place their racial interests above class [or] gender.... The defection of enough of its members ... will set off tremors that will lead to its collapse. *Race Traitor* aims to serve as an intellectual center for those seeking to abolish the white race" (10).[59] Guided by the principle "*treason to whiteness is loyalty to humanity,*" *Race Traitor* envisions treason on a number of fronts, from verbal retorts to racist jokes or commentaries to interracial marriage to cross-racial identifications in politics, fashion, and music (10). "What makes you think I am white?" is the quintessential race traitor question, and its deployment in the face of the police is one of the most heralded abolitionist acts. As Garvey and Ignatiev write in an essay that appears elsewhere,

---

58. Ignatiev and Garvey, *Race Traitor*, 2. Further citations are included in the text.

59. Linda Martín Alcoff discusses the problem of abolitionism in race traitor theory in "What Should White People Do?" While she acknowledges that whites cannot possibly disavow the power that skin privilege confers, and hence that they cannot resurrect their own authority to determine the meaning of race that any project to unsettle white supremacy would necessarily engender, she nonetheless calls for white double consciousness as the means to engineer the end of racism: a "double consciousness requires an ever-present acknowledgment of the historical legacy of white identity constructions in the persistent structures of inequality and exploitation, as well as a newly awakened memory of the many white traitors to white privilege who have struggled to contribute to the building of an inclusive human community" (25). Alcoff is not alone, of course, in moving from a structuralist account of white power that symbolically and materially attaches skin to the psychic life of whiteness and the productive possibility of antiracist attachments, but it is precisely this investment in reforming white subjectivity as an antiracist pedagogy that repeats the paradox of particularity I have sought to track. In an important discussion of Whiteness Studies, Sara Ahmed critiques both the impulse and the consequences of the very question that organizes Alcoff's inquiry. See Ahmed, "Declarations of Whiteness."

the cops look at a person and then decide on the basis of color whether that person is loyal to or an enemy of the system they are sworn to serve and protect.... [T]he cops don't know for sure if the white person to whom they give a break is loyal to them; they assume it.... What if the police couldn't tell a loyal person just by color? What if there were enough people around who looked white but were really enemies of official society so that the cops couldn't tell whom to beat and whom to let off? ... With color no longer serving as a handy guide for the distribution of penalties and rewards, European-Americans of the downtrodden class would at least be compelled to face with sober sense their real condition of life and their relations with humankind. It would be the end of the white race.[60]

In thus forging a "new minority determined to break up the white race," the authors of *Race Traitor* join Roediger in constructing a model of the mobile antiracist subject whose conscious political production not only particularizes whiteness by unmasking its universalizing power but that does so in order to craft for economically disenfranchised whites a generative and ultimately antiracist class politics.[61]

If this description of *Race Traitor* suggests a coherent intellectual and activist project, it is important to stress that contributions to the journal vary widely in political content. This is due in part to the collective nature of the journal and to its mediation between activist and academic political sites. It is also a consequence, it seems to me, of the difficulties that abound in transposing nineteenth-century antislavery abolition into the paradigmatic site for constructing a late twentieth-century antiracist subject. By affirming as heroic and antiwhite the work of such abolitionists as John Brown, leader of the failed slave revolt at Harper's Ferry, *Race Traitor* reinscribes the centrality of white masculine leadership even as it posits such leadership as historical evidence for the abolition of the white race. "How many dissident so-called whites would it take to unsettle the nerves of the white executive board? It is impossible to know. One John Brown—against a background of slave resistance—was enough for Virginia" (13). Overly drawn to masculine models of armed retaliation, *Race Traitor* effectively evacuates altogether the feminist trajectory of nineteenth-century aboli-

60. Garvey and Ignatiev, "The New Abolitionism," 105–6.
61. Garvey and Ignatiev, "The New Abolitionism," 107.

tionism, reproducing instead the white male rebel as the affirmative subject of antiracist struggle. Such affirmation, situated in the context of essays about the Irish and prewhite immigrants, symptomatically demonstrates the oscillation between universal privilege and minoritized particularity that characterizes not only the history of white subject formation in the United States but the critical apparatus of Whiteness Studies itself.

Race Traitor's implicit response to its own critical contradiction of abolishing whiteness in a frame of white masculine heroic narrativity is to situate the African American as the quintessential American. Ignatiev writes,

> The adoption of a white identity is the most serious barrier to becoming fully American.... [T]he United States is an Afro-American country.... Above all, the experience of people from Africa in the New World represent the distillation of the American experience, and this concentration of history finds its expression in the psychology, culture, and national character of the American people. (18, 19)

Thus defining the abolition of whiteness as the precondition for becoming American, Ignatiev retrieves an American exceptionalist logic that displaces the historical white subject as the national citizen-subject for a narrative of national origin cast now as black.[62] In doing so, a metaphorical "America" of national longing supplants the materialist "America" through which state violence—physical, economic, and ideological—has guaranteed the juridical privileges of whiteness. Leaving aside the many ways this formulation eradicates a range of groups and experiences, it is significant how important to *Race Traitor* is the resignification of the nation as part of a reclamation of the "human." "It is not black people who have been prevented from drawing upon the full variety of experience that has gone into making up America. Rather, it is those who, in maddened pursuit of the white whale, have cut themselves off from human society" (21). The abolition of whiteness reclaims

62. "What is the distinctive element of the American experience?" Ignatiev writes. "It is the shock of being torn from a familiar place and hurled into a new environment, compelled to develop a way of life and culture from the materials at hand. And who more embodies that experience, is more the essential product of that experience, than the descendants of the people from Africa who visited these shores together with the first European explorers ... and whose first settlers were landed here a year before the Mayflower?" (*Race Traitor*, 19).

the democratic possibility of human sociality, itself a characteristic of the resignified nation.

My focus on the language of nation and national identity is meant to recall the ideological work of *Forrest Gump* and its mobile protagonist whose fantastic projection of a postsegregationist society entailed the literal and symbolic remapping of the territory of the nation. In Gump's claim to what Berlant calls "the normal," the white male subject reconstructs itself on the grounds of a fabled sentimentality, with all state-based debts paid and a reproductive future of politically uncontaminated subjectivity guaranteed. In *Race Traitor*, the editors seek not so much the normal but the "ordinary" as the contrast to the state: "the ordinary people of no country have ever been so well prepared to rule a society as the Americans of today" (4). This is because, in Ignatiev's words, "few Americans of any ethnic background take a direct hand in the denial of equality to people of color" (16–17). The conscious agency that defines the becoming white of the prewhite ethnic is strategically dissolved in the present where the ordinary person is theoretically divested of taking a committed interest in the perpetuation of white racial privilege. Indeed, whiteness, while the object under investigation and ultimate destruction, is exteriorized to such an extent that the conscious agency heralded as necessary to undo it has no theoretical hold on the interior constitution of the subject. In contrast to Roediger's work, there is here no psychic effect of whiteness as a social construction, merely an interpretative inscription based on skin that can be consciously refused:

> The white race is a club, that enrolls certain people at birth, without their consent, and brings them up according to its rules. For the most part the members go through life accepting the benefits of membership, without thinking about the costs. When individuals question the rules, the officers are quick to remind them of all they owe to the club, and warn them of the dangers they will face if they leave it. *Race Traitor* aims to dissolve the club, break it apart, to explode it. (10–11)

In dissolving the club, in revealing the "costs" of membership to be the failure of whites to be fully American, *Race Traitor*'s postsegregationist antiracist subject emerges, against the power of the state, as emblem of a coherent nation.

The construction of the antiracist subject in *Race Traitor* thus goes something like this: whiteness is understood as the consequence of a universalizing pact between white skin color and white club privilege, one that deprives white people of a positive relation both to humanity and to U.S. national identity. White supremacy is less an effect of individual activities and ideologies than the consequence of institutions of state power, which themselves alienate the ordinary citizen who is neither directly nor enthusiastically involved in the oppression of people of color. In this way, *Race Traitor* assumes, as does Roediger, that cross-racial class alliance is the locus of more urgent and identifiable political interests for the majority of whites, though *Race Traitor* is dedicated to the possibility of a "minority" of traitors—not, as in Roediger, a mass class movement—performing the work of abolishing white supremacy. This work involves making whiteness visible as a racial category by interrupting the "natural" assumption that people who look white are invested in being white. Race traitors must thus mark whiteness as a racialized particular in order to perform their disaffiliation from the universality that underwrites the category, where such performance is understood as the necessary claim to an antiracist subjectivity. This is, it seems to me, the performative force of the race traitor question, "What makes you think I am white?" which simultaneously and paradoxically refuses the position of the universally unmarked by ultimately claiming to no longer be marked by it. In asserting the particularity of white racial identity as preamble to refusing it altogether, the race traitor passes through both the universal and the particular in order to found a new minority of former white people. Counting on the power of individual disavowal of the juridical white subject of state power, *Race Traitor* reimagines an empowered humanist and quintessentially masculine subject whose intent to repeal its own whiteness is consecrated as the central practice of antiracist struggle.

These moves that seek to privilege the conscious intentions, practices, and political attachments of the subject over the body evince a desire for mastery not over bodies per se but over the social as the discursive setting in which a white body comes to have material meaning. This is an interesting turn of the social constructionist project, as it mobilizes the language of antiessentialism to evacuate consciousness from social embodiment altogether, thereby rescuing a humanist subject from the overdeterminations of sociality itself. In *White Trash: Race and Class in America*, Annalee Newitz is especially critical of the abjection of the body that underwrites the conscious production of the antiracist subject in the race traitor school. For her, as for other scholars who turn to the permanent poor as a means for studying whiteness, social construction's de-essentializing project must not abandon the body but resignify it in order to differentiate white identity from the practices and structures of white racial supremacy. As she writes in "White Savagery and Humiliation":

> We are asked [by the abolitionists] to demonize whiteness rather than to deconstruct it. . . . Social problems like unequally distributed resources, class privilege, irrational prejudice, and tyrannical bureaucracy which we associate with whiteness are just that—*associated* with whiteness. . . . They are not essential to whiteness itself, any more than laziness and enslavement are essential to blackness. . . . Informing whites that their identities are the problem, rather than various social practices, makes it sound like whites should die rather than that white racism should. The ideologies of white power which make some white people socially destructive are the symptoms of American inequality and injustice, not its principle causes.[63]

In countering the equation between whiteness and supremacy that inaugurates the race traitor's self-conscious critical move to become "non-white," Newitz pursues a de-essentialized whiteness that can hold its own, so to speak, in the same grammatical gesture as the antiessentialist analysis of blackness. In the process, the empowered privileges of whiteness and the stereotypes that degrade blackness take on an analytical equivalency as whiteness is situated as an identity object in need of the same resignification that has accompanied Civil Rights and black power struggle over and in the name of blackness. "While whiteness is undeniably linked to a series of oppressive social practices, it is also an identity which can be negotiated on an individual level. It is a diversity of cultures."[64] Such diversity points toward the possibility, as Newitz writes with coeditor Matt Wray in the anthology's introduction, of "a more realistic and fair-minded understanding of whiteness as a specific, racially marked group existing in relation to many other such groups."[65]

The desire for a critical paradigm that can approach both black and white on quite literally the same terms—in a mode of theoretical equal opportunity—shapes *White Trash* at a number of levels, providing a means

63. Newitz, "White Savagery and Humiliation," 149–50.
64. Newitz, "White Savagery and Humiliation," 148.
65. Wray and Newitz, *White Trash*, 5. Further citations are included in the text.

not to deny the body but to radically resignify the social meaning evoked by and invested in white skin:

> Our anthology is intended as an intervention in this field [of Whiteness Studies], offering a critical understanding of how differences within whiteness—differences marked out by categories like white trash—may serve to undo whiteness as racial supremacy, helping to produce multiple, indeterminate, and anti-racist forms of white identity. (4)

But even as white trash writers seek to resurrect the possibility of an anti-racist subject who is also white—as opposed to the antiracist subject who has transcended whiteness—the critical apparatus put into play here participates in the fantasy of white injury and minoritization evidenced in other trajectories of Whiteness Studies, no less than in the popular sphere. When the editors write, for instance, that whiteness is "an oppressive ideological construct that promotes and maintains social inequalities, causing great material and psychological harm to both people of color and whites" (3), they inadvertently construct a mutuality-of-harm hypothesis that powerfully appends whites to the harmed position of people of color. This move serves as the foundation for rendering "white trash" "not just [as] a classist slur" but as "a racial epithet that marks out certain whites as a breed apart" (1–2). The double reading of "white trash" as classist and racist is fundamental to *White Trash*'s articulation of itself as an antiracist project, providing the means, first, to link poverty to racial minoritization and, second, to produce such minoritization as a racialization of whiteness from within.

But how does one arrive at a notion that the class oppression that poor whites experience is also a racial oppression, and further that the very category of "white trash" can serve as a model of antiracist forms of white identity? Wray and Newitz begin by noting that the term has been traced to African American origins, being deployed by slaves as a mode of insult and differentiation in relation to white servants. This origin story, they write, "in the context of black slavery and white servitude speaks to the racialized roots of the meaning of [white trash]" (2). Racialized in what sense? As a mechanism of institutional power? As a force of subordination? The authors don't say, and it is this failure to explore the nexus of power embedded in the origin story that allows "white trash" to be cast as a racialization with minoritizing effects. This becomes fully clear, it seems to me, in the introduction's quick turn to the "Eugenic Family Studies" of the late nineteenth and early twentieth centuries, in which poor whites were medically investigated on models of genetic defect previously used to define black inferiority. But the authors do not cite the relationship between eugenics and the long traditions of scientific and medical renderings of biologically based ideas of African and African American racial difference. Instead, their descriptive language of the consequences of eugenics on the enduring stereotypes of poor whites replicates—and comes to stand in for—stereotypes explicitly connected to racist renditions of blackness:

> The eugenic family studies . . . [were] used . . . as propaganda . . . [for] call[s] to end all forms of welfare and private giving to the poor. . . . [T]he stereotypes of rural poor whites as incestuous and sexually promiscuous, violent, alcoholic, lazy, and stupid remain with us to this day. Alarmingly, contemporary conservative[s] . . . have resurrected this line of biological determinist thinking, blaming white trash for many of the nation's ills and . . . call[ing] for an end of the welfare state. Indeed, the widespread popularity of Herrnstein and Murray's *The Bell Curve* speaks to a renewed interest in U.S. social Darwinism as an explanation for cultural and class differences. (2–3)

The political valence of "white trash" in a slave economy in which servitude has very different meanings for blacks and whites is compressed under the weight of the eugenics model, and "white trash" begins to take on the significatory power of a racialized minority itself: "[B]ecause white trash is a classed and racialized identity degraded by dominant whiteness, a white trash position vis-a-vis whiteness might be compared to a "racial minority" position vis-a-vis whiteness" (5).

The consequences of these critical moves are multiple: the insistence on "white trash" as a minoritizing racialization simultaneously disarticulates racism from institutionalized practices of discrimination based on a group's designated racial status and crafts for poor whites a position structurally comparable to that of a racial minority. An antiracist project for whites is thus inaugurated at the site of a harmed and discriminated whiteness. As the editors declare at the outset: "Americans love to hate the poor. Lately, it seems there is no group of poor folks they like to hate more than white trash" (1). The psychological wages of whiteness defined by DuBois and taken up by Roediger are thus supplanted by emphasizing whiteness as a material privilege—and one whose security has been decidedly lessened in the revisionist class politics of the post-'60s: "As the economy and unemployment figures in the U.S. worsen, more whites are losing jobs to downsizing and corporate restructuring, or taking pay cuts. While it used to be that whites gained job security at the expense of other racial groups, whiteness in itself no longer seems a sure path to a good income" (7). In the context of the introduction's larger and at times deeply contradictory framework, the above assertion functions to produce the power of whiteness as a fully (and seemingly only) materialized economic relation; hence when material advantage does not exist, one occupies the position of a racialized minority, albeit within whiteness. In measuring the comparable worth of marginality in this way, *White Trash*'s intervention into Whiteness Studies produces, we might say, a white identity formation that has no compensatory racial debt to pay.

What generates this compulsion for a minoritized whiteness that is not "expensive" to people of color? Or more to the point, why is such minoritization necessary to the critical consciousness sought for in the name of an antiracist field of study? These questions are not intended to dismiss or undermine the importance of reading the boundary-making strategies within whiteness that both police and produce its racial authority and coherence.[66] Rather, they are meant to turn our focus to the identificatory relay that is at work here, where the insistence on "white trash" as a form of minoritization produces the critical movement through a now "blackened" whiteness that is taken to disrupt, analytically, the universalizing presumption of white power as vested in white skin. Such a process of disaffiliation is different from other trajectories of Whiteness Studies. As we have seen, in both the class solidarity and race traitor schools, where whites are encouraged to become race traitors in order to forge class-based alliances, the self-conscious position of disaffiliation that seeks "nonwhiteness" is one contingent on escaping the overdetermined social meaning of the white body In this, the antiracist white subject weds itself to knowledge as a rational production and, with knowledge, to a reclamation of history that raises the instance—in most cases the instance of the Irish—to the level of the episteme. For the academic project, the "fact" of the Irish's originary blackness works to establish and sustain the belief in the transcendent possibility of reversing history, and the scholarly insistence on the conscious formulation of critique/knowledge/political commitment is heralded as the means to

66. See Matt Wray's fuller analysis of the white rural poor, *Not Quite White*.

trump an essentializing body logic every time. The white trash school, on the other hand, works to resist the split between consciousness and embodiment by seeking to undermine the authority of white universalism from within. It thus stakes its antiracism on discerning power inequalities among whites, thereby confounding the seeming homogeneity of white identity. But in the process, it encounters its own reproduction of the discourse of white injury and minoritization, albeit from the other side of the essentialist divide, thereby allowing the white scholar to identify with an object of study who, as I have said, has no racial debt to pay. This is a powerful form of identification, but no less invested than other trajectories of Whiteness Studies in the capacity of the field to forge an antiracist subjectivity for itself.

To cast this in terms of the overarching concern with the political conscious that shapes this chapter, let me say that particularity is neither essentially antiessentialist nor antiracist, nor does its analytic pursuit guarantee that Whiteness Studies can disaffiliate from the racial powers and pretensions that attend universality, regardless of how much attention is devoted to those once or now displaced from the elite formations of whiteness itself. For in the field's elaborate investment in transporting the analytic gaze to the particular, we witness a confounding reiteration of the epistemological privilege that underwrites white racial formation, where the prerogative of individualized subjectivity is grasped by a critical subject now convinced of its ability to negotiate the meaning and effects of its own social identity. While it is true to say that the hyperconsciousness that Whiteness Studies evinces arises in response to the pressure put on white embodiment in the postsegregation years, it is also the case that the field's critical aim toward de-essentialization has the strange effect of working against the link between whiteness and privilege that was so historically hard won in the first place. To take refuge in the fact that the political ideals motivating all this identificatory mobility proceed from the left, not the right, as they surely do, would require that we side with consciousness, criticality, and intention once again. My aim here has been to interrupt just such a move, given my sense that such consciously grasped authority is itself one of the prerogatives of universalizing power. It is the historical endurance of this privilege, *not what the privilege is used for*, that must be understood as part of the reach and flexibility of white power. For this reason, it becomes important to settle into the prospect that there may be no theoretical, historical, or methodological escape from the impossibility of antiracist white subjectivity, precisely because the conscious determinations entailed in generating it have far too much of the universal at stake.

What Was Whiteness Studies?

It may seem ridiculous to spend so much time arriving at this rather unremarkable revelation, since I could have easily jettisoned the issue of antiracist subjectivity from my discussion altogether and spent this chapter analyzing white racial power in other modes of political articulation. After all, antiracism as the political language in which white power is challenged does not need to inaugurate a deliberation on the antiracist white subject per se. Indeed, most traditions of antiracist work do not, as evidenced by the many projects that make inquiries into whiteness under other names, including Ethnic Studies, feminist theory, and postcolonial studies. Still, in order to think about the relay between academic projects and the political desires that both inaugurate and sustain them, I have wanted to read Whiteness Studies in the context of its own social construction, such that its reliance on cross-racial identification, white minoritization and injury, and various strategies of mobility can be seen not simply as opposed to liberal whiteness, but as profoundly imbricated in it. In doing so, I have not meant to suggest a faulty analogy between the liberal whiteness of *Forrest Gump* and Whiteness Studies, nor to elide the film's formulation of injury and poverty (or poverty as injury) with scholarship on the permanent white poor, as if one could move with complete ease across the political, economic, and discursive differences that separate popular culture from the academic enterprise of Whiteness Studies as a whole. Nor have I wanted to underestimate the political and theoretical benefits of distinguishing between having white skin and identifying with white skin privilege. My hope instead has been to trace the circulation of similar tropes in order to demonstrate the complex negotiations over the meaning, social form, and political future of whiteness that characterized the 1990s. In this, my chapter stands neither as an attempt to discourage revisions of the historical record of immigration, labor, and slavery in ways that would allow us to explore the social construction of whiteness, nor as a tacit endorsement of monolithic renderings of whiteness that fail to attend to the complicated local practices through which ethnic identity has been racialized in majoritarian or minoritarian ways. I am arguing instead that what we learn by studying the object relations of Whiteness Studies is just how much rendering whiteness particular will not divest it of its universal epistemological power.

Such a lesson begins by linking the discourses of the academy with the popular public sphere and by tracing the disciplinary discourses that have mobilized Whiteness Studies as an emergent field. The former evokes the historicity of the present that governs the representational forms of white supremacy to which Whiteness Studies was heir and traces those contradictions that reveal how critical explanations of the present do not inoculate us against it. They are rather effects of and struggles with the present's insidious power. The latter facilitates an understanding of the institutional knowledge investments that accompany every disciplinary gesture whereby critical authority is conditioned on the identity and reproducibility of a chosen object of study. The conundrum for identity knowledges keyed to majoritarian identity formations is that legitimate objects of study are never exhaustible; they reproduce themselves in the very process of their critical dissection, no matter if the analytic destination is toward the deconstruction or demolition of the object's power—or not. No academic object of study comes into being without critical justification. Each requires articulation of its methodological and critical authority, and necessitates the reproduction of both for its ongoing critical exploration. In the case of whiteness as an institutionalized object of study, this means establishing an entire disciplinary apparatus, one that justifies the object, its study, and the methods to accompany it, all as the precondition for trying to displace or destroy the social power it wields. The disciplinary apparatus, then, is itself an inoculation against the destruction of the object it has brought into being, which is why I argue at various points in this book that objects of study can resist what we want to make of them. To consecrate the study of white racial identity and power as a field formation called Whiteness Studies is not, then, to divest whiteness of academic authority and power. For neither the epistemological status of whiteness as the implicit framework for the organization of what we know as the Human Sciences nor the epistemological status of white scholars as the authorized agents of institutional knowledge is dismantled by establishing whiteness as a particularized object of scrutiny in a field called Whiteness Studies. This is because the particular, as I have argued throughout this chapter, does not stand in a binary relation to white universalism, but repeatedly— and complexly—underwrites it.

In delivering us to this end, I do not mean to indict Whiteness Studies for lacking the political outcome that accompanied it, as if the fault, so to speak, belongs to it alone. Indeed, as *Object Lessons* maintains, no field of study is outside the historical and social practices that concern it, which means that even radical traditions within modern knowledge formations are not innocently prior to but decisively and unpredictably implicated in the histories and inequalities they track. While all of us committed to identity knowledges have spent time in careful declarations of what the work of our fields means, we know enough about the processes of historical transformation, accommodation, and revision to acknowledge, when pressed, that critical agency is not often, if ever, the chief determination of social change. Critical consciousness does not get at the heart of why so much fails to change, in part because its emphasis offers no perspective to discern why, even in the face of knowledge to the contrary, people continue to cling to certain ways of understanding things. To be sure, there is no knowledge free from the desire that is invested in it, so the point here is not to reproduce knowledge as outside the province of affective attachments or the unconscious. This is perhaps the most salient point that cuts across the chapters of *Object Lessons* as a whole.

The larger questions, of course, concern the academic project itself. What are the consequences of continuing to expect critique to be a successful strategy for inhabiting the political effects we use it for? And how coherently do theoretical innovation and critical commitment line up with the world of living things? These are issues that have haunted left critique of all kinds for decades and have delivered too many conversations into meaningless debates about the faulty politics of theory or the faulty theory of contemporary politics. I for one do imagine that how we think of the world matters, but we're a long way off from understanding precisely how, given the embeddedness of critical life in institutions that shape as much as situate who we are and what we seek to do. If knowledge is prioritized as the means to trump affect or belief—such that white privilege can be historically assessed in order to be disowned—then we enter a theoretical field founded on *the belief in knowledge*, one that is profoundly committed to the idea that "our" knowledge can survive what others will try to do with (or to) it. This is an amazing belief, almost as self-invested as the one that encourages us to take our relationship to objects of study and the fields we consecrate in their names as innocent of motives or consequences that we do not explicitly claim. Both are sustained by an approach to academic production born in discourses of consciousness and conscious political intention.

In this context, what is so striking about the history of Whiteness Studies is precisely how its intentions to counter histories of white self-obsession were consolidated through what in hindsight can only be considered ever more intense forms of white self-obsession. Mike Hill wrote early on about the narcissistic potential embedded in the white pursuit of whiteness as an object of study, almost in the same breath that his own work was given a signal position in formulations of the field's arrival. As he put it, "One might fairly suggest that (the white privilege of) desiring to cast-off 'white privilege' . . . eventually runs up against a rather sneaky inverse narcissism."[67] This narcissism is not the white academic's alone, but part of the larger cultural condition signified by liberal whiteness, which is the framework within which I have tried to read the contradictory but pervasive struggle over the content and meaning of whiteness in the 1990s, in both the academic and popular realms. But let's be clear: the narcissism of the period is not to be found in the mere fact of white universalizing self-obsession, as if that were somehow more extreme in the 1990s than before. (One would be hard pressed to find a moment in U.S. history not utterly oversaturated by white narcissism.) The point is rather that in the cultural ascendency of liberal whiteness, the 1990s were characterized by a narcissistic attachment *to the struggle* that ensued over the meaning of whiteness in discourses and representational practices produced by whites themselves. The difference here—between the narcissism that attends whiteness and the narcissism that attends white struggles to interpret it—is a slim but important one, allowing us to return one last time to consider the field imaginary of Whiteness Studies and the practices that constituted it, including the political grammar it developed in seeking to bring the power of its object of study to a historical end.

If we take Whiteness Studies as a product of media invention, as I have suggested, it is no small irony to note that a field characterized by an emphasis on conscious political intentions had to struggle from its inception against the commodity ethos that turned it immediately into the latest-greatest-white-thing. But all the attention, indeed all the declarations and counternarrations, along with the stunning proliferation of scholarship

---

67. See paragraph 11 of Hill, "What Was (the White) Race?"

and the citational canon it quickly provoked, worked to generate its increasing academic authority and institutional weight. In addition, because whiteness signified a relation to the identity discourse of entities already in existence—Black Studies, Women's Studies, Gay and Lesbian Studies—it inherited the energy and political expectations of their (inter)disciplinary formulations. And yet, as much as it reflected these longer identity traditions, Whiteness Studies was never able to duplicate them, given that its project was founded on a decisive and haunting lack. Its object of study was not only difficult to locate but also bore no resonant antiracist critical inheritance, and it had never had a left social movement formed in its name. Nor did it have the capacity to double as a subject of knowledge, such that the very explication and analysis of the experiences that comprised it would function as a practice of justice. Mimicking identity knowledges, but without the political calculus that brought Ethnic, Women's, and Lesbian/Gay Studies into being, Whiteness Studies garnered its disciplinary shape in a compensatory relation to that which it was not. For this reason, the centrality of labor history is no minor, coincidental feature; it must be read as the very means by which Whiteness Studies marshaled a politicized critical discourse to signify its leftist credentials. In much the same way, the emphasis on race traitor rhetorics authorized the claim that Whiteness Studies was founded on an activist agenda and gave the hint, if never fully the realized fact, that a social movement was available to inspire and guide it. And the critical attention to the super poor made available a scene of minoritization within the terrain of whiteness that gave the field the means to situate whiteness as an identity object of national harm.

But it is the studied attachment to antiracist subjectivity that reveals the critical and psychic stakes of the field's disciplinary dispensation and the political grammar it both reflected and sought to generate. For in the figure of a subject who would come to disavow the power that constituted it, Whiteness Studies could inhabit the longing that lives beneath its disciplinary relations, a longing that was not at all about the desire for abolition, death, or negation but about their inverse: rehabilitation, affinity, and revaluation. Yes, I mean to say, in the face of all the boisterous assertions to the contrary, that the longing that resided in the disciplinary apparatus of Whiteness Studies reflected a profound desire for a white subject that could survive knowing what made it. This is not survival in terms of material life; it is not mere living. The survival at stake is psychic and it arises from the very dualism that Winant so usefully explicates. In the structure of its disciplinary practice, Whiteness Studies sought to resolve what dualism had put into play, with the antiracist white subject being the outcome or consequence of a white subject outliving its own confrontation with what whiteness in the postsegregationist era had come to mean. *Forrest Gump*, as we know, took cover in the resolution of unknowingness, giving us a white subject who survived the racial trauma that the privileges of his embodied history had come to represent by knowing nothing distinct about it, except the exceedingly sentimental lesson of race-blind love. If practitioners in Whiteness Studies wanted to believe in white people studying themselves as the means of doing the right thing, they never imagined an antiracist white subject who would leave the scene of the bus stop alone. The resolution for Whiteness Studies required a social practice of subjective transformation. The antiracist white subject—figured variously as the object of study, the critical perspective that would comprehend it, or the field itself—had to be pulled and shaped from the racist clay. *Made*, not born, in the USA. And the gauge of the transformation rested on the person of color, as analogue or psychic figure if nothing else. Otherwise, there was no means to confirm that transformation had taken place.

In this regard, it would be a mistake to say that Whiteness Studies was, in the final instance, about white folks alone, even in those discourses of white antiracist self-creation in which it is most possible to describe the field in such a way. The white gaze that Whiteness Studies turned toward the self was as constituted by the projection of the other as the more classical colonial epistemology in which the domination of the other as an object of scrutiny produced the fantasy of white superiority that ushered in the modern European self. The difference here was that Whiteness Studies both anticipated and inhabited *the look back* and sought, in ways that were both subtle and overt, for recognition that what the racialized other saw was not the same old white thing. The anticipation of that look is central to the operations of white racial dualism, the psychic means by which counterwhiteness is incorporated into whiteness such that "being white" is cast as a normativity to be both disparaged and feared—by whites themselves. It is difficult to measure the extent to which postsegregationist whiteness has been bound up in trying to win such recognition—difficult to measure because its signs have been everywhere. Think only of the way that white guilt has no meaning apart from the audience, real or imagined, that would engender white self-perception as such, or of the power that the "token" can evoke for whites as the symbolic evidence of their own supremacist transgressions. Or the meaning for a guilty white nation of electing Barack Obama to be its first "real" not simply representational African American president.[68] White racial dualism is not, then, a structure of binary operation, nor merely a divided or doubled relation. What underwrites it is triangulation, such that white self-division (what Winant means by dualism) is constructed by, routed through, and in relation to the figure of color who is ultimately needed to confer the authenticity of the passage from white identifications to antiracist ones. This is not necessarily a literal conferral; as we have seen in the different trajectories of Whiteness Studies, the figure of color can appear in various ways, as a political collaborator, genealogical referent, economic form, or historical analogy.

To be sure, practitioners in Whiteness Studies quickly grew weary of the difficulties that the field's ascendency wrought, so much so that in recent years the entire venture has been demoted in many academic venues to lowercase script: whiteness studies. There are no new calls for special issues devoted to whiteness, and its presence as a topic on the conference circuit has decidedly waned. It would be self-serving to lay this decline at the feet of the epistemological contradictions I outlined above—as if the life or death of a field is determined by the coherence and correctness of theoretical thinking alone. It is much more likely that what worked to deliver Whiteness Studies to its twenty-first-century tomb was the force of commodification that threatened its political intentions and undermined its critical tone. Today, the most well-known project on the topic lives under the moniker "critical whiteness studies" at the University of Illinois, where scholars produced a collective bibliography in 2006 that seeks to resituate the study of whiteness to evoke its interdisciplinary and historical

---

68. In satirizing the narcissism of white antiracism, the *Onion* reflected on white self-congratulation following Barack Obama's 2008 election to the office of the U.S. president.

> First witnessed shortly after President Obama's historic victory, the open and cheerful smiling has only continued in recent months, leaving members of the black community completely unnerved. "On behalf of black people across this nation, I would like to say to our white brethren, 'Please stop looking at us like that,'" said Brown University psychology professor Dr. Stanley Carsons. "We're excited Barack is president, too, and we're glad you're happy for us. But giving us the thumbs up for no reason, or saying hello whenever we walk by, is really starting to freak us out." ("Nation's Blacks Freaked Out by All the People Smiling at Them," February 16, 2009)

reach. The editorial material accompanying the bibliography sets it against the pervasive description of Whiteness Studies as a white project of contemporary academic origin. As Roediger explains in the bibliography's introduction, the critical whiteness studies project was sponsored by the Center for Democracy in a Multicultural Society and was "interracial from its inception," with key roles played by "faculty and students from the university's ethnic studies programs."[69] The bibliography is meant to demonstrate that "the critical study of whiteness is not, as it is too often portrayed in the press, a recent and university-based project undertaken mainly by white scholars" but was "developed most quickly and systematically among racialized, enslaved, conquered and colonized peoples for whom white power and white pretense were urgent problems."[70] As this language makes clear, the force of the introduction's retrospective renarrativization of the origins of the study of whiteness is propelled by the field's commodification as a white academic endeavor. In seeking to interrupt the segregationist effects of this commodification, Roediger casts Whiteness Studies as the representative figure of both an errant form of academic inquiry and of contemporary whiteness, thereby making clear that the political value of "critical" marks the genealogical space in which white antiracism refuses the fantasy of its academic autoinvention.

Can we simultaneously agree on the importance of refusing the fantasy *and acknowledge* that there is something else to be said about how "nonwhiteness," as Roediger called it in *Towards the Abolition of Whiteness*, once again is given the role of extracting the inquiry of whiteness from its overdeterminations as both commodity and narcissistic investment?[71] Or more to the point, is it possible to deliberate on the object relation that is being sought here, in which a racialized genealogy and interracial collaborative form is figured as the necessary guarantee that the inquiry into

69. See Roediger, "Introduction," 5.

70. See Roediger, "Introduction," 5.

71. Future inquiry into these issues might consider the ways in which antiracism is routinely ascribed not only to Ethnic Studies per se but to all social positions of racialized oppression, often occluding the very historicization that would enable us to discern the complexity of political responses to white domination as a series of historical forms. Some of the most important work in both Ethnic Studies and postcolonial studies has engaged the historical complexity of resistance. See especially Chow, *The Protestant Ethnic and the Spirit of Capitalism*; and Lubiano, "Like Being Mugged by a Metaphor."

whiteness will be immune from the epistemological and social power of the object of study? I ask these questions not to deliver my readers into greater frustration by failing to affirm the pursuit of an antiracist formulation of the study of whiteness. But having followed the tropes of liberal whiteness and traced their imbrication in the hyperconsciousness of Whiteness Studies, it seems clear that Roediger's renarrativization does not so much break with the political grammar of the field imaginary as work to correct it, downgrading its arrogance by insisting on interraciality "from its inception" and offering to the inquiry a nonwhite origin. These moves reproduce both the structure of white racial dualism and the critical practice developed in Whiteness Studies that aimed at its resolution by conferring on the study of whiteness a genealogy of color that particularizes antiracist whiteness as itself an interruption of forms of white universalist knowledge and privilege. As I have discussed, this particularization is not essentially antithetical to the epistemological power or social structure of whiteness. It is, on the contrary, endemic to it—which is to say, endemic to the processes by which racial identities have been made and contested within the political grammar that shapes modern U.S. life. Such a grammar has come to include, quite decisively, cross-racial alliance and the figurative consciousness of "nonwhiteness" as the scene of political knowledge and transgression, which is why I suspect that the passage to *critical* whiteness studies for many left scholars will be a secure one. Certainly it undermines white universalism by reversing the terms of epistemological authority and establishes a critical pedagogy that usefully addresses the deficit that racial privilege plays in discerning the form, substance, and reach of white power.

Nevertheless, a crucial question remains: what are the consequences of figuring "nonwhiteness" as the means of carrying critical whiteness studies forward, given the assumption here (and elsewhere) that the political consciousness it represents is free of the power of the object it seeks to isolate and interrogate? This is an important and difficult question, in that it challenges not just white antiracist investments in nonwhiteness as the means of exacting postwhite political affiliations, but the political imaginary that brought Ethnic Studies into being, which rhetorically forwards its attachments to objects and analytics of study as an engaged *project* of antiracism, not a *historical formation* of one. The distinction I am reaching toward here would position antiracism in all of its discursive traditions and trajectories as an object of inquiry from within and not simply against the political grammars in which whiteness as a structure of power has been historically transformed, resuscitated, and politically secured. In this context, both Whiteness Studies and critical whiteness studies, like Ethnic Studies itself, are evidence of the historical formation of antiracism, steeped not simply in the political cultures in which they seek to articulate themselves but in *the culture of the political* that organizes the terrain on which the legibility of their social and critical actions inevitably rests. For antiracist whiteness, this means taking all the ways in which it is evoked, defined, cultivated, and practiced—whether in the language of subject production, as part of a social movement, or in the protocols of critical whiteness studies itself— as the historical locus of analysis, not as background or provocation, not as critical perspective or political intention, but as content and substance. To be sure, the scholar's critical implication in what we seek to discern will be no less constrained, but the point here is to open the space to extract a few lessons before we send Whiteness Studies to its grave.

First, antiracist whiteness is never an antithesis to white racial formation. It is most resonantly part of it, which makes it impossible to know in advance which political ends its elaboration will serve.

Second, antiracism is both a political grammar and the reflection of one. It is formed in the difficult translation between political desire and its fraught materialization, which is why criticality is inadequate as either its means or its political measure.

And third, Whiteness Studies is not alone in failing to confront what it would mean to know any of this.

FOUR

Refusing Identification

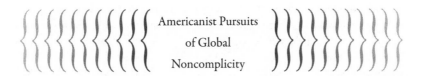

Americanist Pursuits
of Global
Noncomplicity

One does not have to travel very far in the archives of Whiteness Studies before finding herself addressing the force of U.S. national identity as a related and similarly vexed critical problem. This is not simply because white racial formation has been an indelible part of both the structure and idiom of U.S. national identity. It is also the case that each represents a majoritarian identity form whose superordination raises compelling issues for identity knowledges and their commitment to critical practice as a practice of justice. These are *bad objects*, after all, whose power is not to be extended or defended, but undone. By devoting the middle chapters of *Object Lessons* to the hegemonies of whiteness and U.S. national identity, I am exploring the difficulties that arise when critical practice seeks to resist the world-historical authority of the object of study that defines and specifies it. As we have seen, Whiteness Studies was undermined from the outset, as tethering antiracism to a subject conscious of his historical formation reiterated a mode of self-mastery steeped in the very disembodied protocols of Enlightened humanism long considered constitutive of the imperial sovereignty and epistemic reach of the white, masculine, and European subject. In the province of this chapter's chief concern—contemporary American Studies and the pursuit of global noncomplicity that likewise characterizes it—the critic is similarly charged with particularizing her object of study, but the demand to do so raises a rather different set of critical conundrums.[1] For while "America" has to be situated in the specific context of the historical violences that have been germane to its growth as a geopolitical power, it must also be disarticulated from the ideological lineages of exceptionalism that posit it as universally unique and hence as

1. Various terms have circulated in American Studies to describe the field's attempt to attend both to the exceptionalist legacies of its formation in the United States and to transformations wrought by globalization since 1989, including the concepts of the postcolonial, postnational, and the transnational. I am using the "international" as both a general framework for these collective efforts and as a specific discourse, given its use in new organizational bodies (the International Association of American Studies, IASA) and its ubiquity in conversations about American Studies across world regions. In these contexts, internationalization always carries with it a call for the displacement of the centrality of U.S.-based American Studies as a critical authority and global hegemon in organizations of the field. On the specification of "internationalization" for American Studies, see Desmond and Dominguez, "Resituating American Studies in a Critical Internationalism"; Giles, "Virtual Americas"; Lenz, "Internationalizing American Studies"; Shamir, "Foreigners Within and Innocents Abroad"; and Hones and Leyda, "Geographies of American Studies."

For specific discussions of the analytic capacities of the postcolonial, see Cherniavsky, "Subaltern Studies in a U.S. Frame"; King, *Postcolonial America*; Ickstadt, "American Studies in an Age of Globalization"; Edwards, "Preposterous Encounters"; Schueller, "Postcolonial American Studies"; and Park and Schwarz, "Extending American Hegemony."

On the postnational as a critical rubric, see Pease, "National Identities, Postmodern Artifacts, and Postnational Narratives" and "The Politics of Postnational American Studies"; Balkir, "The Discourse on 'Post-nationalism'"; Buell, "Nationalist Postnationalism"; Rowe, *Post-nationalist American Studies*; and Shapiro, "Reconfiguring American Studies."

For considerations of the transnational, see Giles, "Reconstructing American Studies" and "Transnationalism in Practice"; Wald, "Minefields and Meeting Grounds"; Thelen, "The Nation and Beyond"; Moya and Saldívar, "Fictions of the Trans-American Imaginary"; Fishkin, "Crossroads of Cultures"; Kroes, "National American Studies in Europe, Transnational American Studies in America"; Medovoi, "Nation, Globe, Hegemony"; and Traister, "The Object of Study." A touchstone essay in conversations about the transnational, though not focused on American Studies, is Miyoshi, "A Borderless World?"

exceptionally particular.[2] In the oscillation between a universality that arises from its global hegemony and the universal particularity of the exceptionalism that casts America as better than the rest, the Americanist project must come to terms with how and when to particularize. Too much particularity can reiterate a faulty exceptionalism, even of a negative kind, as when the United States is exposed in its global ambitions by figuring its dominance as an exceptional imperialism.[3] Too little particularity can revive the universalism that travels under cover of the generic, as when the U.S. context serves implicitly as the framework for developing the analytic value of any number of critical perspectives, including those called

2. Exceptionalism is always a weighty word to use in American Studies conversations and today exceptionally so, given its characteristic use to critique U.S. American Studies in the heyday of its institutionalization in the post–World War II era, when—as the story goes—the U.S. state began in earnest to use mass education for a nationalist project of citizen building in a global effort both to differentiate itself from a fractured Europe and to counter the growing power of the Soviet Union. Through well-funded agencies, the field was integrated into the geopolitical routes and ideological work of U.S. foreign policy, which sought to affirm the exceptionalist idea that "America" was not simply unique but universally representative of democratic nation formation and hence paradigmatically different from all other nations that had come before. In most intellectual histories of the field, the turn against exceptionalism is coincident with interventions into the academy by U.S. social movements, generating an emphasis on everyday life, minoritized histories, anti-state resistance, and popular cultural forms that shifted the terrain of critical discussion from consensus and shared cultural heritage to contestation and difference, and eventually to the now-familiar framework of multiculturalism. On exceptionalism's critical legacy for the study of U.S. culture, see especially Tyrrell, "American Exceptionalism in an Age of International History"; Shafer, *Is America Different?*; Kammen, "The Problem of American Exceptionalism"; Greene, *The Intellectual Construction of America*; Adams and van Minnen, *Reflections on American Exceptionalism*; Madsen, *American Exceptionalism*; Ross, "Liberalism and American Exceptionalism"; Rodgers, "American Exceptionalism Revisited"; and Pease, *The New American Exceptionalism.*

3. While there are those who will defend the perspective that the United States is an exceptional empire, in the sense that the reach of its global power is historically unique, I would counter this claim by pointing out how the perception of a world-historical uniqueness is intrinsic to empire as a historical form. This is a slightly different claim than that of Ann Laura Stoler, who argues that empire is always an exceptional form. For more on the methodological pursuit of a comparative history of empire, see Stoler, "On Degrees of Imperial Sovereignty" and "Tense and Tender Ties"; and Steinmetz, "Return to Empire."

global and transnational. As these examples indicate, much of what is politically at stake in American Studies has to do with differentiating the critical act from the power the object wields, such that the critical relation to the object of study does not reiterate nationalist ideologies, imperial state agendas, or U.S. discourses that take themselves as referent for the world.[4]

These are familiar issues for identity knowledges organized around a majoritarian object, retracing the dilemma that Whiteness Studies evoked in its attempt to differentiate complicity *as an unconscious condition* and (non)complicity *as a choice*. But the difficulties facing American Studies go further, as its institutional emergence was not born in left critical alliance with identity knowledges and did not proceed through aspirations to destroy the power of its object of study, which grounded Whiteness Studies in the posture of counterhegemonic rebellion from its beginning. The justice project that now shapes American Studies as it is practiced in the U.S. university is more properly understood as the effect of the field's resignification in the aftermath of 1960s social revolt, when a new generation of scholars began to approach U.S. national identity as fragmented, not homogenous, and when the arena of culture became the privileged setting for exploring the contestations of race, gender, sexuality, and class submerged in the mythic narratives offered by exceptionalism.[5] Since 1988, the formation of this resignified field has been called the New Americanism, following a largely negative review by Frederick Crews, who used the phrase to denigrate what he took as a mistaken critical turn away from the formal study of literature and the objectivist disciplinary priorities of historical inquiry toward an overtly politicized scholarship.[6] In the years immediately following the review's publication, scholars would begin to defend the New Americanism in name, crafting a disciplinary identity for it that not only refused the negative value Crews ascribed to politicization but parsed the field's priorities in relation to the Cold War American Studies

4. For a thorough discussion of how the U.S. state has mobilized American Studies, see Anne Marie Logue, "'Telling America's Story to the World.'"

5. The Americanist theorist most important to understanding culture as the scene for contemporary U.S. political struggle is Lisa Lowe. See especially her *Immigrant Acts* and "The International Within the National."

6. See Crews, "Whose American Renaissance?" Please note that additional citations in the text are from the online link, which is not paginated.

project that it was taken to displace. That project, in the terms that New Americanism would tell it, was a protonationalist one, beholden to the ideologies emanating from the security state, and dedicated to forging an entire symbolic vocabulary to accompany the worldwide defense of capitalism that the Cold War period spawned.[7] To differentiate itself from the Cold War project, New Americanism would do more than formulate disidentifications with the object of study. It would also cultivate a politics of identificatory *refusal* aimed at the critical grammar and symbolic attachments of its predecessor. Instead of emphasizing individualism, consensus, and the open wilderness, for instance, it would prioritize community, social struggle, and the violence of dispossession, making clear that the white masculine subject at the heart of Cold War exceptionalism was a particular embodiment whose universalized status was another example of how the story of America being told and the historical record were violently askew.

By foregrounding all that the Cold War apparatus was taken to disavow, New Americanism produced American Studies not simply as a domain for the study of identities or as an umbrella for the accumulated efforts of various identity knowledges, but *as an identity knowledge*, characterized most pointedly by the dedication to critical practice as an agency of justice. To mobilize the vocabulary of *Object Lessons*, we might say that New Americanism founded an investment in identity disarticulated from fantasies of convergence—as in the exceptionalist pursuit of *an* American identity—in order to foreground instead a contentious

---

7. The origin of American Studies as a field is not coincident with its institutionalization in the U.S. university, which is a point that has been made by a small number of scholars interested in tracing how it first emerged in the 1930s as a critique of both Britain's centrality in humanistic inquiry in the United States, and the high-culture imperialism that repeatedly subordinated U.S. culture to the bourgeois customs and histories of western Europe. The popular-front investments of this critique highlighted proletarian understandings of mass culture, labor, and consumption and stressed cultural resistance to the global proliferation of capital's capture of social life. American "identity" in this formulation was not, then, nationalist in the exceptionalist sense that today dominates historical assessments of the field. This is not to say that its earliest formulation was unproblematical, as populist conceptions of labor, culture, and social life were thoroughly mired in racial and gendered hierarchies. But the critical understanding of the object of study that consolidated it was not the same as that which institutionalized American Studies in the 1950s.

U.S. national sphere and the contradictions that struggles for political recognition and national redefinition reflect and engage. From the outset, its critical ambition was directed toward particularity and de-universalization, which is why the symbolic force and territorial logic of "America" was and continues to be both its target and that which it must analytically outrun. Its most prominent rhetorical mode is critique, which orients it toward the future, as critical practice is aimed at converting the forbidden, disavowed, and buried past to contemporary political use on behalf of a world still to come. In all this, New Americanism posits itself as *exterior* to the object of study that names it in order to guarantee an analytic position commensurate with the political desire that animates it—a position that is simultaneously outside the object's geopolitical power but inside the disavowed histories, affects, and violences that attend and support such power. Like Whiteness Studies, it crafts an object relation that differentiates its own political attachments and ideations from the power its object wields, while authorizing a new set of critical priorities and analytic attachments that suture its political and disciplinary commitments together. Unlike Whiteness Studies, however, which was exhausted before it was institutionalized, New Americanism grew throughout the 1990s to become virtually synonymous with the practice of American Studies in the U.S. university as a whole.

The contradictions that arise here are as generative and troublesome as those attending the paradoxes of white particularity explored in chapter 3. For while New Americanism is keyed to a refusal of identification with the Cold War formation of the field it sets itself against, it has taken shape in a vastly different historical and institutional context than its predecessor, as the era of its rise, cultivation, and analytic domination is coincident not simply with the actual demise of the Cold War state and its geopolitical projections but with the generation of new globalizing impulses that stress transnational, postnational, and international perspectives, economies, and institutional missions. In this, New Americanism has become prominent in the U.S. university at the same time as the full bloom of neoliberal governmentality and the internationalization of U.S. markets, state projects, and the knowledge industry, begging the question as to whether— and from whose perspective—the exalted exteriority it sought was in or out of step with the production and transformation of state power that it worked so hard to discern in order to resist.[8] How, after all, could the field be outside the global power of its own object of study and yet ensconced as the leading, indeed hegemonic, discourse of American Studies in the U.S. university when the U.S. university was being transformed from a national to global entity—that is, when the U.S. university was being remade to signify *as worldly*, not national, in a feat of cosmopolitan expansion and resignification that would enable it to extend its dominance of the knowledge industry globally?[9] From this perspective, to be *in* the U.S. university is to be entangled with the forces of U.S. global power, no matter how thoroughly antihegemonic are the analytic dispensations of the field. The disjunction here between material location and analytic dispensation is crucial to the itinerary of this chapter, as the relationship between the critical priorities of New Americanism and the institutional location in which it is forged has become a central issue in the latest Americanist pursuit of noncomplicity: internationalization.[10] Under its auspices, the New

8. These transformations are too vast to record with any nuance here, but generally the concept of neoliberalism is used to foreground the historical disarticulation of the state from the nation that further identified the state with the global market *and* turned governmentality away from hegemonic negotiations toward sheer biopolitical management. Unlike the Cold War state form, the security state of the present is thought to eschew culture as a scene of incorporative national struggle in favor of projects of force, whether military or economic; hence the growth of prisons and the security industry and the deflation of public schools, job training programs, public transportation projects, labor unions, and national welfare of every kind. Within the U.S. university, these transformations have been registered in a variety of ways. Most crucial for identity knowledges has been the rather spectacular fall of the humanities as a curricular priority and the reformation of area studies. Each in different ways has challenged traditional disciplinary organizations that take the nation as a discrete unit of study, making the emergent "global university"—owned and primarily located in the United States but defined by its internationalized address—attentive to the national but on vastly different terms: not as isolatable and distinct, but as porous, multiple, and marketable.

9. My own university is currently in the midst of building a campus in China, while it explores India as a future site. New York University has opened a university satellite in Dubai. These institutions are not alone. Every major research university in the United States is currently reshaping its discourse and material practice around the figure of the "global university." See Marginson, "The Rise of the Global University."

10. At its most generic, internationalization circulates as a powerful political wish to escape the suffocating Americanization of the globe that many see as the inner lining

Americanist project has been particularized in order to undermine its authority as the defining discourse and geopolitical center of the field. It is no longer "American Studies" but U.S. American Studies or, more deftly and at times antagonistically, "American American Studies."[11]

In the following pages, I track the dilemmas that internationalization raises in order to deliberate further on the wish that underlies it: that a critical practice can be found that extracts the study of the U.S. from implication in both the U.S. state project of annexing wealth and producing military alliance and economic dependence *and* the critical hegemony of American American Studies.[12] After all, if the imperative to international-

and greatest threat of contemporary globalization. Hence, it seeks to situate the study of the United States in relation to diverse regional and transnational practices of culture, politics, labor, and people and in such a way that the field does not reiterate the U.S. state project of annexing wealth and producing military alliance and economic dependence *or* the hegemony of U.S. popular culture and its globalizing commodity circulation *or* the expansion of the U.S. university as both the model and leader of a global academic culture. The critical transformations evoked by internationalization are thus expansive and daunting. They entail, at the very least, transcending the critical limits of the nation form; resituating the field within the conversations and epistemologies of postcolonial and postnational knowledges; tracking the transnational circulations of an object of study such that it appears unfamiliar to those who study it; producing a global perspective within which the United States is made secondary, if not also at times marginal, to the large and complex "rest"; and generating new scholarly collaborations, citational networks, and critical habits for practitioners in the field.

11. The origin of the phrase "American American Studies" is not entirely clear, but well after I heard it in American Studies venues outside the United States, I came across its usage in Ron Clifton's 1979 essay, "The Outer Limits of American Studies: A View from the Remaining Frontier," 365. For Clifton, the remaining frontier was American Studies abroad where, he strikingly noted, "many opportunities [exist] to become founding fathers all over" (367). How strange, given the present context, that Clifton saw the possibility of getting "outside" the U.S.-based project of the field as a way to extend the nationalist discourse of "America"! In that same anniversary volume, Robert F. Berkhofer Jr. would take up the topic of the specificity of U.S. American Studies quite differently. See his "The Americanness of American Studies"; and more recently, Kennedy, "Spectres of Comparison."

12. The only academic organization formed explicitly to forward this agenda, the IASA, organizes a conference in diverse parts of the world every two years, houses a journal, and has no formal institutional home, which makes it literally postnational. Numerous other projects have been initiated on a smaller scale to pursue the field's internationalization by attending not only to the analytic dispensations of postnational critical frameworks but the production and circulation of critical authority,

ize is itself a prioritized mission for the U.S. university, such that Ameri-can American Studies is imbricated in the U.S. state's imperializing power regardless of its analytic discernments, what prevents the call to interna-tionalize American Studies from being congruent with the agenda of the U.S. university in its globalizing production as well? More to the point, how does refusing identification with American American Studies place the discourse of internationalization outside the critical grip of a field whose imaginary is itself predicated on an identificatory refusal with the field formation that it critiqued in order to displace? As *Object Lessons* would have it, this chapter is less interested in debating these questions than in affirming the suspicions that motivate them, which means affirm-ing, first, that the call to internationalize American Studies as a means to escape its "Americanness" is in league with the U.S. knowledge industry's globalizing ambitions no matter how often or how forceful practitioners position their critique as an interruption of just such a convergence; and second that the move to refuse identification with American American Studies in order to produce difference from it is fully at home within the field imaginary that internationalization seeks to contest.[13] My aim in say-ing this is not to defend New Americanism against the imperative to par-ticularize it or to taint the promise that internationalization figures by ex-posing how it fails to escape its own institutional or historical complicities. I am more interested with how the contradiction that internationalization

---

including the hegemony of English in American Studies journals throughout the world.

13. For U.S.-based practitioners in American Studies, one effect has been the recali-bration of the relationship between "domestic" and "foreign" study, which has created funding opportunities for research and collaboration outside the territory of the United States that were quite limited two decades ago. At my own institution, the "study abroad" program now includes semester-long residencies in the United States (typically in "global" cities), and much of my American Studies teaching takes place through col-laborations with the Center for International Studies. From this perspective, the im-perative to internationalize is a feature of the contemporary U.S. university and under-scores the ways in which U.S.-based Americanists are now far more likely to travel outside the United States than ever before, provoking the affective and territorial rela-tions I sketch in this chapter where shame and anger on the one hand and proximity and complicity on the other intermingle to provoke the New Americanist into awareness that she might sound and act just like an American Americanist even when she doesn't want to.

evokes—that it replicates the institutional and object relations of the field formation it otherwise critiques—reinforces the *urgency of the central issue it raises*: how to recognize in both analytical terms and practices of knowledge production the fundamental internationalism of a world system of social and conceptual relationships such that the dominating role of the United States can be defined but not overdetermined, interpreted but not reified, particularized but not exceptionalized. For if the discourse of internationalization does not travel very far toward this, its greatest wish, without reproducing the symptoms that generate the need for it, then what matters most are the promises it makes, not its inability to make them come true.[14]

In other words, internationalization is most compelling for *Object Lessons* as a critical aspiration. It makes visible the importance of distinguishing between American Studies as an academic field and the particularities of its practice in the U.S. university. It reinforces the need to interrupt the tacit reliance on nation and national rubrics for organizing knowledge, which allows us to consider how language, culture, labor, commodities, territory, and capital are related in circuits of production, translation, and transformation without reifying either their historical specificity or complexity. Most important perhaps, it puts enormous pressure on the research practices of Americanist scholars by forging a reconsideration of

14. Other issues haunt the wish as well. How, for instance, does one actually achieve an internationalized object of study or, for that matter, produce an analytic that could yield an internationalized field? Is internationalization about new perspectives on the object of study, the United States, from places "outside" its geographical center, such that one has an international American Studies by having a distinctly European American Studies, South Asian American Studies, and American American Studies? Or is internationalization achieved by following the routes of accumulation, "influence," and the forms of culture, power, and of course violence and exploitation that move from the United States to the rest of the globe? Or both? What precisely does internationalization require and how will we judge our ability to deploy it to counter the powerful efforts of the United States to locate itself, quite literally, everywhere on the globe, whether through cultural and economic forms or in the proliferation of its knowledge industry as well? The contradictions that arise in this collision of analytic transgressions, U.S. knowledge hegemonies, and the university's role in extending the cultural work of the U.S. state reveal the complexities of seeking to turn American Studies "outside" its practice in the United States, and raise important issues about the work that identificatory refusal promises to perform on behalf of internationalization.

area and national fields of study, university cultures, and the global knowledge industry more generally.[15] But regardless of the multiple utilities it offers, it does not resolve the issues that it helps to name. Rather, it is most effective in staging, from numerous angles and in various vocabularies of critical passion, many of the problems it anticipates, describes, and seeks to ameliorate. By explicating this conundrum, my destination in this chapter is the rather simple conclusion that an internationalized American Studies is "not one," to trope the famous line by Luce Irigaray.[16] The field's enmeshment, translation, and iteration across national (and increasingly transnational) university systems in various regions of the world, no less than its complex engagement with local knowledge practices, histories of colonialism, class politics, and regional warfare—generate different critical aims, institutional politics, modes of production, *even objects of study.*[17]

15. This chapter is the outcome of my participation in various projects that were designed to reflect on the possibilities of an internationalized field with Americanists from different institutional settings. These included workshops, seminars, and conferences organized by the Nordic American Studies Association, the DFG Network on European American Studies, the Australian and New Zealand American Studies Association, the Italian Association for North American Studies, the Clinton Institute for American Studies in Dublin, and the IASA. In various ways, each of these occasions served to reiterate the need for internationalization, making visible not only the dominance of U.S.-based American Studies, but the critical urgency of reflecting on the field's implication in the globalization of "America" itself. They also demonstrated how deeply problematical is the pursuit of a coherent field of study that eschews national frameworks altogether.

16. See Irigaray, *This Sex Which Is Not One.*

17. I am thinking here of an especially interesting conversation about pedagogy that took place across a number of sessions at the 2004 Australian and New Zealand American Studies Association conference. As they described it, New Zealand Americanists had to work hard to interrupt the anti-Americanism in which issues of U.S. culture were situated in their national political discourse, while colleagues in Australia needed to encourage a critical relation to the object of study, given the Australian state support for U.S. militarism in the early part of this century. This dynamic is often at the forefront of conversations that include scholars who work in different national university systems, making it clear that at the symbolic no less than the material level of its global travels, "America" is not a singular entity. While this fact gives added urgency to the imperative to internationalize, it is also one of the most daunting features of internationalization, as it raises the possibility that I pursue in this chapter of the object's differentiation and openly contentious signification.

Such differentiation, at times incongruity, undermines the imperative to internationalize the field into a coherent global entity from the outset. For this reason, I argue that what "America" means in any of the sites of its articulation and study, including within the territorial boundaries of the U.S. itself, is finally the open question that internationalization helps us to explore, not an answer that it can promise to deliver. This is because the core problem that internationalization raises is not the geographical "fact" or the "imaginary" formation or the epistemological "privilege," or the daunting "exceptionalism" of "America," nor is it the haughty authority of American American Studies to determine the analytic path of the field, but everything that stands in the way of coming to terms with all of this at once, including the habit of reading critical practice as the measure and mode of identifying and ameliorating geopolitical complicity.

Traveling Affect

Let's begin with the story of the American Americanist's critical emergence, which has less to do with place of birth or national venue of employment than with the work that the discourse of internationalization has performed in its various efforts to particularize the formation of the field as it is practiced in the United States. And let's do so by charting my own travels through three scenes of Americanist practice as a pedagogical foray into the critical subjectivities and analytic judgments that internationalization seeks both to foreground and displace.

    1. I was having dinner with American colleagues at the U.S. American Studies Association conference when I reported that I would be visiting Italy for the first time, where I would be speaking at a seminar in Rome called "Pursuits of Happiness." At the mention of the seminar title, my colleagues began to chuckle. "That's so dated," one of them said. "But Rome is magnificent," said another. I understood the assurance that their laughter delivered; after all, "we" had never been so dated.[18] But this "understand-

---

18. No left U.S. academic of my generation or younger would turn willingly to happiness as a topic. It fell out of academic favor in the 1950s after Howard Mumford Jones published *The Pursuit of Happiness*, which spawned a small discussion on the topic, mostly in the form of book reviews. Arthur Schlesinger Jr. offered a few words on whether or not happiness was a fundamental right in a free society in foreign policy debates in the late 1970s, but this conversation moved in a direction contrary to those

ing" quickly turned to shame as I caught a glimpse of what my Italian colleagues might take me to be: another smug American academic, happy to visit Rome, for free.

2. It was 2003 and I was in Leiden at the inaugural International American Studies Association (IASA) Congress. In his presidential address, "Defending America Against Its Devotees," Djelal Kadir promoted his new organization's agenda by critiquing the national insularity and provincialism of American Studies in its U.S. formation.[19] Under the imperative to internationalize, he argued, American Studies needed to differentiate itself from the priorities and perspectives of its national practice; it must "cease," as he succinctly put it in an essay published that same year, "to be American."[20] As the key word of the conference, "provincialism" was raised in every session I attended, including one in which an African American scholar talked about W. E. B. DuBois and the black intellectual tradition. Initially, I was confused. What was so provincial about DuBois or, more to the point, why was the study of U.S. practices of racialization

---

pursued in U.S. American Studies at the time, which had begun to highlight the systemic occlusions and omissions on which the American Dream of happiness seemed to depend. This does not mean that U.S. culture is no longer saturated by happiness as an idiom of ordinary life. Indeed, the phrase is ubiquitous. Rock bands and real estate companies use it, as do politicians and media pundits. It has appeared in the title of a twenty-first-century government report, "Beyond Therapy: Biotechnology and the Pursuit of Happiness," which gives state backing to the pharmaceutical industry and its psychotropical approach to positive feeling for a population that is being diagnosed increasingly with manic depression. In the popular press, happiness appears as part of what needs to be defended, as in the recent *Renewing American Culture: The Pursuit of Happiness*, which hopes to parse a distinction between Western imperialism and the global protection of the value of freedom. And Hollywood regularly recycles it, with the 2006 film *The Pursuit of Happyness* (Columbia Pictures; dir. Gabriele Muccino) moralizing the road to economic accumulation by following Chris Gardner, an African American father, as he struggled from homelessness to wealth in 1980s San Francisco—all wrapped in the star quality of Will Smith, who received an Oscar nomination as best actor for the role. (The film is based on the book, *The Pursuit of Happyness*, by Chris Gardner with Quincy Troupe.)

See Jones, *The Pursuit of Happiness*; Schlesinger, "Human Rights and the American Tradition"; President's Council on Bioethics, "Beyond Therapy"; and Malloch and Massey, *Renewing American Culture*.

19. Kadir, "Defending America Against Its Devotees," 135–52.

20. Kadir, "Introduction," 11.

described as nationalist and critically insufficient? After three days of these encounters—and with the charge of provincialism growing to include chauvinism and "navel gazing"—my confusion turned to anger. How was it, I wanted to know, that in *this* economy of geography and identity, one was immune from the charge of provincialism by being from Leiden or Leeds or Darwin or Kingston or Minsk or Campo Grande or Saporro or Trondheim or 200 miles north of New Delhi—anywhere, that is, outside the geographical territory of the United States? If this was what the international meant, it was not an analytic at all. Rather, it was an identity-oriented perspective grounded in place—and one purportedly capacious in its global reach as long as it did not inhabit the domestic (and indeed domesticated) space of the United States.[21]

3. That was before my last story, which concerns not a conference but a publication. In the years following Leiden, I wrestled with my own defensiveness about the identity politic that internationalization put into play and with both the political and analytic implications of the field's turn to the kind of postnational inquiry that had made its global reorganization so visible and urgent in the first place. The essay that I first drafted set out to consider how difficult it was to definitively parse the distinction that "American American Studies" was being used to generate, not because there was no such thing—there surely was and is—but because American American Studies was not

---

21. What I wanted to protest, let me be clear, was not the proposition that proximity generated complicity. No one, after all, could assume that one's implication in the study of the United States is the same in Hungary, where the postsocialist state must negotiate its relation to a consolidating "Europe," neoliberal economic policy, and U.S. foundations of educational aid, as it is from within the powerful global hegemony of the U.S. knowledge industry. My irritation was with the generic formulation that confirmed the distinction, such that a territorial "outside" became the sole means for determining non-complicity. If in this calculus the non–U.S.-based Americanist was understood to have an international perspective unavailable to his U.S.-based colleague, there was no sense that the "international" scholar could be a U.S. citizen by birth or someone, citizen or not, trained in the U.S. university, which rather confounded the entire calculus for determining who was provincial and complicit and who was not. Given that the conference theme was "How far is America from here?" it felt rather defeating that such a literal take on the question of critical identity was being invoked when the proceedings were aimed precisely at exposing the complexities of nation formation, national identity, and geopolitical relationality in a global context.

and is not solely practiced in the U.S. university.[22] It is not coincident with the national identity of the practitioner nor with her North American venue of employment. Neither is it internally coherent and, most important, for those who are in it or of it or in close proximity to it, it cannot be wished or willed away. Like the object of study that it names and interrogates, American American Studies has a history and is constituted by the political economy and cultural practices that attend the geopolitical fictions in which it is made and circulated, including of course the stories it tells about itself. In considering those stories, especially those that narrated the turn from the Cold War field apparatus to the New Americanism, I was struck by how much the discourse of internationalization specified American American Studies in the same language that New Americanism used to critique both the formation of the field it succeeded and the imperial practices of the U.S. state: as exceptionalist, arrogant, self-obsessed, universalizing, parochial, deluded, paternal, and aggressive. How distinct, then, was the discourse of internationalization from the entity it sought to specify and displace? Or to pose the question from the opposite direction: to what extent was the discourse of internationalization, crafted in antithesis and disidentification with American American Studies, nonetheless reliant on its critical habits and progressivist political imaginary, such that in its critical motion to specify and displace it, internationalization was more aptly producing it? These were the questions that animated my inquiries, until the editors of a volume intended to survey the current shape of the field of American Studies asked me to contribute my essay.

22. In recent conversations about internationalization, the term *American American Studies* has been used in rather confounding ways, sometimes as a synonym for either U.S. American Studies or U.S.-based American Studies, at other times in contradistinction to both. When deployed as a synonym, American American Studies plots a geographical identity that is simultaneously national and nationalist in origin and identification— it is rather literally a field "made in the USA" by people "made in the USA," with all of the familiar self-centered national affections and afflictions attached to the discursive production of "America" in the United States. When used to denote a distinction from U.S. (based) American Studies, American American Studies indicates trajectories of identificatory nationalism in Americanist knowledge practices without analogizing the field to territory and nativity. In this deployment, an Americanist working anywhere, born anywhere, in the world can be an American Americanist, just as a U.S.-based Americanist is not an American Americanist by default. This latter distinction is not widely used; indeed I think it safe to say that a vocabulary for differentiating Americanist scholarship globally has yet to be fully developed.

This is where the core of my third story lives. According to the table of contents, there were only two chapters by scholars from outside the United States and no deliberation other than mine on internationalization per se. I panicked. How, in *this* context, could I argue that internationalization was dependent on the critical habits of that which it most disavowed—American American Studies—when the volume's political economy of knowledge production reiterated the internationalist's most stinging critique: that Americanist scholarship that originated in the U.S. university took itself as constitutive of the field as a whole? How could I defend myself against the inevitable accusation that we were all provincial without abandoning the analysis I was committed to about the ways in which internationalization and American American Studies were more than antithetically linked? In the end, I revised my essay to offer what I phrased as a "friendly critique" of the collection's authorial geography, before venturing into my argument that internationalist discourse was dependent on the New Americanist calculus of inclusion and exclusion that had reshaped the Cold War formation of the field in the United States. I thus tried to have my cake and eat it too: I critiqued the volume's sparse inclusion of scholarship produced outside the United States in order not to be stung by the criticisms I had learned to hear, while demonstrating how the discourse of internationalization drew its critical logics from the rise of New Americanism in the genealogy of American American Studies itself.

When the editors reviewed my essay, they cut my "friendly critique," less to avoid criticism than because they found my criticism off-target and conceptually weak. Their volume, they explained, was organized around the concept of the transnational and had a great deal of work by well-established left academics—Amy Kaplan, José Saldívar, Donald E. Pease, Lisa Lowe, Brent Edwards, Michael Denning, Robin D. G. Kelley, George Lipsitz, George Sanchez, Ruth Gilmore, Phil DeLoria—all of whom had helped turn American Studies from its protonationalist formation during the Cold War era toward understanding the violent force of U.S. imperialism and the routes of transnational migrations of various kinds that had been carved out in support of and resistance to it. Given New Americanism's own investment in critical self-reflection, I was told, the analytic priority of the transnational answered the imperative to internationalize by turning American Studies outside identifications with the imperial project of "America" that characterized its critical predecessor. The conversations that ensued were compelling and useful, and I found the editorial arguments for the analytic utility of the transnational partially persuasive. I understood, for instance, how the emphasis on the transnational performs an important reformulation of the genealogy of Americanist knowledges, such that one could resituate the field in an intellectual history traceable, in one of numerous trajectories, from Marcus Garvey, Frederick Douglass, W. E. B. DuBois, and Frantz Fanon to Paul Gilroy. It made sense to me to use the transnational as the analytic rubric to link this work to the scholarship on the border, immigration studies, the queer diaspora, media cultures, language debates, and various new social movements—indeed, to a whole range of objects of study that allowed for the creative and critical reshaping of the field from what many of us had learned to critique as its myth and symbol hegemonies.

And yet, I remained haunted by the affect that the discourse of internationalization had produced in the various venues in which I had encountered it, and by my own suspicion that no matter how far the transnational might travel analytically, it was not equipped to grapple with many of the dilemmas that internationalization had and was continuing to generate. All this, not because the transnational had no strategic value or lacked critical force, but because it was impossible to imagine a single resolution, let alone an *analytic* one, for the incommensurability between the political aim of American American Studies and the implication of the field in the extensive power of the U.S. knowledge industry. Of this much I felt certain. But what did it all mean? Was the transnational analytic functioning as the vehicle through which American Americanists could inoculate themselves against the critique of our global power and authority, such that we could imagine ourselves outside the nationalizing discourses and imperial agency of our object of study regardless of how inside we were to the globalizing U.S. knowledge industry and the authority it conferred on us to define the priorities and scope of the field?[23] Or was the chasm that opened here, between the analytic capacity of the transnational and the political economy of Americanist knowledge in its global production, a means to explore the differentiated relations that the discourse of internationalization

23. Let me be clear that I am indicting my own work in this charge, as the volume produced from the first half decade of the Futures of American Studies Institute at Dartmouth featured mainly U.S.-based Americanist scholarship in a collective citational practice that reaffirmed the hegemony of U.S. Americanist discourses. See Pease and Wiegman, *The Futures of American Studies*.

exposed, such that the critical task was less about resolution and more about understanding the incommensurabilities between the wish and the symptoms that evoked it? This chapter answers *yes* to both of these questions. This means accounting first for the way that New Americanism reads internationalization as one of its own critical horizons because of its refusal to identify with the imperial nationalism of its Cold War predecessor, before exploring how the discourse of internationalization seeks an outside to American American Studies by relying on the practice of refusal it learns from it. Here, in the mirror formation of *their mutual misrecognitions*, we can track what is fascinatingly congruent about New Americanism's own postnationalism and the discourse of internationalization that simultaneously reflects and contests it: their animated pursuit of critical noncomplicity.

Refusing What?

It is surely no surprise to find the entity that internationalization has so productively identified—the American Americanist—in a certain crisis of self-recognition. If she laughs at the prospect of pursuing happiness and if her laughter ignites a wave of shame, it is not because the topic has no intrinsic critical value, nor that the significance of its historical or cultural meaning has now passed. What "dates" the pursuit is not the pursuit itself but the progressive political narrative that underwrites American American Studies, which seeks to critically unburden the field from its prior nationalist attachments, especially those that have been too identified with "America" and its exceptionalist self-imaginings to manage the necessary critique of its violent imperial ambitions. From this perspective, happiness is a casualty in the field's New Americanist transformation, too weighty an emblem of nationalist self-obsession, too profoundly idealist for the grip of critique through which practitioners seek to defend themselves against the global power of their object of study. So the American Americanist must travel to Rome to pursue happiness. What (and who) does she find there? International observers armed with enough dispassion and globality to be comprehensive in the face of complicit natives, who are too overwhelmed with proximity to know what they see? Of course not. But she does find herself confronted with the critical traveler's dilemma, becoming not only more "American" and more decisively "American Americanist," but more curious about the practices through which she is learning to become what others already take her to be—and more interested too in what they, at such a distance, may not find compelling about the institutional, political, and epistemological entanglements in which she finds herself. All this, even as she also knows that the multiple and disparate relationships in which she and others are made—along with the production and circulation of their objects of study—are never entirely comprehensible, and not simply because there are no perspectives *on* them that are not also produced from *within* them.

From the vantage point of *Object Lessons*, the problem has to do with the difficulty of negotiating the present as much as with the enormity of accounting for the ways in which knowledges, like their practitioners, are situated in a range of differentially produced geopolitical and analytic relations, ones so dense they are difficult to fully imagine, let alone enumerate.[24] From this perspective, internationalization begs the question of whether the field transformation it heralds is about catching up to a present that has already transformed us or producing a relation to the future that can rescue us from what seems like the present's characteristic incoherence. (Why else do so many narratives about the present rely on the idea that it is more complex than any historical present before it?) Field transformation is routinely caught in this temporal dilemma, so much so, it seems to me, that part of the fantasy that propels it is that *practitioners are the agents* of field revision—this, instead of the more fateful supposition that changes in the narrative formation and critical priorities of fields of study are generated by the very processes critics hope to decipher and transform. After all, it is not simply out of nowhere that scholars have

24. These relations include scales of analysis that do not necessarily converge: from the specific implications of place in local, national, regional, hemispheric, and global formulations to the transits of people, commodities, and cultural forms in circulations that mimic and transform the routes of capital, labor, and empire; from the histories of national university systems and the organizations of knowledge in which the study of language and culture has been generated to the powerful ways in which contestations within a national political sphere are played out through struggles over and within the knowledge apparatus as a whole; from the cultural migrations and translations of systems of meaning and interpretative forms to large- and small-scale political economies and labor formations; from practices of belief, modes of belonging, and identity inheritances to legal regimes, forms of governmentality, histories of political contestation, and discourses of identification and resistance. This list, of course, goes on, revealing the complexity in which both objects of study and their practitioners are situated *and* the refracted angles of vision that bring them into view.

learned to read the imperial power of "America" onto the field's critical relations, such that renderings of hierarchy, discrimination, and complicity in critical practice have come to stand as *politics* writ large. This is one of the distinctive marks of New Americanism's own production as an identity knowledge, as the critique of the Cold War consensus model was effected precisely by locating the question of politics at the level of the critical relationship. In learning to situate *itself,* in wish if not always in fact, as resolution to that which it critiqued, New Americanism became relentlessly focused on differentiating its critical act from the power of its object of study. It is this field imaginary that generates the paradox I am trying to track: where the charge of U.S.-centrism and provincialism can remain unintelligible to New Americanism at the same time that the refusal of identification that grounds the internationalist critique is fully at home as a critical maneuver within American American Studies itself. To explicate how this paradox is produced and sustained, I want to delve more fully into the repudiative operations of New Americanism, as the identificatory refusal the field cultivates does not belong to it alone.

In fact, throughout the U.S. university today, scholars rely on *refused identification* to generate a critical practice that evokes their commitment to academic knowledge production as a realm not of neutral or dispassionate observation but of political engagement.[25] It might be true to say that refused identification was first deployed as a tactic for revisionary work in disciplines that had long claimed to be universalizing and objective, even as they routinely occluded both the specificity and the diversity of the human subject in gendered, racial, sexual, and economic terms. It is certainly true to say that whole generations of scholars have now been trained to practice refused identification as the means by which they challenge the normative assumptions of their disciplines, undoing canons, transforming methodologies, and resisting not simply particular disciplinary histories but the privileges such histories ascribe to specific critical vocabularies and habits of thought. Think here of the deliberative refusals of the "critical humanities," which have dismantled universalizing ideas of Western masterworks and the hierarchies of "civilization" and authorial intention that have accompanied them. Or of cultural studies, which refuses to grant

---

25. In a very different context, Judith Butler writes about refused identification in "Melancholy Gender/Refused Identification," in *The Psychic Life of Power,* 132–50.

value solely to aesthetics and its mode of understanding culture as high art by turning to everyday life and the complex agency that renders meaning productive, not merely consumptive. In numerous interdisciplinary projects—from postcolonial studies to Ethnic, Women's, and Sexuality Studies—refused identification has provided the founding gesture, differentiating objects, analytics, and critical habits from those privileged by dominant organizations of knowledge. This does not mean that such knowledges have not also produced their own identificatory practices; indeed, part of what refused identification performs is the transference of identification away from the priorities of the dominant model toward the dispossessed identities and categories of analysis that it is taken to have implicitly or explicitly ignored. These transferences not only transform the field in question by making both legible and legitimate new objects of study, methodological priorities, analytic practices, and critical questions, but they establish an oppositional political imaginary through which practitioners understand their scholarship as socially significant, if not ethical and just.

In U.S. American Studies, refused identification has been the primary response to the purported exceptionalism of the Cold War object of study, opening scholarly investigations to a range of people, practices, and critical questions previously subordinated, if not conceptually excluded.[26] The now-generic narration of the New American Studies as an outcome of the counterhegemonic logics and ambitions of social movement dissent in the 1960s is critical to the refusal the field performs, as it establishes an origin for the field that is external to both the U.S. university and the state apparatus of which it is a part. But the consolidation of New Americanism as the Cold War successor did not take shape in the immediate aftermath of social movement dissent. Tellingly, its narrative began to emerge in 1988, a few short months before the world historical event that would mark the end not simply of a geopolitical era but of living alternatives to capitalism and its global pursuit. In his review essay "Whose American Renaissance?" Crews would register the critical turn by deploying the neologism "New Americanist," and in the next few years, others would generate field-defining statements that countered or differently refracted the critical

26. Gene Wise is often credited with most incisively elaborating the field's struggle with its object of study. See "'Paradigm Dramas' in American Studies"; and more recently, Radway, "What's in a Name?"

present that Crews lamented.[27] Robert Berkhofer Jr.'s essay in 1989, a longer version of a paper he delivered at the American Studies Association meeting in 1988, put forward the idea that there was a "new approach to American Studies, if not a new American Studies."[28] His essay supported the emergence of a new set of priorities: of ethnic and gendered differences over homogeneous national identity, dissensus over consensus, everyday life over aesthetic practice, and interrogations of culture over political history and the official narratives of the state. But Berkhofer was cautious, as the question mark in his title, "A New Context for a New American Studies?" suggests, about whether the new scholarship was developing an equally new critical capacity to handle the complexities of the relationship between text and context on one hand and past and present on the other. Would it, he wondered at his essay's end, be as theoretically sophisticated in its historical narration as it was in its analysis of the social construction of "reality"? Or would it revamp the field in vocabulary and self-narration without substantively transforming the dominant habit of converting "the past into present use"?[29]

27. For Crews, "the New Americanists are broadly poststructuralist in sympathy; they refuse to draw categorical distinctions between literature and history, foreground and background, art and advocacy, and they distrust all 'foundational' claims, whether they be for fixed aesthetic quality, authorial autonomy, a specifically literary kind of discourse, or scholarly detachment. But they scorn the daisy chain of indeterminacies with which the once dandyish but now crestfallen Yale deconstructionists used to caper. For a New Americanist, social struggle must always be kept in view, and any concepts obscuring it—concepts, for example, of the 'American character,' of the representative masterpiece, of the impish freeplay of signifiers—are to be not just rejected but exposed as ideology."

28. See Berkhofer, "A New Context for a New American Studies?"

29. Berkhofer wrote: "Should we assume that the changing vocabularies during the past four decades represent progress in refining our terminology in the light of increasing conceptual sophistication, or merely altered intellectual and political preferences? Should we tell the story as one of changing climates of opinion (old vocabulary) or struggles for intellectual and political hegemony (new vocabulary)? Should it be emplotted according to the trope of irony—or of romance? Has the American Studies movement entered its own postmodern phase because of its engagement(s) with poststructuralist, post-Marxist, postfeminist, and even posthistoricist theory and practice? Does this answer depend upon one's choices of narrative plotting and viewpoint or perspective on discourse and politics? Should we postulate a rupture or continuity, and what difference does each plotting make for what and for whom? Will the return to a neo-Progressive

The answers to his questions seem not to have been extensively debated, perhaps because Crews's essay, cast as a review of seven recently published works of Americanist scholarship, was so negatively inclined toward the New Americanism it named and so prominently published (in the twenty-fifth anniversary issue of the *New York Review of Books*) that it generated immediate repudiation.[30] (The ending was especially acerbic: "The New Americanists," Crews wrote, are "destined to become the next establishment in their field. They will be right about the most important books and the most fruitful ways of studying them because, as they always knew in their leaner days, those who hold power are right by definition.") By the spring of 1990, Donald E. Pease had collected a set of new essays and published an introduction to them as the now signatory statement, "New Americanists: Revisionist Interventions into the Canon."[31] Pease had not one but two books under review by Crews, and a good many pages of "Whose American Renaissance?" used these works to delineate the failures of the New Americanism.[32] "What chiefly marks Pease as a New Americanist," Crews

---

version of American history as overall context bring back a simpler link between text and context, between language and social reality that denies the more skeptical implications of the linguistic turn for interpretive security and political certainty? Only the future can reveal the answers to these questions, but will the construction of that history be plotted any differently in form than what now converts the past into present use?" ("A New Context," 606).

30. The books were: Michaels and Pease, *The American Renaissance Reconsidered*; Reising, *The Unusable Past*; Bercovitch and Jehlen, *Ideology and Classic American Literature*; Pease, *Visionary Compacts*; Tompkins, *Sensational Designs*; Reynolds, *Beneath the American Renaissance*; and Fisher, *Hard Facts*.

31. Pease, "New Americanists." This essay was later republished by Pease in an edited collection for his New Americanist book series at Duke; see *New Americanists: Revisionary Interventions in the Canon*. A second special issue of *boundary 2* edited by Pease appeared in 1992, also to be subsequently published as a collection. See *National Identities and Post-Americanist Narratives*.

32. Philip Fisher, also a figure whose work was under review by Crews, edited a special issue and volume of essays in the early 1990s. That collection, *The New American Studies: Essays from Representations*, might be thought of as the road not taken, as it offered a pragmatist map of the new American Studies, shifting critical emphasis from myth to rhetorics and from national unity to regionalism—with race and gender serving as the material content of the regional. As Carolyn Porter pointed out in a 1994 review essay, Fisher's formulation neutralized the very revision of the field that he sought to remap. "[A] field so defined," she wrote, "relieves its practitioners of any theoretical need

wrote, "is his eagerness for moral certainties about the relation between the books and the politics he admires." In the end, Crews faulted the New Americanism for "self-righteousness," along with "its tendency to conceive of American history only as a highlight film of outrages, its impatience with artistic purposes other than 'redefining the social order,' and its choice of critical principles according to the partisan cause at hand."

Pease's subsequent essay—what might properly be called the founding manifesto of New Americanism—repudiated Crews's repudiation and established refused identification as foundational to New Americanism's critical mode. Where Crews questioned what he saw as the New Americanist conflation of culture and politics, Pease affirmed their inextricable relation and read Crews's resistance as symptomatic of the political unconscious of the Cold War's liberal anticommunist consensus, which had operated through repression, including the repression of the historical violence of conquest. Pease thus defined the New Americanist project as linking the "repressed sociopolitical contexts *within* literary works to the sociopolitical issues *external* to the academic field," such that "questions of class, race, and gender" could be returned to the field.[33] In this way, New Americanists "occup[ied] a double relation": "For as *liaisons between* cultural and public realms, they are at once within the field but external to it. Moreover, as representatives of subjects excluded from the field-Imaginary by the previous political unconscious, New Americanists have a responsibility to make these absent subjects representable in their field's past and present" (31). In Pease's hands, Crews's essay became not only an ungenerous attempt to reclaim the field for the Cold War consensus but a politically inflected psychic map of the ideological crisis that the New Americanism had already effected—one that did more than forward a set of new texts or critical questions. Indeed, for Pease, the New Americanism was an interruption of the field imaginary that had become dominant in the 1950s

---

or capacity to address cultural differences. . . . It also—and not accidentally—affords no critical standpoint on the cultural work of American literature other than the pragmatist's. . . . It is precisely because of these deficiencies, in my view, that this version of 'the new American studies' is all too likely to prevail" (496). While Porter's prediction missed its mark, her discussion of the field's possible futures is a stunning explication of the critical terrain of the early 1990s. See "What We Know That We Don't Know."

33. Pease, "New Americanists," 16, 32. Further citations to this text are given parenthetically.

and that underwrote the institutional consolidation of American Studies in the U.S. university during the postwar period. It exposed the field's "fundamental syntax—its tacit assumptions, convictions, primal words, and the charged relations binding them together" (11). While Crews was unable to register the identifications that had come to legitimate his own authority as a practitioner within the field imaginary that governed him, Pease's refusal of identification with it both demanded and made possible the narrative transformation of the field that his essay celebrated as New American Studies.

But how exactly did the New Americanist gain critical insight into the Cold War field imaginary without becoming subsumed by the "fundamental syntax" its critique put into place? Or more to the point, what enabled Pease to herald New Americanism as the alternative to the Cold War formation of the field without worrying about its own disciplinary determinations? After all, in Pease's definition, "A field specialist depends upon th[e] field-Imaginary for the construction of her primal identity within the field. Once constructed out of this syntax, the primal identity can neither reflect upon its terms nor subject them to critical scrutiny. The syntactic elements of the field-Imaginary subsist instead as self-evident principles" (11–12). In these terms, a field practitioner is immune to knowledge of the identifications that compel her because disciplinarity is the effect of the unconscious operations of the field imaginary. For this reason, Pease cast the New Americanist as "at once within the field yet external to it," which gave practitioners the ability to not only narrate but inhabit the conscious political intentions that defined it (31). Hence when a New Americanist "makes explicit the relationship between an emancipatory struggle taking place outside the academy and an argument she is conducting within the field, the relationship . . . can no longer be described as imaginary. Such *realized* relations undermine the separation of the public world from the cultural sphere" (19). From a position of exteriority, then, the New Americanist project refuses identification with its predecessor's imperial object of study in order to claim the political force of social movement *as its own critical agency*. In doing so, Pease figured the significance of New American Studies as nothing less than the means to "change the hegemonic self-representation of the United States' culture" (32).

There is, of course, much to say about the political desire that underlies New Americanist claims—the desire, that is, to retrieve the repressed interiority of the field's Cold War imaginary without risking complicity with it or with the ideological sphere in which "America" might be said to secure its imperial and universalizing self-definition. To be situated in the mobility of "outside/in," as Pease called it, enabled the New Americanism to assert its authority for field transformation from within the political imaginaries established by social movements, thereby placing it outside the field of American Studies—or in contemporary terms, outside American American Studies, conceived not as a territorial or identity formation but as the field's fundamental syntax in the Cold War period. Because the terms of that syntax are inexplicable to the subject constructed within it, "an Americanist," Pease writes, cannot delineate "uncritically held assumptions without disaffiliating himself from the field of American Studies" (3). He must, in other words, be outside the field in order to have analytic purchase on what lies inside its dominant logics. While critics might take issue with the psychoanalytic vocabulary (of primal scenes, repression, and trauma) by which Pease delivers New Americanism to this complex location, most U.S.-based Americanist scholarship produced in the last two decades is beholden to the double relation that Pease defined, which not only casts critical practice as an alternative political agency but rejects the possibility that a new disciplinary apparatus guides it. The consequences of these investments on American Studies today are far reaching, especially given the fact that New American Studies has established its authority, as Crews predicted, as the dominant formation of the field in the United States.

As preamble to understanding how refused identification underwrites the discourse of internationalization that shapes the present, I want to devote the next section to reflecting on some of the most prominent trajectories of scholarship that might now be said to have resituated U.S.-based American Studies within the field imaginary that New Americanism defines. In their collective turn away from the Cold War project of the field—through questions of empire, transnationality, borders, and diaspora, and in critical frameworks aligned with postcolonial, postnational, hemispheric, and comparative studies—each of these trajectories takes its externality to the nationalist "Americanness" of American Studies as the means to found its own critical and political self-definition. Their use of refused identification is profoundly a self-conscious maneuver, one aimed at disarticulating field practices from what are generally considered past complicities with an exceptionalist object of study and a field imaginary in service, not resistance, to the state. Each trajectory thus marshals the utility of its own investigations and critical attachments as a committed formulation of the left politics of the field, and each perceives itself, often quite explicitly, as essential to current critical efforts to attend to what has been called the "worlding of American Studies."[34] Understood less as a cartography of new subject orientations in the field than as a remapping of its political desires, these trajectories demonstrate how familiar internationalization is *as an idiom* within the New Americanist field imaginary and thus prepare the way for considering the paradox that internationalization's own turn to definitive self-narration entails: being at once a discourse aimed at getting outside the Americanness of American Studies at a time when the dominant field imaginary in the United States understands itself to be committed to precisely the same thing.

Inside and Out

In the years following the publication of his New Americanist manifesto, Pease began working with Amy Kaplan to chart more precisely the repressed history of imperial ambition occluded by the Cold War warriors. Their 1993 *Cultures of United States Imperialism*, now a landmark in the field, signaled the New Americanist shift from the powerfully iconic object of "America" to the more mortal figure of the "United States." Other scholars—most notably Laura Briggs, David Kazanjian, Gretchen Murphy, Lora Romero, Shelley Streeby, Cheryl Walker, and Laura Wexler—have followed in this vein, turning Cold War American Studies on its head by explicating the project of empire in U.S. nation-state formation, often with careful dissection of the dynamics of domestic/foreign and citizen/alien that have shored up the ideological narratives and subjects of conquest.[35] As a whole, this scholarship has been especially important in identifying a new archive for historical study, from the discourses and contexts of settler colonialism to forgotten U.S. wars (with Mexico, the Philippines, and Korea) to

34. See the special issue "Worlding American Studies," edited by Gillman, Gruesz, and Wilson.

35. See Kaplan and Pease, *Cultures of United States Imperialism*; Briggs, *Reproducing Empire*; Kazanjian, *The Colonizing Trick*; Murphy, *Hemispheric Imaginings*; Romero, *Home Fronts*; Streeby, *American Sensations*; Walker, *Indian Nation*; and Wexler, *Tender Violence*. Also see Kaplan, "Manifest Domesticity" and *The Anarchy of Empire in the Making of U.S. Culture*.

the counternationalist discourses produced in empire's wake. By establishing the critique of U.S. imperialism as the generative force and critical destination of the field, this work refuses identification with both the exceptionalist state and its disciplinary formalization in American Studies programs in the U.S. in the mid-twentieth century.[36]

Alongside this work is a *second* trajectory of scholarship shaped by the New Americanist emphasis on empire, what Lisa Lowe calls "the international within the national," which disrupts the persistence of nativist approaches to cultural identity by foregrounding histories of transnational migration, such that the field turns its attention to the "material legacy of America's imperial past [as it] is borne out in the 'return' of immigrants to the imperial center."[37] Lowe's specific case is Asian American Studies and the subject formation it studies and transcribes, which she approaches not as a project of protonationalism on the part of a minoritized population, but as a response to the political economy of U.S. imperialism and the migrations of people which the routes of empire beget. Other scholars working in this vein—Eithne Luibhéid, David L. Eng, and Martin Manalansan—continue the New Americanist critique of the Cold War knowledge apparatus by focusing on the contexts, ruptures, and continuities of migration and subject formation in the ongoing imbrication of capital formation and coloniality.[38]

A *third* trajectory of New Americanism follows the concern with histories of imperialism to refute notions of both an epistemological and territorial inside/out by focusing on what José David Saldívar has generatively defined as border studies.[39] Along with Jeffrey Belnap, Raúl Fernández, Mary Pat Brady, Maria DeGuzmán, Kirsten Silva Gruesz, and Ramón Saldívar, this work challenges the conflation of the United States with the American hemisphere, engages scholarship from Latin American Studies, and redefines culture and cultural practices in multilinguistic and postcolonial formulation: all in order to think about transcultural and transnational identities and the forms of cultural production, political practice,

36. In a review essay, Susan Gillman considers the "main moves, terminologies, and innovations in US empire studies, post-1998" (196). See "The New, Newest Thing."

37. Lowe, "The International Within the National," 29.

38. See Luibhéid, *Entry Denied*; Eng, *Racial Castration*; and Manalansan, *Global Divas*.

39. See Saldívar, *Border Matters* and *The Dialectics of Our America*.

and everyday life that cannot be adequately discerned from within the territorial or cultural logics of nation.[40] Its signatory refusal collates around the geographical imaginaries that have sutured state formations to both identity and culture in earlier modes of American Studies, such that much of its scholarship explores the history, meaning, and force of a hemispheric imaginary.[41]

A *fourth* and compellingly related trajectory, Black Diaspora Studies, draws most heavily from the intersection of African American and African Studies and proceeds from new projects on modernity, the Black Atlantic, Black Europe, and other configurations of black intellectual traditions from Fanon and C. L. R. James to Stuart Hall and Paul Gilroy.[42] In many ways, this scholarship builds on even as it critiques the nationalizing discourse of U.S. Ethnic Studies, as in work by Carole Boyce Davies, Brent Edwards, Saidiya Hartman, Nikhil Singh, and Michelle Stephens.[43] Its geopolitical imaginary is multisited and increasingly grapples with the minoritized status of Africa in studies of globalization and in the discourse on diaspora more generally. New Americanist critique in this vein privileges displacement as an axis of interrogation and has the difficult task of attending to the symbolic weight of the United States in global histories of black identity formation. Its identificatory refusals take shape against nation-state organizations of knowledge and culture, and, in the hands of

40. See Belnap and Fernández, *José Martí's "Our America"*; Brady, *Extinct Lands, Temporal Geographies*; DeGuzmán, *Spain's Long Shadow*; Fox and Sadowski-Smith, "Theorizing the Hemisphere"; Gruesz, *Ambassadors of Culture*; and Saldívar, *The Borderlands of Culture*.

41. Numerous notable journals have featured special issues on hemispheric studies in recent years. See Kadir, "America, the Idea, the Literature"; Moya and Saldívar, "Fictions of the Trans-American Imaginary"; Shukla and Tinsman, "Our Americas"; Fox, "Critical Perspectives and Emerging Models of Inter-American Studies"; and Levander and Levine, "Hemispheric American Literary History."

42. See especially Fanon, *Black Skin, White Masks*; James, *Beyond a Boundary*; Morley and Chen, *Stuart Hall*; Hall, "Cultural Identity and Diaspora"; and Gilroy, *The Black Atlantic*.

43. See Davies and Ogundipe-Leslie, *Moving Beyond Boundaries*; Davies et al., *Decolonizing the Academy*; Edwards, "The Uses of *Diaspora*" and *The Practice of Diaspora*; Hartman, *Lose Your Mother*; Singh, *Black Is a Country*; and Stephens, *Black Empire*.

some scholars, the Cold War era is itself being rewritten to rethink the relationship between anticommunism and U.S. Civil Rights.[44]

A *fifth* trajectory of New Americanist scholarship calls for a comparative perspective that decenters the United States from its universal representation as the quintessential national form, thereby locating operations of culture in cross-national formulations that are multinational in both critical practice and analytic scope. This work, represented by John Carlos Rowe, Gunter Lenz, Rob Kroes, Rob Wilson, Paul Giles, Djelal Kadir, and others, situates itself within reconfigurations of the knowledge industry on a global scale as it encounters and seeks to rethink area studies models with more fluid and flexible ideas about nations as imaginary formations with deeply material effects.[45] Its identificatory refusals are aimed at exceptionalist approaches to U.S. nation formation and the state-based organizations of knowledge that have ensued.

My *sixth* and last trajectory builds on much of the preceding work to explore the relationship between the national and the international in the modes of knowledge production at work in American Studies as a global scholarly enterprise. Elaborated by Ron Robin, Jane Desmond, Virginia Dominguez, Sheila Hones, Julia Leyda, and others, it pays attention to the uneven distribution of power—in resources, cultural capital, and critical authority—that accompanies the production and circulation of American Studies across national university systems, and calls attention to, as Desmond writes, "the different goals, stakes, and histories of U.S.-based, and non-U.S. based scholarly communities."[46] Within this framework, which is often allied with comparative and postnational approaches, scholars have begun to map the political economy of American Studies in the local,

---

44. See Baldwin, *Beyond the Color Line and the Iron Curtain*; Borstelmann, *The Cold War and the Color Line*; and Dudziak, *Cold War Civil Rights*.

45. See Rowe, "A Future for 'American Studies'" and *The New American Studies*; and his edited collection, *Post-nationalist American Studies*; Lenz, "Toward a Dialogics of International American Culture Studies"; Kroes, *If You've Seen One, You've Seen the Mall*; Wilson, *Reimagining the American Pacific*; Giles, *Virtual Americas*; and Kadir, "Introduction."

46. See Robin, "The Outsider as Marginal Scholar"; Desmond, "Transnational American Studies and the Limits to Collaboration"; Torres, "US Americans and 'Us' Americans"; and Hones and Leyda, "Toward a Critical Geography of American Studies." The citation is from Desmond, "Transnational American Studies," 19.

national, and regional contexts in which it is embedded, which has had the triple effect of rendering American American Studies both critically distinct and an object of internationalist critique, *and* of placing New Americanism in closer proximity to its Cold War predecessor than it would otherwise choose to think.[47] A key component of this trajectory of work entails reconsidering the priority placed within New Americanism on race, gender, and sexuality (or multiculturalism more generally), such that a "critical internationalism" emerges as distinct from any project that locates itself within the province of peoples or cultures of a territorially bounded United States.[48]

47. A number of scholars—most notably Eva Cherniavsky, Donatella Izzo, Scott Lucas, and Sabine Sielke—are working on the intellectual and geopolitical specificity of American Studies programs, paying attention in various degrees to national and regional political histories, funding patterns, and organizations of knowledge that shape the field's frames of reference, critical vocabularies, and research priorities as well as its relation to U.S. American Studies and "America" itself. The "thick" history being developed thus demonstrates the conflicting and multiple stakes of American Studies. Cherniavsky's work focuses on postsocialist eastern Europe and various funding agencies (such as the Soros Foundation) that have and continue to underwrite the development and expansion of American Studies programs there, where universities seek to negotiate their relationship to westernization, understood as both western Europe and the United States. Izzo charts the history of American Studies in Italy and its complex relation to fascism in intranational and European debates in the mid-twentieth century, while Lucas discusses the formation of British American Studies. In a lengthy consideration of the practice of American Studies in Germany, Sabine Sielke traces field-forming conversations about methods and theories across disciplinary domains to consider its potential transdisciplinary future. See Cherniavsky, "Post-American Studies, or Scattered Reflections on the Cultures of Imperialism"; Izzo, "Outside Where?"; Lucas, "USA OK?"; and Sielke, "Theorizing American Studies."

48. For instance, Kadir writes of the "postnationalism" of the New Americanism as "a more capacious nationalism that reinscribes a nationalist project, whose cultural dominant proves nothing less than a more variously differentiated nationalism," one that serves "the perennial nationalist project of self-affirmation through self-differentiation, broadened in its scope, base, and illusionary political unconscious to the identity formations of 'minorities' or 'disenfranchised groups'" ("Introduction," 19). In a less scathing tone, Jane C. Desmond and Virginia R. Dominguez remark on the tendency of scholarship on multiculturalism "to limit discussion of cultural diversity . . . to issues affecting populations living within the United States. . . . Although it is important that contemporary U.S. debates about cultural diversity produce an expansion of courses, textbooks, and museum representations of, by, and about minoritized U.S. populations, it had been

This list is meant to be suggestive, not definitive or comprehensive. Scholars work in more than one area; areas overlap; and there are significant arenas of contemporary criticism that I have failed to make coherent or legible. Hemispheric studies, for instance, could be a trajectory of its own or allied with comparative postnationalism. Diaspora might operate as a generic formulation, used to include the Pacific Rim or to frame queer theoretical emplotments of sexuality and globalization. Comparative Ethnic Studies and the diverse histories of colonialism and sovereignty that such perspectives generate could also be highlighted, or the entire list could be fashioned around theoretical attachments (new historicist, feminist, cultural studies, psychoanalytic, Marxian, intersectional, etc.). My point, however, is not to seek to *represent* the breadth of content or even the contours of all the scholarly trajectories that have been generated by the critical turn to New Americanism but to offer a glimpse of how thoroughly reliant they all are on refused identification as the means to generate the externality that Pease identified as fundamental to the field and that I read here as its defining characteristic. In those trajectories that critique the imperial state, scholars position themselves outside the nationalist discourses of the Cold War object of study in order to trace, through prenational and postnational frameworks, the colonial paths of U.S. economic, military, and ideological expansion from the false unity and domestic enclosure of its territorial "inside," an "inside" peopled well before European arrival. When the destination of critique extends to the configurations of people and cultures that are displaced by the brutality of nation building, as in both border and diaspora studies and in the incorporative modality that Lowe calls "the international in the national," New Americanists attend to the transnational routes of travel that empire has generated, the imaginary delineations it has drawn between people, and the modes of affiliation and collective life it has engendered, often through resistance, in the process. At this scale of analysis, Cold War models of cultural and national homogeneity are rejected, and New American Studies makes culture and nation both antagonistic and distinct. In this way, the critic's identificatory refusal works to restore to cultural and critical legi-

---

our hope that these debates about cultural diversity would also produce ... dialogues about the many other societies, cultures, and issues elsewhere in the world, including the perspectives of foreign scholars on the humanities in the United States" ("Resituating American Studies in a Critical Internationalism," 476).

bility the subjects, processes, and cultural forms of production that have been exteriorized by official national U.S. culture and by the prior field formation that tacitly endorsed it.

The pivotal distinction here between cultural formation and the apparatus of the nation-state grows less discernible in the latter trajectories I have defined, as the critical externality to the object is increasingly performed by the analytic dispensation of a geographical outside. These projects are deeply invested in decentering the United States from within the scene of its academic self-reference by thinking at a comparative scale of analysis about nation and region, and by establishing both international venues and internationalized genealogies for the collaborative production of the United States as an object of knowledge. The latter point is most clear in the collaborative and multinational inflection of the scholarly genealogies I cite, where non-U.S.-based Americanists have produced some of the most influential theoretical accounts of transcultural and comparative studies. Still, it has to be noted how the very history of competitive empire that shaped the founding nationalist gesture of U.S. colonial migration from western Europe is symbolically and materially traceable in the scholarly collaborations documented here, giving credence to the sense, apparent elsewhere, that the self-consciousness with which Americanists now approach the project of internationalization is the effect of contemporary urgencies whose histories are not, critically speaking, our own. I will have more to say shortly about the tendency in American Studies to manage the historical situatedness of its practitioners in dehistoricized and increasingly moral terms, such that the reliance on conscious refusal perpetuates a critical idiom overwhelmed by the fantasy specter of noncomplicity. For now, however, the point is simply this: that regardless of their divergent critical agendas, each of the trajectories I cite participates in materializing what the field imaginary of New Americanism has promised to make real—that through the cultivation of new scholarly attachments and critical vocabularies, Americanists can situate their work outside not only the imperial state apparatus and the national mythos that accompanies it, but the history of the field's implication in each.

Time Zones

Mappings of every kind, of course, tend to flatten the terrain over which they hover, requiring for actual travel a more proximate rendering of the territory one inhabits, encounters, or hopes to flee. But proximity in U.S.

American Studies has long been the key problem that the field has sought to correct, not a situation that it desires, let alone a political goal. To be in the interior, on the ground, at home, or in any of its nationalizing time zones has been and continues to be the affectively loaded scene of contamination and abjection; indeed, it is a primary source of shame for the New Americanist traveler, as I have been discussing. Hence, the New Americanism works hard to exchange the imaginary of the wilderness that enabled a mythological outside to the trauma of colonial extermination for the knowledge orientations provided by recovering the scene of violence, a scene of violence unassimilable to the national mythos. It does this from the complex psychic and epistemological spaces of exteriority, where anger, guilt, disidentification, and mourning coalesce into an investment, to repeat Pease's terms, to "change the hegemonic self-representation of the United States' culture" (32). This investment is no minor political desire, even if it might be taken, as it has, as a self-aggrandizing grasp for power or as the mirror inversion, through the syntax of dissent, of the kind of provincializing nationalism of that which it sought to displace. Both of these critiques rehearse, in gesture as well as plot, the mood and manner of New Americanist disaffiliations from the Cold War field imaginary that it has come repeatedly, I want to say compulsively, to cite. This compulsion is an important feature of New Americanism—indeed I take it to be constitutive, which means that as much as it narrates its own historical supersession, the New Americanism cannot live a day without the figure of the Cold War consensus to define that which it is not. This is no surprise, of course, because in a certain sense, New Americanism *invented it*: invented the very monolithic power of the Cold War apparatus it now foundationally rejects. Invented it by consolidating all of its contradictions into a narrative of complicitous identification with the state. And now, in much the same motion, internationalization promises to pay New Americanism the same honor, refusing identification with it as a means of constructing its own generative authority, one in which the promise of exteriority can free the field once and for all from the complicity of "America and its studies," as Kadir put it.

These are impossible desires, of course, which is the very reason we cannot afford to dismiss them. Indeed, I take seriously the work that refused identification performs, even if I find its relentless commitment to consciousness and the ethical utility of its own critical agency exhausting. After all, transformations of any field, including American Studies, are effected by much more than critical or political intention. They arise from historical forces, institutional impulses, and political ir/rationalities quite separate from the subjects who come to identify with and against them. And yet the critical exercises through which identity fields of study have come to be narrated have their own familiar cast of characters, with omniscient narration, totalizing evil, and heroic resolution—or in even more familiar terms, prescient critics, corrupting state power, and a sophisticated theoretical agenda armed for radical change. The temporal structure of these exercises typically splits the past from the present and the dead from the living (or the nearly retired from the more recently employed), such that the future is always owned by the present; indeed it is what the present lives for. If the language I use here relies on the technologies of fiction, not the determining social realities sought by documentary history, it is not that narratives of field formation jettison claims to material authority. In fact, what is striking is how often they present themselves as historical description against the animating failure of the field's past complicitous projections.[49] Hence, the double relation that authorizes New American Studies organizes the field into two time zones: a past that can never *not* be unconsciously aligned with the imperial state, and a present and future that thrive on their conscious and conscientious escape from such complicity.[50] That this psychic temporality is oedipal is certain—the New Americanism is mobilized by a critique of founding fathers, and its rebellion is routinely emplotted as the refusal to be domesticated by ideological fictions and state managements of various kinds, which is why, in the logic of its "newness," it is forever young. But when taken up by proponents who call for a wholly new internationalized field, New Americanism is stopped dead in its tracks, its animating self-propulsion returned, in temporal retrogression, to prototypical national time where it shares kinship with its Cold War predecessor.[51] The refusal that internationalization

49. There are numerous examples of the generic form I am citing here. For additional diagnosis of the operations of the field-forming narrative in American Studies, see Wiegmen, "The Ends of New Americanism."

50. For an interesting meditation on the status of the state as the complicity object in American Studies, see Bérubé, "American Studies Without Exceptions."

51. In his controversial essay "On Recovering the 'Ur' Theory of American Studies," Leo Marx makes an argument similar to Kadir's but for entirely different analytic reasons. Arguing that the New Americanists share continuities with the Cold War field

generates here is double edged. It takes the New Americanist revolt as a failure of critical self-recognition, resituating it within a continuous history of American Americanist identificatory attachments; in doing so, it consolidates the New Americanism as symptom and agent of the imperial ambitions of the state, refusing the former as a means of generating dissent from the latter.

I take Kadir's founding presidential address to the IASA conference in 2003, "Defending America Against Its Devotees," as a signal moment in establishing internationalization as the historical impetus and critical force of a field-transforming turn, one that shares the familiar emplotment from proximity to externality, from complicitous past to hopeful future. In it, he situates the war in Iraq as the watershed event that has "paradigm-altering" implications for American Studies, as large as those of the Vietnam War, but "with the difference that the global scope of American Studies as an international field today will resist the re-absorption of these changes into a national and nationalist project of US Americanism."[52] His manifesto begins, to trope Pease, in the rhetorical gesture of turning America outside itself.[53] Once an "object of devotion," "a generator of epistemic paradigms for its own assessment," "a continentally defined geopolitical territoriality," "an unquestionable ideological imaginary," and a nationalist "sponsor of American Studies," America today, he writes, has been fundamentally

---

apparatus that they refute, Marx seeks to rescue his own generation from political condemnation. See Marx, "On Recovering the 'Ur' Theory of American Studies"; and responses to it by George Lipsitz ("Our America") and Amy Kaplan ("A Call for a Truce").

52. Kadir, "Defending America Against Its Devotees," 135. Further references to this work are included parenthetically in the text.

53. In her response to Kadir, Amy Kaplan, then president of the U.S. American Studies Association, agreed that the field "must address the current international crisis" and that this would require "both new collaborative efforts of international networks of scholars and the emergence of new archives to remap the terrain of the object of study" (154). But she warned against the slide in his essay from American American Studies to American Americanist and the problematic reification of geography thus inscribed as an unquestioned "politics of location": "The production of knowledge circulates too globally, unevenly, and circuitously to fit neatly into this inside/outside model.... Furthermore, if one posits the possibility of viewing the United States from a purely external vantage, one risks recuperating a vision of the nation as a monolithic, cohesive, and unitary whole, even from a critical perspective" (155). See Kaplan, "The Tenacious Grasp of American Exceptionalism."

resituated "as an international object" and "subject of investigation" ("Defending," 136). He thus calls forth the "common endeavors" of the IASA to foreground the study of America from "criteria and scholarly principles that do not originate in America itself," which means placing at the forefront the perspectives of "non-Americanized Americanists"—those who "have known all along" that the United States was not the center of the world ("Defending," 136, 143, 146). To be sure, Kadir acknowledges that American Studies in the United States ceased "some time ago" to approach its object of study as "a univocal, celebratory occasion"; nonetheless, he repeatedly positions the New Americanism as part of a recuperated exceptionalism that is deaf to its own insularity, such that the turn it inaugurated remains nationalist, in part because it never traveled into the global arena but stayed, as he characterizes it, within the domain of "inequities in America's racial, ethnic, economic, and gender history" ("Defending," 139, 148).

The full force of Kadir's critique of New Americanism emerges later in 2003 in an essay I have already referenced, which serves as the introduction to a special issue of *PMLA* on hemispheric American Studies called "America and Its Studies." In this essay, which names the names that his public address at the IASA conference did not, Kadir refers to Janice Radway's presidential address to the U.S. American Studies Association in 1998, "What's in a Name?" as a "national soliloquy" of "nation-centered and nationalist discourse," and chastises the New Americanism for its work as yet "another tactical turn in the predictable pattern of chronic self-reconsolidation through self-disruption" that characterizes "American discourse."[54] The focus of his strongest identificatory refusal is Pease, whom Kadir positions, with no self-irony, as an agent of self-canonization, the self-promoted leader of the New Americanist guild. For Kadir, the externality that Pease ascribes for New Americanists, as wrought by the political imaginary of social movements and captured by the concept of postnationality, "emerges as a more capacious nationalism that reinscribes the nationalist project, whose cultural dominant proves nothing less than a more variously differentiated nationalism . . . a ruse in the perennial nationalist project of self-affirmation through self-differentiation, broadened

54. Kadir, "Introduction," 22–23, n. 3. Further references to this work are included parenthetically in the text.

in its scope, base, and illusionary political unconscious to the identity formations of 'minorities' or 'disenfranchised groups'" ("America," 19). In this,
Kadir continues, there is "no space between these variegated American
identities and the identification of American American studies taken in as
naturally and as inexorably American. All fissures have been sealed, the
circumscription completed, the wagons impenetrably circled, and America, once again, is securely interred within itself" ("America," 20). The
sweep of Kadir's historical condemnation pivots on an ironic juxtaposition
of the baptism, as he calls Crews's 1988 essay, of New Americanism with
George H. W. Bush's postsocialist declarations of the New World Order
following the official end of the Cold War. Indeed, for Kadir, this is more
than juxtaposition; it is an "uncanny simultaneity" that begets an unconscious affiliation, a way for American Americanists to banish all recognition of the United States as one nation among many to forward instead
the self-narrating and self-fulfilling image of itself, automythic and still
innocent everywhere it goes. By this logic, he writes, in his essay's most
astounding rhetorical moment, "To do American studies as a non-
American . . . is to engage in un-American activities, or—as Bush II would
have it in his historic congressional address on terrorism, counterterror-
ism, and their regimes of truth—if you are not with us, you are one of
them" ("America," 19).

As is no doubt clear, Kadir's masterful reduction of New Americanism
to a repetitious discourse of self-confirming national narcissism simultaneously tropes, even as it refuses, the critical idioms and historicizing logics
of New Americanism in its own gestures of Cold War disavowal. But
more than this, the goal that he seeks—of "an exogenous assessment of
America"—echoes the very externality claimed by Pease even as he excori-
ates Pease, in the tenor of Pease's earlier excoriation of Crews, for being
retrogressively invested in nationalizing mythologies and in orders of
knowledge that make no identificatory break with "America" ("America,"
22). Thus, when Kadir insists that Americanists must "resist interpellation
into the ideology of state apparatuses" and "pursue, consciously and assidu-
ously, a comparative and relational refocusing of America in the larger
world context," he hears no echo of his project in New Americanism, in
part because the psychic temporality of past and future has been split and
the roles of complicity and its negation consigned ("America," 22). Internationalization—no agency of state power, no discourse of recuperative
potential, no product of national imaginaries—stands now on the other

side of the new great divide between what was and what is not yet: an American Studies that, in Kadir's words, will "cease to be American and an instrument of official state policy and become, instead, an independent, international field of inquiry and teaching" ("America," 11).

But what is an independent international field? And on what terms can we ascribe things deemed American to an unquestioned conjunction with the official operations of the state? After all, if the New American Studies is formulated in various ways by the impact and idiom of internationalization, and if its focus on identity and difference can be read as transnational and transcultural, not simply as insular and internal, as it surely can, then how do we arrive at this new Manichean framing of Americanist knowledges? Or more to the point, what position or analytic or epistemological perspective enables the transcendent recoding that inspires it, and precisely how will critics know when the study of "America" has been banished from complicity with the object once and for all? These questions are impossible to answer without undermining the internationalizing impulse altogether, which is why I stated at the outset that its most important contribution was the aspiration it named, not the various arguments put forward to materialize it. And there is nothing in Kadir's argument that leads me to second his call for an "independent international field"—certainly not *one* that seeks to account for relationality on a global scale by generating a critical calculus that knows in advance how to measure the relationship between national subjects and their political complicity. This is why I say that the discourse of internationalization is most interesting as a performance of the critical complexity of everything that it so urgently seeks to correct.

But let me not turn toward the end of this chapter by simply reciting the critical tendency to habitual reinscription, as that would risk leaving my readers with the idea that the main problem to be addressed is Kadir's reliance on refused identification, which places him within the imaginary of the field he seeks to reject. When it comes to the conundrum of internationalization, there's more going on than this. After all, if Kadir's refusal of identification with New Americanism is at home within it, then New Americanism bears the capacity to incorporate even those critiques that most pointedly seek to challenge it, putting the project of getting outside American American Studies right in the middle of it. Such incorporative power has long been understood to belong to hegemonic operations of all kinds; indeed, as Kadir discusses, the appropriation of dissent has been central to America's exceptionalizing idiom, as it absorbs critiques of the history of imperial violence and structural discrimination by converting them into projected ideals, to be forwarded around the world as uniquely America's own.[55] All this could quite powerfully suggest that New American Studies departs in identification from its object of study only long enough to restore it, albeit on less offensive grounds. And yet it is also clear that internationalization is no less burdened by the difficulty of fulfilling its aspirations than is New Americanism, which is why we can read its attempt to escape the hegemonic force of America as the very vehicle that extends and renews it as an internationalized object of concern. In the face of these mutual failures to outrun complicity, we have to say *yes*, as I indicated at the outset. Yes to reading the refused identification of New Americanism as a tactical investment in the object of study, one produced by demonstrating the history of U.S. democratic failure as the means to undermine the exceptionalist alibi routinely used in America's imperial pursuits. Yes too to the failure of internationalization to remain unimplicated in the project of globalization that accompanies the U.S. university's increasingly triumphant interests in transnational and post-national critical frameworks. But also *no*. No to the assumption they both share that takes critical practice as a privileged domain—indeed *the* privileged domain—for simultaneously discerning and doing battle with "America" itself.

Not One

It is no doubt strange for me to ascribe so much seeming agency to a critical operation, as though internationalization actually *is* something. But in what sense is this not true? Left critique in the United States has long been convinced that ideas have material effects (think ideology) or that, in fact, they *are* material (think race). But there is no agreed-upon understanding of precisely how ideas take on a life of their own, which is why at this late date the publishing industry still shows a healthy interest in work that pits the utility of theoretical abstraction against the empirically real.

55. I must remark here on how completely attuned to this rhetorical project was Barack Obama's bid for the U.S. presidency, as demonstrated in any number of his campaign speeches, but see especially his victory speech following the Iowa caucuses on January 3, 2008: "Video: Assessing the First Round," *New York Times* Web site, January 3, 2008, www.nytimes.com/interactive/2008/01/03/multimedia/20080103_IOWA_VIDEO.html#.

The more salient point for my purposes is that conceptual entities such as internationalization may lack ontological or material definition, but they nevertheless *do* something, and that something is often more immediately tangible in the realm of affect and critical investment than in everyday life as a disaggregated whole. This is why I began my discussion by suggesting that the primary value of internationalization is its aspiration and by situating my reading of it less in terms of the effectivity of its claims than the force of the desires that compel it—not, then, as a matter of its ability to revolutionize the ways in which Americanist knowledge is produced and practiced around the world but in the affective domain where the passages of shame, anger, and resistance begin to register the subject forming stakes of doing so. Affect, not conscious formulations. Relationality, not refusal. Implication, not noncomplicity. Differentiation, not opposition.

At the same time, this chapter has made two distinct observations about the internationalizing project. First, I have argued that through its generative impulse to refuse identification with American American Studies, internationalization confirms its commitment to the field imaginary of the entity whose power it hopes to undo by reiterating the field-forming syntax in which refusal, exteriority, and political consciousness are fused. In thus seeking a means to overcome critical complicity not only with "America" as an imperial and globalizing historical entity but with its nation-based institutional study, the discourse of internationalization does not break with the disciplinary demands of New American Studies but defines and defends itself from within them. My second point proceeds from the first but casts its gaze in the opposite direction in order to demonstrate how the disciplinary apparatus of New American Studies is fortified, not threatened, by the challenge that internationalization brings to it. This is the case not only because New Americanism shares the same aspirations that internationalization names, as evidenced by the various scholarly trajectories developed in the past two decades—diaspora, border studies, the postnational, etc.—that have similarly sought to overcome the limits of a nation-based conceptual framework. Even more important is the way that the disciplinary apparatus of New American Studies is generated by the pursuit of critical complicities, such that the exposure of error and failure has a strategic function in sustaining the promise of resolution that stokes the reproduction of the field. Paradoxically, then, the discourse of internationalization is internal to the operations of New American Studies precisely because of the exteriority it claims, which means that in the very act of critiquing New Americanist complicities, internationalization helps to extend the foundational promise that inaugurates the field.

In forwarding these observations, my chapter has not sought to find a way to effect the transformations that internationalization desires, no matter the fact that I wholly endorse the urgency of the concerns it raises for American Studies as a disciplinary formation and academic practice in universities around the world. Nor have I promoted the possibility that other conceptual frameworks—the global or transnational for instance— might fulfill its aspirations by better addressing the problems that currently undermine its critical efforts. Instead, I have gestured toward the idea that American Studies cannot be organized into an internationalized field precisely because "the field" it invokes is not a singular formation. This suggestion, let me emphasize, is not offered as the inaugurating supposition of a new paradigm nor does it carry with it a defining critical agenda for remaking the field. It means to summarize instead the very condition of Americanist knowledge production in order to attend to the disciplinary apparatus in which the commensurability between critical practice and the agency of the object of study is congealed.

The difficult issue my discussion raises then is not about ascribing false agency to internationalization. It has to do instead with what lurks beneath internationalization's aspiration to craft a set of critical practices and priorities that relieve American Studies from being implicated in the global power of its object of study. This is not simply the belief, as I have suggested above, that the relationship between the practitioner and her object of study is both an index and inscription of the social relations of U.S. global hegemony, but that practitioners can attend to the one as a means of attending to the other. In the end, such an investment in critical practice as a political agency is enabled less by the specific determinations of the field imaginary in which Americanist knowledge is produced, internationalist or not, than by the *imaginary of the field* through which the pursuit of noncomplicity takes hold. This imaginary confers political agency on every gesture of field transformation, not only in American Studies but in other fields of study, as *Object Lessons* explores. It is the practitioner's first and most enduring disciplinary romance. It is this imaginary that promises to carry internationalization from the complicities that variously incite it to the fantastic wish for an uncontaminated future that it stands for.

FIVE

....

Critical Kinship

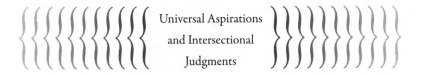

Universal Aspirations
and Intersectional
Judgments

If the critical aspiration of internationalization was meant to generate distance between the critic and the toxic power of her object of study, the imperative to intersectional analysis under scrutiny in this chapter works to an opposite end.[1] Not distance but proximity; not the refusal

1. For signal work that addresses intersectionality, see Crenshaw, "Demarginalizing the Intersection of Race and Sex" and "Mapping the Margins"; Culp, "Colorblind Remedies and the Intersectionality of Oppression"; Caldwell, "A Hair Piece"; Collins, *Fighting Words*; Hutchinson, "Identity Crisis"; Brah and Phoenix, "Ain't I a Woman"; McCall, "The Complexity of Intersectionality"; Zack, *Inclusive Feminism*; Nash, "Rethinking Intersectionality"; Davis, "Intersectionality as Buzzword"; Peterson, "Interactive and Intersectional Analytics of Globalization"; Weber, *Understanding Race, Class, Gender, and Sexuality*; Berger and Guidroz, *The Intersectional Approach*; and Dill and Zambrana, *Emerging Intersections*.

Various journals have had special issues on the topic. See especially *Journal of Intercultural Studies* 31.1 (2010); *International Feminist Journal of Politics* 11.4 (2009); *Politics*

of identification but intimacy and attachment. In its contrast with the projects we have just examined, intersectionality is not chiefly interested in superordinated identity forms or in the prospect of wrenching political intention from unconscious complicity in order to sustain belief in political futurity. On the contrary. It takes the key impediment to identity-oriented justice as the problem of *partial attention* and locates such partiality in the universalizing effects that attend the institutionalized monotheism of identity as a solo sojourn, now compartmentalized—if not departmentalized—under the singular rubrics of race, gender, sexuality, or nation. By posing itself as a counter to single-axis analysis, intersectionality pursues not only complexity but particularity, specifically through the critical location attributed to both black women and black feminism *and* in such a way that no configuration of identity as a constructed social relation of power and subordination is thought to be beyond its analytic reach. In this, it promises to overcome partiality through comprehensive attention, generating a critical practice that gives difference to identity in order to discern identity's multiple and proliferating intensities, inequities, and political agencies. Given its citational ubiquity no less than the optimism it can afford, it is no exaggeration to say that intersectionality circulates today as *the* primary figure of political completion in U.S. identity knowledge domains. This is especially the case in field conversations collated to feminist ends where, in the words of Naomi Zack, intersectionality is a "leading feminist paradigm" if not, as Leslie McCall cites it, "the most important theoretical contribution that women's studies . . . has made so far."[2] In the discourse of program documents and national field organizations, it is repeatedly posited as both a core pedagogical tenant and a field-defining analytic and institutional goal.[3] In-

---

and Gender 3.2 (June 2007): 229–80; *European Journal of Women's Studies* 13.3 (July 2006); *American Literature* 77.1 (March 2005); *Feminist Economics* 8.2 (2002); *Journal of Contemporary Legal Issues* 11.2 (2001); *Social Text* 52/53 15.3–4 (1997); and *Hastings Law Journal* 48.6 (August 1997).

See also the "post-intersectionality" archive: Valdes, "Sex and Race in Queer Legal Culture"; Kwan, "Intersections of Race, Ethnicity, Class, Gender and Sexual Orientation"; Hutchinson, "Out Yet Unseen"; Ehrenreich, "Subordination and Symbiosis"; and Chang and Culp, "After Intersectionality."

2. Zack, *Inclusive Feminism*, 1; and McCall, "The Complexity of Intersectionality," 1771.

3. My home department is no exception, as our mission is described, in language I helped to draft, as an exploration of "the meaning and impact of identity as a primary

deed, faith in its promise to be commensurate with the political desire that calls it forth is so far reaching that any inquiry into the field imaginary of identity knowledges would be incomplete without attending to the affective investments that are produced and refracted by its critical commitments.

To be sure, this description is a far more accurate reflection of intersectionality's critical reputation and frequent rhetorical invocation than an encounter with either the intricate details of its analytic emergence or the ongoing controversy over how best to put its intentions to use.[4] But I open this chapter by rehearsing the expansive aspirations that are now attached to it in order to foreground the paradox that attends it: that while intersectionality draws its critical courage and reputation by positing particularity in the face of universalizations of all kinds, it routinely travels unaccompanied by a rich *critical* particularity of its own. By this, I mean that the narratives that frame its academic circulations are not keyed to the specific disciplinary and political conjunctures that have shaped its critical history. Rather, these narratives partake in just the kind of extrapolations that mark my description above, where the failure of partial perspective is overcome by the promise of a paradigmatic resolution, and the particularity of black women's identity position functions as the formative ground for a critical practice aimed at infinite inclusion. The leaps engaged here are most arresting if set in slower motion. On what terms, for instance, can the commitment to particularity take paradigmatic shape without sacrificing its force as a counter to universalizing tendencies? Or more to the point, how can particularity retain the specificity it evokes when the destination it inscribes is to render critical

---

though by no means transhistorical or universal way of organizing social life by pursuing an *intersectional* analysis of gender, race, sexuality, class, and nationality. In the classroom, as in our research, our goal is to transform the university's organization of knowledge by reaching across the epistemological and methodological divisions of historical, political, philosophical, economic, representational, technological and scientific analysis. In our Program's dual emphasis on interdisciplinarity and intersectionality, we offer students new knowledge while equipping them with a wide range of analytical and methodological skills" (http://womenstudies.duke.edu/about, accessed August 25, 2010).

4. According to Kathy Davis, there are three key debates about intersectionality: "how the concept should be defined, its appropriate parameters, and how it should be used" ("Intersectionality as Buzzword," 77).

practice not simply coherent but comprehensive in its analytic capacity and scope? Both of these questions point to the tension between intersectionality as a commitment to the particularity of black women's minoritization and its redeployment as the means to claim paradigmatic mastery over both the experiences of women of color and identity's historical, social, political, and psychic complexity as a whole. But in the circuits in which intersectionality moves as a critical aspiration and analytic tool, such a contradiction is not only *not* disabling, it is positively sustaining as it provides a relation to the universal that does not have to be feared. In this, feminist commitments to justice can be disarticulated from the errors of *women's* overreach to pursue the possibility of a critical practice that never excludes. "What more could one desire from feminist inquiry?" Kathy Davis asks, in an argument that defends intersectionality's utility precisely because of the way that its lack of definition and analytic specificity generates the expansiveness of its political claims.[5] Because of its "ambiguity . . . vagueness and inherent open-endedness," she writes, intersectionality enables a "process of discovery which not only is potentially interminable, but promises to yield new and more comprehensive and reflexively critical insights"; in these terms, its critical value is sustained by the paradox that attends it, as the "infinite

---

5. Davis, "Intersectionality as Buzzword," 77. Not all scholars would agree with Davis's defense of intersectionality on the basis of its lack of analytic distinctions and critical definition. Many seek to confirm its importance by enhancing its critical rigor. Dorthe Staunæs, for instance, argues for more attention to lived experience in order to better understand how the intersections between "gender, ethnicity, race, age, sexuality and class" are inhabited ("Where Have All the Subjects Gone?," 101). Sunila Abeysekara wants to explicate the importance of ethnicity and of ethnic conflict in thinking about women's particularity in various world regions ("Racism, Ethnicity, and Peace"). Marjo Buitelaar seeks to foreground first-person narration, thereby understanding both narrative practice and subjective formation as predicated on intersectional relations ("'I Am the Ultimate Challenge'"). Nira Yuval-Davis argues for the "need to differentiate carefully between different kinds of difference" in order to expand intersectional understanding from a "focus on the particular positions of women of colour" to "more general terms, applicable to any grouping of people, advantaged as well as disadvantaged" ("Intersectionality and Feminist Politics," 199, 201). Gill Valentine argues for intersectional engagements with the case study ("Theorizing and Researching Intersectionality"), while Ange-Marie Hancock forges intersectionality as a "normative and empirical paradigm" that can "more comprehensively answer questions of distributive justice, power, and government function" ("Intersectionality as a Normative and Empirical Paradigm," 249–50).

regress built into the concept . . . allows endless constellations of intersecting lines of difference to be explored."[6]

This is not to say that intersectionality travels without a distinct citational history. It certainly does, which is why its inaugural theorist, Kimberlé Crenshaw, is familiar to students and scholars in every identity-based field. But while Crenshaw focused explicitly on the relations between race and gender, and on the intersectionality "of Black women's experience," the work that has developed under its critical framework assumes a much farther-reaching capacity, one that seeks to account for both familiar and emergent formations of race, gender, class, sexuality, nationality, religion, and increasingly health, age, and ability.[7] Indeed, it is quite striking how often scholarship passes over a substantive engagement with Crenshaw's arguments, taking intersectionality instead as a paradigmatic address against any universalism or single-axis analysis of identity and difference on behalf of black women or more generically women of color—and not as a concept originating in a very specific emplotment of power and subordination. In the narrative gestures that write intersectionality as a critical discourse aimed at feminism's completion, Crenshaw's work is thus figured as the expression of impulses and aspirations that preceded it, not as the origination of the project that intersectionality is taken to name. In the 2006 special issue on intersectionality of the *European Journal of Women's Studies*, for instance, the guest editors produce a narrative that is now familiar: "Long before the term 'intersectionality' was coined in 1989 by Kimberlé Crenshaw, the concept it denotes had been employed in feminist work on how women are simultaneously positioned as women and, for example, as black, working-class, lesbian or colonial subjects."[8] For this reason, the editors take intersectionality to be "useful as a handy catchall phrase that aims to make visible the multiple positioning that constitutes everyday life and the power relations that are central to it."[9] Crenshaw's "coinage" of intersectionality is similarly positioned in other critical histories as the consolidation, even the critical summation, of ongoing efforts.[10]

6. Davis, "Intersectionality as Buzzword," 77.

7. Crenshaw, "Demarginalizing the Intersection of Race and Sex," 139.

8. Phoenix and Pattynama, "Editorial," 187.

9. Phoenix and Pattynama, "Editorial," 187.

10. Most often these efforts are located in second-wave feminism, but scholars have also used black women's political struggles in the nineteenth century as the temporal

For Patricia Hill Collins, the term evokes black feminist critiques of single-axis analysis in favor of explicating what she first called "the matrix of domination" and what others have termed "double jeopardy," "multiple jeopardy," the "simultaneity of oppression," and "interlocking systems of oppression."[11] Jennifer C. Nash's recent "Re-thinking Intersectionality" locates intersectionality similarly, citing Crenshaw's formulation as part of a history of black feminist theorizing: "Myriad feminist scholars have destabilized the notion of a universal 'woman' without explicitly mobilizing the term 'intersectionality,' arguing that . . . the experience of 'woman' is always constituted by subjects with vastly different interests. To that end, intersectionality has provided a name to a pre-existing theoretical and political commitment."[12]

The narrative of intersectionality's belated arrival is an especially interesting one for the itinerary of *Object Lessons*, not the least because of its contrast with the general habits of feminist critical practice, which routinely confer on *the namer* much more than citational status and rarely posit a scholar's articulation of a term in the lower register that "coinage" infers. Indeed the namer is more often than not elevated in stature, becoming both the referent and agency for the analytic tradition she is taken to inaugurate and represent. Think here of Judith Butler's figural status in poststructuralist feminist theory or Gayatri Spivak's signatory representation of postcolonial deconstruction or Donna Haraway's canonical designation

---

framework for narrating the origin of intersectional commitments. For the former, see Collins, "It's All in the Family"; for the latter see Jordan-Zachery, "Am I a Black Woman or a Woman Who Is Black?"

11. On "the matrix of domination," see Collins, *Black Feminist Thought*; "double jeopardy," see Beale, "Double Jeopardy"; "multiple jeopardy," see King, "Multiple Jeopardy, Multiple Consciousness"; "simultaneity of oppression," see Hull et al., *All the Women Are White*; and "interlocking systems of oppression," see Combahee River Collective, "A Black Feminist Statement."

12. Nash, "Re-thinking Intersectionality," 2. In addition to the works already cited, intersectionality's prehistory is typically drawn to include: Dill, "The Dialectics of Black Womanhood"; Carby, "White Woman Listen!"; Davis, *Women, Race, and Class*; hooks, *Ain't I a Woman?* and *Feminist Theory*; Lugones and Spelman, "Have We Got a Theory for You!"; Moraga and Anzaldúa, *This Bridge Called My Back*; Smith, *Home Girls*; Giddings, *When and Where I Enter*; Glenn, "Racial Ethnic Women's Labor"; Spelman, *Inessential Woman*; and Mohanty, "Under Western Eyes."

as the originator of cyborgian feminism or even Nancy Hartsock's textual centrality to feminist standpoint epistemologies. In these instances, the feminist archive has elaborated a conversation through ongoing argument, contestation, and critical dissection about the analytic capacities and political utilities of each author's work *and* the texts that found or extend the tradition they represent. In some cases, the context in which they argued and the ideas they cultivated from conversations with others have been deleted entirely from the archive, thereby dispensing even more critical capital to the signature that comes to preside over a shared body of work.[13] Given these kinds of contextual effacements, it is certainly compelling, even commendable, that the narrative about intersectionality's critical origin refuses the lure of the signature in favor of a history of collective critical and political endeavor.[14] But what happens in the process to the theoretical contours of the term as Crenshaw developed it and to the specificity of her opening argument, which located the critical problem of attending to black women's subordination in the operations of antidiscrimination law? Is Crenshaw's intersectionality theoretically commensurate with the critical aspirations now ascribed to it as the means to generate comprehensive accounts of the operations of identity and subordination in the social world as a whole? Does it revise or invent, elaborate or subvert, extend or

13. This is why I often begin my feminist theory graduate seminar with texts from the 1970s, including Gayle Rubin's "The Traffic in Women," in order to demonstrate that the 1990s was not the origin of (1) feminist interest in critical theory; (2) a rigorous anti-essentialism; (3) attention to the organization of gender outside the United States; or (4) interest in the question of women's differences from *woman*. When students later read Monique Wittig, they are surprised to "discover" that poststructuralism is not the only way to think about symbolic systems, just as they are surprised to learn that Audre Lorde regularly relied on poetry, not critique, to forge commitments to feminist cross-race analysis and alliance. See Rubin, "The Traffic in Women."

14. While not the destination of this chapter's inquiry, a much longer conversation is needed to explore the way that the narrative of intersectionality's origins often condenses a wide range of overlapping and divergent political interests in the 1980s, as multiple feminist political projects—black feminism, socialist feminism, lesbian feminism, anti-imperialist feminism, and all of the permutations and cross traffic in between— were working on the theorization of what some activists and theorists jokingly called the holy trinity, "gender, race, and class." For a very selective look at the socialist feminist literature, see Haraway, "A Manifesto for Cyborgs"; Mies, *Patriarchy and Accumulation of a World Scale*; and Sacks, "Toward a Unified Theory of Class, Race, and Gender."

limit the multiple projects and general destinations that have been used to represent intersectionality's political commitments? In other words, what is the relationship between intersectionality's theoretical origin as a concept and framework and the term's massive circulation as the name of a body of scholarship that is taken simultaneously to both precede and outlive it? And what does it mean that intersectionality functions today by tacking back and forth between a demand for the particular and a promise that through it every relation of subordination can be brought into critical view?

The discussion that follows is organized around the assumption that Crenshaw's theorization of intersectionality has been de-referentialized in its interdisciplinary travels, such that the direct address to the state that attended her initial reading of the operations of race and gender in antidiscrimination doctrine has undergone a transformation, generating the sense, now pervasive in academic uses of the term, that intersectionality is *in itself* ameliorative, which is to say that its use does more than explicate black women's experience: It works against their domination by revealing the relations of exclusion that link their subordination across the otherwise disparate spheres of law, activism, and theory. To be sure, Crenshaw's theorization encouraged just such a critical extrapolation, as the concept was initially developed by twinning a radical rereading of the atomization of race and gender in U.S. discrimination law with an equally radical, indeed devastating, critique of the way that both black antiracist politics and feminist theory repeated the law's tactical mistake. In the first of her two foundational essays, "Demarginalizing the Intersection of Race and Sex," Crenshaw analyzed a series of court cases with black female plaintiffs by examining the doctrinal "tendency to treat race and gender as mutually exclusive categories" in order to rethink "the entire framework that has been used as a basis for translating "women's experience" or "the Black experience" into *concrete policy demands*."[15] The state was thus the central and, I will argue, paradigmatic agency of power toward which the political stakes of intersectionality, no less than its rhetorical invocation, were turned, which formally constituted the practices of antiracist activism and feminist theory as political projects in an explicitly juridical sense—as contestatory, plaintiff-based, and representational. Hence it is no exaggeration to say that Crenshaw's

15. Crenshaw, "Demarginalizing the Intersection," 140, emphasis added.

inaugural formulation worked to confer statelike authority on its own critical discernments, inaugurating intersectionality as a figure of value set not simply against the law but toward the fulfillment of justice that the juridical state was said to inadequately deliver.

Today of course intersectional analysis travels well beyond the disciplinary domain of law and its strategies of representation and resolution, and yet it is my sense that the juridical imaginary first emergent in Crenshaw's theory continues to govern intersectionality wherever it goes. Even Crenshaw's work participates in the de-referentialization I identify here, as her subsequent essay, "Mapping the Margins," turns away from antidiscrimination doctrine to address the "structural, political, and representational aspects of violence against women of color" as a collective entity.[16] In a footnote, Crenshaw articulates the political commitment that underwrites this critical expansion, reiterating as intersectionality's own juridical truths the conclusions that the analysis of antidiscrimination law helped to deliver.

> I explicitly adopt a Black feminist stance ... cognizant of several tensions that such a position entails. The most significant one stems from the criticism that while feminism purports to speak *for* women of color through its invocation of the term "woman," the feminist perspective excludes women of color because it is based upon the experiences and interests of a certain subset of women. *On the other hand*, when white feminists attempt to include other women, they often add our experiences into an otherwise unaltered framework. It is important to name the perspective from which one constructs her analysis; and for me, that is as a Black feminist. Moreover, it is important to acknowledge that the materials that I incorporate in my analysis are drawn heavily from research on Black women. *On the other hand*, I see my own work as part of a broader collective effort among feminists of color to expand feminism to include analyses of race and other factors such as class, sexuality, and age. I have attempted therefore to offer my sense of the tentative connections between my analysis of the intersectional experiences of Black women and the intersectional experiences of other women of color. I stress that this analysis is not intended to include falsely nor to exclude unnecessarily other women of color.[17]

16. Crenshaw, "Mapping the Margins," 1244.
17. Crenshaw, "Mapping the Margins," 1244, n. 8, emphasis added.

What interests me most is the anxiety that accompanies Crenshaw's description of her critical investments, for in the double usage of the phrase "On the other hand," she rather confoundingly depicts the tripartite relationships among black women, white women, and "other women of color" according to a binary division. While this division allows for the consolidation of women of color against white feminist exclusions, it inadvertently reveals the analytic difficulty that accompanies the wish that inspires it, as Crenshaw was clearly concerned that an overemphasis on black women's experience as the evidentiary ground for discerning the domain of "violence against women of color" would repeat white feminism's blindness by similarly subordinating some women's experiences in favor of those of others. As this chapter develops, I will pay attention to the consequences of the analytic relations arrayed here, between the rhetorical function of intersectionality to address white feminist exclusions and the resonant difficulty of projecting black women's experience as the paradigm of racialized gender for women of color as a whole. At the same time, I will be interested in how the rhetorical power that is amassed in this critical expansion is contingent on the juridical foundation that ushers intersectionality into its theoretical distinction and commits its rhetorical voice and analytic perspective not simply to the particularity of black women's experience but to the critical location in U.S. feminist theory from which such a perspective departs. In this, feminist theory is simultaneously approached and inhabited through the juridical imaginary that defines intersectionality as a critical act of political intervention.

The work that intersectionality performs as the privileged figure of justice in interdisciplinary feminist domains is thus complex and contradictory: Its power emerges precisely from its origin in law and in rhetorics of address to the state that generate the juridical imaginary that governs it even as its analytic limit is reached in the equation it repeatedly exacts between critical practice and legal justice. By addressing the ways in which the juridical imaginary founds intersectionality's critical power, this chapter pauses over the analytic impasse it cannot help but engender: where its figural resolution as a comprehensive, inclusive, and multidimensional approach to the intersections of race and gender not only renders "Black women's experience" paradigmatic, but stakes intersectional reason on the force of the protocols of paradigmatic reading it hones. To demonstrate why I take this to be so, the chapter follows a circuitous route across different and at times incommensurate archives, from legal cases stoked by disputes over property and personhood arising from assisted conception, to feminist theory and its keen interest in reproduction, to popular culture where national narratives about race and sex are managed and transformed. Through my central case study, in which a white woman gave birth to a black child whose embryo was not her own, I explore the difficulties that ensue for an intersectional feminism already committed to gestation as the means to achieve resolutions that prioritize black women's experience and interests. At the same time, I expand on earlier discussions in *Object Lessons* about the pedagogical influence of Civil Rights on the reconstruction of white subjectivity in the postsegregation era, where emergent emphases on multicultural and multiracial commitments sought to refigure white supremacy's historical violence in new modes of cross-racial feeling, identification, and affiliation. As the title indicates, "kinship" is this chapter's central figure, serving both to define the wish that mobilizes intersectional commitments and to foreground the trope that links the different kinds of materials it arrays, all of which grapple with the fiction of the monoracial family that attends the historical convergence of race, sex, and nation. The theoretical arc of the chapter is thus dedicated to assembling incongruent sites of discussion—legal cases, feminist theory, and popular film—to pose questions both about the paradigmatic protocols of intersectional reading and the difficulty of rendering coherent the conflicted relations of race, sex, and reproduction today.

What follows, let me be clear, is not a critique of intersectionality; I am trying neither to rewrite its theoretical operations nor to reformulate its critical or political utility.[18] Nor do I take up this discussion to claim, as does Wendy Brown, that race, gender, and sexuality are incommensurate in their juridical constitution, social formation, and/or psychic configuration such that law displays the impossibility that Women's Studies and other identity domains inherit, which is to account for "the complex, compound, internally diverse and divided subjects that we are."[19] The point, to follow the idioms and intuitions of *Object Lessons*, is to pay attention to the critical densities of the political desire that has been invested in intersectional analysis, which more forcefully than anywhere else in the archives

18. For an argument that takes these approaches, see Puar, "'I Would Rather Be a Cyborg Than a Goddess.'"

19. Brown, "The Impossibility of Women's Studies," 92. See my response, "Feminism, Institutionalism, and the Idiom of Failure."

of identity knowledges has made a claim on "black women's experience" as its own. If the previous chapter analyzed the field imaginary of the New Americanists as a defense against implication in the global power and imperial violence of the field's object of study, this chapter seeks to discern intersectional investments as the means to do justice through critical kinship with its object of study. In doing so, in exacting its obligation to the figure that compels its analysis, intersectionality becomes enthralled to an object of study that must conform to the shape of its critical desires, which is to say to the shape of the authority it draws *from her* perspective and social position in order to confer *on her* the very epistemological priority and legal autonomy it promises *to her*. To take the disciplinary apparatus I discern here as an indictment of intersectional analysis is to hear a judgment I do not intend, as this chapter is not concerned with measuring the value of the promises that intersectionality makes but with the lessons at stake in fully inhabiting them. What interests me most is how intersectionality as a critical practice is motivated by love.

Case and Context

On April 24, 1998, Donna Fasano, a white woman, and Deborah Perry-Rogers, a black woman, underwent in vitro fertilization at a fertility clinic in midtown Manhattan.[20] While each woman received her own fertilized eggs, Donna was accidently given three of Deborah's embryos as well. Only Donna, the white woman, became pregnant, and in December 1998 she gave birth to two boys, one of whom, DNA tests showed, was not genetically hers. As the media declared, Donna Fasano had delivered "twins," "one white, one black," but the status of her motherhood was immediately

20. I am drawing my information on this case from both legal and media sources. On the former see *Perry-Rogers v. Fasano*, 715 N.Y.S.2d 19 (App. Div. 2000); *Perry-Rogers v. Obasaju*, 282 A.D.2d 231 (N.Y. App. Div. 2001); *Fasano v. Nash*, 282 A.D.2d 277 (N.Y. App. Div. 2001); Bender, "Genes, Parents, and Assisted Reproductive Technologies"; and Felder, " 'Perry-Rogers v. Fasano.' " On the latter see especially Grunwald, "In Vitro, in Error—And Now, in Court"; Newman, "Visiting Rights Denied in Embryo Mix-Up Case"; Rohde, "Biological Parents Win in Implant Case"; and various articles by Jim Yardley, "After Embryo Mix-Up, Couple Say They Will Give Up a Baby," "Health Officials Investigating to Determine How Woman Got the Embryo of Another," "Sharing Baby Proves Rough on 2 Mothers," and "Pregnant with Meaning."

challenged as Deborah and her husband Robert filed for custody of Joseph Fasano, who was determined to be their genetic child.[21] In March 1999, the couples reached a custody agreement: The Fasanos would give Joseph to the Rogerses if the twins would be raised as brothers. "We're giving him up because we love him," Donna Fasano explained to reporters.[22] In May, one day after Mother's Day, as the *Washington Post* duly noted, the Fasanos relinquished the child to the Rogerses, who renamed him Akeil.[23] The custody agreement was short-lived, however, and by the end of June, the couples were in court. The Fasanos claimed that the Rogerses had broken the agreement by refusing to allow Akeil to spend a weekend at their home; the Rogerses cited Donna's disregard for their parental authority, as she continued to refer to herself as the child's mother and assured him that "mommy is here."[24] David Cohen, the Fasano attorney, explained the Fasanos's perspective: "[They] don't see [Joseph] as someone else's black baby; they see him as their baby."[25] Or in Donna Fasano's words, "He has two mothers. I am his mother, and Mrs. Rogers definitely is his genetic mother."[26] Rudolph Silas, attorney for the Rogerses, countered, "The child can only have one mother, and on that we're very adamant."[27] The court agreed and

21. In using the language of "mother" and "child" here, I am troping the discourse of the courts and the contesting adults, all of whom participated in reproducing social kinship forms from the processes of technological reproduction. The sheer enormity of trying to indicate the passage from the socialization of "nature" to a naturalized "social" is part of what this chapter explores, even as I admit to having failed to find a way to interrupt the language that consolidates these relations. At earlier stages of its writing, the chapter marked each figure—mother, father, child, brother, family—through the grammatical index of the quotation, but in the end this was far too burdensome and so numbing as to become ineffectual. More important to note is how the naturalized language that shapes the domain of assisted conception is repeatedly under assault by the very forms of technological assistance the fertility industry provides. Its own market-oriented need to convince consumers of its "naturalness" is just one of the reasons for the aggressive assertion of the normative logics of reproduction, biology, and kinship in a domain dedicated to addressing the failure of nature to do its normative work.

22. Quoted in Grunwald, "In Vitro, in Error—And Now, in Court."

23. Throughout this chapter, I use both "Akeil" and "Joseph" to refer to the contested child, depending on which family's perspective is being referenced.

24. Quoted in Yardley, "Sharing Baby Proves Rough on 2 Mothers."

25. Quoted in Grunwald, "In Vitro, in Error—And Now, in Court."

26. Quoted in Yardley, "Sharing Baby Proves Rough on 2 Mothers."

27. Quoted in Yardley, "Sharing Baby Proves Rough on 2 Mothers."

in September 1999 it declared Deborah Perry-Rogers both the biological and legal mother.[28]

But the struggle over Akeil continued for another year, as the Fasanos sought to defend their right to a relationship with the child, in part by emphasizing that bonding had occurred both during pregnancy and in the first months of life. In the end, the New York appellate court rejected the Fasanos' argument and annulled the custody arrangement along with the Fasanos' right to visitation altogether. The decision reasoned that "any bonding . . . was the direct result of the Fasanos' failure to take timely action upon being informed of the clinic's admitted error. Defendants cannot be permitted to purposefully act in such a way as to create a bond, and then rely upon it for their assertion of rights to which they would not otherwise be entitled."[29] For the court, the Fasanos would not have been otherwise entitled because they were not biologically related to the Rogerses, nor were the children borne by Donna Fasano related—at least not under domestic relations law, which, the court pointed out, had no mechanism to confer legal recognition on "gestational siblings" who were "biological strangers" as only human beings born together who were tied " 'by half or by whole blood' " were legally entitled to recognition as brothers.[30] As the court emphasized, "where defendants knew of the error not long after it occurred, the happenstance of their nominal parenthood over plaintiff's child should have been treated as a mistake to be corrected as soon as possible."[31] To be sure, the court affirmed that the gestational mother had legal standing to sue and that, as one analyst of the case put it, "the term 'genetic stranger' alone . . . can no longer be enough to end a discussion of this issue."[32] But the authority of the mistake and the contractual intentions that underwrote it set the terms in which both intimate affect and

28. In the well-known Baby M case, the woman who was the surrogate in a contract-based conception was designated the child's biological mother, but legal custody went to the person who had initiated the contract and donated the sperm. More often, however, the legally designated biological mother retains legal custody as well. See Allen, "Privacy, Surrogacy and the *Baby M* Case"; and Patterson, "Surrogacy and Slavery."

29. *Perry-Rogers v. Fasano*, 715 N.Y.S.2d 19 (App. Div. 2000), at 26.

30. *Perry-Rogers v. Fasano*, 715 N.Y.S.2d 19 (App. Div. 2000), at 26.

31. *Perry-Rogers v. Fasano*, 715 N.Y.S.2d 19 (App. Div. 2000), at 26.

32. National Legal Research Group, "The Liability of Reproductive Laboratories for Mistakenly Provided Genetic Material."

proper belonging were legislated, making the Fasanos' attachment to Joseph an error.

While earlier court cases involving reproductive technologies raised similar issues about the authoritative status of genetics versus gestation, *Perry-Rogers v. Fasano* is importantly unique in the history of assisted conception in the United States. It features the first woman, Donna Fasano, to be defined as both genetic mother (to the white child) and gestational mother (to the black child) in the same live birth.[33] In addition, it foregrounds the medical reality of black infertility, which is almost wholly illegible from within a dominant cultural discourse overwritten by notions of hyperreproductive and socially vampiristic black maternity.[34] How Deborah Perry-Rogers secures her claim to natural maternity is in part a story about twin contracts: with the fertility clinic that offered technological assistance for genetic reproduction, and with the state that sanctioned and naturalized, via the patriarchal marriage contract, her (hetero)sexual activity and the procreative property it might beget. At work in both of these contract relations is the property logic of liberal personhood, by which I mean the formation of social subjects within a modern state apparatus that recognizes and confers personhood on the basis of contractual relations—on the ability to enter into and stand as a responsible agent in a

33. She is not, however, the first white woman to give birth to two children genetically classified as racially different. In 1993 a Dutch fertility clinic mistakenly fertilized a woman's eggs with the sperm of both her white husband and a black man. She gave birth to twin boys and the white couple is now raising both of them under the legal standard that gives custody to the biological mother and to her husband, regardless of whether or not he is the child's biological father. This case is interesting because the white couple purposely went looking for the genetic father after the mistake became known in order to engage him—if he were so willing—in the life of his genetic son. See Simons, "Uproar over Twins, and a Dutch Couple's Anguish"; Elliot and Endt, "Twins—With Two Fathers"; and Liebler, "Are You My Parent?" The case is also referenced by Yardley, "Health Officials Investigating," and discussed briefly by Roberts, *Killing the Black Body*, 252.

34. According to statistics widely cited on this point, black infertility rates in the 1990s were 1.5 times higher than those of whites, while nearly twice as many whites sought medical assistance for infertility. See New York State Task Force on Life and the Law, *Assisted Reproductive Technologies*; Roberts, "The Nature of Blacks' Skepticism about Genetic Testing"; Wilcox and Mosher, "Use of Infertility Services in the United States"; and Ikemoto, "The In/Fertile, the Too Fertile, and the Dysfertile."

contract obligation to both the state (as citizen) and to other citizens (as transactors of labor and property ownership on one hand and as recognized heteronormative married subjects on the other).[35] These domains of contract obligation—of citizen, spouse, and laborer/owner—have operated historically as powerful pedagogies for both the production and excision of "proper national subjects," mediating the terrain of formal state inclusion and its expression and exercise in everyday life as evinced in the birth certificate, the voting card, the draft card, the passport, and the marriage license. Despite its pedagogical double bind—where entitlement is the biopolitical mechanism of discipline and obligation—liberal personhood in U.S. racial and sexual narratives bears the symbolic figure of democratic institutionalization, which means that political mobilizations that have succeeded in unraveling its racialized and sexual exclusions have also worked to suture the idea of "freedom" to it. Winning under its auspices is a contradictory inheritance, but it is here that Deborah and Robert Rogers secure their status as the natural biological parents of Akeil—an outcome that stands in contrast to a much longer history of legal judgments against African American claims for property rights in the realm of reproduction.[36]

And what of Donna Fasano, a white woman who gave birth to a black child she hoped to legally claim as her own?[37] As the beneficiary of the clinic's mistake, she inherited property that was not, legally speaking, her

35. Patricia Williams has written eloquently about the institution of contract law and the complexity of "self-possession" in U.S. life. See her "Fetal Fictions." See also Naffine, "The Legal Structure of Self-Ownership."

36. According to stories run in *Jet* magazine about the case, Deborah Perry-Rogers worked as a nurse, while Robert was a teacher, and the Fasanos were in finance. Both couples lived in New Jersey. Donna was thirty-seven at the time of the first court case, while Deborah was thirty-three. See "White Couple Gives Baby to His Black Genetic Parents."

37. Let me note here that in using the language of "black" and "white" in my own references to the children, I have purposely chosen not to speak of their identities in terms of national-racial cultures, as in Anglo- or European American and African American. While the discourse of color is frequently critiqued (and rightly so) in critical race theory, the postulation that the children bear cultural identities that proceed from their corporeal descriptions carries the risk of de-essentializing the discourse of race in the domain of the body by re-essentializing it in the domain of culture. In other words, it is just as difficult to ward off essentialism in talking about culture, cultural traditions, and cultural identities as it is in approaching the domain of the physical body. For a discus-

own, which made her part of a longer history in which whiteness is linked to improper property acquisition.[38] From this perspective, Donna Fasano's attempt to privatize her own reproduction, to make her body speak the authority of gestation—of labor and belonging—is both a defense against the symbolic historical positioning she inherited from the clinic's mistake and a historical repetition of the property logic of race. And yet, it is not simply a repetition, in the sense that her desire to authorize white maternity of a black child, to have her body recognized as the agency of black life, places her in the realm of what I want to call *multiracial desire* as it relates to but is distinct from the interracial, which has haunted the "American family" for more than two centuries. Imagine the conjuncture. In November 1998, as Donna Fasano was about to enter her eighth month of pregnancy, the journal *Nature* published the first account of genetic research that offered to settle the debate over Thomas Jefferson's sexual relation to his slave, Sally Hemings: "DNA analysis confirms that Jefferson was indeed the father of at least one of Hemings' children."[39] The controversy over Jefferson's paternity was of course a controversy only to some. To a host of scholars in American and African American Studies the historical evidence had long been convincing.[40] Still, many of the white descendants

sion of the culturalist turn in racial thinking, see Pascoe, "Miscegenation Law, Court Cases, and Ideologies of 'Race' in Twentieth-Century America."

38. See Harris, "Whiteness as Property"; and Lipsitz, *The Possessive Investment in Whiteness.*

39. Lander and Ellis, "Founding Father," 13. See also Foster et al., "Jefferson Fathered Slave's Last Child" and "The Thomas Jefferson Paternity Case."

40. The evidence in favor of viewing Jefferson as the father of all of Hemings's children included the first-person testimony of Madison, Sally Hemings's fourth child; the 100 percent correlation between the timing of Hemings's pregnancies and Jefferson's presence at Monticello; and the strong physical resemblances between Jefferson and several of Hemings's children. Annette Gordon-Reed's two book-length studies collect these and other forms of knowledge about Jefferson's relation to Sally Hemings. See *Thomas Jefferson and Sally Hemings* and *The Hemingses of Monticello*. See also DuCille, "Where in the World Is William Wells Brown?"; and Chinn, "Reading the 'Book of Life.'"

For some defenders of the racial "integrity" of the Jefferson line, the authority of DNA was crucial to dislodging their long-standing objections. The Thomas Jefferson Association, which owns and operates Monticello, launched its private investigation of the genetic study and publicly affirmed the "high probability that Thomas Jefferson fathered Eston Hemings, and that he most likely was the father of all six of Sally

of Jefferson remained unconvinced. Monticello Association President Nathaniel Abeles expressed the perspective of the largest organization of Jefferson's white descendants: "They have not provided conclusive evidence that Thomas Jefferson had a relationship with Sally Hemings."[41] The wish this disavowal represents for sexual allegiances to white origins is the powerful manufacture of fantasy under whose tutelage facts, no less than human beings, have been born. In this context, it is hardly a surprise that the scientific truth of *Nature* proves inconsequential to the white Jeffersons' need to maintain belief that their wish for purity is true.[42]

However large their number—and however overwrought their proclamation—the white Jeffersons represent an increasingly minority opinion in the longest controversy about sex and race in U.S. history. In the context of the case that mobilizes my discussion here, they stand in stark contrast to the Fasanos, who exhibit forms of cross-racial feeling in the domain of family unimaginable, indeed uninhabitable, by those who call themselves Jefferson's white heirs. If the Jefferson descendants are living within the monoracial ideology of family that suppresses knowledge about the interracial sexual terrain of slavery, the Fasanos display white identity affiliations born in a vastly different racial order, one whose coexistence with the aggressive fantasy of white purity speaks to the mobility of white identifications that has become a distinct part of the postsegregationist era. These identifications are not legible from within the structural forms, discursive productions, and affective conditions of segregationist

---

Hemings's children." Quoted in Check, "Jefferson's Descendants Continue to Deny Slave Link."

41. Quoted in Check, "Jefferson's Descendants Continue to Deny Slave Link."

42. With the election of Barack Obama as U.S. president in 2008, a great deal of media attention turned not only to his racial identity and history, but to that of his partner, Michelle Obama, whose family lineage is traceable to enslavement. Her maternal history, as the *New York Times* reported in October 2009, could be followed to her great-great-great grandparents, "a slave girl and a white man, and their son." To explore the implications of her genealogy for U.S. culture, the editors asked a panel of writers and academics, "Why has it taken so long for Americans to appreciate these deep multiethnic connections?" The language of the question reflects the disavowal that the question is meant to uncover by wanting "appreciation" and "multiethnicity" in a genealogical narrative that would require attention precisely to a political order in which "a slave girl and a white man" figure as sexual precedents. See Swarns and Kantor, "In First Lady's Roots, a Complex Path from Slavery" and "One Family's Roots, a Nation's History."

white supremacy—not because their cultural dispensations bear no investment in whiteness but because those investments are quite different from segregation's supremacist ones. Elsewhere in this book I have called these differences *liberal whiteness* and have sought to demonstrate how the pedagogies of Civil Rights reform worked to fracture white subjectivity in increasingly self-conscious ways, producing forms of affiliation and identification that turned *against* dominant monoracial discourses born in white nationalism and segregationist white supremacy. But while liberal whiteness must be understood as challenging the myths of racial purity and white national origins produced by earlier white supremacist discourses, its multiracial attachments do not necessarily entail a direct confrontation with the history of sexual violence and human expropriation that otherwise resides in the material life of kinship as a national history of interracial heterosex. In this context, one of my tasks will be to consider the figure of the white father, the missing master term, if you will, in the national narrative of race and the family. Indeed *he* is the nation's most spectacularly absent father, the only one who has never been made to account for his paternal dispossessions—not even in the 1990s when both popular and political discourse worked hard to manage the symbolic repertoire in which he could come to stand as father of the emergent multicultural nation. How this rehabilitation was staged is a story beyond the scope of this chapter, but there is no way to encounter the seemingly eccentric figure of Richard Fasano, who claims the black child born to his white wife as his own, without contending with the transformations of white paternal affect that accompany multiracial desire in the postsegregationist era.

In the following section, I deliberate on the stakes of adjudicating the legal case in either woman's favor before offering two different frames of analysis for this chapter's discussion. The first situates the figure of the gestational surrogate in the feminist critical archive where the realm of reproduction has been given priority in discerning the historical consequences of racial slavery for understanding hierarchies among women. The second turns to popular culture to consider how representations of assisted conception engage with national narratives of race and sex in ways that revise and recode their historical prohibitions. My goals are thus diverse. I want not only to discern some of the distinct features of the legal case and the critical and cultural contexts that affect its interpretation, but to foreground the role of the case study in shaping the terrain of evidence, precedent, and prediction that accompanies feminist intersectional analysis which, I argue, relies on a juridical framework as its primary methodological mode. At the same time, I am interested in how popular representations of family and familial relations can be read in relationship to the broader arc of multiculturalism and the transformations of images and affects that it has evoked. Hence, I argue that the circulations of discourses about reproductive technologies, no less than the increased use of them in medical procedure, have played an increasingly crucial role in the production of new and often conflicting narratives of kinship since the early 1990s, providing technological assistance in the making of the *multicultural nation* by helping to forge multiracial kinship relations without the crisis that interracial sex as the narrative of national origin begets. One of my destinations, then, is to consider how cross-racial feeling is culturally framed, even nurtured, as part of multiculturalism's reformulation of national narratives of race and sex—and in ways that position blackness as the symbolic value to be possessed in order to exact the equivalence that multiculturalism promises to deliver. The other is to situate, more as juxtaposition than analogy or contrast, how feminist attempts to adjudicate black women's minoritization in discourses of all kinds—legal, reproductive, and critical—are important engagements with the possibilities and limits of shaping multiracial commitments to feminist ends. In this context, intersectionality is not simply the name for a theory aimed at comprehending the densities of race and racialization, but an instance, indeed an insistence, on the political value of the critical kinship it sets out to hone.

The Lure of Judgment

In the end, then, the courts dismissed Donna Fasano's claim to maternity and restored the rights of reproductive inheritance to the monoracial family by way of the gene. Does this mean that its decision was wrong? Some would certainly say so. Law Professor Leslie Bender has argued, for instance, that the appellate court was sex biased in its privileging of genetics over gestation and race biased in its "genetic essentialism," by which she means its conception of "the essence of a human being . . . [according to] his or her genetic code."[43] For Bender, genetics-based decisions *always* privilege men's role in reproduction and routinely engender "a new kind of biological

43. Bender, "Genes, Parents, and Assisted Reproductive Technologies," 40.

racism" by reiterating the ideology of race as membership in biologically discrete groups.[44] For these reasons, she argues for a uniform standard to protect gestational maternity. Countering this position, Ilana Hurwitz finds that any recourse to a hierarchy of motherhood threatens to displace the needs of the child in each case, arguing therefore for a child-centered instrument to replace the taxonomies of maternity.[45] Other legal scholars such as Raizel Liebler view the case as the consequence of an unregulated industry, such that emotional harm (not to mention expensive litigation) is the inevitable result for all parties when fertility clinics have no enforceable standards of care.[46] Liebler proposes heightened regulation and new consent policies as a means to begin to manage, in advance, the possibility of error. The popular discourse is split between a fascination with the mistake as a spectacle, as the high-pitched language of the mix-up and its revelatory two babies, "one white, one black" indicates, and sympathy for either one or the other potential mother, and sometimes even for both. For the African American magazine *Jet*, the court's decision implicitly affirms a Civil Rights vision, while the *National Right to Life News* takes the case as support for the belief that life begins at fertilization, and *20/20* wastes no time registering its primary attachment, calling the story it aired, "Losing Joseph."[47]

It is hardly a surprise, of course, that legal scholars work within a decision-based rhetoric in citational forms congruent with the argumentative traditions of professional litigation culture, while the media follows the emotional contexts that render any attempt to discuss the stakes of legal justice a matter of conflicting opinion; its interests after all are firmly keyed to the immediacy of sales and ratings. But legal scholarship is weighted quite differently, being turned toward the future and toward forms of interpretative practice in which judgments matter most not simply for what they do in the case in question, but for how they might condition the future direction of legal decisions. This is no doubt why the courts, much like the scholarship it cites and provokes, routinely sets forth its interpretative criteria, both to clarify the terms on which it bases its written

44. Bender, "Genes, Parents, and Assisted Reproductive Technologies," 54.
45. Hurwitz, "Collaborative Reproduction."
46. See Liebler, "Are You My Parent?"
47. See "White Couple Gives Baby to His Black Genetic Parents"; Fee, "Embryo Mix-Up Shows Why Roe v. Wade Is Outdated"; and Walters, "Losing Joseph."

judgment and to specify how that judgment can and cannot be read. Interpretation, in this regard, is outcome based and future oriented, which is why it is commonplace to expect every study of a legal case to address the court's decision in a manner that assesses its actions. Indeed, in the many years that I have been thinking about race and reproduction through the lens of *Perry-Rogers v. Fasano*, I have been asked more times than I can remember to whom I believe the child in question rightfully belongs. Usually the question comes in the shape of the simple opposition I have troped above: Was the decision right or wrong? Did it correct one harm by imposing another? And if so, which harm is more harmful? I have found it nearly impossible to escape the disciplinary hold of these questions, given how swiftly the answers—I'm not sure, or I don't know, or that is not what is most interesting—betray the conditions on which the stature of the legal case study garners its authority to begin with.

If I say, for instance, that the courts merely compounded the clinic's mistake by making one of their own, I become beholden to a concept of the social relation of family lodged in the agency of the womb and to an argument that requires me to refute the Rogerses' claim to the entitlements of liberal personhood, which have been achieved in the long history of racial struggle in the United States with significant and at times profound effort. To be sure, I can still feel sympathy for the Rogerses, and I can understand and even foreground how they might have experienced historical déjà vu upon learning not only that a third party misappropriated the property of their persons but that a white man's patronymic marked the birth record of their genetic child.[48] But individual sympathy would not ground my legal reasoning, as my commitment to gestation would be primary, aimed in part at correcting a long history of stolen maternity in which the gestational mother is the one who has most acutely borne the exclusionary effects of hierarchies of race, class, and gender. Indeed, I could even go so far as to argue that a decision on behalf of Donna Fasano would be a decision with precedent-setting capacities for the future of gestational rights in the con-

---

48. Following Hortense Spillers and Saidiya Hartman, Nancy Bentley takes up the problematic of kinlessness as a condition of the Middle Passage and North American slave law to argue that "the modern concept of race is not an extension of kinship, as if race were a family or class identity writ large . . . [but] a practical negation of kinship morphologies," one that pivoted on "propagation and not as the creation of kin" (272, 280). See Bentley, "The Fourth Dimension."

text of medical negligence and malpractice for everyone. In the process, I could claim that Joseph shares both a biological and a social relation to the Fasanos or, to be more exact, that gestation *is* a social relation: between fetus and birth mother and between the fetuses as well. That there is currently no language in domestic relations law to name these relations does not mean that they do not exist; it merely indicates the importance of developing a more capable grammar for technologically assisted reconfigurations of kinship. In this way, I would counter the reasoning of the court—which crafted the Fasanos' affective attachments as nominal, happenstance, and willfully *mistaken*—by affirming gestation as an embodied priority around which the future of legal judgments should be made. And I could do this even as I registered the gender essentialism involved, which converts a woman's capacity to bear children into a figure of maternity and assumes that gestation is a natural process of embodied attachment. I could do this because the alternative choice, to concede to the authority of the gene, is far too likely to displace and devalue women's labor in reproduction—which is a story we already know too well.

If, however, I simply cannot sustain a commitment to gestation in the face of the clinic's mistake or in the context of the history of white property entitlements to black reproduction, I can side with the courts' opinion and return "the African American child," as the infant in question was sometimes called in the legal proceedings, to his genetic parents. To be sure, this would write Donna Fasano's embodied labor out of the story and risk subordinating the affective attachments that were cultivated there. And, much like the argument in her favor, it would reinforce the dominant ideology that kinship resides in the realm of the biological, even as my judgment would reverse priorities and take heredity and parenthood as belonging to the authority of the gene.[49] I could still acknowledge the complexity of Donna Fasano's maternal attachments, especially given the emotional trauma that often accompanies infertility, and I could even consider, as did the first court in 1999, the extent to which psychological bonds between the twins had formed both before and after their births.[50] But those attachments would have no legal

49. For a history of the emergence of the "genetic family," see Dolgin, "Choice, Tradition, and the New Genetics"; and on the rise and fall of a nonbiological racialism in the study of the gene, see Fausto-Sterling, "Refashioning Race."

50. In the 1999 lower court decision that established the Rogerses' claim to legal custody, the judge affirmed the Fasanos' claims of emotional connection to Joseph by sup-

bearing, because I too would take genetics as the more powerful and more authoritative relation. The child, after all, was said to look just like Deborah Perry-Rogers's mother, and while we can offer historically nuanced explications of the social fiction of race, it is less easy to be dismissive of the importance of learning early and well how to arm oneself against the tactile violence of its concrete deployment as hierarchy in everyday life.[51] For this reason, I might even want to argue that the court failed to deliver on the important question of the "good of the child" by pretending throughout its decision to be "race blind," even as I would endorse the ability of any couple to raise a child who was not, in the indexical language that perpetuates the leap from the social to the biological and back again, "from their own background." To the extent that the antiessentialist language I would want to craft here is difficult to muster from within reproduction's biologically essentialist frame, I could simply say that, given the social world in which we live, the court's decision was right by being the lesser harm. And I would no doubt want to admit that I found it baffling that the Fasanos never tried to locate the Rogerses, especially given that they learned, at week five of Donna's pregnancy, that the clinic had made a mistake.[52] Still, that bafflement is simply a projection, which is why I would have to resist following the court's knuckle-rapping discipline that chastised the Fasanos for not taking proper action to ward off emotional investments in "property" not theirs. (What actions would those be, anyway? And proper to whom?[53]) In arguing

---

porting their plea for visitation and by calling for additional psychological study to determine the extent to which the (then) six-month-old infants had bonded. The Fasanos claimed that the boys "loved each other" and that their psychological health required that visitation not be annulled. The Rogerses, as we now know, sought a higher court's opinion and eventually won their claim. See Maull, "Oddly Enough."

51. Richard Rogers recounts his first sighting of Akeil—"I looked at him and said, 'Oh my goodness, he looks like Debra's [sic] mother.' The spitting image!" See "Lasting Consequences," 4.

52. The Fasanos' behavior is contrasted by a recent case in which a woman seeking in vitro fertilization (IVF) treatment became pregnant with an embryo not her own. Upon learning of the clinic's mistake, Carolyn Savage and her husband decided to carry the fetus to term and to transfer the child to its genetic parents upon birth. See "Embryo Mix-Up at Fertility Clinic Resolved Amicably."

53. Following news of the mistake, Donna Fasano underwent DNA testing and thereby discovered, at a date that I have not been able to discern from the narratives available, that only one of the fetuses she carried was genetically hers. In interviews, she

in favor of the court's decision, if not wholly in agreement with the terms by which it was rendered, I could give support to the court's wish that without the clinic's mistake, families would have been assisted in reproducing only on their own terms—or, more accurately, only on the terms that their turn to the contract was meant to yield: monoracial family arrangements.

There are, of course, other ways to argue for or against the court's decision, but the performative aim of this section lies in foregrounding the limits of just such an itinerary for engaging the densities of race, gender, and reproduction that are so powerfully arrayed in the case but subordinated by the juridical form that shapes it—which requires, by definition, a final decision. The risk for identity knowledges of taking up "the case" as a point of departure lies here: where critical analysis is conditioned from the outset by the court's judgment, such that the rhetorical practices honed no less than the political imaginary inscribed are keyed to the priorities and assumptions of legal reason. In the structure of argument that ensues, critical authority is founded on the opposition between affirmation and dissent, which makes *taking a position* the only authoritative position possible. To be sure, this is precisely what has been attractive for identity knowledges about the case study—legal or not—as it emphasizes the kind of paradigmatic mode of reading referenced at the outset. But what happens to feminist critical practice when the destination sought is wrapped up in winning a judgment that has been made commensurate with changing the social world as a whole? Or more to the point, what are the consequences when the field imaginary that frames our turn to the case is steeped in legal reason and the argumentative and interpretative practices it conditions and begets?

These questions are bound to the argument I am pursuing, which is that unlike Crenshaw, whose analysis began with the legal structure of antidiscrimination law before analogizing its agency to feminist theory and antiracist activism alike, feminist scholarship that travels under the framework of intersectionality today routinely reverses the analogic relation, reading feminism and feminist texts as if their occlusions were and are

---

recalled that medical professionals at the fertility clinic advised that she abort, but the couple adamantly refused. It hardly seems possible that the New York appellate court was suggesting abortion as the proper action to accompany knowledge of the mistake. But in its emphasis on the Fasanos' misbegotten attachment, the court reveals a moral conception of the obligation that attends the contract.

juridical discriminations. Indeed the interchange and at times explicit exchange of epistemic and state violence is very much at stake in the theorization of critique as a mode of political address which underlies the way that theory has been analogized in feminist critical practice to the terrain of the state, its content imbued with the destinies of state discourse, and its authorship read as a mode of near-magisterial power. And yet, the actual presence of the state as a target of address in its distinct juridical form is displaced. For this reason, I want to suggest that *the transformative agency we grant to critique reflects a melancholic attachment to those state discourses in whose absence it primarily speaks,* but which it has no avowed means to address or confront.[54] This is not to say that the state and its discourses are not implicated in, even structurally productive of, scholarship as a whole, but it is to foreground a tension that matters considerably to the conversation of this chapter: between, on the one hand, the generic force of the imperative toward justice that underwrites identity knowledges and leads to a shared cross-disciplinary and widely interdisciplinary emphasis on transforming contemporary social conditions by critiquing them and, on the other hand, the analytic travels of the juridical imaginary and law-based rhetorics as they move across the methodological, disciplinary, and epistemological divides that comprise the interdisciplinary study of identity.

The Mistake

But how, you might ask, can I make so much out of what begins with a fertility clinic's mistake? This is, after all, a crisis of kinship by accident, not design. As such, my analysis lacks the authoritative agency cultivated

54. Bill Readings provides a compelling angle on the U.S. university's contemporary neoliberal absorption of critique and criticality into "excellence," such that the kind of work that rose to left critical prominence in the 1980s and early 1990s—largely denoted by the interface between critical theory and cultural studies, and widely produced by scholars who brought increased social diversity to the faculty ranks—could be managed by emergent market/consumer discourses. While the vociferousness of the culture wars and the right's assault on the university tempers the sense in which the university of excellence comes to power through its accommodating capaciousness, many of Readings's predictions about the university's "use" of fields and perspectives that arose to challenge it remain germane. While he ends his analysis with a call for thinking, it seems to me that by the time his book was published, it was already too late in the process of the university's neoliberalization for *that* as a counterstrategy. See Readings, *The University in Ruins.*

from the critical practices I have described above, where the legal case is taken as a paradigmatic entry into discerning the intersectional nature of power, and the critical act emerges as an ameliorative counter to the social violences repeated by legal judgment. How can I arrive anywhere, let alone into the vocabulary I am using—about the case study, liberal personhood, juridical reason, and multiracial desire—from within the seeming disorder and radical contingency of the spectacular exception? How, especially given that the critical idiom I have adopted draws from the insistence of *Object Lessons* a commitment to inhabitation, not resolution, and hence makes no argument for methodological consistency or equivalence, let alone repair? These questions have haunted this work from its beginning when colleagues at its inaugural venue (an interdisciplinary workshop called Race, Nature, and the Politics of Difference) challenged me to account for the failure of the case *to represent* a pervasive cultural condition or legal situation which, methodologically speaking, is precisely what the use of a case study is supposed to do.[55] Some colleagues urged me to conduct interviews with the disputing parties, along with their attorneys, relatives, and friends, so that I could garner interpretative authority by constructing an archive of feeling, to trope Ann Cvetkovich, against the anti-affective dispositions of the law.[56] Others thought that the case could open into a more extensive ethnography about race and kinship in the fertility industry, which could build on feminist work in anthropology on the topic. Or I could follow not just this case and its mistake, but custody cases that have arisen from mistakes more generally in order to consider the ways in which courts, clinics, and media were addressing the failure of human intention to find a match in technological romance.[57] So intrigued

55. My thanks to Donna Haraway for initially pressing this point and to Donald Moore for inviting me to the event, where my presence served as an exception to the group's primary orientation toward cultural anthropology. Thanks as well to Bill Maurer for a crash course on anthropological investments in kinship.

56. Cvetkovich's project seeks to track the ephemera of affect in ways that raise compelling issues about the relationship between the study of cultural forms and the subjects who negotiate identity within and against them. See Cvetkovich, *An Archive of Feelings*.

57. For work that does this, see especially Noble-Allgire, "Switched at the Fertility Clinic." Noble-Allgire offers a protocol for judgment that is quite detailed, but the overall gesture is that the gestational mother has a priori standing, unless the genetic mother contests, in which case a two-mother solution is preferred. The courts have repeatedly

was I by the prospect of transcending my own disciplinary limitations that I left the workshop full of hope for effecting a methodological transformation, one that could lend greater authority to my analysis by foregrounding some combination of the political and affective economies of lived experience such that both my assemblage of disparate archives and my reliance on speculation could be anchored in the methodological security of embodied evidence. In this way, the case study could become the very means for settling interdisciplinary discontent by focusing the argument on its paradigmatic, not exceptional or accidental, content.

But in the end, I was more intrigued by what my colleagues wanted from my object of study than the prospect of delivering it to them, which is why the essay that appeared in the workshop proceedings followed my own disciplinary inclinations by turning from the case to popular culture to register the thick entanglements of representation, race, gender, and reproduction I found there. To be sure, I acknowledged the methodological challenge the mistake posed by staging my contribution as a meditation on the difficulty of negotiating disciplinary identities in interdisciplinary settings. "Critical kinship" emerged as the conceptual framework for understanding disciplinary attachments and the priorities they inscribe about the criteria of evidence, the value of procedure, and the authority of one's critical archive—in short, the terms of legitimacy on which the academic professional can make any claim to know. In linking disciplinarity to kinship, I was aided by the force of kinship as the ur-language of anthropology and by my own need for a defensive maneuver, especially as I sought no methodological relation to the participants in the case and hence no relation to the authority of the human subject whose everyday world had been radically remade by the mistake's intervention.[58]

---

rejected the two-mother solution as harmful to the child, but Noble-Allgire argues that the courts need to find solutions that match the complexity of contemporary kinship issues in assisted conception.

58. In the course of these deliberations, it has become clear that what we now take as the interdisciplinary interrogation of *race* is shaped by the divergent critical priorities and political assumptions of the various disciplines that have engaged it. Hence, a study of the economics of racial slavery can be read from one disciplinary perspective as sheer disregard for the subject's lived experience, even as the economic detail will be necessary in another disciplinary domain to register the incredible theft that underwrote European colonialism. Or, to take another example, the analysis of the workplace experience

This is part of the reason that my ongoing elaboration of the case study of mistaken implantation resisted—and continues to—the demand for a critical practice aimed at coherent representation, not because such a strategy has no value but rather because of the way it has been held forth as the means to resolve the antiparadigmatic implications of a case arising from a fertility clinic's mistake. But it is precisely because agency is so fully awry in this case and the legal apparatus of liberal personhood called on to correct it so completely unable to bring reproduction back into the authority of embodied heteronormativity that it has seemed important to me not to seek methodological resolution by turning to the individual's self-reflective articulation to measure or represent the meanings of "the case." This refusal is dicey to be sure, but it is consonant with the way that *Object Lessons* has wanted to question the resonant investment in critical authority to master the relation between the subject and object of knowledge. My approach has been to inhabit the conundrums in order to consider the various disciplinary routes of redress that have come to attend to the gaps between not only political aspiration and critical practice, but the object of study and the agencies we do and don't invest in them. In the context of this chapter's specific deliberations, the mistake is an important condition, less an exception than the very emblem of the nonparadigmatic force of living that is repeatedly disavowed by the methodological imperatives of modern disciplinary thought. While the courts seek to reverse the mistake and the imperative toward methodological correction seeks to resolve the difficulties it raises, I take it as the means to draw attention to the disparate but linked authorities of normativity, consistency, and critical intimacy that underwrite knowledge production altogether. By addressing this chapter's inability to situate its analysis in such paradigmatic terms—and hence to situate the case as a paradigm of contemporary social power—I want to

---

of African Americans in corporate culture will be taken as a political displacement of the racial formation of contemporary capitalism in one context while serving in another as valuable evidence for understanding the contemporary distribution of race and capital within economic sectors. Much more work needs to be done to address the multiple ways in which *race* has been constituted as a conceptual framework and political figure. For a more extensive discussion of these issues, see Stoler, "Racial Histories and Their Regimes of Truth"; Dominguez, "Implications"; Roediger, "A Response to Stoler"; Wacquant, "For an Analytic of Racial Domination"; and Mehta, "The Essential Ambiguities of Race and Racism."

emphasize the central tension that resides in *Object Lessons*: between on the one hand the hopeful expectation that the critical act is commensurate with the social world it engages and often takes itself to be "tracking" and the prospect, on the other hand, that it never can be. My assumption is that the desired relationship between critique and its political ambitions can find no guarantee in paradigmatic reading, no matter the security such an interpretative protocol offers for rendering our perception of the world not simply coherent but more potently "true."

From this point of view, the mistake is both a challenging and useful form of interruption into the systemizing habits of critical practice, as its authoritative rebuttal to paradigmatic reading affects not only my critical relation to "the case" but all the participants that comprise it. Consider once again the images it puts before us: of a white woman believing passionately that she is the mother of a black child; of a black woman claiming natural kinship with the child nurtured by a white woman's womb; of a white man declaring paternity of the black child his wife bore; of a black man hoping to give his name to his genetic son. If the entire case is, so to speak, "pregnant with history," it is clear that there are different racial histories operating here, not just the echo of slavery and its evocation of white theft of black personhood as property or liberal personhood's transformative counter to slavery—not simply the history, then, of unlawful, violent, and nationally denied interracial sex—but also the contemporary multicultural reconstruction of racial affect that makes it possible for the white family to imagine itself the natural home for multiracial twins. These images are startling in their novelty and so affectively and historically dense that one might *want* to believe with the courts that the mistake should be undone and the grammar of race resecured to the reproductive authority of intention offered by heterosexuality as the natural origin of monoracial kinship. But the mistake is profoundly pedagogical, which is why paradigmatic reading is no match for managing the questions of justice and judgment it raises. As a pedagogy, the mistake functions as the means to inaugurate and dispense the multiple hierarchies of value that differently position the contending couples' conflicting claims, while establishing not only what the court determines it can rightly know but the moment in which "knowing" is said to matter altogether: "where defendants knew of the error not long after it occurred, the happenstance of their nominal parenthood over plaintiff's child should have been treated as a mistake to be corrected as soon as possible, before development of a parental relationship." Here, under the pedagogical authority of the mistake, the court casts any action not formed in obligation to it as an ethical misstep. In doing so, the court affirms the promise invested in liberal personhood: that the contractual citizen has a right, borne of fulfilling its obligations to the state, to inhabit only the forms of sociality and intimacy that the subject can be said to want.

Donna Fasano, of course, takes the pedagogy of the mistake in an altogether different direction, cultivating its consequences in the language of embodied affect and seeking—even after losing the status of legal maternity—for the boys she birthed to be raised as "brothers." As a lawyer said of the Fasano perspective, they "don't see [Joseph] as someone's else's *black* baby; they see him as their baby." To read this quote as a postracial fantasy is to miss the pedagogical work that the mistake performs in situating both couples in different discursive terrains of race and racialized reproduction. For by taking Joseph as their baby, the Fasanos mark his racial inheritance as performed by the gene as secondary to the authority of gestation as a naturalized mode of familial belonging. In television interviews, the Fasanos talked openly about the social challenge of raising a black child in a white family while images of the family in their home showed toys that featured figures in both black and white. To see Joseph as "their baby" is not, then, a definitive refusal to see the child as black; rather, it is a refusal to index his blackness as that which would naturally locate his belonging elsewhere.[59] For the Rogerses, however, the mistake is indisputable proof that no social kinship can be assembled from the happenstance of the gestational bond, as they repeatedly refused the idea that the boys could be brothers. For them, brotherhood required a relation of genetic kinship with a shared parent; hence the boys were twins because of their life in the uterus but they were not and could not be "brothers." The war established here between conceptions of race that naturalize it in two ways—as genetic/propertied and as familial/affective—is an important

59. This is not to say that the actions and affects of the Fasanos are antiracist—multiracialism is not in itself an antiracist formation, but in the terms I conceive it, it is also not white supremacist. France Winddance Twine's work on the white mother has been important for thinking through some of these issues. See Twine, "Transracial Mothering and Antiracism" and "Bearing Blackness in Britain."

feature of the contemporary terrain of reproductive technologies and the cultural imaginaries they beget, making it difficult to discern in advance which discursive logics will be mobilized and to what—or whose—end.

Setting Precedents

The history of black maternity is at the center of intersectional scholarship on reproduction, where the economic and moral effects of slavery's negation of all forms of legal personhood are explicated in their distinctly raced and gendered dimensions.[60] By paying attention to the two most powerful forms of chattel dispossession—the loss of ownership of one's person and of one's reproductive "issue"—this scholarship has consciously worked to construct a discourse of maternal value to pose against the white masculinist traditions inscribed in both dominant social and legal opinion. For scholars with a special interest in the twentieth century, the emergence of the fertility industry has been an important arena for continued exploration of the subordination of black maternity, especially in legal disputes over biological parentage that involve surrogacy. Here, the U.S. legal system has been faulted for its reliance on three hierarchies of value that support both patriarchal and white racial outcomes: (1) the contribution of sperm donorship over the contribution of the ovum, (2) the biological authority of the gene over gestation and delivery, and (3) the relationship de-

60. The archive that takes up both slavery's reproductive economy and its legacy in ideologies of black maternity in the present is too extensive to account for in its entirety, but key contributions include: Jones, " 'My Mother Was Much of a Woman' "; Davis, *Women, Race, and Class*; White, *Ar'n't I a Woman?*; Omolade, "The Unbroken Circle"; Spillers, "Mama's Baby, Papa's Maybe"; Austin, "Sapphire Bound!"; Allen, "Surrogacy, Slavery, and the Ownership of Life"; Rutherford, "Reproductive Freedoms and African American Women"; Lubiano, "Black Ladies, Welfare Queens, and State Minstrels"; Davis, "The Private Law of Race and Sex"; Cherry, "Nurturing in the Service of White Culture"; Smith, *Welfare Reform and Sexual Regulation*; and numerous works by Dorothy E. Roberts, including "Racism and Patriarchy in the Meaning of Motherhood," "Punishing Drug Addicts Who Have Babies," "The Genetic Tie," "Privatization and Punishment in the New Age of Reprogenetics," "Race, Gender, and Genetic Technologies," and *Killing the Black Body*.

For a survey of the impact of race and class in the domain of assisted conception, see Ehrenreich, "The Colonization of the Womb."

fined by and established through the contract over everything else.[61] Intersectional analysis has argued against these hierarchies by emphasizing embodied labor—regardless of whether or not the gestational mother contributes genetic material—and by exposing the political economy of reproductive technologies in general, given the wealth and whiteness of the population these technologies tend to serve.[62] In much of the intersectional archive, in fact, there is a strong sense that the gestational mother is extracted from the authority of her own reproductive labor by the combined forces of both patriarchy and white supremacy, such that the proliferating medical management of infertility must be read in the context of a longer history of white racial formation as a fantasy of blood purity. If we use the language of the sanctity of life here, in an arena of inquiry dedicated to women's choice in all matters reproductive, it would reference the political value accorded to embodied labor and the critical commitment to figuring maternity outside the conceptual framework of commodity

61. The medical establishment of course is also deeply implicated in the political warfare over the meaning of technological *assistance* for "biological" reproduction. Consider, for instance, what assumptions underlie a diagnosis of "infertility," when the term refers to the failure to get pregnant after a year of unprotected heterosexual sex. What notion of the fecundity of heterosexual sex is at work here? What would happen to the idea of infertility if the period of "failure" was, say, five years? And what does it mean for technology to offer *assistance*, especially in such cases as IVF, where sperm and ovum can be extracted from people who not only have never met one another, but who have not met either the contracting "parents" or the woman who might serve as their surrogate? If some seemingly natural process is being assisted, what substance or form does nature in this process take? Why the language and pretense of *assistance* at all?

62. Infertility is notoriously expensive to treat. In one woman's personal account of her attempts at IVF pregnancy—and her eventual turn to a surrogacy arrangement—a single cycle of egg harvest, fertilization, and implantation cost $8,000, with an additional $4,000 for medication. See Kuczynski, "Her Body, My Baby," 44. When the author gave up her own attempts at pregnancy, after her eleventh IVF cycle, she and her husband, an investor, hired a surrogate, who was paid $25,000. The contracting mother described her pleasure that the surrogate and her family were "college-educated," lived in a suburb, and were "not so different from us" (48). The photos accompanying the story demonstrate that all the parties are white except for the baby's nurse, who stands in the background wearing a white uniform. For other discussions of the political economy of reproductive technologies, including the relationship between the regulatory systems of law, medicine, and the market, see Ikemoto, "The In/Fertile, the Too Fertile, and the Dysfertile."

exchange, especially on behalf of the poor women of color who serve disproportionately as surrogates.

It is in this context, where the gestational mother is given priority over the contract and embodiment emerges as the countervalue to the hegemony of the gene that the Rogers-Fasano case becomes especially interesting, if not vexing, for scholarship that takes its critical reading of legal cases as a practice of transformative justice. For when the court awarded Deborah Perry-Rogers legal maternity, it departed from what was at the time a much-embraced legal standard in the United States where, in nearly every state except California, the gestational mother held legal status.[63] While the standard was applied inconsistently, it nonetheless established, in terms that feminist scholars and reproductive activists have supported, the priority of embodied labor as a state-sanctioned discourse of biological belonging. A controversial exception to the rule came in 1991 when the first surrogate who was not genetically related to the child she bore for a wealthy white and Filipina couple sued for custody. *Anna J. v. Mark C.* has been written about extensively in the intersectional archive on gender, race, and reproduction because of the ways in which the court, to paraphrase Deborah Grayson, could not conceive of Anna Johnson, a single black woman, as mother to any child except a black one.[64]

63. Cited in Grunwald, "In Vitro, in Error—And Now, in Court." This standard evolved from more traditional custody disputes and seems reliant on the suture between what is now thought of as gestational and genetic maternity. Its application has had a diverse scope, in that the lack of surrogacy laws in some states or the actual criminalization of paid surrogacy arrangements in others means that the gestational mother has won legal maternity simply because the surrogacy contract is unenforceable or outlawed. For instance, in 2009 a case in Michigan featured contestation over a child born in a surrogacy arrangement who had no genetic tie to any of the contesting parties. The contracting couple bought both egg and sperm from anonymous donors and paid for IVF implantation of a surrogate. The surrogate and her husband now have custody, after contesting the contracting couple's right to be named legal guardians, given the revelation that the intended mother had a mental health condition. See Saul, "Uncertain Laws on Surrogates Leave Custody at Issue." According to Saul, in 2009, ten states had laws that allowed for surrogacy but imposed restrictions on its conduct, including that at least one of the intended parents share a genetic relationship to the child. For a discussion of the legal terrain of assisted conception in the early 1990s, see Blankenship et al., "Reproductive Technologies and the U.S. Courts."

64. See *Anna J. v. Mark C. et al.*, 286 Cal. Rptr., 372 (Cal.App.4 Dist. 1991); and *Johnson v. Calvert*, 851 P.2d 776 (Cal.), *cert. denied*, 510 U.S. 874 (1993). For Grayson's discussion of the case, see "Mediating Intimacy."

In privileging the contracting couple's intention to have their own genetic child, the court denied Johnson's petition in the midst of media discussion of her scandalous "character."[65] When the *Perry-Rogers v. Fasano* decision cited the case as a precedent for denying Donna Fasano's gestational claim to maternity, it reinforced the seemingly monoracial belief that black women are the natural mothers of black children, but it did so by calling forth the very legal mechanisms that underwrote the decision against Anna Johnson: the intention of the contracting couple to reproduce their own biogenetic family. There are a number of ways to read this outcome: (1) that Deborah Perry-Rogers is an exception in the legal archive of black maternity in that what she inherited in her relation to the gene was otherwise a reward of white privilege; (2) that the biological authority of the monoracial family, so alive in the discourse of the gene, can actually work in black women's legal favor; (3) that the bourgeois entitlements of liberal personhood confirmed by the contract are weighted by class and heterosexual advantage as securely, if not at times more surely, than by racial disadvantage; and/or (4) that the mistake so overdetermined this legal encounter that nothing *paradigmatic* about the contemporary terrain of race and reproduction can be made of it at all.

What would it mean to say that each of these interpretations is true or, to be more precise, that each is as potentially true as the other? To try to proceed in this way would require opening the precedent to the different temporalities in which legal opinion, like critical practice and everyday life, operates, which would mean reading the precedent as never fully commensurate with the uses to which it might be put. This entails resisting the circulatory system of legal authority in which the precedent secures the claim to a normative and stable grounding *that citing it is taken to mean*: in short, that circulatory system in which the precedent is an enabling fiction for law's authority, organizing retrospectively the incidental and mobile particularities that attend a case into equivalent interpretative frames that can stand as the basis (or alibi) of future judgments. As most scholarship in feminist and critical race theory attests, procedure narrows what law takes as part of its interests, thereby suturing its epistemological capacity to the register of method, and method to the outcome of equivalence. This is what is taken as the deep flaw of antidiscrimination law since it makes a fetish of

65. Hartouni, "Breached Birth." Further citations are included in the main text.

equivalence—to the point of rendering the court unable to discern when harm and advantage are being multiplied under its tutelage. It is no surprise then that the court makes minor in *Perry-Rogers v. Fasano* what are in fact the very circumstances at stake in the case when it likens the fertility clinic to the maternity ward and unanimously orders the babies to their genetic families. The case, writes the court, "bears more similarity to a mix-up at the time of a hospital's discharge of two newborn infants, which should simply be corrected at once, than to one where a gestational mother has arguably the same rights to claim parentage as the genetic mother."[66] The quest for methodological coherence locks the decision into "readable time," discerning the mistake as the origin of the contest and thereby bracketing the temporal disorder of its living consequences. Here is where the contracting couple's intention becomes the deciding rule; the mistake, after all, was not meant to happen. If one wanted to risk overstatement, she could say that securing the precedent is always a project of disarticulating human error from law's claim to justice, which is necessary to the institutional authority of legal decision as procedurally and methodologically beyond the mistakes that incite it.

These temporal problematics are legible not only across the entire institution of legal opinion (by which I mean the courts, the professional culture in which practitioners are trained, and the theoretical writing that arises from both) but in the protocols of U.S. identity knowledges, where the work of the past four decades has entailed an enormous effort to recast the historical time of the nation according to a different calculus of precedent and opinion.[67] Here, the logic of the precedent requires a return to dominant national narration what the institution of the state via the law has rendered external to its judgment, which is to say external to the normative procedure on which its authority is repeatedly secured: cultural discourses, experiential histories, subaltern knowledges, and entire worlds of affect and attachment that have no legibility within the population politics and policies of the state. That much of this work has explicitly addressed the state and self-consciously defined itself as policy oriented is neither accidental nor incidental; it marks these fields' imbrication in the university's own institutional project of nation building, where "knowl-

66. *Perry-Rogers v. Fasano*, 715 N.Y.S.2d at 25.

67. The nation is not, of course, the only "time" in which identity knowledges operate, as other chapters in *Object Lessons* discuss, but it is not insignificant, no matter the current imperative toward transnational analytics in all the fields I discuss.

edge for society" is part of a complex struggle from within the auspices of professional expert culture over the meaning and making of the "social." There is certainly much more to say about the consequences for identity knowledges of its own professional location and the ways in which its identifications with the state's disposable knowledges and peoples is marked by a profound class divide, one that scholarly emphasis on community, identity, and affiliation can never fully elide.[68] For now however I want to foreground the collision, if you will, of two kinds of precedents—the legal and the critically historical—and the authority they are each used to wield in contestations that frame one of the primary political stakes of identity knowledges, which is to transform the historical record as a means to elucidate not only the present but the capacity of the future to interrupt continuities of subordination and dispossession such that political critiques of the violence of normativity in all its social registers can be heard.

To do this, I will look more closely at the critical conversation attending *Anna J. v. Mark C.* in order to begin charting the path of nineteenth-century slavery and its property logic of kinship as it moves through the case of contract-based conception that serves as the precedent for authorizing reproductive intentions in *Perry-Rogers v. Fasano*. As the first instance in the United States in which a "genetic stranger" fought for legal custody of the child she bore, the case reveals the legal distinction that reproductive technologies in the 1990s began to yield: that biology as the epistemological foundation for the naturalness of human reproduction could be hierarchicalized, with gestation and genetics vying for priority in determinations of legal maternity. Since the 1991 case, surrogacy has witnessed a taxonomic division into "traditional" and "nontraditional" forms. "Traditional" references a contractual

---

68. In *The Protestant Ethnic and the Spirit of Capitalism*, Rey Chow discusses the ways in which the protesting ethnic subject is caught in a racialized discourse in which she must repeat her discursive condition of racialization in order to register a protest against it. From this perspective, the ethnic scholar of Ethnic Studies in the white university is in an especially vexed position, being on one hand a representative of ethnic subjectivity to the university and on the other hand the figurative expert of those subjects who have been externalized by the institution's own racialized formation—in terms of both its social body and its organization of knowledge. In being both the ethnic subject and the ethnic subject's professionalized representative, the scholar must continually negotiate her status as the bourgeois representative of a racialized folk whose absence from the institution is itself the defining political condition on which the discourse of the field is organized to speak.

situation in which a surrogate performs, through artificial insemination, the role of both gestational and genetic motherhood. Nontraditional—what Sarah Franklin calls "total surrogacy"[69]—identifies the now more frequent situation in which the gestational and genetic roles are not embodied in a single individual.[70] In the total surrogacy relations of *Anna J. v. Mark C.*, it is the distinction between genetics and gestation that operates to define custody—and it is this distinction that underwrites the decision in *Perry-Rogers v. Fasano* to affirm black legal maternity and cast Donna Fasano as both a gestational mother and a genetic mother in the same birth. While the intersectional archive emphasizes the outcome of *Anna J. v. Mark C.* as a disavowal of the historical precedent of slavery and hence as a refusal to incorporate into legal judgment the history of black women's reproductive subordination, I am interested in the instability of the historical precedent to function paradigmatically in its travel through the densities of the relationships produced in the evolving kinship complexities of assisted conception. To emphasize this instability is not a refusal to consider how slavery marks the legal or cultural status of black maternity in the twentieth century. But it is to suggest that its authorizing value as a precedent reaches a critical limit in the distinctly disordered racial logics of the present, where the contract formulations of liberal personhood reconfigure (which is different from overthrowing) the discursive and state terrains in which embodiment and conception continually evince, undergo, and resist racialization.

Slavery and Surrogacy

Let me then contend with what both the media and scholars found insignificant about the *Anna J. v. Mark C.* case: that the child Johnson bore was—to use the commonsense language of race—racially mixed.

---

69. Franklin, "Romancing the Helix," 70.

70. Given legal contestations over custody in surrogate contract relations, commentators note a discernible rise in the number of total surrogacy situations in the first decade of the new century, in part because of the belief that maternal-fetal attachments decrease in intensity under the conditions of genetic strangeness. In situations of transnational surrogacy—where, for instance, a U.S. couple contracts with a woman in the global south to serve as surrogate—the disarray in international governance of reproduction is relied upon as a further guarantee that the surrogate would be unable to win a claim on custody of the child.

Dorothy Roberts, for instance, interprets the case as a concerted effort on the part of the U.S. courts to guarantee white racial reproduction. "By relying on the genetic tie to determine legal parenthood," she writes, "the courts in the Johnson case ensured that a Black woman would not be the 'natural mother' of a white child."[71] While Roberts notes that Crispina Calvert was not white, "the press," she emphasizes, "paid far more attention to Anna Johnson's race than to that of Crispina Calvert. It also portrayed the baby [Christopher] as white."[72] Hence Roberts follows the media presentation by emphasizing the child's whiteness, as does Deborah Grayson, who defines Crispina Calvert as an "honorary white" by pointing to white cultural stereotypes that depict Asian Americans as the "model minority."[73] In this consolidation of a triangle of racial identities into a dualism between black and white, Grayson and Roberts both struggle to establish *Anna J. v. Mark C.* within the property logics of race and (non) personhood that governed nineteenth-century slave culture and that have served to define notions of analytic justice in the scholarly archive that takes up the intersections of race, gender, and reproduction. Writes Grayson,

> The continuing legacy of miscegenation laws that used . . . the "one drop rule" to maintain distinctions and separations among groups of people place a high value on white skin—white blood—because those who can have it are strictly limited and monitored. . . . To say that Johnson could be a mother to baby Christopher would be to indicate a willingness on

71. Roberts, *Killing the Black Body*, 281.

72. Roberts, *Killing the Black Body*, 281.

73. Grayson, "Mediating Intimacy," 529, n. 10. Significantly, the "model minority" label is itself unevenly distributed within the many ethnicities that coalesce under the sign "Asian American," with Japanese and Chinese taking cultural precedence over Southeast Asians and Pacific Islanders, including Filipino/as. In fact, in a recent assessment of education in the state of California, Filipino/as were found to be more on par (which is to say similarly economically and racially oppressed) with Latinos than with several of the ethnic groups within Asian American. At the University of California–Irvine, as elsewhere in the state, there has long been student interest in detaching Filipino/a from Asian American, which has controversial implications for Asian American Studies as a program and field. For a discussion of these field formation issues, see Toribio, "The Problematics of History and Location of Filipino American Studies within Asian American Studies."

the part of the courts and the public to relinquish or, at minimum, to blur racial-familial boundaries.[74]

And states Roberts, "The vision of Black women's wombs in the service of white men conjures up images from slavery. . . . In fact, Anna Johnson's lawyer likened the arrangement Johnson made with the Calverts to a 'slave contract.'"[75]

In constructing the notion of a "slave contract," Johnson's lawyer was no doubt hoping to mobilize the history of enforced kinship and state control over black women's reproduction as a discursive tool in arguing against the wealth and marital status that conferred privilege to the Calverts. But to the extent that critics reiterate the analogy between slavery and surrogacy, they fail to distinguish between these two forms of human property relations, overlooking at least two crucial issues: (1) that being married to a white man does not make Crispina Calvert white, nor does it make her children unambiguously white; and (2) that Anna Johnson is not a slave woman; she has access to the liberal rights of personhood that enabled her to enter into the contractual relation with the Calverts in the first place. While such contractual rights do not enable Johnson to enter either the court or the media on par with Mark Calvert, it is important to articulate the specificities of racialization through which Johnson is disempowered here. As Saidiya Hartman discusses, the transformation from slavery to contractual personhood that took place in the Reconstruction era (and that has been furthered with the demise of official segregation as a national policy) did not "liberate the former slave from his or her bonds but rather sought to replace the whip with the compulsory contract. . . . [L]iberal notions of responsibility modeled on contractual obligation, calculated reciprocity, and most important, indebtedness . . . played a central

74. Grayson, "Mediating Intimacy," 545. This comment is preceded in the article by Grayson's deliberation on Crispina Calvert's statement, quoted routinely in the press, that the baby "looks just like us." Grayson interprets this to be "a sign for blood—for the closed, racialized membership of family and race" (545). Here, again, is the condensation of the interraciality of the Calverts into a discourse of white racial homogeneity, one that functions in Grayson's text as the vehicle for rendering temporal continuity between the practices of slave culture and those of reproductive technologies.

75. Roberts, *Killing the Black Body*, 282.

role in the creation of the servile, blameworthy, and guilty individual."[76] From this perspective, it is Johnson's status as an indebted liberal subject that explicates the mode of racial subjection operating here where her responsibility to the social world that recognizes her as worthy of universal inclusion makes her guilty—guilty of the failure to honor the contract, a failure that is made manifest in the media discourse by representing her as a former welfare cheat.

None of this is to say that the history of slavery has no significant bearing on *Anna J. v. Mark C.*; far from it. But its bearing is less analogical than discursive, which is to say that the case transmutes the ideology of the racialized system it fails to fully reenact through the descriptions of Johnson as a default queen, the one who risks social chaos by discarding her responsibility to fulfill the obligations of the social, borne through the contract. This is, then, a historical trace of the transformations that black maternity in the United States has been forced to yield: where, first, reproduction in the slave economy writes black women as naturally hyperproductive (and thereby increases productivity in fulfillment of the property logic of accumulation), and second, freedom engenders a palpable fear about monstrous reproductivity in the context of a cultural discourse about native black social irresponsibility. Anna Johnson's *value*, we might say, arises from her obligation to contractual personhood and its twentieth-century reformulations of racialized servitude. Thus, while the media representation of *Anna J. v. Mark C.* ignored Crispina Calvert's racial identity in order to privilege the white father's paternity over both the genetic and gestational mothers, the subsequent reinstallation of such an analytic in feminist discussions of the case disables our ability to render historically palpable racialization as a multiply scripted cultural and historical process, *and* to attend to the status of contract as a means of securing the liberal entitlements of personhood. It also critically negates the significance of the marital contract between Mark and Crispina Calvert, which, while offering

---

76. Hartman, *Scenes of Subjection*, 6, 9. Focusing on the official transformation from slavery to freedom, Hartman argues that "the vision of equality forged in the law naturalized racial subordination while attempting to prevent discrimination based on race or former condition of servitude" (9). Hence, *Plessy v. Ferguson* "illuminates the double bind of equality and exclusion that distinguishes modern state racism from its antebellum predecessor" (9).

a state sanction to interracial sexuality, places their sex fully within the law as a disciplinary practice for normative heterosexuality and monogamous reproduction. The Calverts' desire for a child that "looked like them" repeats, ideologically, the fantasy of merger that the romance narrative of heterosexuality repeatedly effects, naturalizing the equation between the founding of culture and the act of hetero-procreative sex.[77] But, importantly, that naturalization is not materially realized in this case, as reproductive technology begets a multiracial child who is decidedly not the consequence of interracial sex. This is a point I return to below.

The analytic adopted by Grayson and Roberts is not unfamiliar to those reading the intersectional archive on reproductive technology, as it works to counter the patriarchal political economy of surrogacy with a moral and/or political clarity about the racialized history of the gestating body. While giving birth to a child that the law refuses to name as legally one's own does repeat the theft of the body that slavery enacted, reproductive technologies in assisted conception produce the contract as a form of social mediation that differentially commodifies the relation between bodies and life. In this new economy of the body, the contract serves to secure the ideology of liberal personhood as that which, precisely, differentiates the past from the future. It is this differentiation that functions to place liberal personhood within the progress narrative of modernity, transforming the violence of "bodily theft" under slavery into the seemingly benign social relations of autonomy and choice that the contract is made to speak. This does not mean that for Anna Johnson the contract was not coercive; but it does differentiate among forms of coercion that enable us to examine and anatomize the racializing apparatus of the state after slavery's official dissolution and that underwrite, as we shall see, the deployment of various naturalizing discourses of race in the context of reproductive technology today. More to the point, the contract logic of liberal personhood is central to understanding the racial complications of the Rogers-Fasano case, where genetics replace gestation as the foundational language of property-as-life, and maternal affect is rerouted in the language of the law from the discourse of the body to the property life of the gene. For the Rogerses, this is the dream of liberal personhood from its other side, where the contract obligation borne by the fertility clinic and its manipulation of bodily

77. On this point, see especially Schneider, *American Kinship*.

material enables the nonreproductive black woman to succeed in attaining legal maternity. The theft of the body that characterized slavery—in which maternal affect was unrecognizable as either human or real—and that wrote the gestating black body out of maternity is replaced by capital's authority to mediate two mistakes: nature's "mistake" of infertility and the clinic's mistake of improper property implantation. In paying for a service that promises to give nature-as-reproduction "back" to the province of the body, the Rogerses can guarantee their right to liberal personhood through the contract. In this way, Deborah Perry-Rogers comes to own the labor of another woman's gestation, as the property logic of personhood extends itself to the level of the gene.

The question to be asked here, of course, is why the critical discussion of *Anna J. v. Mark C.* takes the media representation of the case as coterminous with the ideological shape of the court's decision no less than as the authoritative measure of its cultural meaning, imposing the precedent of slavery even while acknowledging that the details of the case exceed its terms. The answer to this question has something to do, I am suggesting, with the authority that the precedent grants to the political calculus in which intersectional analysis operates, such that it can be situated as equivalent to (precisely by virtue of its political difference from) the court's state-based authority. In "Breached Birth: Reflections on Race, Gender, and Reproductive Discourse in the 1980s," Valerie Hartouni situates her discussion of the Johnson-Calvert case in the context of Reagan-era discourses of black theft from the public coffers, the emergence of the "fetal person," and the heralded utility of assisted conception to usher the childless white career woman into maternal fulfillment. In this racialized nexus of enthusiastic pronatalism, Anna Johnson is disciplined by both the media and the courts for her errant attachments in a racialized ecology of long-standing historical subordination. In this context Hartouni argues that "the color of Anna Johnson's skin set the terms in which the larger issues raised in this case were addressed and settled," even as she acknowledges that Crispina Calvert "while not exactly brown . . . was not exactly white either" and that the "outcome of the case—as opposed to the contests that structured it—would not have been significantly different had Anna Johnson been white" (87, 83, 87). On this latter point, she cites the Baby M case, in which the white surrogate lost custody of her genetic child to the white contracting father who donated the sperm. The incommensurabilities of the precedent-setting logics at work here are multiple and serve to displace even as they evoke a series of important distinctions between (1) the legal discernments of traditional (Baby M) and total surrogacy (Johnson-Calvert); (2) the black-white binary of race and the identities of the participants involved; and (3) the racialized discourses at work in the court's decision and the decision's failure to mark paradigmatically the genetic tie as white. Still, Hartouni writes that "the proceedings as well as the decision . . . clearly worked to safeguard the prerogatives of race and class privilege—indeed, both worked, as Johnson's lawyer succinctly put it, to ensure that the white baby was given to the white couple" (83).

In the end, then, it is the court's decision that is described as doing the work of "contain[ing] the potentially radical effects of new and currently evolving reproductive practices," such that the "'natural' family" is preserved "as a biologically rooted, racially closed, heterosexual, middle-class unit" (88, 87). In this argumentative strategy, slavery's historical repression is made to counter the legal text as the key determining precedent for understanding Anna Johnson's subordinated status within the linked structures of white supremacy and heteronormativity. By exposing this ideological compact, the critical act becomes a political weapon of its own, serving as the means to demystify the organization of power it names "and in that," Hartouni affirms, "lies a political beginning" (88). This assurance is both familiar and politically inviting as it transfers interpretative power from the legal judgment to the critical act, allowing the feminist critic to plead the surrogate's case in an attempt to win a positive judgment for her outside of (even against) the terms that delegitimated her court claim.[78] But

78. Hartouni struggles in her defense of Anna Johnson in ways that are interesting for identity knowledges as a whole. In an endnote, she tries to deal with the charge that Johnson used the custody controversy to make money on the talk-show circuit.

> While Johnson may have been approached by various talk-shows, in point of fact she appeared only on the "Donahue Show" in order to counter what she took to be widespread media misrepresentations of her claims. Although she apparently received payment for her appearance—$4600, or precisely the amount required to repay Social Services [for welfare overpayments she received]—she testified that she knew nothing of this payment and did not personally receive it. While this seems, on the surface, to be somewhat farfetched, it is entirely possible that any fee Johnson received for her appearance was negotiated by and channeled through her lawyers. Contrary to public perceptions, talk-show guests rarely

the cost of doing so is the premature closure of the legal text's meaning, as the critical argument can only proceed by making the case conform to a paradigmatic reading of black female experience. To be sure, white paternity was set directly against black gestational maternity in this case and won the day, but the court's decision on behalf of the contracting couple was not an endorsement of the "racially closed" family unit as Hartouni contends—at least not if one acknowledges the agency of the *other* woman of color, Crispina Calvert, whose contribution to reproductive life is as crucial as her husband's but whose racial identity is not coterminous with his. Hence, as I have suggested, the racial ideology at stake in the court's decision was not committed to monoracial belonging as the intersectional archive has insisted, as the court's decision is not an unambiguous reiteration of a white masculine hegemony intent on its own racial reproduction.

Why, then, the seemingly studied insistence by scholars to the contrary? Or more to the point, why this insistence as the means to fulfill intersectionality's hope of addressing the multiplicity of women's differences and the specificity of black women's experience in criticism and law at the same time? The answer lies in part in the very promise that intersectionality makes when it designates critical practice as the scene of justice. For by wagering its interpretation against that of the state in order to challenge if not transform the political effects of discriminatory judgments, intersectionality inhabits a juridical imaginary in which its own interpretative strategies and affective attachments serve *as precedent-setting* values. Hence, we might say that it is intersectionality's own critical authority that is most urgently at stake in the paradigmatic strategies of interpretation it both authorizes and demands. To read *Anna J. v. Mark C.* within a racialized ecology that renders the court's decision commensurate not only with the white racial state and its investments but with the deployment of race,

---

receive compensation for their participation beyond airfare and hotel accommodations. ("Breached Birth," 88, n. 3)

Acknowledging that Johnson's self-defense is "farfetched," Hartouni mounts a stronger defense by offering her own explanation, thereby consolidating the equation between harm and innocence at stake in the media's sensationalist coverage. One of the compelling issues rarely addressed in identity knowledges arises here, in the seeming necessity of figuring our objects of study as innocent, which weds the political commitment to social justice to the authority of moral judgments.

gender, and class in both law and culture is thus a means to confirm inter-sectionality's authority to exact interpretative justice where there has been none.

My point in working through the precedent-setting case of *Anna J. v. Mark C.* is less to refute the critical attention paid to white masculine he-gemony than to wonder over the terms of its analysis, which emphasize a paradigmatic approach to both white paternity and black female experi-ence that repeatedly consigns the details of the case to a set of overarching and prior historical predictions. By retrieving the child's multiracial in-heritance and foregrounding the contest between women of color over maternity, I have wanted to explore the ways that the commitment to in-tersectionality falters on the very protocols of paradigmatic reading that attend the juridical imaginary that inspires it. Anna Johnson's loss, after all, is Crispina Calvert's gain, and it will become Deborah Perry-Rogers's as well, demonstrating that black women's interests, no less than those of women of color as a group, are not uniformly arrayed within the racial log-ics of reproduction that frame claims to maternity. To be sure, we can argue that the fertility clinic's mistake makes the ruling in favor of black maternity exceptional, thereby rendering *Perry-Rogers v. Fasano* immate-rial to considerations of past and present subordination of African Ameri-can reproduction. But such a reading repeats the insistence on paradig-matic reading as the authoritative and ameliorative strategy for rendering justice, thereby assuming that black women's experience in law and culture can be paradigmatically known. While this assumption gives intersection-ality a powerful critical voice and inscribes its authority as the generative means to stand with and as the black female plaintiff in the court of legal, cultural, and theoretical opinion, it does so through a set of assurances that intersectionality's own dedication to the complexity of power would encourage us not to ignore: that women of color might have distinct in-vestments not only in their differences from white women but from one another as well. On this point, it matters very much *which* black women come to serve as paradigmatic of black women's experience and how the intersectional archive not only pleads their case but chooses them in the first place. In this, Anna Johnson may indeed be a paradigmatic figure—less of black women's experience per se than of intersectionality's own criti-cal commitment to render a counterdecision to the state as a means to craft its authority as an intervention. It is the commitment to *this* decision that underlies the analysis of the case across the various texts that now comprise its feminist archive, as Anna Johnson plays a role not only in the Calverts' mission to fulfill their biogenetic reproductive desires but in the critical province of intersectional analysis as well, where the desire to demystify the powers that shape both subjects and their social worlds founds the authority it wagers on behalf of its own formulations of justice.

All of this is to say that the foreclosure of the case's meaning effected by the intersectional approach to *Anna J. v. Mark C.* functions to affirm and sustain the very critical authority that intersectionality so powerfully generates. If Anna Johnson is made to *serve* the intersectional archive as its paradigmatic figure, her service is almost certainly disavowed by the rhetorical structure and political vision that generates the intersectional imperative, as nothing in its critical archive enables us to ask why the scholar's defense is routinely taken to be in her interests, not the scholar's own. But in making Anna Johnson the paradigmatic black woman by figuring the case of her gestational surrogacy as the paradigm of subordination, the scholarship that defends her must attest to its own precedent-setting authority and in this intersectionality can be seen within the disciplinary apparatus that has come to define it, one that works to transfer both the power and political effect of the law to itself. No wonder, then, that intersectionality has so much critical authority in feminist practice, as its aspiration toward justice serves as proof that critical practice has been wrenched from complicity and exclusion, which offers unwavering assurance that the critical voice it commands is immune to error and insignificance. My attention to this—the disciplinary demand of intersectionality—is not meant to argue with the power of its powerful investments. But it is to draw attention to the wish that inspires it: for a critical practice that counters the law by establishing its own.

Multiracial Desire and White Paternity

If contestations over race and maternity are brought into view by following the precedents on which the court based its decision in *Perry-Rogers v. Fasano*, it is not yet clear what understanding of white masculine hegemony underlies my challenge to the *Anna J. v. Mark C.* critical archive, especially in the context of the distinctions I offered at the outset between white segregationist supremacy and liberal whiteness on the one hand, and between interracial sex and multiracial desire on the other.[79] Certainly the point has already been made that when the court endorsed the Calverts' intention to have a biological child of "their own," it did not, as Hartouni and others have claimed, follow the ideology of monoracialism that has underwritten white supremacist logics, no matter how much the couple's privileged access to liberal personhood (via class and the heteronormativity of the marriage contract) helped them defeat Anna Johnson's claim. But the Calverts' intention was not white racial reproduction—and it is this that requires attention not simply as a matter of deciphering a key detail of the case but for a broader consideration of the symbolic function of white paternity in the contemporary discourse of the multiracial nation. For in the figures of the two white men before us—Mark Calvert and Richard Fasano—we can read powerful commitments to cross-racial feeling that have very little legible resonance in the repertoire of either popular or historical cultural narration before the 1990s.[80] In chapter 3, I contextu-

79. In moving from a discussion of black and white maternity to white paternity, this chapter reflects the organization of power that has repeatedly occluded the black male's claim to paternity in the narratives of race and sex that found the discourse of both reproduction and nation. That occlusion might be regarded as a history of two differently arrayed repressions: the first is consecrated in slave-based social formations where kinship is subordinated violently to the property regime and patriarchal gender is denied, as Hortense Spillers has so evocatively articulated. The second follows the keynotes of liberal personhood and confers heteronormative privilege through the marital contract while de-authorizing it through a host of state-based subordinations of black paternity. In this second mode, the heteronormative privilege of marriage is trumped by the economic formation of the racialized welfare state. For a more comprehensive discussion of the black male's status in both feminist theory and in U.S. national narratives of race and sex, see my earlier work, *American Anatomies*. For Spillers, see "Mama's Baby, Papa's Maybe."

80. How the white father came to be represented in the 1990s as a paternal signifier for cross-racial feeling and multicultural life is complex, but his resignification was managed in no small part by the "cool" masculinity that characterized William Jefferson Clinton's tenure in the White House. While Clinton is often called the first black president, it is more apt to understand him as the first father of the U.S. multicultural nation. Unlike presidents before him, Clinton avowed his cross-racial feelings and deployed them for political gain. When his presidency threatened to dissolve in sex scandal, it was no small irony that his defenders used the story of Thomas Jefferson as his alibi. Sex scandal, they asserted, was a national tradition. In many ways, this was true, but what made sex a scandal? It was not about "having" sex per se but about having it in ways that

alized this claim by locating the historical emergence of liberal whiteness in the post–Civil Rights era as part of the reconstruction of white subjectivity that accompanied the dissolution of segregation as the official state form of white supremacy. As I argued, liberal whiteness nurtures modes of affect and affiliation that stand in stark contrast to public discourses of separation, segregation, and violence that marked earlier dominant forms of white supremacy in which paternal authority was predicated on legal, psychic, and epistemological investments in national whiteness.[81] It was my contention that liberal whiteness rejected those forms of white supremacy that sought, violently, to preserve the unpreservable (racial purity), and it was within its cultural context that I placed the rise and fall of Whiteness Studies as a specific project aimed at crafting white antiracist subjectivity.

To further that discussion here entails projecting onto both Mark Calvert and Richard Fasano a startling transformation of white masculinity's grammar of racial affect in the form of what I am calling *multiracial desire*. That this multiracialism can be set against blackness, as in the media discussion of the Calvert case, or found illegitimate by the courts, as in the Rogers case, is part of what interests me, as contemporary white racial hegemony is not achieved by a uniform racial ideology, but is secured and unmoored, contested and reformulated by intentions as much as accidents, by structures as much as the subject's negotiation of them, by drastic change as much as the leveling torque of the familiar, by contradictions and instabilities as much as hierarchical entrenchments. Hence my emphasis throughout this chapter is on the multiple contending and contradictory discourses of race, biology, and kinship as they encounter intersectionality's paradigmatic approach to black women's experience in a calculus of power that

---

violated both the taboos that normalize sexual acts and activities *and* the ideologies of white paternal leadership that construct the nation as family and the leader as its father.

81. It is perhaps not coincidental that the major cultural text I read in my discussion of liberal whiteness earlier in this book is *Forrest Gump*, which, while framed by the South and the history of slavery, nonetheless pairs a white male and an Asian American woman as the model for a nonviolent, multicultural future. This alignment has a great deal to do with the film's articulation of a compensatory narrative concerning U.S. involvement in Vietnam, but it is important to note how Asian American female subjectivity mediates the racial dynamic of black/white both here and elsewhere as part of the contemporary multicultural dynamics of racialization. For an important conversation about these issues, see Kim, "The Racial Triangulation of Asian Americans."

replays the precedent of slavery as the determining condition for encoun-
tering the contemporary contractual subject. To argue against this precedent is not to argue against the fact that slavery haunts U.S. culture and
plays a decisive role in the ongoing elaboration and contestations of racialized power in social life. But it is *to situate the historical struggle against
white racial hegemony as an agency of its transformation* and to pursue a
mode of interpretation that resists the lure of paradigmatic reading. To say
that white supremacy is both historically disorganized and disorganizing—
even for those subjects who are considered identical with it—is to grapple
with its power not to diminish it. The point, then, is that the proliferations
of discourses of white multiracial desire in the 1990s do not negate the history of segregationist white supremacy nor do they uniformly extend it.
Rather they respond, contend, and struggle with it, which is why the figures of Mark Calvert and Richard Fasano are so interesting, raising the
specter of white men who pursue their desire for multiracial family at a
historical juncture increasingly willing to reward them for it.[82]

What, then, propels Richard Fasano's claim of kinship with Joseph? It
is not, as in the case of Mark Calvert, the fantasy of normative biogenetic
kinship that heterosexuality affords, as Richard is a genetic stranger to Joseph and has no means to rewrite his relation to the pedagogy of gestation
and birth through which the patriarchal master narrative of romantic heterosexual merger has long emerged. His only means to enter the legal terrain of the case is through the marital contract, and it is precisely that
contract that renders his paternity coextensive with Donna's gestational
claim.[83] In claiming an obligation of kinship to the black child his wife

82. The point is not that discourses of white multiracial desire in the 1990s described,
explained, provoked, or produced Mark Calvert or Richard Fasano—the relationship
between any particular subject and the cultural discourses that represent that subject is
far more dense than our reading of cultural production generally yields. What I offer is meant
to suggest the pedagogies of public affect that have reshaped white hegemony in the "official"
afterlife of state-authorized white supremacy and its aggressive racial nationalisms.

83. In fact, had they not been legally married, Robert Fasano would have had virtually no paternity claim, as paternity is legally recognized first through the marital relation to the birth mother and second, though far less frequently, through genetic relatedness alone. In another case of a fertility clinic's mistake, the court awarded legal
maternity to the gestational mother and legal paternity to the sperm donor, given that
the gestational mother was not married. And in another case, in which the contracting
father divorced the contracting mother before the child was born, the court decided that

bore, Richard Fasano is an arresting figure in the national tradition of white supremacist paternity, one established by the kinship practices of slavery, which consecrated, through the hierarchical arrangements of property and (non)personhood, the cultural disavowal of violently extracted interracial reproduction. One thinks again of Thomas Jefferson and his angst-ridden white descendants. For Richard Fasano, however, the affirmation of paternity situates him outside, indeed against, monoracial conceptions of white reproductive family and national racial purity, thereby marking him as a white paternal subject not subjected to the racial reason of segregation in ways we have come, analytically speaking, to expect. And yet, what is compelling about this case is the pedagogy of the mistake that ushers the white family into cross-racial feeling, for it is under its authority that Richard Fasano comes to imagine himself as Joseph's father—an authority that enables white multiracial desire to emerge in a context made safe by the eradication of sex itself. This is quite different from those situations in which white couples choose to use the agencies of assisted conception for the purpose of producing multiracial families, as the Fasanos arrive at cross-racial feeling without intention. The affective power of nonintention is fascinating as a way to both figure and index the compromise that multiculturalism might be said to offer in its discursive emergence in the 1990s, where the challenge it raised to confront U.S. racial history as the centerpiece of nation formation was countered by a liberalizing concession to equivalence. Multiracial desire, then, not interracial sex.

Nowhere in popular culture have these issues been more cogently portrayed in the context of reproductive technologies than in the 1993 film *Made in America* (dir. Richard Benjamin). The film was no box office hit, to be sure, but it represents one of the first attempts to explore in popular cinema the new reproductive technologies as an arena for cultural rearticulations of race, kinship, and national belonging. Starring Whoopi Goldberg as Sarah Matthews and Ted Danson as Hal Jackson (and writing their very public affair of the early '90s into cinematic history), the film is, narratively speaking, a paternity plot. It opens in biology class where Sarah's daughter Zora (Nia Long) and her friend Tea Cake (Will Smith) complete an assignment to determine their personal blood type. What Zora learns

---

he had no status as the child's "father," given the absence of a genetic relationship, and therefore was not liable for child support. For a discussion of allocations of paternity in the context of fertility clinic mistakes, see Noble-Allgire, "Switched at the Fertility Clinic."

sends her on a quest that yields, at least initially, a twin discovery: that artificial insemination was her conception's sexless primal scene and that her biological father, Hal Jackson, is white. In this, the film engineers a paternity plot in which the origin and existence of multiracial families is born in the detachment of reproduction from procreative, interracial sex. And yet, even this disembodied reproduction is not in the end safe enough. So anxious, in fact, is the film about the specter of interracial sexual reproduction that its final discovery must reverse its inaugurating one: Hal is not Zora's biological father after all. The fertility clinic's records, it turns out, were woefully scrambled when it sent its handwritten documents "overseas" for translation to computer. This last small detail seems hardly worth repeating, except that it provides an ideologically salient displacement, making the origin of confused racial origins external to the nation; it happened "overseas." The plot thus refuses by its end the technological compromise it seemed initially willing to accept, settling instead on the ideologically normative representation of reproduction as a monoracial domain. In this, *Made in America* makes sure that both racial *and national* categories maintain their biogenetic distinction; Hal has not fathered a black woman's daughter; Zora is not a white man's child; the fertility clinic's records have been miscegenated by "foreign" forces. If interracial union, then, is disavowed through the focus on artificial insemination and artificial insemination as a vehicle for biracial reproduction is ultimately rendered impossible, how precisely does the film manage to produce a multiracial family as the cultural destination for a distinctly new American kinship relation, one that rehabilitates the threatened image of the white father to restore his record in national narratives of race and sex that the discourse of the multicultural nation comes to reframe?

It does this by offering the proposition that white acceptance of the idea of interracial kinship is itself a healing pedagogical power, both for individuals and for the nation. When Hal consents emotionally to the possibility of his paternity of a black child, he is transformed from a neoliberal-racist bachelor who lives in a white mansion on a hill to a member of a black family, indeed its new father/husband figure.[84] The construction of the

84. Significantly, Hal's reconstruction is accompanied by financial success (commercials that inadvertently feature Sarah revive his car dealership). This is of course the ultimate white liberal fantasy, that personal no less than national transformation will always be materially advantageous.

scene that marks his affective conversion is crucial to understanding the national discourse that reverberates throughout *Made in America* (the title, displayed in the opening credits in red-white-and-blue script, certainly makes no effort to conceal its national dedication). Sitting alone drinking beer and watching television, Hal becomes emotionally transfixed by the triumphant final scene of *The Little Princess* in which Shirley Temple, that icon of white American girlhood, is reunited with her soldier father, and the two embrace. In a wistful identification with this father-daughter reunion, set against the backdrop of melodramatic nationalism, Hal sentimentally accepts Zora as his own. The pedagogy of this moment of white liberalism is life transformative; embracing the idea of his parentage of a black woman's child, Hal quits a whole range of bad habits, including his emotionally empty attachment to his white girlfriend. The film thus mobilizes the idea of multiracial kinship as a pedagogical lesson in soulful living, thereby rescuing the white man from the very dangerousness that he has come to inflict on himself (through drinking, smoking, reckless driving, and emotional detachment). This lesson is so successful that Hal becomes dejected when he learns that Zora is not his biological daughter. But in the end, the pedagogical lesson requires *only the acceptance of the idea of white paternity of a black child* and not its literalization, Hal's sense of loss is recuperated in the final scene as Zora calls him "my father." Through these plot maneuvers, *Made in America* transforms the specter of interracial procreative sexuality into nonprogenitive multiracialism, as the multiracial family form emerges, distinctly, through something other than sex.

To a certain extent, one could argue that this last fact demonstrates the film's own understanding of the anthropological distinction between social and biological parenting, as the narrative works to denaturalize the cultural insistence that genetic relatedness grounds the affective economy of kinship. The film's ideology of family pivots, after all, on the idea that acknowledging the possibility of fathering a biracial child provides the proper feeling to maintain the psychological link otherwise thought to be initiated by blood. But while the escape from kinship's biological grounding is ideologically enticing, even this social constructionist reading lacks the power to fully rehabilitate the film's invested desire in sentimental feeling as itself a natural domain for the multiracial family's national belonging. For in the translation of Hal's paternity from a biological claim to a symbolically patriotic one that arises from sentimental feeling, the film does not relinquish the discourse of nature, it simply relocates it, and in the process of this relocation, it manages to leave intact the fantasy of distinct bioracial lines. To be sure, *Made in America* does not bar interracial sexuality on the whole, for the romance narrative between Hal and Sarah is quite classically one defined by bodily desire, even if of the PG-rated kind. But their status as a (nearly) postreproductive couple disengages sexual activity from procreative activity. It is for this reason, I believe, that the film labors through a potential sex scene with Zora and Diego, a Latino who works at Hal's dealership. By raising the specter of *this* interracial activity, which is also potentially procreative, *Made in America* confirms its narrative refusal to challenge U.S. ideologies about the naturalness of race at the level of their most intimate threat: sex.

Zora's date with Diego functions in a second important way. It demonstrates that while the film's primary racial form, via Sarah and Hal, is black/white, its broader commitment is not uniformly fixed on this binary configuration. Indeed, the secondary cast of characters affirms a representational multiracialism, with named Latino, Asian American, and African American bit players. But while Hal Jackson's world is peopled with racial "diversity," it is significant that the film offers no other named white male character, which means that the crisis of subjectivity being explored in *Made in America* is precisely that of a now-singular white masculinity facing the possibility of its own erasure. Hal's sentimentality is ultimately the means by which the film manages this subjective crisis, and it is in the nature of his kinship feeling that he comes to be rescued from a vacuous, dead-white life. While such a narrative in which black people give soul to whiteness is nothing new—a version of it underwrites antiracist whiteness wherever it goes—its reiteration here rewrites the threat of white subjective disintegration in the context of a liberal multicultural public discourse that defines racial diversity and inclusion as coextensive with national democratic achievement itself. That the film offers as cultural difference only a commodified representation of Afrocentrism (via Sarah's ownership of African Queen, a book and novelty store) is less a contradiction than a strategic redeployment of all signs of "difference" into the discourse of class and consumption. And it is this redeployment that functions to make "equality" and "equivalence" the founding sensibility of the language (and leger) of personhood characteristic of the emergent multicultural nation.[85]

85. To trace various assessments about the radical and recuperated aspects of multiculturalism's deployment in the public sphere, see Goldberg, *Multiculturalism*; Gordon and Newfield, *Mapping Multiculturalism*; Gutmann, *Multiculturalism*; Escoffier, "The

In the narrative movement that I have now charted—where the initial specter of sexual coupling is denounced in favor of a discourse of cross-racial feeling—we witness the film's ambivalence about the genre conventions of romance that it seems to reiterate: The couple form here must struggle to define itself outside the very conventions of embodied intimacy that locate the romance genre in a narrative discourse about the origins of kinship. In *Made in America*, the ambivalence arises precisely from the potential violation of romance's unspoken affiliation with racial sameness— an affiliation that becomes apparent by noticing how narratives of interracial love are more often organized under the genre terms of tragedy or sentiment than of romance itself. Tragedy witnesses the inability of interraciality to sustain itself, often in narratives that feature passing characters whose "real" blood identity is ultimately discovered, and the lovers must part. Sentimentalism, on the other hand, negotiates the consequences of interracial sexuality by emphasizing not sexual but familial love and founding that love in a broader discourse about moral and national responsibility. In popular texts of the nineteenth century, including some of the most canonical slave narratives, for instance, sentimental discourse defines family and equality as coextensive in order to link black humanity to blood ties and rewrite slavery as the horror of enslaving one's own kin. While sentimental rhetoric was less a challenge to the economic structure of slavery than to its affective economy, it worked by naturalizing, as a form of feeling, the familial discourse that underwrote the monogenetic Christian belief in the total unity of man. Its strategy was a powerful, if not unproblematical, counter to the slavocracy's legal armature, which substituted property for personhood and repeatedly consigned the slave woman's reproduction to accumulation as a desexualizing and defamilializing economic end. And yet, precisely because of its tie to the violence of slavery, sentimental discourse in the nineteenth century turned to cross-racial feeling not to inaugurate a national discourse about multiracialism as the essence, if you will, of national identity, but rather to right the wrong of slavery, understood primarily through the specter of interraciality as the domain of violation and violence.[86]

Limits of Multiculturalism"; Spivak and Gunew, "Questions of Multiculturalism"; and Giroux and McLaren, *Between Borders*.

86. See Yanagisako and Delaney's edited collection, *Naturalizing Power*, for an important set of critical models that historicize the family plot's ideological origins at the

Made in America both lives up to this description of sentimental narrative and departs significantly from it—a departure that importantly registers the historical transformation in ideologies of racial identification that multiculturalism both generates and now governs. On one hand, its narrative trajectory is aimed toward establishing cross-racial feeling and a sense of the implicit kinship between racially differentiated groups of persons. On the other hand, it works to obviate altogether the possibilities that interracial sexuality might serve as the foundation for inculcating this affective economy of kinship. In this contradictory dynamic between biogenetic and social relatedness, the filmic narrative works to extradite Hal, as the emblem of white masculinity, from a history of racialized property relations while simultaneously ensconcing him in the domain of cross-racial feeling. These narrative moves are made possible by the presence of new reproductive technologies which enable a vision of social reproduction that is not dependent on the biogenetic encounter that has come to be written as the originating moment of both nation and culture in sex. We are left, then, with a discourse of cross-racial feeling that sanitizes affect from embodiment, and thereby rewrites the nineteenth-century sentimental tradition from a recognition of inequality and violence into nonsexual romantic comedy, which is to say that *Made in America* achieves the multiracial feeling necessary to the liberal consciousness of multiculturalism itself. In doing so, the film ends up repeating what the *Perry-Rogers v. Fasano* decision assumed with all the confidence that DNA provides for anchoring the truth of blood and nature: that families are racially distinct. As the newspaper reports of the mistake declared, one twin was black, the other white.

Critical Kinship

Throughout this chapter I have been using the Rogers-Fasano story as the originary occasion for considering the messiness of affect, property, and personhood that dis-organized the racialization of reproduction and kinship in late twentieth-century U.S. culture. My archive has been eclectic, even idiosyncratic; and my deliberations on and through the case have

---

intersections of modernity, industrialization, secular humanism, scientific Nature, and liberal personhood.

been less comprehensive than mosaic, circulating as I have done around three different points: (1) how the intersectional archive has insisted on an analogy between surrogacy and slavery as its chief analytic for understanding the contestatory domain of legal kinship; (2) how this insistence has theoretically ignored the contract which serves as the defining feature not only for new reproductive kinship relations but of liberal personhood, which is arguably the dominant subject formation within which racialization now takes place at the level of the state; and (3) how, in the production of liberal whiteness, new reproductive technologies provide the technical assistance to imagine multiracial families without engaging the "living horror" of miscegenation as the fleshiness of interracial sex. In all of this, I have been concerned with the way new reproductive technologies raise knowledge questions about the meaning and origins of both persons and life and simultaneously reiterate and reconfigure the naturalized assumptions that have enabled the most common of kinship terms—family, mother, father, brother—to operate as if they require no critical attention to their social constitution. At the same time, I have tried not to place the issue of reproductive technologies in the context of temporal historical progress, as if the discursive operations of culture ever enable the seemingly new to replace without a living trace the old. Instead, I have used the Rogers and Fasano case to read the realm of reproductive technologies as an incoherent primal scene where embodied relatedness mingles with the genetic authority that has now set Nature in conflict with Life and remapped the body as an engine of replication (the gene) and not reproduction (gestation). In this primal scene, the scientific worldview struggles to establish its hegemony over the blood discourses of everyday life, even as this discourse exacts its revenge by carrying forward the idea of monoracial family and belonging in the language of the gene.

Understood, then, as contestatory knowledge projects, new reproductive technologies engage the "incoherent" intersection of various cultural discourses and social domains and make possible, in their articulation in and through the cultural imaginaries they both inherit and transform, a way to consider how race as a discourse of origin is figured and reconfigured in thoroughly contradictory ways in the United States today. To say that white supremacy is secured by these contradictions would be to offer a decision that forecloses one of the points I have pursued: that white hegemony under the auspices of the multicultural nation is shaped in contradistinction to supremacist discourses of white purity. The contests that arise here demonstrate vastly different affective responses and modes of national longing for the presumptively black and white alike. So on one hand, we witness black reparative politics intersecting with the reconcilatory desires of white multiracial nationalism to insist in different political languages on the restoration of the Hemings line to the story of Jefferson's national founding and white paternity, and on another hand the decisive rebuttal signaled by the Rogerses, who concede that Akeil and Vincent are twins, born together, but in no sense blood relations and hence not "brothers." In the incommensurabilities that arise from these and other juxtapositions in the chapter as a whole, I have been interested in the remaking of the racial logics of kinship in the 1990s such that the reconstruction of the long historical disavowal of the blood discourse of relatedness emerges in the midst of white multiracial desire to make legible the living consequences of the paternity plot of U.S. slavery. This reconstruction challenges the multiracial nation to make good on the core stakes of its own promise, and yet the cultural circulation of white multiracial desire is most palpably expressed in venues of cultural and human reproduction that bypass the terrain of sexed embodiment itself. These re-emplotments of the stories I have been exploring are neither conclusions nor decisions. At best, they are negotiations of the multiple and contradictory fictions of race whose living consequences are real enough to compel us to establish facts even when we know there are none. The racial family is perhaps this chapter's most elaborate fiction, and I have deployed it to define not only the social positions people are ascribed to but the identity forms they inhabit and the contestations that arise when the logic of monoracialism is affirmed or transgressed, whether by accident, imagination, judgment, or gestating intention.

The larger arc of the chapter has been framed by two different meditations on critical practice, both of which array issues germane to the obsessions of *Object Lessons* as a whole. The first has to do with the epistemology of the mistake as a condition of knowing that overwhelms my critical ability to situate the case as a paradigmatic entity—thereby making it impossible to produce and assert the necessary authority to say what, precisely, the case means as a model for contemporary practices of racialization or their amelioration. Under the tutelage of the mistake, I have been compelled to consider instead the contingency of critical practice, which haunts the disciplinary imperative to prove, no less than to provide, continuity and order—especially in those academic domains keyed to the political as their animating agency. It has been in the context of these considerations that I have made little attempt to provide a single overarching argument that can link the discursive sites that I have assembled to read the contestatory affects and cultural images at stake in *Perry-Rogers v. Fasano*. In my failure to commit to the epistemological optimism provided by argumentative closure and secured through the authorizing agencies of paradigmatic reading, I have followed the pedagogy of the mistake to learn not only how it situated the parties whose lives it so radically transformed, but what work its hegemony did to me, the voice that struggles to find a way to live in critical practice without giving in to arguments that are never adequate to the world they stand for—even as I do and have and am giving in. After all, that is the only way that any of us gets the work of criticism done.

The issues raised by the epistemology of the mistake sit at an angle to those addressed by this chapter's second meditation on critical practice, that of intersectionality. While many of its participants array themselves as I do, as both participant and critic, I have stressed from the outset that my purpose is not to exact a more effective or theoretically congruent analytic from the intersectional archive. To be sure, I agree with such scholars as Jennifer C. Nash, whose incisive discussion of Crenshaw's work is in many ways the best to date, when she identifies four problems with intersectional theory: "the lack of a clearly defined intersectional methodology, the use of black women as prototypical intersectional subjects, the ambiguity inherent to the notion of interesectionality, and the coherence between intersectionality and lived experiences of multiple identities."[87] We could of course add others, including the numerous problems that arise from the U.S.-centricity of intersectionality's founding theory of power, history, and subordination. All these problems add up to the strange lacuna that Nash locates at the center of intersectional theory, which is its inability to discern an issue that it would otherwise seem intent on addressing: "whether *all* identities are intersectional or whether only multiply marginalized subjects have an intersectional identity" (9). In considering this problem, Nash points out how the emphasis in intersectionality on multiple marginalization has inadvertently cast black women as a unitary group, such that race and gender

87. Nash, "Re-thinking Intersectionality," 4. Further citations are in the text.

are "treated as trans-historical constants that mark *all* black women in similar ways" (7). As a counter, Nash calls for intersectionality "to abandon its commitment to sameness" by emphasizing the coconstitution of "privilege and oppression" that its reliance on "multiple marginalizations" cannot adequately explore (11–12). Such an emphasis would prioritize considerations of class, nationality, sexuality, and religion as they shape black women's relation to one another, "producing a potentially uncomfortable disunity that allows for a richer and more robust conception of identity" (12). In the process, she contends, new forms of interpretation could emerge, specifically those unencumbered by "the 'logic of the trial'" that has so dominated intersectional thought. As a comprehensive refashioning of intersectionality's critical commitments, Nash also urges greater attention to race and gender as "social processes," not just identity markers, and hence to their intertwined and "*distinctive* . . . technologies of categorization" (13).

In its rhetorical form, Nash's essay is a manifesto for intersectionality's future, as she puts pressure on the three most important critical commitments that have come to define it: "that identity is complex, that subjectivity is messy, and that personhood is inextricably bound up with vectors of power" (13). But I am struck by the way that her critique requires an engagement precisely at those points of theoretical consolidation that have enabled intersectionality to gain its critical power: in the paradigmatic explication of "black women's experience" and in the assumed homogeneity of theoretical and activist deployments of race and gender. For while scholarship committed to intersectionality has been hesitant to take up the vexed intersection of privilege and oppression *when it comes to black women*, it is precisely the intersection with privilege in the cases of both black men and white women that underwrites the necessity of attending to "black women's experience" in the first place, inaugurating the analytic move from antidiscrimination law to the domains of both theory and practice that generates the force of intersectionality's political critique (11). As Crenshaw explains in her founding essay, "Black women are sometimes excluded from feminist theory and antiracist policy discourse because both are predicated on a discrete set of experiences that often does not accurately reflect the interaction of race and gender."[88] In figuring black women's experience as the means to achieve such an accurate reflection, Crenshaw is

88. Crenshaw, "Demarginalizing the Intersection," 140.

doing more than positing intersectional analysis as a fuller account of the complexity of identity; she is wielding black women's experience as a countervalue to other projects meant to address their subordination. The retrospective recasting of her work as the theorization of an already existing tradition lies here, in the massively weighted investment in positioning black feminism as a counterdiscourse of justice in feminist theory itself. For this reason, we could say that Nash's call to explore the paradoxes of intersectionality's theoretical foundation would require abandoning the power and proliferation of Crenshaw's rhetorical point.

In the end, Nash locates the value of Crenshaw's formulation as its precedent-setting success, such that now, with intersectionality's arrival as both "an institutionalized intellectual project and the dominant tool for excavating the voices of the marginalized . . . it is time . . . to begin to sort out the paradoxes upon which its theory rests in the service of strengthening its explanatory power" (13–14). Nash does not address what it means to cast intersectionality as both institutionalized and dominant, but from various perspectives we might say that this is surely a paradox worth pondering. It brings to the foreground the significance of the institutional setting in which intersectionality has garnered its critical authority, such that a theory of marginalization can become dominant even when the majority of those represented by its object of study have no access to the ameliorative justice its critical hegemony represents. This paradox is not the consequence, as many might want to assume, of theory's predilection for abstraction; indeed the success of intersectionality to secure itself as an institutionalized intellectual project arises precisely because of the transference its juridical imaginary effects in casting the state and theory as commensurate. For this reason, I would say that the present configuration in which feminist theory is read as a legislating discourse akin to the juridical state while intersectionality achieves institutional hegemony points toward two different considerations: the overreach of critical investments in the political capacities of theory and the underreach of critical attention to the contradictions and incommensurabilities of the politics of authority wielded and relinquished in diverse institutional settings. While I can agree with the topography defined by Nash for intersectionality's theoretical advancement, I would also want to insist that left theory of any kind does not simply construct an analysis of power as a way of discerning social relations; it lives the complexity of those relations, just as surely as human subjects do. This is why what interests me most in *Object Lessons* is not theoretical resolution, as if any of us can master the meaning of the relations we inherit from worldly actions we did not intend. If I am convinced of anything, it is that no matter what we do, mistakes will happen—and that knowing this is no compensation for the fact that living means living unprepared.

SIX

The Vertigo of Critique

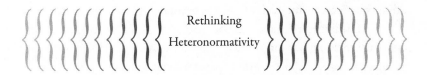

Rethinking
Heteronormativity

While intersectionality serves as a signal figure for political resolution in identity knowledge domains, it is not exceptional in its ability to forward a future-generating project even as its own methodological aspirations remain largely unfulfilled. This is because the political desire invested in it has the entire apparatus of disciplinary reproduction on its side, which does not simply use but requires failure as the resonant condition for generating and sustaining critical authority. As many have noted before me, failure is intrinsic to desire—no matter of what kind—but as I hope to have demonstrated throughout these pages, it operates in rather distinct ways in identity knowledge domains where the incapacity of the present propels the political desire that both founds and characterizes critical commitment. As each of the chapters has explored, it is under the auspices of the political imperative to do justice that the critical value of identity knowledges is forged, giving shape to their object and analytic priorities as heavily vested political relations. My tactic in reading these relations has not been drawn toward arguing with or confirming their authority. Rather, I have sought to elucidate the field imaginary that governs them as a way to inhabit the critical terrain that is formed by the multiple and at times deeply contradictory disciplinary demands that ensue. For this reason, each chapter has been engaged in discerning the formation, force, and consequences of the distinction that organizes *Object Lessons* as a whole: between the political desire that animates identity investments and the objects of study that are taken to reflect, refract, confound, or utterly disable them. In pursuing these relations, I have wanted to emphasize—more accurately to perform—their intrinsic mobilities, which has entailed tracing both the productivity and incapacity of objects to deliver what critics have wanted from them. In doing so, my goal has been to render palpable the ways in which identity knowledges amass their influence, not simply from the work they enable and encourage, but from the belief they help to sustain about the world-building agency of critical inquiry itself. Because this agency is always beset by the poverty of its materialization, the disciplinary subjectivity offered by identity knowledges is simultaneously alluring and reassuring, enabling practitioners to train their attentions on failure as the necessary means for traveling beyond it. Hence, the centrality of critique as the rhetorical and methodological staple of identity knowledge domains: melding authority with pleasure, it reiterates the disciplinary promise to rework failure for transformative ends.

The previous chapter addressed these issues by focusing on feminist critical investments in intersectionality as a counterweight to the now-famous failure of *women* to adequately represent the diversity collated within its majoritarian frame. But while critics have staged intersectionality as a project bent toward evading all universalist attachments, I read the political desire that mobilizes it as predicated on that which it self-consciously seeks to undo. For what intersectionality demands is not the dissolution of all hope for a *we* that can survive *women*'s political overreach, but minute attention to the failures that now condemn it as preamble, even method, for overcoming them. In making the argument that intersectionality pivots on a universalist desire that cannot be avowed, I tracked the complicated transferences it imparts to feminist critical practice, where the commitment to justice becomes literalized in the paradigmatic reading protocols it hones. Here, where critical acts are given the status of juridical judgments, intersectionality promises to resolve the ongoing impasses of identity by conferring critical authority on *and as* knowledge of *women*'s error. Intersectionality's political aspirations thus reside in its determination to render the error—and not the wish that guides practitioners toward it—as the very center of attention, if not the characteristic mark of its own passionate critical disposition. In this it moves in a different direction from the general itinerary of *Object Lessons*, which has followed the agency of the wish as it generates a disciplinary apparatus to grapple with that which interrupts, evokes, negates, or disguises it. Such a pursuit is not meant to give priority to the wish over the failure that generates it, as if attention to the desire for political resolution should (or even could) outweigh critical investments in counting what delays it. Nor is this turn toward the wish a way to resurrect a fantastical *we* that can be inhabited in identity knowledges without dissonance or contradiction. The point, in fact, has been the opposite: that the political desire borne by the wish is itself so fantastical that evidence of it resides almost wholly in practices (both social and theoretical) committed to detailing the ways in which its materialization fails. In the complexity of these generative but vexed disciplinary operations, one cannot track the error without reviving the wish, just as one cannot inhabit the wish without being devoted to discerning the error. This is the conundrum that *Object Lessons* has sought to explore.

In this final chapter, I want to turn more directly to the performative rhetorics of critique and the failure that both propels and haunts it. As I have done before, I begin by telling a story about my own critical engagement with an object of study—in this case heteronormativity, which I take to be both the central political term for a distinctly queer approach to the study of sexuality and the animating agency of its ongoing academic institutionalization. While Michael Warner deployed the concept first in 1991, its analytic origin is routinely traced to critical developments the year before, when two books changed the way identity knowledges would figure gender and sexuality as objects of study altogether.[1] In *Epistemology of the Closet*, Eve Kosofsky Sedgwick offered a theoretical understanding of sexuality that measured the force of heterosexuality's disciplinary compulsion without conforming to it, while Judith Butler's *Gender Trouble: Feminism and the Subversion of Identity* critiqued "the heterosexual matrix" that attended familiar feminist approaches to gender.[2] Soon, Warner with Lauren

---

1. See Warner, "Introduction," 8.

2. Neither Sedgwick nor Butler used the term "heteronormativity," but it is safe to say that there is no contemporary use of the term that does not draw on the critical maneuvers these critics put into play. In *Epistemology of the Closet*, Sedgwick writes,

Berlant on one side of the Atlantic and Jonathan Dollimore on the other would consider the social and psychic operations of heteronormativity, insisting on the importance of differentiating it from heterosexuality per se as part of a larger critical agenda elaborated and embraced as *queer theory*.[3] In this way, queer critique emerged into theoretical distinction by developing heteronormativity as one of its core concepts, thereby extracting the ideological compact between heterosexual and gender regimes that rooted both in nature *from nature* to generate new analytic terrains.[4] Not just: how might scholars critically calibrate the relationships between and among sex, sexuality, and gender without reproducing heteronormativity, but also: how were norms made, circulated, lived, desired, transformed, and resisted? Not just: how were we fucked by gender, but also: was it possible to fuck

My own loose usage in this book will be to denominate that problematized space of the sex/gender system, the whole package of physical and cultural distinctions between women and men, more simply under the rubric "gender." I do this in order to reduce the likelihood of confusion between "sex" in the sense of "the space of differences between male and female" (what I'll be grouping under "gender") and "sex" in the sense of sexuality.

For meanwhile the whole realm of what modern culture refers to as "sexuality" and *also* calls "sex"—the array of acts, expectations, narratives, pleasures, identity-formations, and knowledges, in both women and men, that tends to cluster most densely around certain genital sensations but is not adequately defined by them—that realm is virtually impossible to situate on a map delimited by the feminist-defined sex/gender distinction. (29)

In *Gender Trouble*, Butler's focus on the "heterosexual matrix" serves as the means to discern normativity as a centerpiece of modern power and governmentality.

3. See Dollimore, "Bisexuality, Heterosexuality, and Wishful Theory"; and Berlant and Warner, "Sex in Public."

4. This is not to say that queer critique was *the first* critical discourse to analyze heterosexuality or to define the ways in which its social operations, in Adrienne Rich's famous words, are compulsory. Feminist work might be understood as aiming its critique at *normative heterosexuality* or what Chrys Ingraham has called "heterogender." See the entire collection in which Rich's essay, "Compulsory Heterosexuality and Lesbian Existence," appears: *Powers of Desire*, eds. Snitow et al., along with core criticism that constitutes what is now called women of color feminism, especially as represented by Moraga and Anzaldúa, *This Bridge Called My Back*. For Ingraham, see "The Heterosexual Imaginary." For a useful critique of heterogender, see Jackson, "Sexuality, Heterosexuality and Gender Hierarchy."

without fucking *with* gender?[5] And most important: from which conception of power, what theory of the social, and whose understanding of both the subject and embodiment would the most effective and nuanced critique of heteronormativity come? These questions have produced an enormous amount of critical commentary, yoking together different kinds of academic projects into a shared intellectual endeavor more expansively called Queer *Studies*.[6]

The slide from queer theory to an interdisciplinary field name, Queer Studies, is a temporally short one, but for the conversation here, its critical significance is far reaching.[7] For in the consolidation of queer "studies" as an institutionalized project of antinormativity, queer critique has undergone its most sustained and confounding normalization, one that operates to define the contours of the field and the core critical grammar that drives its political intentions—all this, no matter the fact that the core feature of the field's contemporary self-definition pivots on its commitment to a liberating body of critical reflection, one that promises to resituate the social, psychic, and historical complexity of sex and sexuality on antinormative

5. The language here is borrowed from an exchange between Judith Butler and Carolyn Dinshaw at the February 7, 2002, panel, "Who Owns Gender?" at New York University, organized by the Center for the Study of Gender and Sexuality.

6. On field-documenting collections and textbooks, see Haggerty and McGarry, *A Companion to Lesbian, Gay, Bisexual, Transgender, and Queer Studies*; Corber and Valocchi, *Queer Studies*; Beemym and Eliason, *Queer Studies*; Johnson and Henderson, *Black Queer Studies*; Lovaas et al., *LGBT Studies and Queer Theory*; and Hall, *Reading Sexualities*.

7. In much contemporary scholarship, "queer theory" and "queer studies" are used interchangeably. In "Reflections on Queer Studies and Queer Pedagogy," for instance, Judith Halberstam writes, "I have heard colleagues and students alike comment upon the possible decline of queer theory. Some say that queer theory is no longer in vogue; others characterize it as fatigued or exhausted. . . . Is queer studies in some kind of slump?" (361). For reasons that will become clear, I find it important to differentiate the two entities, which have interrelated critical genealogies, but are not synonymous in either disciplinary or institutional form—queer theory being far more attached to the province of the humanities, especially literary study in its disarticulation from the literary object via critical theory, and queer studies being the interdisciplinary frame for work that shares no specific theoretical preference or priority but is defined more generally as part of a critical project shaped by antinormative critical intentions.

terrain.[8] By exploring the work that heteronormativity performs for the field of study that now writes itself against it, I close this study by tracing the rise and fall of one of my most coveted critical investments, less to dwell on the particularities of Queer Studies than to engage with the rhetorical forms and political intuitions that attend left identity critique in its multiple travels. In the context of *Object Lessons*'s overall intentions, this chapter is a meditation on the problem of arguments—both their progress and detour—and the strange course that concepts take in academic work, including the ways in which they can stop meaning what critics want them to. Such a problem is only slightly less alarming than the way they can occlude the complexities of what they stand for. The chapter is also about the discursive labor of academic inquiry and what I think of as the critical sensibility of being word heavy, argument oriented, and concept driven—the critical sensibility, in short, that attends identity knowledges and the subjects they cultivate, privilege, and reward. These are subjects who believe in explication; who are willing to stake the world, including its very future, on interpretation; and who find both pleasure and despair in what words do. If you are reading this, I am pretty sure that there's a shoe nearby that fits you.

Questionable Arrivals

The story begins simply enough. I was invited to speak at a conference.[9] While the invitation made it clear that the goal was to forward feminist understandings of gender and heteronormativity, I planned to use the

8. David Halperin early on lamented the "normalization of queer studies," but he did so in a rather nostalgic embrace of what he took to be its founding radicality. I want to insist here that my focus on the normativity of antinormativity in contemporary Queer Studies is *not* forwarded as a lament and is not figured as preamble to any suggestion for how best to retain, restore, or preserve a radical signification for the concept, theory, or even identity of things deemed *queer*. In this, I part ways with some of the most respected and authoritative scholars in the field. See Halperin, "The Normalization of Queer Studies," as well as Eng, "Queering the Black Atlantic, Queering the Brown Atlantic," which parses the terrain of contemporary queer studies to determine which kind of scholarship "works to keep queer studies queer" (204).

9. The conference "Heteronormativity: A Fruitful Concept?" was held at the Norwegian University of Science and Technology in Trondheim, Norway, June 2–4, 2005, organized by Trine Annfelt, Agnes Bolsø, Britt Andersen, and Elin Havelin Rekdal

occasion to travel in a different direction. The year was 2004 and I was captured—I suppose I should say "captivated" because the feeling was not yet constraining—by the way queer critique marshaled its theoretical commitments through a performative resistance to heterosexuality as a normalizing regime. Indeed, like many of my peers, I thought it true to say that the theoretical weight of heteronormativity had been elaborated most productively in queer critical and cultural venues where everyday understandings of gender and sexuality were transformed by the priority accorded to unruly organizations of bodies, desires, and identifications—so much so that I took it as axiomatic that the institutional and critical power of queer critique lay in its antinormative intuitions.[10] The conference would be an opportunity to engage the richness of this position by demonstrating how queer critique worked to counter powerful social narratives and the histories they referenced and distorted, less as a project of revision than as one of insurgent redefinition. I wanted to trace queer critique's world-building aspiration, the way it thought that wherever queers pursued a life made meaningful not simply from their own acknowledgment of antinormative desires and identifications but from a collective intention to garner social space, legal protections, religious recognition, and medical

---

from the Center for Feminist and Gender Studies and the Department of Interdisciplinary Studies of Culture. In seeking "to challenge and explore new ideas associated with the concept of heteronormativity," the conference posed a series of opening questions: "What are the theoretical implications and effects of heterosexual expectations in different contexts and historical periods? How can new understandings of 'heteronormativity' help refine and deepen feminist analysis of gender relations? And can analytical tools like heteronormativity be utilised in the humanities and in social sciences alike?"

10. The contemporary scholarly archive on heteronormativity is extensive, appearing in conversations in fields as diverse as nursing studies, sports and sports writing, outdoor education, hunter-gatherer studies, aged care studies, mental health, language study, food studies, military sociology, communications, curriculum studies, and the more traditional disciplines: political science, history, literature, and anthropology. For representative usages of it across the disciplines, see Jackson, "Gender, Sexuality and Heteronormativity"; Hutchinson, "Ignoring the Sexualization of Race"; Ferguson, "The Nightmares of the Heteronormative"; Luibhéid, "Heteronormativity and Immigration Scholarship" and *Heteronormativity, Responsibility and Neo-liberal Governance in U.S. Immigration Control*; Chambers, "'An Incalculable Effect'"; Roseneil, "Why We Should Care about Friends"; Seidman, "From Identity to Queer Politics"; and Pérez, "Queering the Borderlands."

assistance for that life's pursuit, heteronormativity was forced to reveal and defend itself. But more than this, I wanted to show how Queer Studies used heteronormativity to transform gender. Not heteronormative gender in its dyadic coupledom, but sexy, mobile, proliferate gender. Transitive gender. Open, unapologetic, nonconforming gender. Gender like grandma never knew! As I prepared to write my conference paper, it was this that most intrigued me: the seemingly gradual, suddenly ubiquitous resurrection of gender as an object and analytic able to vie with sex and sexuality as the animating center of queer critique's analytic domain.[11] Here, then, was the heart of the talk I wanted to give: to explore how queer critique was committed to demonstrating all the ways in which gender refused to be lived, in psychic and social life, in critical theory as well as ethnographic inquiry, according to heteronormative rules. Queer gender. I even thought it possible to argue that the queer recasting of gender was refiguring the critical boundaries, scope, and meaning of sexuality itself.

I formulated an opening statement: that recent efforts to posit "female masculinity" and its nonidentical correlate, "masculinity without men," were only the latest manifestations of a queer critical and cultural organization staked, rather profoundly, around a desire for gender's transitivity. The signs of this cultural organization, I planned to argue, were everywhere, not simply in the growth of transsexual politics and cultural practices or in the proliferation of boi culture and new transgendered embodiments, but in the longer histories of sexual inversion, cross-dressing, drag, and butch-

---

11. Numerous scholars have discussed this now pervasive shift. In the "Thinking Sex, Thinking Gender" debate in *GLQ*, Heather Love ties the resurgent life of gender as a (if not *the*) central object of inquiry in Sexuality Studies to the emergence of trans criticism. Love writes,

> Although sexuality studies remains as interesting and important as it used to be, it does seem to me that transgender criticism is now addressing questions that were not and could not be addressed at one time. I sometimes find it ironic that queer studies has come back to a central focus on gender, since the founding of the field seemed to entail the liberation of sexuality from gender. The recent work is sometimes heavier than the early work in queer studies, but this is perhaps inevitable, given that the newer critics have once again taken up "the coarser stigmata of gender." ("'Oh, the Fun We'll Have,'" 260)

This chapter is a meditation on the persistent failure of sexuality as object or analytic to anchor the field.

femme that had dominated the queer cultural lexicon in the twentieth century, especially in the United States. My aim, however, would not be to establish historical or critical continuity for these practices nor to heal (though who could object) the rifts that had emerged between trans and queer political articulations and their more academically inclined critical agendas. Rather I would work within the conference's agenda to say something about how such delineations were operating today as an incessant, perhaps even aggressive, queer critique of heteronormativity. This tactic promised to let me share pleasure in the way that the queer pursuit of gender transitivity rendered heteronormativity and its dedication to dimorphic gender the monotonous height of monotonous sameness. Queer desire, I could lovingly affirm, was many things, but the heteronormative idea that it was "same-sex" attraction or worse, a mimicry of gender conformity, was truly absurd.

At the same time, I assumed that if I made my approach to the transitivity of gender expansive—figuring it as embodiment, psychic identification, and social identity, as well as erotic practice and sexual form—I could interrupt some of the ways in which gender had become the node around which various antagonisms between feminist and queer theory had congealed into monolithic caricature. You know the scenarios: queer theory, the angry feminist asserts, faces the Left's exhaustion at the real challenge of revolutionary change by throwing a party. It invites and cultivates gender dissidence; dresses up individualism to simulate political commitment; celebrates the feminine through drag; and always leaves time at the end of the night for some gay-male-only canonical fun. Feminism, the queer theorist says with a sigh, is so indebted to sexual subordination that her masochism requires the repetition that masochism always loves. Every act of theoretical or activist engagement returns her to original sin: gender hierarchy, sexual oppression, material inequality. The self-righteousness of feminism's traffic in material violence, the queer theorist says, is a pornography of its own. There have been significant internal lines of discord, of course, within such monoliths; feminist sex radicalism has long interrupted sexual subordination feminism's reach, just as queer of color critique has unraveled the authorial privileges of queer theory's anti-identitarian theoretics. But what I hoped to get at was the profound intellectual and political intimacy that the debate sustained, an intimacy so analytically underappreciated as to be overtly dismissed by each of the dominant strategies adopted to address it: the progress narrative, which tries to make everyone happy by giving to each some individual space, and the queer theoretic break, which takes analytic abstinence as the means for trying to disarticulate all kinds of attachments. In both of these modes, the stakes of debate are strangely deferred, even as the pretense toward resolution can make us believe that the strategic goal is not postponement. I wanted instead to consider how attending to the transitivity of gender could be interesting in the present critical conjuncture for feminist and queer theory alike.

This meant that my talk would need to pay careful attention to those scholarly projects that had most ushered me into my own thinking, even if in doing so, I would be required to attend to the differences that such intimacy would generate. Two kinds of projects seemed, initially, most important: those that had sought an understanding of sexuality irreducible to gender identifications and identities, and those that had sought to capture the sexuality and eroticism of gender identifications without reiterating either gender or sexuality according to heteronorms. If Sedgwick was most often noted for foregrounding the former and Butler for making the gender trouble necessary to the latter, Gayle Rubin's earlier "Thinking Sex" provided some of the political rationale and analytic capacity that enabled both.[12] My debts, however, were even more recent, as readers of *Object Lessons* well know. Janet Halley, following Rubin and Sedgwick, had made compelling arguments about the importance of "taking a break from feminism" in order to develop a queer theoretic in law that could provide a rigorous approach to sexuality shorn of moralisms and romantic domesticities while intervening in the state-based protectionism of MacKinnonite feminism, whose sexual harassment legislation had become a tool for homophobic persecution.[13] As I discussed in chapter 2, Halley sought to counter

12. See Rubin, "Thinking Sex." The essay was also reprinted as the first piece in the signal volume Abelove et al., *The Lesbian and Gay Studies Reader*. While more than enough has been made of Rubin's polemic against feminism in "Thinking Sex," it is her essay's attention to the relationship between the good/normal/natural on one hand and the bad/abnormal/unnatural on the other that resonates throughout contemporary queer critique and has made it a foundational essay for Queer Studies as a field. See Judith Butler for a critique of the way that the introduction to the *Reader* narrowed the feminist genealogy in which Rubin's work is situated, in "Against Proper Objects."

13. See chapter 2's discussion of Ian Halley, "Queer Theory by Men." See also the longer work by Janet Halley, *Split Decisions*.

the legally institutionalized legacy of second-wave feminism's seeming ownership of the category of women by situating "Queer Theory by Men" as an antidote to the suffocating logic of gender as intrinsic hierarchy. While Ian's argument was an echo of the critique of feminist theories of power already sounded in queer theory, it cast its political desire against the demand for state solutions while presenting sex as the scene of psychic dissolution and unknowability. It was from this essay's critique of "convergence"—where all indifference, pain, inequality, and hierarchy would be analytically and socially ameliorated in one movement or theory, one broad law or paradigm—that I learned to take seriously the incommensurability between the idioms of social movements, their theoretical projections, and the academic institutionalization of identity. Most important, "Queer Theory by Men" provided the means to think about divergence as a powerful aspect of historical change itself, both in institutions and the knowledge itineraries they inscribe and in social practices of identity formation more generally.

While Halley's project jettisoned feminism in order to generate a divergence between gender and sexuality, other scholars, most notably Judith Halberstam, have wanted to consider how gender identities and identifications, nonnormatively cast, were deeply imbricated in sexual practices and cultures. Halberstam's book, *Female Masculinity*, quite soundly critiqued U.S.-based lesbian feminism for its insistence on woman identification and androgyny, and it laid the groundwork for thinking newly about both the gendered and sexual identifications of the stone butch. Today, it still seems possible to say that *Female Masculinity* was the first critical rendering of a "stone butch hermeneutic."[14] Its critique of feminism operated less as a threat to leave feminism than as a reminder, indeed celebration, of the desire for masculinity that had been living in feminism's very midst. Such masculinity, of course, was critically conceived against two common and inadequate assumptions: that masculinity was always a form, expression, or performance of domination and that it belonged, unequivocally, to men. While Halberstam shared with nearly every tradition in feminism the question, "what sexual world did gender create?" her answers always involved the suggestion that lived practices were far more complicated, contradictory,

14. In a study group at Duke University, Laurie Shannon used this phrase to refer to Halberstam's *Female Masculinity*.

and unpredictable than the languages that critics often used to describe them. In her critical perspective, queer scholarship needed not to deprioritize either gender or feminism as a self-constituting rule, but to explore in ever more nuanced ways the transforming relationship between gender and sexuality—in identifications, identity formations, sexual practice, public cultures, and embodied life. If her project never fully escaped the critical enmeshments of identity, as Halley's queer theoretic would want, its failure to do so could be reinterpreted as one of the most interesting and important consequences of her inquiry, no matter how analytically submerged: that gender, not just sexuality, had an erotic life of its own.[15] What was compelling about *Female Masculinity*, then, was the way it could be read to shift the stakes of the segregation of gender and sexuality by trying to locate the erotic practice and potential in the very terrain that lesbian feminism, along with queer theory, had felt compelled to dismiss: gender identity.

My interest in queer desire for gender transitivity was initially situated in the breach between these two kinds of projects. While I agreed, with Halley, that sexuality was indeed excessive to coherent dimorphic gender identity, and planned to attend, with Halberstam, to the sexual life of gender identity, I also wanted to consider queer desire as the simultaneous effect and articulation of a social and psychic traffic in gender transitivity that could not be reduced to gender identity, whether normative or not. I wanted, in other words, to differentiate between the operations of identity formation that were coalescing in a series of trans identities and the way that so much of the sexual life of queer culture—its iconography, affect, language of desire, even the details of sex itself—required a sexual imaginary animated by the lustiness of open-ended, proliferate, transitive gender. My project would thus refuse to oppose sexuality to gender or to secure sexuality through gender identity by seeking instead to trace all the ways in which queer criticism and culture have been invested in making

15. One of the persistent critiques of *Female Masculinity* is that while it presented itself on the side of anti-identity theoretical formulations, its deeper intellectual depths and instincts seemed to reinforce certain identitarian practices, chiefly by proliferating identities, not deconstructing or transcending them. See especially Adams, "Masculinity Without Men"; and Noble, *Masculinities Without Men?* In contradistinction to these critiques, my interpretation of the critical force of Halberstam's work is interested in what it means that her project was unable to leave gendered identity behind.

something sexy—bodies, identifications, acts, and interpretations—by putting gender *on the move*. And further, I would approach gender's transitivity not as antithetical to feminist theory but as part of a broader left critical investment in using the analytic domain for generating world-building projects necessary for emancipatory change. In this case, the change that I wanted to help imagine had to do with intervening more precisely into the operations of heteronormativity, whose past and present confusions over the relationship between sexuality and gender invited not simply ongoing critical objection, but more finely argued outrage as well.

So there I was: finally equipped with a title, an opening statement, paid debts, and the best of critical intentions. I needed only to determine a coherent route to my destination. I decided to organize the talk into three sections: the first on heteronormativity as a critical tool in contemporary queer theory, the second on the return to gender in recent queer scholarly and activist writings, and the third on what it would mean to read a desire for gender transitivity as implicated in and politically necessary to each. Truly, I thought, the talk would write itself.

The Vertigo of Critique

But critique of any kind is a curious sort of work. The actual labor of it requires endurance, and like most kinds of endurance it is easy to be tricked by the fantasy of closure necessary to arrive at the end. This is why some of us invest overly in the plan as if it holds the power of the future's perfection, while others interpret the cultivation of immunity to doubt as sheer bravado and self-assertion. Because critical anxieties tend to coalesce around the threat of endless postponement, it is routine to be relieved by any kind of arrival, even those that portray its author as disheveled or half-dead. Prematurity, on the other hand, is hardly a risk, since academic life never considers early arrival at the finish an ill. The fantasy of closure refuses the possibility that talent lies in the ability to let the process itself prevail. This is the case, I think, no matter how valuable scholars might actually find the practice of critical thinking, or how pleasurable it can be to inhabit the struggle with language that the labor of writing entails. Closure is, after all, *necessary*, not just for the academic professional in need of a recent publication, but also, more urgently, for the political demands implicit in left identity critique. How else will the failure of the future be averted, if it is not possible to find better ways to understand the world we seek to change, or if we fail to understand the change we need to imagine or, worse, if we cannot imagine the change we need to understand? These questions demonstrate the broader stakes of any project's devolution and why critique is most often the device used to discern how *other people's* ideas are inadequate to the desires *we* have invested in them, not the means of tracking the failures and inconsistencies in our own.

So how did my own fantasy of closure fail? Had I begun with the wrong question? Did my title misconceive? Was my opening statement weak? Or did I simply misapprehend what mattered about the question when it arrived into critical legibility? These are all possibilities, but it is most likely that I *enjoyed* the fact that the value of the question lay in what it allowed me to ignore. There's pleasure, after all, in thinking that we can think our way somewhere, and more than a little pleasure in thinking that we might get there when others cannot. This is not a pleasure identity knowledge workers typically acknowledge, in part because we are too busy making claims for the world-making labor that critique entails, which repeatedly cloaks professional investments in the noble rhetoric of the political desire that incites it. But to openly embrace the pleasure that comes from the limits and prohibitions which the question routinely orders? *That* risks revealing much more than we want to know, including our love of disciplinary blindnesses and the methodological circumscriptions that guarantee them, as well as our need to reward ourselves by accomplishing tasks that bolster our belief that we can. This might be one way of explaining why the rhetoric of critique can function as a practice of self-assurance or how, to put it slightly differently, the present is overwhelmed, if not overdetermined, by the anxiety and compulsion of arriving at the end. Anticipation may be admissible as a kind of pleasure, but deferrals and dead ends are serious forms of deprivation.

Let me sketch, then, the three biggest problems that my initial presumption gave me freedom to ignore. The *first* emerged from my attempt to locate the specificity of gender transitivity as a desire intrinsic to queer culture, which was connected to the *second*, the fraught translations between identity projects in the public sphere and the utopian political attachments of analytic enterprises.[16] How, after all, could I seek to delink the desire for

16. In "Sex, Panic, Nation," Bruce Burgett makes an important notation about the distinction at stake in my discussion here. He writes, "Treating the three core concepts of sex, sexual, and sexuality as *analytically* distinct and decoupling each of them from questions of identity and nationality does not mean that any of them can be *descriptively*

gender transitivity from an investigation of identity formation when the evidence for the very proliferation of gender mobility that I was poised to praise—where transgender is not transsexual is not lesbian is not dyke is not butch is not FTM—was taking shape in the rights-bearing logic of contemporary personhood as a set of discrete identities, such that errors in taxonomic precision were increasingly perceived as violent political efface-ments, and the very use of transgender and transsexual rubrics was inter-preted by some activists as a queer theoretical theft of trans identities and political agendas? In this context, how could I pursue a critical inquiry that wanted to resist identity consolidations and the disciplinarity of the

---

disarticulated from identitarian and nationalist cultures and politics in any given his-torical conjuncture" (69). Following Foucault, his project calls for an account of the his-torical emergence of the concepts of sex and sexuality, such that contemporary queer in-quiry not repeat the myth of their transcultural and transhistorical "realness." In the process, his essay calls for a methodological resolution that should be familiar to *Object Lessons* readers: "The point is that those cultures and politics can be properly understood only if our critical and historical epistemologies—our ways of knowing about them—do not reproduce the embedded assumptions of the social and historical formations in and through which they are enacted" (69). For Burgett, this means emphasizing trans-national analytics, intersectionality, and interdisciplinarity in order to challenge the "isolation of sex and sexuality as discrete interpretive categories and objects of analysis" (70). But if historicization is the counter to social and conceptual essentialisms, it is not clear how these frameworks can be simply taken as antithetical to the normalizing pro-cedures of critical thought, as if *their* political effects are already known to be precisely the ones we most want. The very formulation of power, history, and culture that Burgett so incisively relies upon suggests otherwise, demonstrating that even critical alternatives and their invested significations are not alternatives *to* the social and historical forma-tions they are set against, but alternatives *within* them. To put this another way: the on-going transformation of the political horizons of left criticism is not a progress narrative of critical mastery, but the substance and struggle of a complex historicity. How to en-gage *this* aspect of identity knowledges is harder than pointing to the violences and injus-tices of a social world that make such knowledges both necessary and vital. As I have said before, I don't believe that any of us can participate in identity studies without repeating the critical habits that make such work legible and credible within the political imagi-nary of the fields that we belong to. This means that *Object Lessons* is not about rescuing us from our habits so that we can do different, if not "better," work; I'm more inclined to think that our habits are incredibly interesting and need to be rescued from us. See Bur-gett, "Sex, Panic, Nation"; along with Blum, "A Response to Bruce Burgett." As a coun-ter to my use of his work here, see Burgett's compelling analysis of the problems attend-ing the writing of the history of sexuality in "Between Speculation and Population."

state (re: Halley) without in some sense positioning my project as a rejection, or worse condemnation, of group aspirations for identity-oriented recognition and legal protections? And what about the general framework of "queer culture" or "queer desire" to begin with? Did I actually want to collate the kinds of proliferations, migrations, and circulations that I had set out to chart into a composite entity that could so comfortably house them all? What traction could *desire* wield if there was no aspect of the pursuit of gender's transitivity that left anyone unfulfilled?

In a general sense, these questions were not new to critical and cultural struggles around identity, as they seemed to reflect the various incommensurabilities between the spheres in which identities are socially produced, analytically conceptualized, experientially inhabited, and both politically claimed and resisted. If I wanted to learn to take incommensurability seriously, as Halley taught me I must, I would have to refuse the compromises that my question offered: I would have to resist the desire not only to cast the desire for gender transitivity as a coherent, mutually shared and historically legible cultural and critical organization, but also the consequent impulse to posit one domain of inquiry (the cultural) as intrinsically related, if not ultimately referential and epistemically privileged, for the other (the theoretical). The seeming impasse between something called theory and something called culture could not be resolved, then, by something called queer desire, nor could I let the word "queer" do so much suturing work. What, after all, was this *queer culture* that the diversely queer belonged to?[17] How much tautology (queers belong to queer culture; queer culture is crafted by queer hands; queer theory is the consequence of queer culture; queer theory is queer culture) could my inquiry withstand? To be sure, I witnessed this conflation in all kinds of well-regarded "queer texts," but I sensed something a little desperate about my own need to make such claims on behalf of the very queer culture I assumed was the origin and locus of the desires I was projecting onto it.

If the intractability of the divides generated here between theory and practice on one hand and the suturing coherence of "queer culture" on the other were not heavy enough, it was the *third* problem—the relationship between gender transitivity and heteronormativity—that quite literally

17. Kevin Floyd takes a historical look at the problem of "culture" in queer theory. See his "Making History."

stopped me in my tracks.[18] Remember that I had taken queer critical interest in heteronormativity as a means for rendering legible—as identity, embodiment, politics, and practice of living—all the ways in which queers refused to live according to heteronormativity's intransitive gender rules, which meant that heteronormativity was the reference and text against which queer gender did its most inventive, antinormative, and decidedly transitive work. But just how coherent, comprehensive, and generative was heteronormativity as a theory of gender? Did it explain what scholars used it to discern? As much as I was convinced by the queer desire for gender transitivity as a political expression, I grew less certain about its analytic dispensation when I stared down my foundational assumption: that gender under heteronormative compulsion was not simply tacitly, but definitely *intransitive*. Really? How so? How precisely was dimorphic gender— that allocation of two sexes as two genders—intransitive? Certainly the organization of bodies, identities, identifications, affects, ideations, and intuitions across the historically diverse relation of sex and gender was not static, universal, or historically transcendent; this queer critique knew and used to its own analytic advantage. So what picture of which historical social formation enabled me to assume that an increasingly privileged conception of sex, used to define an increasingly privileged destination of gender, was an intransitive formation? Or, in Wittigian and later Butlerian formulation, what historical conditions generated the rendition of gender I was citing, in which sex was to be dimorphically conceived, and why was I willing to take *that* particular traffic in embodiment and identity as intransitivity? Couldn't the story be told in exactly the reverse: that in its historical emergence, heteronormativity inherited and mobilized a vast cartography of sex and gender whose transitivities it reworked to its own remarkable and transitive ends, giving us dimorphic heterogender? Couldn't it be the

18. I use theory and practice here as a shorthand for what I would prefer to call the conceptual categories of lived experience and critical imagination, which might begin to capture something of the different forms of abstraction that constitutes each. This formulation is counter to much contemporary scholarship, which tends to position "experience" as the "ground" against which abstraction is rendered superfluous to social change, which in turn requires that "experience" be consciously and concretely delivered. This flatlining of the complexity of experience requires that we misrecognize the way it functions *as an analytic category* and leads to rather impoverished understandings of the work of memory, narrative, identification, and desire.

case that any configuration of sex and gender, any formulation of their in-terrelation, even those that refused completely to converge them along with all those that thrilled to merge them, were *always transitive*: always about some version of mobile itineraries of gender and sex whose meaning emerged in specific historical context? In short, how could gender ever be intransi-tive, if it was the productive force that engineered the social meaning of sex? If queer critique assumed this point regardless, taking heteronormativity as the agency of gender's intransitivity, wasn't it reiterating heteronormativi-ty's effect as the very means to critique it?

To be sure, there was no way to pursue these speculations without risk-ing the critical authority promised by fidelity to the field's antinormative intentions, and I was not keen to abandon the optimistic attachments that I had taken as my own. But the inquiry that shaped my conference paper had begun to unravel, leading me to a debilitating suspicion: that the cri-tical authority derived from critique belongs not to the critic but to the questions she learns to hone.

Objects and Their Wishes

Still, it is impossible to know precisely how far the question goes in making its maker, which might explain why the matter is typically settled at the outset in the maker's favor. The maker, after all, is enormously productive. S/he must amass and organize long traditions of critical reflection, ingest and develop argumentative strategies, and attract and convince an audi-ence devoted to both similar and divergent aims, all while trying to find an answer that delivers her animating question to a satisfying end. In this, the question can be lived as an instrument of self-creation, making it difficult to imagine that the force of its urgency is not always—certainly not only—the worldly conditions it references in order to redefine. And what of the critical authority that shapes our objects of study, compelled as they are into the heart of our self-animating questions? Formed by affection, attachment, identification, disavowal, refusal, aspiration, intention, want, or need, our objects of study are bound to duty, invested with the fantastic expectation that they will fulfill all our dependent needs. But as *Object Lessons* has sought to evince, we no more own our objects of study than we possess the ideas we use to authorize them, which is why I said at the outset that our objects of study, like all objects, have wishes of their own. They can refuse what we try to make of them. This is one way of explaining, in the near-perfect narrative logic of retrospection, why my objects—heteronormativity and queer desire for gender transitivity—could so spectacularly elude me. But it says nothing yet of how I eventually faced this. *That* requires a grammar lesson.

Transitivity, I started to remember, is the property of a verb that must take a direct object; in this, it is the mechanism for mediating the relation between the sentence's subject and the action it takes toward an object. An intransitive verb does all the work on its own; it is both action and object for the subject. Transitive verbs, some of us once learned, were dependent, and back in the days when we diagrammed sentences, we were taught that they were weak because they could master no action on their own. Solid writing, many English teachers affirmed, emerged from a vocabulary of sturdy verbs that required nothing. Over time, however, many of us learned the pleasure of finding words to elaborate the object, of sentences that held their breath while they traveled elsewhere. There ware all kinds of pleasures that came in finding objects for our subjects, which is just one way of saying that we earned something for ourselves when we learned to constitute a subject through the objects that we named. Dependence, it became clear, was the real condition of the subject, and that dependence was not a matter of linguistic structure alone. Words meant in context and context proliferated. While I learned early that a masculine object was necessary to my sexual subjectivity, it took longer to know that this object could never be legibly bio-male—and longer still to understand what that object's gender made (and continues to make) of my own.

What this grammar lesson started to suggest to me, among other things, was that no gender formation escapes the subject/object relation because no gendered subject is possible without an object on which its ability to act as a subject depends. This is not to subscribe to a notion of sexuality that constructs it as wholly object driven, nor to produce the object as materially separate or external to the "self." Both of these interpretations would merely reproduce the fantasy of coherence that the recognition of the subject's profound dependency otherwise suspends. Rather, the grammar lesson served to open a space within the framework of my initial question about the queer desire for gender transitivity to consider the possibility offered above: that gender is constitutively, inherently transitive, in terms of both its embodied productions and the circuits of desire it circulates within as well. Whatever fixity it seems to achieve in the processes of normalization does not render it intransitive; such fixity merely identifies normalization as one mechanism for delivering the animating phantasm: that masculinity, for instance, is originally, naturally referentially male, not the consequence of a social operation that produces this very insistence. To assume otherwise, especially within queer critique, might say more about a desire for the political reach of the concept of heteronormativity than about a distinction (between transitivity and intransitivity) that properly accrues to gender itself.

In the political and critical spheres of transgender analysis, of course, grammar is no insignificant issue, and the seemingly coercive dimorphism of subject pronouns has been under intense debate for quite some time. One trajectory of discussion, characterized by Sandy Stone, Kate Bornstein, and Leslie Feinberg, has always seen the bipolarism of normative sex-as-gender as an impossible demand that diminishes the fluidity and intense psychic mobilities of both sex and gender.[19] Another, keynoted in academic circles most prominently by Jay Prosser, has sought to reject celebrations of gender instability by granting authority to the desire to render psychic identifications stable in the referential materiality of embodied sex.[20] The latter work, in particular, has challenged the queer theoretical link between gender instability and radical politics, in part by interrupting the notion that transsexual destinations in legible sex are mere instances of heteronormative conformity. More recently, Bobby Noble has traversed the seeming difference between these perspectives by forwarding a critique of both taxonomic impulses and notions of sex/gender coherence without relinquishing the ground of struggle as one engaged with the everyday political consequences of living trans sexed.[21] Noble's "post-queer" articulation of "incoherence" sits at a compelling angle to both feminist politics and queer theory, neither of which are expendable or adequate, in his terms, on their own. Susan Stryker follows suit but ups the affective pitch into a field-setting proclamation, one that figures the difference between queer theory and Transgender Studies in such performative gusto that readers of *Object Lessons* will no doubt experience déjà vu. She writes, "If queer theory was born of the union of sexuality studies and feminism, transgender

19. See Bornstein, *Gender Outlaw*; Feinberg, *Trans Liberation*; and Stone, "The Empire Strikes Back." See as well two essays by Cheryl Chase, "Hermaphrodites with Attitude" and "Affronting Reason"; and the anthology by Nestle et al., *GenderQueer*.
20. See Prosser, *Second Skins*.
21. See Noble, *Sons of the Movement* and "Refusing to Make Sense."

studies can be considered queer theory's evil twin: it has the same parent-age but willfully disrupts the privileged family narratives that favor sexual identity labels (like *gay, lesbian, bisexual*, and *heterosexual*) over the gender categories (like *man* and *woman*) that enable desire to take shape and find its aim."[22] The reproductive language that Stryker uses here to authorize the divergence between trans and queer mimics queer theory's earlier de-ployment as the term for critically transcending feminism and its various discourses of gender normativity. When Stryker writes, then, that Trans-gender Studies investigates "forms of embodiment and subjectivity that do not readily reduce to heteronormativity, yet that largely fall outside the analytic framework of sexual identity that so dominates queer theory," it is not surprising that Transgender Studies is offered as the emergent emblem to fulfill the "radical queer potential" that queer theory cannot.[23]

As I have discussed in chapter 2, what is often at work in these fraught moments of divergence between projects deeply related—feminist and queer theory, for instance, or queer theory and Gay and Lesbian Studies, or Transgender Studies and queer theory—is a temporal mode of emer-gence that requires, by its very logic, a claim to critical succession. While such succession is never more than a heartbeat away from generational warfare and the psychic modalities of family romance (Noble's book is called *Sons of the Movement*), the point is not to seek to cleanse scholarly discourse of all manner of reproduction, genealogical, metaphorical, or otherwise. I've become much more interested in the way that the gender transitivities most at stake for me as I followed my conference paper's devolution re-vealed some interesting things about the critical engine of divergence it-self: that these fraught moments are, first, subject constituting, by which I mean that they produce new positions of critical authority as well as con-firmations of the legibility of new categories of personhood in the social formation as a whole; and two, that they are consolidating in both their critical and political effects, by which I mean that they help organize the target from which they most self-consciously diverge into the very coher-ence that is articulated in turn as the target of their critique. Women, gay and lesbian, gender, feminism, queer: none of these categories were ever as stable and knowable as the critical discourses that claim divergence *from*

22. Stryker, "Transgender Studies," 212. See also Stryker's edited volume, "The Trans-gender Issue."

23. Stryker, "Transgender Studies," 214, 215.

them have tried to suggest. This is as true of queer theory's divergence from feminism based on a notion of feminism's intractable reliance on heteronormative gender *as it is* of Gender Studies's analytic supersession of *women*'s exclusive universalisms *as it is* of Transgender Studies's divergence from queer theory based on the latter's seeming failure to differentiate itself from LGBTQ's identitarian reach.[24] And it will be true of future divergences within the crosscurrents and contradictions of critical formulations that emerge from the overlapping but not coeval signs of embodiment marked as transsex or transgender, especially in their profound and differential imbrications with the analytic pursuit of race and its divergences from discourses of ethnicity and culture on one hand and biology and genetics on the other. Condensing this into the terms of an object lesson would entail repeating this: that the consolidation of any identity form into the figural fulfillment of the political desire that brings it into being is tentative and transitory, the site not only of ongoing revision and differentiation, and of optimism and attachment, but of predictable disappointment, if not at times political despair. Such affective failure is as necessary as the inaugural ambition, in part because it restores the horizon of possibility by delivering optimism for new objects or analytics to achieve the political resolution invested in them.

The purpose of tracing my path from grammar's transitivity lesson to the topic of divergence is not to subordinate the content of the critique of queer theory in trans scholarship nor merely to append some of the most urgent recent debates to a tableau of prior critiques and their field-forming successions. Rather, I mean to chart how my critical passage through the present nexus has served as the route for my own necessary return to the problem of the political imperative on which my initial question seemed to depend. For if one of the major interventions of transgender critique was its refusal to forward queer as a critically or culturally inclusivist noun, the other was its criticism of critical acts that call every embodied, psychic, or relational alignment of sex and gender heteronormative. Hence, if a FTM who dates women cannot be called heteronormative in any, well, heteronormative sense, and if the whole emergent archive of Transgender Studies seeks a rethinking of the terrain of gender transitivity and embod-

24. It is also the operation that New Americanism engaged in its self-definitional turn away from the Cold War apparatus it would cogently identify, as I discussed in chapter 4. See also Wiegman, "The Ends of New Americanism."

ied sex, what was the bar that separated heterosexuality from sharing in the desire for gender transitivity itself? And if there was no distinct bar, how could queer critique continue to operate as the privileged analytic perspective for discerning the translation of heterosexual gender presumptions into heteronormative rule? If the proliferation of gender transitivity that I set out to track as a queer cultural refusal of heteronormativity was meaningful, it had to be meaningful as, well, something else.

That something else has come to live in the story of my conference paper as an erasure: not the queer desire for gender transitivity, as I initially tried to think it, but more sparsely and yet more expansively *the desire for gender*, a desire that I would now say accrues across various domains in which gender travels: not simply to Queer Studies or Feminist Studies or the acts and identities that either field takes as a challenge to the heteronormative script, or to Transgender Studies, which takes a desire for gender as embodied sex as its inaugural event, not just in those realms of everyday life in which the human serves as gender's most precise object, but also in the practices, modes of desire, and discourses of gender within heteronormativity and the compulsory heterosexuality it begets. This last move, as I have insinuated earlier, delivers me to an arresting and counterintuitive claim born in my paper's devolution into conceptual failure: that the heteronormative social apparatus that generates dimorphic gender masquerading as bio-real sex is not adequately conceived as an insistence on gender *intransitivity*. On the contrary, the heteronormative insistence that gender serves as the privileged mode of signifying the meaning of sex—and hence that gender *is* the body's meaning—is part of a broader, if contradictory, social and psychic desire for gender, a desire animated by profound, incommensurate, and proliferating investments in the look and feel, the language and symbolics, the erotic life and the everyday manifestation, as well as the mutability and transitivity of gender. If gender was to be acknowledged as a term constitutively, irreducibly steeped in transitivity, what precisely had my critical project, initiated to account for the creative and resistant agencies of queer culture, become? Why, in short, give the desire for gender to everyone?

This last question seemed to be at the theoretical heart of whatever conference talk I could imagine trying to give, but instead of turning my attention wholly toward it—which would have meant scrapping the detour and beginning again—I felt compelled to continue following the failure of my originating intentions. After all, my objects of study had gone wild, refusing the political investments I had invested in them and producing new issues that my initial question had foreclosed, including what to do with so-called straight subjectivity and with those modes of sexual identification, embodiment, and desire that found no adequate measure from within the homo/hetero script. Why had my theoretical interest in gender transitivity assumed it to be resonant in queer critique and culture alone, such that heteronormativity was so completely congruent with the subjects it sought to master that only queer life evinced any psychic difference from it? And if queer critique turned the tables on heteronormativity by making normativity itself pathological, what then could we understand about normalization and the political and psychic work of normality itself?[25] Or more to the point, what did we really learn by taking the struggle against normativity as the normative emblem of political good? I was certainly not prepared to encounter these questions, nor could I have imagined arriving into the startling conclusion that making every aspect of normativity pathological was simply to participate in the knowledge project of normalization itself.

But more than this, I was confronted with the difficulty of maintaining my own commitment to divergence, which I had already taken up as a means to side with queer theory without having to cast aspersions on feminism or to consolidate its political meaning according to what others took to be the most egregious versions of "her." How, in the one instance, could I argue so strongly for letting feminism be nonidentical in its historical and political formation such that the theoretic attachments that moved me were neither overcome nor undone by feminism's worldly travels and ongoing struggles with its own complicities, while in the other instance I was happy to converge the political animations of my theoretical acts with the cultural forms in which I found their expression? With all the interest I had

25. This is the conundrum of Michael Warner's *The Trouble with Normal*, which makes a claim for an ethics of queer life that is the critical consequence of queer communal rejections of the norms of sexual subjectivity, relationship, and affect ascendant in dominant heterosexual culture. But because the ethics he touts is dependent on the conceptual framework of normativity for its own meaning, the project's satisfying polemic is achieved only through a specious consolidation of all desires for normativity—including lesbian and gay ones—with the social processes of normalization. The consequence of this, as I discuss at the end of this chapter, is that antinormativity becomes the disciplinary measure of queer critique's own tautological "queerness."

shown in the importance of allowing identity attachments, political movement discourses, and academic theories to travel away from one another with no insistence that they might reach any kind of consensus or mutual reflection, my conference paper nonetheless began inside the disciplinary move that I had been spending a great deal of time apprehending, if not trying to suspend: that move which begins by already knowing what it sets out to study because the position from which it has constituted its object bears all the epistemic privileges of the identity of the subject that attends it. All the pomp, then, to give queer theory its anti-identitarian teeth by refusing to marshal an argument either for queer theory by men or against feminism's privileged women was so easily cast aside when the pleasure of the critical act lay precisely in refusing to know the difference not simply between queer culture and queer theory but between the object of study, the theoretical act, and the subject I had become through the converged intellectual and political attachments that collated under the sign of the *queer* in the first place. If every deployment of *queer* as a theoretical lever relied on the epistemic value already invested in it, then my inquiry's purported destination in the practices of queer culture was not one: not a destination, except as the circuitous return to the location in which my itinerary began, where *queer* stood in fierce opposition to the cultures and practices of normalization from which it had *by definition* already diverged. In this, "queer culture" was the epistemic value I was banking my critical authority on even as I sought analytically to discern precisely what queer culture could yield for an antiheteronormative critical practice.

Focusing on the itinerary of failure was the only way to rescue myself.

Here, then, is a rather different premise from the one I was originally prepared to use: that the critical pursuit of gender is never different from the political desire invested in it. I see the evidence of this everywhere, as gender has been arrayed to discern a wide range of social, psychic, and conceptual relations, including the embodied translations between and among these three domains. Whether it is deployed with affection or aggression, for analytic precision or autopoetic pleasure, with the force of discipline or for unabjected celebration, the critical pursuit of gender is premised on the political vision that defines it as a primary need. If feminist, queer, and trans inquiries currently provide the framework for conceiving the different but related stakes for the pursuit of gender, this does not mean that one is the truer, more accurate, more useful, more urgent account of gender than the others (though there will always be those who make such claims).

Rather, from the vantage of *Object Lessons*, their multiple and contending ambitions underscore the political desires that shape the divergent answers they propose to a set of questions they mutually share. What, they all ask, is gender? What does it do? Who wants it? What does it animate or congeal? When does it fascinate? When does it do us in? By locating the critical pursuit of gender as the consequence of the political desire that divines it, this chapter arrives finally, no doubt simplistically, at *yes*. Yes to gender. Yes to gender as a social system, as a division of labor, as a structure of inequality; as a mode of dis/identification; as an occasion for sex; yes to gender as a habit of thought, a terrain of recognition; a source of shame, a practice of pleasure, a language of being; yes, in short, to gender as the critical means to describe, inhabit, represent, embody, critique, applaud, and resist. And consequently, yes to two final directions: one that supposes that there's more to learn from the incommensurate ways that gender has been wielded to challenge heteronormative compulsions; the other that wants to specify what the slide from queer theory to Queer Studies might tell us about all this. The final moves of this chapter begin by taking both things first.

Antinormative Normativities

While every scene of departure entails some kind of arrival, it is always difficult to know exactly where one is until the force of the familiar takes shape in the new place. Arrivals have little to do with inhabitation; they mainly play a dramatic role in retrospective narration, which means that as much as I can master the story of my conference paper's dissolution into failure, the subsequent challenge of explicating the meaning of *being here* requires a different narration. Here, where what must be considered is the familiarity of the quest to outrun the familiar and the disciplinary demand that regenerates it; where objects of study are constituted, coveted, and condemned in relation to their ability to deliver what the critic wants from them; and where the field imaginary is calibrated to the belief that critical practice is a world-historical agency of its own, no matter the repeated anxiety that it is not. Here is the place that *Object Lessons* has tried to inhabit all along, where attention is paid not only to the disciplinary commitment to justice and to the political desire that underwrites and propels it, but to the rhetorics of critique and the critical authority it simultaneously collates and dispenses. Inhabitation then: which is not about studying identity knowledges in order to leave, change, or perfect them, but to pay attention to what they make of us and why practitioners cannot recognize ourselves as such without the aura and allure, the suspicion and belief, the love and aggression that comes in pursuing the promises they promise to keep. To be sure, the structure of this ongoing relation is confoundingly circular, as political desire propels identity's academic formation and shapes the field imaginary that comes to define critical authority, primary objects, and privileged methodologies as part of the priority of doing justice, all while producing practitioners who take their relation to the field not as discipline but as political investment—most often by taking the political as what we bring to the field, not what the field demands, cultivates, and hones as its primary discourse and disciplinary relation. This is not a diagnosis of complicity, since that diagnosis is staked to the possibility of arriving into a conceptual if not material relation where complicity is not. For this reason, *Object Lessons* has spent no time lamenting institutionalization or arguing that with just the right object of study, critical concept, or analytic perspective, the routes and routines of critical practice can be disarticulated from the disciplinary apparatus that now governs and reproduces identity-based fields. Nor have I wanted to use this project to say that if we just stop all this disciplinary investment, we can cultivate political agencies that are not weighed down by their imbrication in institutional, professional, or disciplinary authority. After all, the critical practice that brings me *here* was learned from within the very frameworks I am trying to discern.

The point is rather that the operations of identity in identity-based fields of study are not limited to the object of study or to the social identity of the practitioner, but steeped in a disciplinary apparatus calculated to produce identity too. This *disciplinary identity* is always a complex imbrication of relations of reflection, dis/identification, and representation to the field's primary object of study, whether in the inaugural value form, as I called it in chapter 2, or in its poststructuralist and postidentity reframings. In this complexity, the particular formation of disciplinary identity within each identity-based field has its own distinctions, being bound to diverse social histories, multiple and even conflicting logics of embodiment and personhood, and a dense array of critical discourses that have been brought to bear on it. If *Object Lessons* has been interested in how identity knowledges produce disciplinary identities in their translations of identity production and forms of critique from social movements to the university, the story I have sought to tell has not been that there is just one mode or method for doing so—nor that the disciplinary relation to be discerned in moving across identity domains is a paradigmatic one. I have been compelled instead by how identity's different points of departure entail and require different kinds of critical and institutional negotiations, which is why I have thought that the object lessons that ensue need to be deciphered—not just assumed—in their relationship to the beliefs and projections that inaugurated them. While this is most true in contrasting the domains collated around minoritized objects of study and superordinated ones (such as whiteness or the imperial U.S. nation), it is important to stress that there is no simple congruence between fields that address minoritization in the three most insistent academic forms in which it is currently arrayed: race, gender, and sexuality.[26] Indeed, as I indicated in the previous chapter, even the political desire that generates intersectionality as a demand to attend to identity's inherent complexity and the exclusivizing itineraries of the single-figure academic domains carries its own universalizing hope, making it important to pay attention to the ongoing quest for a *we* that can survive its confrontation with difference to stage a cogent, if contingent collectivity. *Collectivity*: that absolutely vital, potent synonym for the wish at the heart of identity knowledges, which underscores and enlivens the political commitments that have shaped and transformed them all. It was this wish that lived in my conference paper's founding emphasis on *queer culture* as the locus and impulse of the desire for gender transitivity.

This is also the wish that attends the seemingly incidental slide from queer theory to Queer Studies that I referenced at the outset, which has significance for deciphering what it means to be *here*.[27] Queer theory, let's

26. The status of class as an object of academic inquiry is an interesting one, as it has never accrued institutional attention as an identity knowledge. In fact, as I read it, identity knowledges were crafted in the divergence of race and gender *from class analysis*, primarily through the critical figure of Marx, giving rise to a split within left political theory that remains animated, if not at times quite toxic for understanding how structural inequities and identities are formed today.

27. I have made the potentially erroneous decision in this section to refrain from attributing my characterizations of "queer theory" and "Queer Studies" to specific scholarly actors, choosing instead to organize my comments in terms of governing narratives drawn from institutional documents and research collections that speak to and for the

remember, took self-conscious shape as a divergentist critique of both Feminist and Gay and Lesbian Studies, and sought from within the framework of mostly humanistic inquiry to challenge the Enlightenment legacies of a willful, self-knowing subject such that sexuality might emerge as something analytically distinct from dimorphic sex, gender role, and both gender and sexual identity. In doing so, it resisted the identity practices of knowledge production through which one arrives into critique on the epistemological ground of a shared social experience, which means that it sought a certain kind of distance from the inaugural value form where critical authority was dispensed according to the practitioner's own identificatory relationship to the object of study that her social position implicitly represented and named. Without intimacy with a subject of knowledge made credible by her experience, queer theory's critical practice privileged deconstructive maneuvers, explicitly exchanging identity objects of study for analytic formulations, with *queer* being the key term for discerning sexuality's travels in various networks of power, including those that would most insist on its divergence not just from gender as a mode of subordination or from the normative postulations of M/F that accompany it, but from the generative structures of heteronormativity that have been understood as foundational to each. With these critical priorities, queer theory sacrificed much of the proof-making apparatus that liberal humanism had made politically necessary and familiar, seeking instead to unsettle the framework of sexuality as coherent identity by moving the study of sexuality onto other critical grounds, chiefly those of antinormativity. Herein lay the centrality of Foucault—not only his signal work on the history of sexuality but his long-standing attention to genealogical inquiry and the formation of the modern episteme.

Today, of course, the queer theoretic has been critiqued as harboring its own universalizing pretensions, privileging the already privileged and installing a very specific critical agent at its center: the white gay male scholar.[28]

---

field. On program documents, see n. 33. On special journal issues, see especially Eng et al., "What's Queer about Queer Studies Now?"; Murphy et al., "Queer Futures"; and Halley and Parker, "After Sex?" On special forums and discussions, see Glick et al., "New Directions in Multiethnic, Racial, and Global Queer Studies"; and Jagose and Kulik, "Thinking Sex/Thinking Gender."

28. For work that critiques the normative subject of queer theory in a variety of registers, see Hemmings, "What's in a Name?"; Johnson, "'Quare' Studies"; Namaste,

Its critical archive has been faulted for muting the importance of analyzing geopolitical arrangements and the normative bind of modern knowledge formations as they reiterate nationalist epistemological frameworks, which is read as the means to subordinate critical attention to the political present, routinely signified by the terms globalization, neoliberalism, and imperialism.[29] Most crucially, its analytic itineraries have been considered narrow, individualistic, and overly indebted to Western frameworks—so much so that even the term "queer" has been read for its geopolitical provincialism, if not as a symptom of the imperialism of U.S. cultural and conceptual idioms altogether.[30] These criticisms reflect not only queer theory's inability to satisfy the multiple desires that have been brought to it, but the fact that its animating critique has never been free from the identitarian logics it sought to decipher, no matter its aim and aspiration to the contrary. It is this that the institutional emergence of Queer Studies—the capitalization in relation to queer theory is important here—both registers and accedes to.[31] For in accommodating identity's irresolution in queer theory, Queer Studies dis-

---

"'Tragic Misreadings'"; Harper, "Gay Male Identities, Personal Privacy, and Relations of Public Exchange"; Giffney, "Denormatizing Queer Theory"; and Seidman, "Deconstructing Queer Theory."

29. See, for instance, Harper et al., "Queer Transextions of Race, Nation, and Gender"; Hennessy, "Queer Theory, Left Politics" and "Queer Visibility in Commodity Culture"; Morton, "The Politics of Queer Theory in the (Post) Modern Moment," "Birth of the Cyberqueer," and "Global (Sexual) Politics, Class Struggle, and the Queer Left"; and Cruz-Malavé and Manalansan, "Introduction."

30. For various perspectives on the geopolitical provincialism of queer theory, see Povinelli and Chauncey, "Thinking Sexuality Transnationally"; and Wesling, "Why Queer Diaspora?" For discussion of the individualist predilections of queer theory, especially as formulated through the perceived hegemony of psychoanalysis in the field, see especially Ferguson, "Administering Sexuality"; and Grewal and Kaplan, "Global Identities." For a counterargument on the question of psychoanalysis and queer theory, see Freccero, *Queer/Early/Modern*.

31. To be sure, practitioners in Queer Studies routinely disavow the field's (no less than their own) institutionalization, but the very usage of the term reflects and mimes the dominant language of field authority in the contemporary U.S. university. This does not mean that Queer Studies has succeeded in establishing well-endowed programs in its name at the majority of U.S. universities, even if it has been used to designate curricular forms and to expand already existing program entities, creating LGBTQ Studies and the like. The point is not about the materialization of Queer Studies as a funded institutional entity, but about the imaginary of the field that its usage both invokes and *comes to*

penses the sign of the *queer* across the incommensurate registers that comprise its social and intellectual itineraries—and with far less debate, consternation, or critical stress than in the past. Gone are the days when every conference exploded around the possibility that a queer theorist might not be gay, or that the very demand that a theorist be gay might not be queer.[32] Instead, queer has come to be wielded, even in critique, as a term of

---

represent, and hence about the multiple and expansive critical territories that its recitation enables practitioners to claim.

Let me emphasize this point. While the practice of Queer Studies outside of its own autonomous institutional sites is different from the practice within it, both are institutional projects. The difference they reflect is *in the kind of institutionalization they evince.* Any claim for a noninstitutionalized Queer Studies is not simply a contradiction in terms, but a disavowal of the authority garnered by those who speak to, within, and as practitioners in the field, though part of the point of my discussion here is to draw attention to the way that claims to be against institutionalization is one of the surest means of performing the disciplinary identity that Queer Studies dispenses. For a telling look at how central is the issue of anti-institutionalization for the political idealizations of queer critique, see Berlant and Warner, "What Does Queer Theory Teach Us about *X*?"; Halperin, "The Normalization of Queer Studies"; and Dinshaw, "The History of *GLQ*, Volume 1."

32. Important recent exceptions include the Gay Shame conference at the University of Michigan in 2003, and the much less discussed Queer Matters conference at King's College, London, in 2004. The Gay Shame conference erupted over two different but familiar issues: the relationship between academia and activism on one hand, and the white racial hegemony of queer critical authority (as evidenced in the paucity of scholars of color as key presenters) on the other. For a discussion of the former, see Mattilda, "Gay Shame"; and Love, "Epilogue." For the latter, see Halberstam, "Shame and White Gay Masculinity"; Perez, "You Can Have My Brown Body and Eat It, Too!"; and the collection of papers from the conference itself edited by Halperin and Traub, *Gay Shame*.

For an account of the Queer Matters conference, see the forum organized by the AsiaPacifiQueer (APQ) Network, "Replacing Queer Studies." In the introduction, Peter A. Jackson, Fran Martin, and Mark McLelland summarize their concern over the conference's narrow geopolitical engagement, specifically "the ongoing dominance of US-based research and researchers within the field":

> Several aspects of the conference sparked such reflections. These included: the lack of any non-England/US-based speakers in the conference's plenary sessions (indeed, even British voices were a rarity amid the massive dominance of US-based scholars); the casual disregard—despite well-meaning declarations of American "humility"—that was shown by most of the US-based plenary speakers for sexual cultures anywhere outside of the United States; and the tendency for

mobility and de-referentialization while also collating a host of identifica-tory projects (including those that render *it* a category of identity). Thus, the *queer* of Queer Studies can name a subject position, a category of identity, a historical experience, a subjectivity, an identification, a critical analytic, a gender discourse, a practice of embodiment, a sexual formation, an ethics, a politics, a theoretic, a mode of interpretation, a practice of reading, a knowl-edge project, and an agenda for social change.

Through its own self-animating antinormative intentions, then, Queer Studies gets to have its cake and eat it too: it can function as an organizing referent for queer theory while simultaneously forging an interdisciplinary critique of it; it can promise to fulfill queer theory's anti-identitarian com-mitments while proliferating identity commitments of its own; it can re-fuse institutionality while participating in and generating its own institu-tionalized forms. If it consequently misrecognizes the scope and increasing hegemony of its own institutional power, it is not because it operates on bad faith or critical arrogance, or that it simply has fallen prey to the rou-

---

questions about cultural difference to turn inevitably into questions about ethnic difference *within* the US nation-state, while the issue of differential national-cultural positioning was all but ignored. Problems also arose as a result of the streaming of papers according to geographic area, which produced an unfortu-nate "ghetto-ization" of Asian queer issues.... Finally—and very forcefully—a central problem was brought home to us by the statement made by one plenary speaker who, defending the US-based journal *GLQ*'s apparent lack of interest in publishing translations of non-English-language queer studies work, flatly as-serted that the "default" language of queer studies today is, in any case, English. (300)

What's interesting about the juxtaposition of these two conferences and their cri-tiques is how race or, in APQ's usage, ethnicity is figured quite differently. In Hiram's essay, for instance, the exclusion of scholars of color and of critical race work reveals a foundational white patriarchal nationalism in queer theory, with the excision of queers of color functioning to uphold the historical abstraction of citizenship and belonging to whiteness and maleness. In APQ's critique of the geopolitics of queer critique, the figure of the U.S. queer of color as a referent for race and queer race studies confirms instead of interrupts the nationalism of the U.S. formation of queer studies. Both critiques, of course, can be correct at the same time, even as their confluence suggests not only the incapacity of U.S.-based interventions into American nationalism to travel internationally, but the difficulty of race to be wholly disaggregated from the national specificity of its scene of articulation.

tines of generational transmission that characterize authority transfer throughout academe. The point to be made is that queer theory's critique of identity as a normative feature of modern governmentality has been no match for the antinormative itineraries that found Queer Studies. The distinction that has emerged is subtle but exacting. *It is not the normativity of identity as a form of modern biopolitics that is chiefly under assault in the slide from queer theory to Queer Studies, but normative identities, along with normativity itself.*[33] Or to put it another way we might say that in

33. An increasing number of programs use the nomination Queer Studies. While precise data are really difficult to locate (as many academic resources do not differentiate between Sexuality Studies, LGBT Studies, LGBTQ Studies, and Queer Studies), well-known Queer Studies concentrations, minors, or majors exist at California State University–Northridge, Wesleyan College, Smith College, Denison University, Humboldt State University, and the University of California–Irvine. Nearly all of these use the concept of norms and (anti)normativity in their official descriptions of the field. For instance, according to one popular program on the West Coast, Queer Studies "questions normative constructions of sexuality and gender" by focusing "on histories, contemporary experiences, and community-based knowledges of lesbians, gay men, bisexuals, transgender people, intersexed people, queers, and others who occupy non-heterosexist and non-normative gender positionalities. The program explores how heterosexism, heteronormativity and transphobia intersect and collide with national, ethnic, racial, class and other identifications, fostering a community of learners who grapple with issues of diversity, gender, sexuality and social justice." Another defines Queer Studies as "an emerging interdisciplinary field whose goal is to analyze antinormative sexual identities, performances, discourses and representations in order ultimately to destabilize the notion of normative sexuality and gender. Queer studies comes out of a critique of identity politics. It rejects essentialized conceptualization[s] of sexuality, gender, and sexual identity as innate or fixed. It represents a deconstruction of hegemonic conceptions of sexual and gender categories within straight, gay and lesbian communities. In queer studies, the interpretation, enactment, and destabilizing of sexual identities is linked to that of gender categories." And a third describes Queer Studies as "the study of how norms are produced and come to be taken for granted, and, conversely how they are destabilized either through their own internal contradictions or through the interventions of activists seeking social justice. Thus the field shares intellectual affinities with the interdisciplinary fields of women's studies, gender studies, ethnic studies, critical legal studies, and cultural studies. Interdisciplinary insights from area studies, religious studies, science and technology studies, and visual studies also enrich this field of study." In a brief survey of the mission statements of LGBT programs, I found none that did not use the language of norms and normativity to describe their curricular focus. Anonymous citations are intended.

institutionalizing queer theory's theoretical commitments, Queer Studies reinterprets its assault on identity by making normative identities as well as the structures in which sexual and gender normativities are produced and protected its primary disciplinary identity and critical aim. It is for this reason that the term "queer" can be appended to the very identity markers its critical divergence was cast against, begetting LGBTQ Studies and similar conglomerations, not as contradictions but as elaborations, even proliferations, of the subjects, objects, and sites of the field's interdisciplinary engagements. In the kinds of paradoxes that identity seems repeatedly to stage, this makes the reproduction of normativity absolutely central to disciplinary authority, which is why so much effort in Queer Studies is currently expended to name and at times even to shame those normativities that are inhabited, desired, and pursued *within* gay, lesbian, trans, and queer discourses and political projects as well as outside of them. In this, antinormativity serves as the single most important disciplinary norm for critical legibility in the field.

What, then, of heteronormativity? To the extent that its analytic capacity has generated much of the field imaginary of Queer Studies, it has become less an object of study than a precondition for the field's self-constitution and managed incoherence. As with other field-forming designations, the precondition necessarily circumscribes a domain of inquiry (no matter how expansive it is), defines its political aim, and routes its practitioners to the horizons, habits, and formulations thus inscribed—all of which function to impart modes of authority and belonging in the field. Is it strange to say then that heteronormativity is the engine through which Queer Studies has consolidated itself, underwriting the generic force of normativity as the target and rationale of its field imaginary and the political project that is routinely ascribed to it?[34] Surely not, if we consider that no

34. Against an increasing critical insistence, I would argue for *greater specificity* in the critical deployment of the concept of queer to resist consolidations of the term into a generic framework that organizes all social groups, practices, and evidences that can be found exterior to normative U.S. ideologies and cultural forms. For instance, in tracing the relationship between sexuality and racial modernity, Roderick A. Ferguson's work often comes to stand as evidence for a kind of zero-degree analogy between racialized difference and homosexuality, even as his work is quite explicit in citing the analogy's genealogical origins in canonical sociology. The fact that African Americans are historically (in and in the wake of plantation slavery) in excess of bourgeois familiality does not

identity knowledge—indeed no minoritized identity form, no matter how self-critical and anti-identitarian in political commitment—can actually succeed in dismantling the target of its resistance without fundamentally undoing itself, and that undoing is ambivalent at best. To put this conundrum another way, we could say that there is always a good reason for refusing to acknowledge what the survival of our desire requires us to ignore. So even if this discussion might lead to the conclusion that Queer Studies must now reinvent itself, either by shifting its sights from normativity or giving normativity a far more historical specification, or by opening its idealization of antinormativity to critique, there will be no way to arrive into a newer version of the field cleansed of strategic foreclosure. Like it or not (and mostly, I think, we do like it), fields of study, regardless of their content, are identity formations precisely because that is what disciplinarity confers. As is true of field formations of every kind, one becomes a Queer Studies scholar by participating in its conversations, theoretical priorities, discursive tropes, methodological practices, and citational histories. How utterly paradoxical that the reproduction of the critique of normativity is one of the surest ways to secure belonging in the field! (The other, as I discuss in earlier chapters, is to claim to be outside the field as the performative condition of residing within its terms.)

To be sure, this explanation is less than critically fulfilling. What can be more antithetical to the contemporary sign of the queer than the inability to cultivate a little political optimism in and through it? Even the best architects of queer negativity offer enormous political pleasure in defying affirmative conceptions of sociality and the attachments to futurity that

---

mean that they are "queer" or "queered subjects" unless the term "queer" has been universalized as the transhistorical sign of the nonnormative. To be sure, a great deal of scholarship is now leaning in precisely this direction, making all signs of social abjection, deviance, and counterbourgeois socialities into figural elements of a queer critical imaginary. But the collectivity imagined in the process arises at times in flagrant disregard of the ideological commitments and experiential complexities of the subjects arrayed within it, for whom the queer political imaginary cannot be assumed to be legible, let alone hospitable, to their desires, identifications, and attachments at all. For an interesting discussion of queer critique as a methodology for analyzing race, see Ford, "What's Queer about Race?"; and for a consideration of nonnormative heterosexuality and the problem of binary consolidations of identities in queer political activism, see Cohen, "Punks, Bulldaggers, and Welfare Queens." For Ferguson, see *Aberrations in Black*.

compel them.[35] Why, then, the absolute failure to make failure our political guide, given how masterful queer critique has been at rendering loss into survival, mourning into militancy, and melancholia into productive resistance—indeed, in investing in the very alterity that our valued distance from heteronormativity confers on us? Why all this pondering of the necessary omissions, conflations, and refusals that produce the alternative political imaginary signified by the queer, especially when I have been moved so deeply by it, not once but many times before *and* when everything I was taught to value is at stake in the failures I have followed and enacted here? Am I giving up, turning scared, or is this an effect of middle-class middle age, which calms itself by looking at the world and acting bored? Or maybe the problem to be grasped is simply this: that repetition does breed a kind of exhaustion, such that what was once a salve can become an aching sore. (Consider, once again, the persistent irritation that is now the category of *women*.) In such a context, there can be a certain relief in following failure—not just because it addresses a range of symptoms but because it promises new diagnoses right up to the end.

So let's consider what the devolution of my critical attachments has revealed about the figure—gender—that initially compelled me. First, we might say that as gender has been pursued as an object of study, it has proliferated meaning, traveling across experiential, analytic, and theoretical domains where it has been deployed by different critical projects to varying, at times incommensurate, ends. In this proliferation, gender is most decisively made and remade according to the political desire that finds it valuable in the first place. Second, as in all matters of desire, we must grant the object we pursue the authority of its own ungraspable difference, which means that there is always the possibility that it will resist what we want to make of it. The gap we encounter here, between what we critically seek and the object that may fail to deliver it, renders the pursuit of gender perpetually incomplete. This situation is to be neither resolved nor lamented. Rather, the point is that much more is at stake in our object relations than what we take their pursuit to mean. As I use the term here, "object relations" references two different levels of interdependence: between the knower and the

---

35. Lee Edelman is currently at the forefront of the queer critical elaboration of the negative as the scene of political critique. See his "Antagonism, Negativity, and the Subject of Queer Theory," "Ever After," and *No Future*.

object of study s/he critically constitutes and investigates, and between the knower and the political investment the critical pursuit is meant to sustain and confirm. If much contemporary debate has been engaged in arguing over the terms by which gender will be critically addressed and analytically known, much less has been said about the political desires that propel its pursuit altogether. It is this that "The Vertigo of Critique" has been meant to explore.

Summation

Every ending requires its own retrospection, if only as a means for completing the rhetorical project of narration. So after so many pages of detour, let me offer a few points of summation, less a conclusion than a series of potential implications that arise from inhabiting identity knowledges and their resonant aspirations.

1. Whenever we constitute an identity object of study, we are trafficking in a desire for critical practice to do emancipatory work. If we find ourselves disappointed that our objects and analytics don't live up to what we need from them, as we inevitably do, the problem we face cannot be resolved simply by finding something new. As *Object Lessons* has tried to prove, some attention needs to be paid to the disciplinary demands that govern what we *expect* our objects and analytics *to do*.

2. If the desire for gender explored in this chapter seems inescapably ludic, wrapping politics as it does in the realm of fantasy where desire is routinely thought to live, I can only wonder who imagines that politics of any kind are possible without fantasy coordinating some of the footwork. From this perspective, the problem for identity knowledges is not how to make our conception of politics accord with reality alone, but how to register the projections, transferences, anxieties, and aspirations that comprise it.

3. In the end, the desire for gender is not simply about wanting or not wanting gender. It is not about having the gender we want or getting everything we want from gender. It is not even about extracting from gender an account of the world worth wanting. It is neither a heuristic nor an agenda, not a detour or a destination. In the context of *Object Lessons*, it is a figure for foregrounding the anxieties of incompletion that the priority of critique is meant to heal.

4. If my use of "the desire for gender" remains murky, it might be because the phrase lacks critical ambition. It is not a formulation that explicates a problem, nor an analytic that struggles toward resolution. It has no distinct political agenda, and its critical capacity is amassed for the sake of the general, not the specific. While it would be nice if the case were otherwise, it harbors no insight into the urgency of the present. The most that it delivers is an intuition: that the desire for gender will leave none of us alone.

And Yet

No argument is ever finished, but that rarely stops us from performing our arrival at a definitive end. There's happiness in the resolute conclusion and a certain relief that we have survived the final stroke. I, for one, take enormous pleasure in the concluding flourish, even if I know that what remains to be said is often more interesting than whatever I can declare *done*. So let me delay just a bit longer to ponder the analytic road not taken—the one that lies on the other side of all this noise about contemporary queer critique's animating attachments to gender. After all, when queer theory turned up to dress feminism down, it made a lot of promises about prioritizing sexuality that it failed to keep.[36] If Queer Studies now seems enthralled by gender, what might we say about the sex queer theory once sought so defiantly to have? Did its bold declaration for critical monogamy undermine its desire from the outset, igniting passion for the very thing (gender) that its commitment to sexuality categorically refused? Or should we craft a psy-

---

36. This is not to ignore the prescient "Thinking Sex" by Gayle Rubin, or Pat Califia's biting *Public Sex*, or Leo Bersani's angry "Is the Rectum a Grave?" or Cindy Patton's brilliant "Visualizing Safe Sex," or Douglas Crimp's pedagogical "How to Have Promiscuity in an Epidemic," or Michael Warner's castigating *The Trouble with Normal*, or Juana María Rodríguez's haunting "Gesture and Utterance," or Kiss and Tell Collective's riotous *Her Tongue on My Theory*, or Selena Whang's unnerving "The White Heterosexual Couple," or Tim Dean's eviscerating *Unlimited Intimacy*, all of which take on sex as practice and relation, as embodiment and self-shattering form. Nor am I suggesting that when queer theories seem not to be talking about sex, they are saying nothing about it at all. The issue I raise here concerns the extent to which queer theory has ever achieved the kind of critical intimacy with sex that its narrative of origin has claimed. On this latter point, see the special issue of *South Atlantic Quarterly* called "After Sex? On Writing Since Queer Theory," edited by Janet Halley and Andrew Parker.

chic account of the historical situation, one that traces how the investment in sex as analytic aim was so profoundly embedded in counterhegemonic rage against the homophobic nationalism of dominant responses to AIDS that there was no way *not* to become exhausted by it?[37]

Or maybe, under the influence of the vertigo that has led us here, we might consider the possibility that queer theory's theoretical project to attend to sex was undone by the very political ambition that emerged to characterize it—that is, by the priority accorded to the critique of heteronormativity, which has made antinormativity, as I discuss above, the primary political gesture of the field. How else might we understand the structuring paradox that underlies contemporary queer critique, where scholars simultaneously reject taxonomies of the normal and abnormal while privileging precisely those acts, identities, and identifications abjected by normalization? Hence, the field both refuses the logic of normalization and incessantly revives it in order to mark its relation of alterity to it. Readers of *Object Lessons* have seen this critical motion before. So, on the one hand, scholars work stridently to counter the discourse of normality and perversity that founds heteronormativity, offering new sexual vocabularies along with radically different moral scales for understanding the vast collection of acts and identifications that live at the outer reaches of its regulatory regime. No sex practice that violates any of heteronormativity's rules is considered perverse according to the counterlogics and refused identifications cultivated by queer critique. On the other hand, with antinormativity as the highest critical value, the field must cultivate, often to the point of idealization, the most resolutely alternative—that is, the most radically perverse and socially unassimilable—in order to do justice to the project of alterity and difference invested in the sign of the queer. It is this latter emphasis that is seen in the ongoing critique of gay marriage and homoreproduction for their reiteration of heteronormative induction, accompanied as it is by a resounding scholarly silence on the Civil Rights aspects of the marriage movement or the political desires that might now be collated or condensed within it, including those arising from the historical trauma of the first decade of the AIDS epidemic.[38] This

37. One of the most evocative and moving essays to trace queer theory's relation to the emergency of AIDS is Nunokawa, "Queer Theory."

38. I am certainly not the first to suggest that both the baby boom of the 1990s and the marriage movement of this century need to be contextualized as compensatory

is not to jump on the marriage wagon, as I carry no brief for it, but it is to point out how the shape and scope of the scholarly conversation is pitched to reveal and confirm the field's antinormative intentions.

Let's consider the paradox I am tracking here another way. Imagine attending with critical rigor to sex itself—to embodied acts, erotic forms, fantasies, affects, identifications, and cultural organizations of bodies and desire—while trying to ensure that our investigation takes political aim against normativity.[39] Fist-fucking, BDSM, polyamory, sex with friends, erotic vomiting, stone femininity. What kind of critical attention can avoid the slide into analytic normativity that description and referentiality entail? Does ethnography suffice? What about historical inquiry, genea-logical analysis, narrative interpretation, sociological survey, or autobiog-raphy? Which methodological approach can protect our critical invest-ments in the antinormative value and stature of our object of study from the normalizing protocols of the very knowledge regimes that we would

---

mourning strategies for communities rocked by overwhelming loss in what some com-mentators take to be the genocidal first decade of the AIDS epidemic. The stories are now legend of lovers and partners denied access to medical decisions, hospital visita-tions, funerals, and the remains of shared households, including children. If "marriage" figures as a broad compensatory response to these exclusions, it is not adequate to render the entire movement as one motivated by normative desires without offering a history and context in which our understanding of normativity takes material form. This is not to deny that a more radical antistate politics could be created by seeking to abolish mar-riage altogether and to interrupt the consolidation of race, class, and national privilege that marriage begets. The point is rather that very little queer studies scholarship has been interested in historicizing the emergence of normativity in queer communities and politics, both in relation to the psychic impact of AIDS and to other resonant materiali-ties. More often, the accepted critical interpretation reads gay marriage at the level of macropolitical life, linking it with neoliberal governmentality and/or the U.S. state's incorporation of homosexuality into the normative project of empire, thereby casting the subject's everyday negotiation of the horizons of political inclusion in binary terms, as either liberal complicity or queer antinormative rebellion.

39. "Sex itself" is, of course, an impossible formulation, but I pursue it here as part of the rhetorical performance of this chapter, which is different from producing a critique to represent the analytic truth of my political desire. This stage of the chapter is meant to grapple with the terminological difficulty that sex raises as an object of study for a field bent on achieving antinormativity as an analytic, critical, and political goal. For an ex-cellent discussion of the difficulty of analytically apprehending various sexually over-marked acts and bodily parts, see Franke, "Putting Sex to Work."

use to discern it? And further, how can scholars pursue a critical interest in the specificity of sex without reiterating the discursive formation and ideological predispositions of heteronormativity as the primary lens of analysis, as indeed the governing framework not simply in modern social life but in our analysis of it? That is, how can we wrestle both the category and the domain of sex from heteronormative definition if our critical project begins with the supposition that the contemporary organization and practice of sex is a consequence of it? Each resistant act is bound to its reigning definition; indeed there is no resistance without first establishing heteronormative definitions.

How, then can the field cultivate the antinormative without being committed to the normative? And once we are so committed, what precisely differentiates heteronormativity's hold on the social organization and imagination of sex and sexuality from its critical, analytical hold on us? Is there satisfaction with the field-forming answer: because *we* know how to critique it, because *that* is what we mean when we use the word "queer"? These twists and turns are all consequences of the disciplinary formation of antinormativity as the guiding frame and political guarantee that shapes the field. Hence, too much sexual specificity in ethnographic attention or narrative description can pose a threat to the sexual imaginary of the field by rendering nonnormative practices familiar and potentially unremarkable on their own terms. The problem deepens when one considers how even the most socially abject sexual acts, affects, and identifications are prone to their own normalizing scripts, social rules, and ideological routines, which means that their emblematic "perversity" and counternormativity can be fantastically undermined by the specific sexual grammars, affective forms, and erotic bonds that attend them in the very community formations in which they emerge into social distinction. Is it enough, critically speaking, for queer critique to claim their antinormativity on the basis of its own antinormative investment in the sign of the queer—in other words, to call the sex queer because the subjects who engage it or the acts they engage violate the prescriptions of the sexual domain defined as heteronormativity by the field?

At the heart of the antinormative enterprise, then, is a deceptively simple but as yet unanswered, perhaps unanswerable, question: What is the sex that queers so queerly have? Or more pertinently, what is the queer sex that queers so nonnormatively have? And *how* will we know it when we see it? These questions are impossible to answer, in part because antinormativity is finally not about the object of study per se but about the relation of aspiration that discerns, prioritizes, and, yes, disciplines it. For this reason, it seems possible to say that sex—by which I mean the specificity of acts, the diversity of identifications, the (de)materialization of desire, and the imbrications of soma, psyche, and sociality—is a rather queer object of study, even for the field that has come to claim and represent it.[40] Does this mean that queer critique has never quite had the sex it so famously is thought to have had? To say yes to all these suppositions makes it possible to think this: that under the tutelage of its project of antinormativity, queer critique has been animated less by sex than by its *proximity* to sex, a proximity that has proliferated objects, transformed identifications, and elaborated all kinds of analytic capacities not in spite of but because of the way that the field has been variously fascinated, unnerved, haunted, bored, overdetermined, or indifferent to sex, but never finally committed to it as its primary object of analysis, no matter how often it has tried, no matter how much certainty has been amassed in the belief otherwise.

Where, then, does this conversation leave us? Somewhere in the midst of the alluring and confounding puzzle that the queer critical apparatus was initially marshaled to settle, where the divergences and convergences between sex, sexual difference, and sexuality comprise the fraught terrain in which political desires have come to live. This terrain is constituted not just by the talk of sex or by the social or analytic force of sex, or even by the incommensurabilities of the domains in which the meaning of sex is lived, but by the kinds of contradictions and evasions that attention to sex provokes, including the sheer impossibility of getting a grip on anything so dense and disconcerting, so ephemeral and material, so intrinsically related and decidedly abstract as an antinormative account of "sex itself." Believe me, I know how preposterous it is to have detoured, postponed, and withheld so many routes of critical exploration in order to arrive into this, the paradoxical simplicity of what the vertigo of critique reveals: that *queer*

40. One of the most interesting recent essays to enter the complexities of this domain is Rodríguez's "Gesture and Utterance," which seeks to travel the distance from how "our racialized bodies fuck in the world" to how sexual imaginaries are inhabited and represented in queer criticism (280). To be sure, her essay's organizing question, "what gives queer sex queer meaning," repeats the tautology of *queer* as referent and object of study that I am tracing here, but the performative emphasis of her essay is especially compelling (281).

inquiry cannot have the sex it says it wants without losing what it wants most from having had it. Of all the object lessons framed and followed by the discussions arrayed in this book, it is this one that might be taken to recast the tensions that reside in identity knowledges as a whole, where what they offer is no match for what we want from them, even as what we want from them is bound to the shape of the questions they teach us to pose.

Object Lessons has been my way of trying to register the affective and analytic complexities of this. Each chapter has traced the aspirations and priorities of an identity object or analytic in order to discern the relationship between the disciplinarity of identity knowledges and the political desires that animate them. My aim has never been simply to expose such discipline, let alone to refuse it, nor to argue against any of the practices that bind us to it. When I have trained my attention on critique, I have wanted to inhabit, not resist, the tension between anxiety and assurance that so powerfully sustains it—the way it pulls us forward in the belief that critical practice is necessary to world transformation while crafting a critical itinerary resolutely dependent on excavating inadequacy and error. Inhabitation is not, then, the means to arrive somewhere else, but the agency of a much different critical ambition, one that has tried to show why identity knowledges are so compelling by attending to the promises they make and the wishes and prohibitions that sustain them.

BIBLIOGRAPHY

....

Abel, Elizabeth, Barbara Christian, and Helene Moglen, eds. *Female Subjects in Black and White: Race, Psychoanalysis, Feminism.* Berkeley: University of California Press, 1997.

Abelove, Henry, Michèle Aina Barale, and David M. Halperin, eds. *The Lesbian and Gay Studies Reader.* New York: Routledge, 1993.

Abeysekara, Sunila. "Racism, Ethnicity, and Peace: Some Initial Thoughts on Intersectionality." *Canadian Woman Studies* 22.2 (Fall 2002/Winter 2003): 36–39.

Adams, David Keith, and Cornelius A. van Minnen, eds. *Reflections on American Exceptionalism.* Staffordshire: Keene University Press, 1994.

Adams, Rachel. "Masculinity Without Men." *GLQ* 6.3 (Summer 2000): 467–78.

Adler, Libby. "The Dignity of Sex." *UCLA Women's Law Journal* 17.1 (Winter 2008): 1–52.

———. "The Future of Sodomy." *Fordham Urban Law Journal* 32.2 (March 2005): 197–230.

Ahmed, Sara. "Collective Feelings: Or, the Impressions Left by Others." *Theory, Culture and Society* 21.2 (February 2004): 25–42.

———. *The Cultural Politics of Emotion.* Edinburgh: Edinburgh University Press, 2004.

———. "Declarations of Whiteness: The Non-performativity of Anti-racism." *borderlands* 3.2 (2004): http://www.borderlands.net.au/vol3no2_2004/ahmed_declarations.htm.

———. *The Promise of Happiness.* Durham, NC: Duke University Press, 2010.

Alcoff, Linda. "Cultural Feminism versus Poststructuralism: The Identity Crisis." *Signs* 13.3 (Spring 1988): 405–36.

———. "What Should White People Do?" *Hypatia* 13.3 (Summer 1998): 6–26.

Allen, Anita. "Privacy, Surrogacy and the *Baby M* Case." *Georgetown Law Journal* 76.5 (June 1988): 1759–92.

———. "Surrogacy, Slavery, and the Ownership of Life." *Harvard Journal of Law and Public Policy* 13.1 (1990): 139–49.

Allen, Judith A., and Sally L. Kitch. "Disciplined by Disciplines? The Need for an *Interdisciplinary* Research Mission in Women's Studies." *Feminist Studies* 24.2 (Summer 1998): 275–99.

Allen, Theodore. *The Invention of the White Race.* Vol. 1. London: Verso, 1994.

Americans for a Fair Chance. "Anti-Affirmative Action Threats in the States: 1997–2004." Washington, DC: Americans for a Fair Chance, 2005: http://www.civilrights.org/publications/aa-in-the-states/aa-in-the-states-2005.pdf.

Anderson, Terry H. *The Pursuit of Fairness: A History of Affirmative Action.* New York: Oxford University Press, 2004.

Angelides, Steven. *A History of Bisexuality.* Chicago: University of Chicago Press, 2001.

Anna J. v. Mark C. et al. 286 Cal. Rptr. 372 (Cal. App. 4 Dist. 1991).

Arondekar, Anjali. "Border/Line Sex: Queer Postcolonialities, or How Race Matters Outside the United States." *interventions* 7.2 (July 2005): 236–50.

Aronowitz, Stanley. *The Knowledge Factory: Dismantling the Corporate University and Creating True Higher Learning.* New York: Beacon Press, 2001.

Asad, Talal, Wendy Brown, Judith Butler, and Saba Mahmood. *Is Critique Secular? Blasphemy, Injury, and Free Speech.* Berkeley: University of California Press, 2009.

AsiaPacifiQueer Network. "Replacing Queer Studies: Reflections on the Queer Matters Conference (King's College, London, May 2004)." *Inter-Asia Cultural Studies* 6.2 (May 2005): 299–311.

Auslander, Leora. "Do Women's + Feminist + Men's + Lesbian and Gay + Queer Studies = Gender Studies?" *differences* 9.3 (Fall 1997): 1–25.

Austin, Regina. "Sapphire Bound!" *Wisconsin Law Review* (1989): 539–78.

Ayers, Edward L. *Vengeance and Justice: Crime and Punishment in the Nineteenth Century American South.* New York: Oxford University Press, 1984.

Babb, Valerie. *Whiteness Visible: The Meaning of Whiteness in American Literature and Culture.* New York: New York University Press, 1998.

Baker, Bruce E. "Under the Rope: Lynching and Memory in Laurens County, South Carolina." In *Where These Memories Grow: History, Memory, and Southern Identity.* Ed. William Fitzhugh Brundage. Chapel Hill: University of North Carolina Press, 2000: 319–46.

Baldwin, James. *The Price of the Ticket* (dir. Karen Thorsen). San Francisco: California News Reel, 1990.

Baldwin, Kate A. *Beyond the Color Line and the Iron Curtain: Reading Encounters Between Black and Red, 1922–1963*. Durham, NC: Duke University Press, 2002.

Balkir, Irem. "The Discourse on 'Post-nationalism': A Reflection on the Contradictions of the 1990s." *Journal of American Studies of Turkey* 1 (Spring 1995): 25–31.

Ball, Howard. *The Bakke Case: Race, Education, and Affirmative Action.* Lawrence: University of Kansas Press, 2002.

Barnard, Ian. *Queer Race: Cultural Interventions in the Racial Politics of Queer Theory.* New York: Peter Lang, 2004.

Bar On, Bat-Ami. "Marginality and Epistemic Privilege." In *Feminist Epistemologies.* Ed. Linda Alcoff and Elizabeth Potter. New York: Routledge, 1993: 83–100.

Barrett, Lindon. "Identities and Identity Studies: Reading Toni Cade Bambara's 'The Hammer Man.'" *Cultural Critique* 39 (Spring 1998): 5–29.

Beale, Frances. "Double Jeopardy: To Be Black and Female." In *The Black Woman: An Anthology.* Ed. Toni Cade. New York: New American Library, 1979: 90–100.

Beemym, Brett, and Mickey Eliason, eds. *Queer Studies: A Lesbian, Gay, Bisexual, and Transgender Anthology.* New York: New York University Press, 1996.

Bell, Roseann P., Bettye J. Parker, and Beverly Guy-Sheftall, eds. *Sturdy Black Bridges: Visions of Black Women in Literature.* Garden City, NY: Anchor Books, 1979.

Belnap, Jeffrey, and Raúl Fernández, eds. *José Martí's "Our America": From National to Hemispheric Cultural Studies.* Durham, NC: Duke University Press, 1998.

Bender, Leslie. "Genes, Parents, and Assisted Reproductive Technologies: ARTs, Mistakes, Sex, Race, and Law." *Columbia Journal of Gender and Law* 12.1 (2003): 1–76.

Bennett-Haigney, Lisa. "New Fronts in the Citadel Battle." *NOW National Times* (November 1995): http://www.now.org/nnt/11-95/shannon.html.

Bentley, Nancy. "The Fourth Dimension: Kinlessness and African American Narrative." *Critical Inquiry* 35 (Winter 2009): 270–92.

Bercovitch, Sacvan, and Myra Jehlen, eds. *Ideology and Classic American Literature.* Cambridge: Cambridge University Press, 1986.

Berger, Maurice, Brian Wallis, and Simon Watson, eds. *Constructing Masculinity.* New York: Routledge, 1995.

Berger, Michele Tracy, and Kathleen Guidroz, eds., *The Intersectional Approach: Transforming the Academy Through Race, Class, and Gender.* Chapel Hill: University of North Carolina Press, 2009.

Berkhofer, Robert R., Jr. "The Americanness of American Studies." *American Quarterly* 31.3 (September 1979): 340–45.

———. "A New Context for a New American Studies?" *American Quarterly* 41.4 (December 1989): 588–613.

Berlant, Lauren. *The Queen of America Goes to Washington City*. Durham, NC: Duke University Press, 1997.

———. "The Subject of True Feelings: Pain, Privacy, and Politics." In *Transformations: Thinking Through Feminism*. Ed. Sara Ahmed, Jane Kilby, Celia Lury, Maureen McNeil, and Beverley Skeggs. London: Routledge, 2000: 33–47.

Berlant, Lauren, and Michael Warner. "Sex in Public." *Critical Inquiry* 24.2 (Winter 1998): 547–66.

———. "What Does Queer Theory Teach Us about X?" *PMLA* 110.3 (May 1995): 343–49.

Bersani, Leo. "Is the Rectum a Grave?" *October* 43 (Winter 1987): 197–222.

———. "The It in the I." In *Intimacies*. Leo Bersani and Adam Phillips. Chicago: University of Chicago Press, 2008: 1–30.

———. "Sociality and Sexuality." *Critical Inquiry* 26.4 (Summer 2000): 641–56.

Bérubé, Michael. "American Studies Without Exceptions." *PMLA* 118.1 (January 2003): 103–13.

Bethel, Lorraine, and Barbara Smith, eds. "The Black Woman's Issue." Special issue, *Conditions* 5 (1979).

Blankenship, Kim M., Beth Rushing, Suzanne A. Onorato, and Renee White. "Reproductive Technologies and the U.S. Courts." *Gender and Society* 7.1 (March 1993): 8–31.

Blee, Kathleen M. "Contending with Disciplinarity." In *Women's Studies on Its Own*. Ed. Robyn Wiegman. Durham, NC: Duke University Press, 2002: 177–82.

Blount, Marcellus, and George P. Cunningham, eds. *Representing Black Men*. New York: Routledge, 1995.

Blum, Virginia. "A Response to Bruce Burgett." *American Literary History* 21.1 (Spring 2009): 87–93.

Bobo, Jacqueline, Cynthia Hudley, and Claudine Michel, eds. *The Black Studies Reader*. New York: Routledge, 2004.

Bonilla-Silva, Eduardo. *White Supremacy and Racism in the Post-Civil Rights Era*. Boulder, CO: Lynne Rienner, 2001.

Bonnett, Alastair. "'White Studies': The Problems and Projects of a New Research Agenda." *Theory, Culture and Society* 13.2 (May 1996): 145–55.

Boone, Joseph A., and Michael Cadden, eds. *Engendering Men: The Question of Male Feminist Criticism*. New York: Routledge, 1990.

Bordo, Susan. *The Male Body: A New Look at Men in Public and Private*. New York: Farrar, Straus, and Giroux, 1999.

———. "Reading the Male Body." *Michigan Quarterly Review* 32.4 (1993): 696–737.

Bornstein, Kate. *Gender Outlaw: Men, Women, and the Rest of Us*. New York: Routledge, 1994.

Borstelmann, Thomas. *The Cold War and the Color Line: American Race Relations in the Global Arena*. Cambridge, MA: Harvard University Press, 2001.

Bowles, Gloria, and Renate Duelli Klein, eds. *Theories of Women's Studies*. New York: Routledge, 1983.

Boxer, Marilyn. "For and about Women: The Theory and Practice of Women's Studies in the United States." *Signs* 7.3 (Spring 1982): 661–95.

———. "Unruly Knowledge: Women's Studies and the Problem of Disciplinarity." *NWSA Journal* 12.2 (Summer 2000): 119–29.

———. *When Women Ask the Questions: Creating Women's Studies in America*. Baltimore, MD: Johns Hopkins University Press, 1998.

Boyle, Karen. "New Man, Old Brutalisms? Reconstructing a Violent History in *Forrest Gump*." *Scope: An Online Journal of Film Studies* (December 2001): http://www.scope.nottingham.ac.uk/article.php?issue=dec2001&id=280 &section=article.

Brady, Mary Pat. *Extinct Lands, Temporal Geographies: Chicano Literature and the Urgency of Space*. Durham, NC: Duke University Press, 2002.

Bragg, Rick. "Converted by Love, a Former Klansman Finds Ally at Black Church." *Washington Post* (July 27, 1997): A3.

———. "In a South Carolina Town, a Klan Museum Opens Old Wounds." *New York Times* (November 17, 1996): 1:16.

Brah, Avtar, and Ann Phoenix. "Ain't I a Woman: Revisiting Intersectionality." *Journal of International Women's Studies* 5.3 (May 2004): 75–86.

Briggs, Laura. *Reproducing Empire: Race, Sex, Science and U.S. Imperialism in Puerto Rico*. Berkeley: University of California Press, 2002.

Bright, Susie. *Sexwise*. Pittsburgh, PA: Cleis Press, 1995.

———. *Susie Sexpert's Lesbian Sex World*. Pittsburgh, PA: Cleis Press, 1990.

Brinson, Betsy. "Teaching Black Women's Heritage." *Women's Studies Newsletter* 8.4 (Fall/Winter 1980): 19–20.

Britzman, Deborah P. *Lost Subjects, Contested Objects: Toward a Psychoanalytic Inquiry of Learning*. Albany: State University of New York Press, 1998.

Brod, Harry, ed. *The Making of Masculinities: The New Men's Studies*. Winchester, MA: Allen and Unwin, 1987.

Brown, Wendy. "The Impossibility of Women's Studies." *differences* 9.3 (Fall 1997): 79–101.

———. "Resisting Left Melancholy." *boundary 2* 26.3 (Fall 1999): 19–27.

———. *States of Injury: Power and Freedom in Late Modernity*. Princeton, NJ: Princeton University Press, 1995.

———. "Suffering the Paradoxes of Rights." *Left Legalism/Left Critique*. Ed. Wendy Brown and Janet Halley. Durham, NC: Duke University Press, 2002: 420–34.

Buell, Frederick. "Nationalist Postnationalism: Globalist Discourse in Contemporary American Culture." *American Quarterly* 50.3 (September 1998): 548–91.

Buitelaar, Marjo. "'I Am the Ultimate Challenge': Accounts of Intersectionality in the Life-Story of a Well-Known Daughter of Moroccan Migrant Workers in the Netherlands." *European Journal of Women's Studies* 13.3 (2006): 259–76.

Buker, Eloise A. "Is Women's Studies a Disciplinary or an Interdisciplinary Field of Inquiry?" *NWSA Journal* 15.1 (Spring 2003): 73–93.

Bulkin, Elly, Minnie Bruce Pratt, and Barbara Smith. *Yours in Struggle*. Brooklyn, NY: Long Haul Press, 1984.

Burgett, Bruce. "Between Speculation and Population: The Problem of 'Sex' in Our Long Eighteenth Century." *Early American Literature* 37.1 (2002): 119–53.

———. "Sex, Panic, Nation." *American Literary History* 21.1 (Spring 2009): 67–86.

Burgoyne, Robert. *Film Nation: Hollywood Looks at U.S. History*. Minneapolis: University of Minnesota Press, 1997.

Butler, Judith. "Against Proper Objects." *differences* 6.2–3 (Summer/Fall 1994): 1–26.

———. *Excitable Speech: A Politics of the Performative*. New York: Routledge, 1997.

———. *Gender Trouble: Feminism and the Subversion of Identity*. New York: Routledge, 1990.

———. "Non-thinking in the Name of the Normative." In *Frames of War: When Is Life Grievable?* London: Verso, 2009: 137–64.

———. *The Psychic Life of Power: Theories in Subjection*. Palo Alto, CA: Stanford University Press, 1997.

———. "What Is Critique? An Essay on Foucault's Virtue." In *The Political*. Ed. David Ingram. Malden, MA: Blackwell, 2002: 212–26.

Butler, Judith, and Joan W. Scott, eds. *Feminists Theorize the Political*. New York: Routledge, 1992.

Byers, Thomas B. "History Re-membered: *Forrest Gump*, Postfeminist Masculinity, and the Burial of the Counterculture." *Modern Fiction Studies* 42.2 (Summer 1996): 419–44.

Caldwell, Paulette. "A Hair Piece: Perspectives on the Intersection of Race and Gender." In *Critical Race Theory: The Cutting Edge*. Ed. Richard Delgado. Philadelphia: Temple University Press, 1995: 267–77.

Califia, Pat. *Public Sex: The Culture of Radical Sex*. Pittsburgh, PA: Cleis Press, 1994.

Campt, Tina, and Deborah A. Thomas. "Editorial: Gendering Diaspora: Transnational Feminism, Diaspora and Its Hegemonies." *Feminist Review* 90.1 (October 2008): 1–8.

Carby, Hazel. "White Woman Listen! Black Feminism and the Boundaries of Sisterhood." In *The Empire Strikes Back: Race and Racism in 70s Britain*. Ed. The Centre for Contemporary Studies. London: Hutchinson, 1982: 211–35.

Carrigan, Tim, Bob Connell, and Jon Lee. "Toward a New Sociology of Masculinity." *Theory and Society* 14.5 (September 1985): 551–604.

Carver, Ann Cathey. "Building Coalitions Between Women's Studies and Black Studies: What Are the Realities?" *Women's Studies Newsletter* 8.3 (Summer 1980): 16–19.

Chabram-Dernersesian, Angie, ed. *The Chicana/o Cultural Studies Reader*. New York: Routledge, 2006.

Chambers, Samuel A. "'An Incalculable Effect': Subversions of Heteronormativity." *Political Studies* 55.3 (October 2007): 656–79.

Champagne, Duane, and Jay Stauss. *Native American Studies in Higher Education: Models for Collaboration Between Universities and Indigenous Nations*. Lanham, MD: AltaMira Press, 2002.

Chandler, James. "Introduction: Doctrines, Disciplines, Discourses, Departments." *Critical Inquiry* 35.4 (Summer 2009): 729–46.

Chang, Robert S., and Jerome McCristal Culp Jr. "After Intersectionality." *University of Missouri-Kansas City Law Review* 71.2 (2002): 485–91.

Chapman, Rowena, and Jonathon Rutherford, eds. *Male Order: Unwrapping Masculinity*. London: Lawrence and Wishart, 1988.

Chase, Cheryl. "Affronting Reason." In *Looking Queer: Body Image and Identity in Lesbian, Bisexual, Gay and Transgendered Communities*. Ed. Dawn Atkins. Binghamton, NY: Haworth, 1998: 205–20.

———. "Hermaphrodites with Attitude: Mapping the Emergence of Intersex Political Activism." *GLQ* 4.2 (Spring 1998): 189–211.

Check, Erika. "Jefferson's Descendants Continue to Deny Slave Link." *Nature* 417 (May 16, 2002): 213.

Cherniavsky, Eva. *Incorporations: Race, Nation, and the Body Politics of Capital*. Minneapolis: University of Minnesota Press, 2006.

———. "Neocitizenship and Critique." *Social Text* 27.2 (Summer 2009): 1–23.

———. "Post-American Studies, or Scattered Reflections on the Cultures of Imperialism." Paper presented at the American Studies Association Meeting, Philadelphia, October 16–19, 2007.

———. "Subaltern Studies in a U.S. Frame." *boundary 2* 23.2 (Summer 1996): 85–110.

Cherry, April L. "Nurturing in the Service of White Culture: Racial Subordination, Gestational Surrogacy, and the Ideology of Motherhood." *Texas Journal of Women and the Law* 10 (2001): 83–128.

Chinn, Sarah E. "Reading the 'Book of Life': DNA and the Meanings of Identity." In *Technology and the Logic of American Racism: A Cultural History of the Body as Evidence.* London: Continuum, 2000: 141–67.

Chow, Rey. *The Protestant Ethnic and the Spirit of Capitalism.* New York: Columbia University Press, 2002.

———. "When Whiteness Feminizes . . . : Some Consequences of a Supplementary Logic." *differences* 11.3 (Fall 1999/2000): 137–68.

Clatterbaugh, Kenneth C. *Contemporary Perspectives on Masculinity: Men, Women, and Politics in Modern Society.* 2nd ed. Boulder, CO: Westview Press, 1997.

Clifton, Ron. "The Outer Limits of American Studies: A View from the Remaining Frontier." *American Quarterly* 31.3 (September 1979): 364–68.

Clough, Patricia Ticineto. "Affect and Control: Rethinking the Body 'Beyond Sex and Gender.'" *Feminist Theory* 4.3 (December 2003): 359–64.

Clough, Patricia Ticineto, with Jean Halley, eds. *The Affective Turn: Theorizing the Social.* Durham, NC: Duke University Press, 2007.

Cohan, Steven. *Masked Men: Masculinity and the Movies in the Fifties.* Bloomington: Indiana University Press, 1997.

Cohan, Steven, and Ina Rae Hark, eds. *Screening the Male: Exploring Masculinities in Hollywood Cinema.* New York: Routledge, 1993.

Cohen, Cathy J. "Punks, Bulldaggers, and Welfare Queens: The Radical Potential of Queer Politics." *GLQ* 3.4 (May 1997): 437–65.

Collins, Patricia Hill. *Black Feminist Thought: Knowledge, Consciousness, and the Politics of Empowerment.* New York: Routledge, Chapman and Hall, 1990.

———. *Fighting Words: Black Women and the Search for Justice.* Minneapolis: University of Minnesota Press, 1998.

———. "It's All in the Family: Intersections of Gender, Race, and Nation." *Hypatia* 13.3 (Summer 1998): 62–82.

———. "The Social Construction of Black Feminist Thought." *Signs* 14.4 (Summer 1989): 745–73.

Combahee River Collective. "A Black Feminist Statement." In *All the Women Are White, All the Blacks Are Men, but Some of Us Are Brave.* Ed. Gloria T. Hull, Patricia Scott Bell, and Barbara Smith. Old Westbury, NY: Feminist Press, 1982: 13–22.

Connor, Eric. "Black Church Seeks Control of 'Klan Museum.'" *Greenville News* (September 3, 2008): 3A.

Corber, Robert, and Stephen Valocchi, eds. *Queer Studies: An Interdisciplinary Reader.* Malden, MA: Blackwell, 2003.

Cornwall, Andrea, and Nancy Lindisfarne, eds. *Dislocating Masculinity: Comparative Ethnographies*. New York: Routledge, 1994.

Craine, Barbara, Elizabeth Grosz, and Marie De Lepervanche, eds. *Crossing Boundaries: Feminists and the Critique of Knoweldges*. Sydney: Paul & Co. Pub. Consortium, 1988.

Crenshaw, Kimberlé. "Demarginalizing the Intersection of Race and Sex: A Black Feminist Critique of Antidiscrimination Doctrine, Feminist Theory and Antiracist Politics." *University of Chicago Legal Forum* 140 (1989): 139–67.

———. "Mapping the Margins: Intersectionality, Identity Politics, and Violence Against Women of Color." *Stanford Law Review* 43.6 (July 1991): 1241–99.

Crews, Frederick C. "Whose American Renaissance?" *New York Review of Books* 35.16 (October 27, 1988): http://www.nybooks.com/articles/4278.

Crimp, Douglas. "How to Have Promiscuity in an Epidemic." In *AIDS: Cultural Analysis/Cultural Activism*. Ed. Crimp. Cambridge, MA: MIT Press, 1987: 237–71.

Cross, T., F. Klein, Barbara Smith, and Beverly Smith. "Face-to-Face, Day-to-Day, Racism CR." *Women's Studies Newsletter* 8.1 (Winter 1980): 27–28.

Cruz-Malavé, Arnaldo, and Martin F. Manalansan IV, eds. "Introduction: Dissident Sexualities/Alternative Globalisms." In *Queer Globalizations: Citizenship and the Afterlife of Colonialism*. New York: New York University Press, 2002: 1–11.

Culp, Jerome McCristal Jr. "Colorblind Remedies and the Intersectionality of Oppression: Policy Arguments Masquerading as Moral Claims." *New York University Law Review* 69.1 (April 1994): 162–96.

Cuomo, Chris J., and Kim Q. Hall, eds. *Whiteness: Feminist Philosophical Reflection*. Lanham, MD: Rowman and Littlefield, 1999.

Curry, George, ed. *The Affirmative Action Debate*. Reading, MA: Addison-Wesley, 1996.

Cvetkovich, Ann. *An Archive of Feelings: Trauma, Sexuality, and Lesbian Public Cultures*. Durham, NC: Duke University Press, 2003.

Dandridge, Rita B. "On Novels by Black American Women: A Bibliographical Essay." *Women's Studies Newsletter* 6.3 (Summer 1978): 28–30.

Daniels, Jessie. *Cyber Racism: White Supremacy Online and the New Attack on Civil Rights*. Lanham, MD: Rowman and Littlefield, 2009.

———. *White Lies: Race, Class, Gender, and Sexuality in White Supremacist Discourse*. New York: Routledge, 1997.

Darder, Antonia, and Rodolfo D. Torres. "Mapping Latino Studies: Critical Reflections on Class and Social Theory." *Latino Studies* 1.2 (July 2003): 303–24.

Davies, Carole Boyce, Meredith Gadsby, Charles Peterson, and Henrietta Williams, eds. *Decolonizing the Academy: African Diaspora Studies*. Trenton, NJ: Africa World Press, 2003.

Davies, Carole Boyce, and Molara Ogundipe-Leslie, eds. *Moving Beyond Boundaries: Black Women's Diasporas*. New York: New York University Press, 1995.

Davis, Adrienne. "The Private Law of Race and Sex: An Antebellum Perspective." *Stanford Law Review* 51.2 (January 1999): 221–88.

Davis, Angela Y. *Women, Race, and Class*. New York: Vintage, 1983.

Davis, Kathy. "Intersectionality as Buzzword: A Sociology of Science Perspective on What Makes a Feminist Theory Successful." *Feminist Theory* 9.1 (April 2008): 67–85.

Dean, Tim. *Beyond Sexuality*. Chicago: University of Chicago Press, 2000.

———. *Unlimited Intimacy: Reflections on the Subculture of Barebacking*. Chicago: University of Chicago Press, 2009.

Dean, Tim, and Christopher Lane, eds. *Homosexuality and Psychoanalysis*. Chicago: University of Chicago Press, 2001.

DeGuzmán, María. *Spain's Long Shadow: The Black Legend, Off-Whiteness, and Anglo-American Empire*. Minneapolis: University of Minnesota Press, 2005.

Delany, Samuel R. *Times Square Red, Times Square Blue*. New York: New York University Press, 1999.

Delgado, Richard, and Jean Stefancic, eds. *Critical White Studies: Looking Behind the Mirror*. Philadelphia: Temple University Press, 1997.

Desmond, Jane. "Transnational American Studies and the Limits to Collaboration: Implications Drawn from the Russian-US Relationship." *American Studies International* 41:1–2 (February 2003): 17–27.

Desmond, Jane, and Virginia R. Dominguez. "Resituating American Studies in a Critical Internationalism." *American Quarterly* 48.3 (September 1996): 475–90.

Digby, Tom, ed. *Men Doing Feminism*. New York: Routledge, 1998.

Dill, Bonnie Thornton. "The Dialectics of Black Womanhood." *Signs* 4.3 (Spring 1979): 543–55.

———. "Race, Class, and Gender: Prospects for an All-Inclusive Sisterhood." *Feminist Studies* 9.1 (1983): 131–50.

Dill, Bonnie Thornton, and Ruth Enid Zambrana, eds. *Emerging Intersections: Race, Class, and Gender in Theory, Policy, and Practice*. New Brunswick, NJ: Rutgers University Press, 2009.

Dinshaw, Carolyn. "The History of *GLQ*, Volume 1: LGBTQ: Studies, Censorship, and Other Transnational Problems." *GLQ* 12.1 (Winter 2006): 5–26.

Di Stefano, Christine. *Configurations of Masculinity: A Feminist Perspective on Modern Political Theory*. Ithaca, NY: Cornell University Press, 1991.

Doane, Ashley W., and Eduardo Bonilla-Silva, eds. *White Out: The Continuing Significance of Racism*. London: Routledge, 2003.

Doane, Woody. "Rethinking Whiteness Studies." In *White Out: The Continuing Significance of Racism*. Ed. Ashley W. Doane and Eduardo Bonilla-Silva. London: Routledge, 2003: 3–18.

Dobratz, Betty A., and Stephanie L. Shanks-Miele. *The White Separatist Movement in the United States: "White Power, White Pride!"* Baltimore, MD: Johns Hopkins University Press, 2000.

Dolgin, Janet L. "Choice, Tradition, and the New Genetics: The Fragmentation of the Ideology of the Family." *Connecticut Law Review* 32.2 (Winter 2000): 523–66.

Dollimore, Jonathan. "Bisexuality, Heterosexuality, and Wishful Theory." *Textual Practice* 10:3 (Winter 1996): 523–39.

Dominguez, Virginia R. "Implications: A Commentary on Stoler." In *Political Power and Social Theory 11*. Ed. Diane E. Davis. Stamford, CT: JAI Press, 1997: 207–15.

DuBois, W. E. B. *Black Reconstruction in America, 1860–1880*. (1935). New York: Atheneum, 1975.

DuCille, Ann. "Where in the World Is William Wells Brown? Thomas Jefferson, Sally Hemings, and the DNA of African-American Literary History." *American Literary History* 12.3 (Autumn 2000): 443–62.

Dudziak, Mary L. *Cold War Civil Rights: Race and the Image of American Democracy*. Princeton, NJ: Princeton University Press, 2002.

Duggan, Lisa. "The New Homonormativity: The Sexual Politics of Neoliberalism." In *Materializing Democracy: Toward a Revitalized Cultural Politics*. Ed. Russ Castronovo and Dana D. Nelson. Durham, NC: Duke University Press, 2002: 175–94.

Duggan, Lisa, and Nan D. Hunter. *Sex Wars: Sexual Dissent and Political Culture*. New York: Routledge, 1995.

Dyer, Richard. "White." *Screen* 29.4 (Autumn 1988): 44–65.

———. *White*. London: Routledge, 1997.

Edelman, Lee. "Antagonism, Negativity, and the Subject of Queer Theory." Forum: Conference Debates. The Antisocial Thesis in Queer Theory. *PMLA* 121.3 (May 2006): 821–23.

———. "Ever After: History, Negativity, and the Social." *South Atlantic Quarterly* 106.3 (Summer 2007): 469–76.

———. *No Future: Queer Theory and the Death Drive*. Durham, NC: Duke University Press, 2004.

———. "Redeeming the Phallus: Wallace Stevens, Frank Lentricchia, and the Politics of (Hetero)Sexuality." In *Engendering Men: The Question of Male Feminist Criticism*. Ed. Joseph A. Boone and Michael Cadden. New York: Routledge, 1990: 36–52.

Edwards, Brent Hayes. *The Practice of Diaspora: Literature, Translation and the Rise of Black Internationalism*. Cambridge, MA: Harvard University Press, 2003.

———. "The Uses of *Diaspora*." *Social Text* 19.1 (Spring 2001): 45–73.

Edwards, Brian T. "Preposterous Encounters: Interrupting American Studies with the (Post)Colonial, or *Casablanca* in the American Century." *Comparative Studies of South Asia, Africa, and the Middle East* 23.1–2 (2003): 70–86.

Edwards, Tim. *Erotics and Politics: Gay Male Sexuality, Masculinity, and Feminism.* New York: Routledge, 1994.

Ehrenreich, Nancy. "The Colonization of the Womb." *Duke Law Journal* 43.3 (December 1993): 492–587.

———. "Subordination and Symbiosis: Mechanisms of Mutual Support Between Subordinating Systems." *University of Missouri-Kansas City Law Review* 71.2 (2002): 251–324.

Elam, Diane. *Feminism and Deconstruction. Ms. en Abyme.* London: Routledge, 1994.

———. "Taking Account of Women's Studies." In *Women's Studies on Its Own.* Ed. Robyn Wiegman. Durham, NC: Duke University Press, 2002: 218–23.

Elliot, Dorinda, and Friso Endt. "Twins—With Two Fathers; The Netherlands: A Fertility Clinic's Startling Error." *Newsweek* (July 3, 1995): 38.

"Embryo Mix-Up at Fertility Clinic Resolved Amicably." *New Haven Register* (September 24, 2009): http://nhregister.com/articles/2009/09/24/news.d3 -embryo3rd.txt.

Eng, David L. "Queering the Black Atlantic, Queering the Brown Atlantic." *GLQ* 17.1 (2010): 193–204.

———. *Racial Castration: Managing Masculinity in Asian America.* Durham, NC: Duke University Press, 2001.

Eng, David L., Judith Halberstam, and José Esteban Muñoz, eds. "What's Queer about Queer Studies Now?" *Social Text* 23.3–4 (Fall–Winter 2005): 1–17.

Eng, David L., and Shinhee Han. "A Dialogue on Racial Melancholia." *Psychoanalytic Dialogues* 10.4 (August 15, 2000): 667–700.

Eng, David L., and David Kazanjian. "Introduction: Mourning Remains." In *Loss: The Politics of Mourning.* Ed. David L. Eng and David Kazanjian. Berkeley: University of California Press, 2003: 1–25.

———, eds. *Loss: The Politics of Mourning.* Berkeley: University of California Press, 2003.

Escoffier, Jeff. "The Limits of Multiculturalism: Identity Politics and the Transformation of the Public Sphere." In *American Homo: Community and Perversity.* Berkeley: University of California Press, 1998: 190–201.

Evans, Mary. "The Problem of Gender for Women's Studies." In *Out of the Margins: Women's Studies in the Nineties.* Ed. Jane Aaron and Sylvia Walby. London: Palmer, 1991: 67–74.

Ezosky, Gertrude. *Racism and Justice: The Case for Affirmative Action.* Ithaca, NY: Cornell University Press, 1991.

Fanon, Frantz. *Black Skin, White Masks*. (1952). New York: Grove Press, 1994.

Fasano v. Nash, 282 A.D.2d 277 (N.Y. App. Div. 2001).

Fausto-Sterling, Anne. "Refashioning Race: DNA and the Politics of Health Care." *differences* 15.3 (2004): 1–37.

Fee, Thomas F. "Embryo Mix-Up Shows Why Roe v. Wade Is Outdated." *National Right to Life News* 26.6 (May 11, 1999): 20.

Feinberg, Leslie. *Transgender Liberation: A Movement Whose Time Has Come.* New York: World View Forum, 1992.

———. *Trans Liberation: Beyond Pink or Blue*. Boston: Beacon Press, 1999.

Felder, Myrna. " 'Perry-Rogers v. Fasano' ": Who Is a 'Parent'?" *New York Law Journal* 225.111 (June 11, 2001): 3.

Ferguson, Roderick A. *Aberrations in Black: Toward a Queer of Color Critique.* Minneapolis: University of Minnesota Press, 2004.

———. "Administering Sexuality; or, the Will to Institutionality." *Radical History Review* 100 (Winter 2008): 158–69.

———. "The Nightmares of the Heteronormative." *Cultural Values* 4.4 (October 2000): 419–44.

Fine, Michelle, Lois Weis, Linda C. Powell, and L. Mun Wong, eds. *Off White: Readings on Race, Power, and Society*. 2nd ed. New York: Routledge, 2004.

Fiscus, Ronald. *The Constitutional Logic of Affirmative Action*. Ed. Stephen Wasby. Durham, NC: Duke University Press, 1992.

Fisher, Ali. "The Janus-Faced Development of 'New American Studies.' " *49th Parallel* 2 (Autumn 2006): http://www.49thparallel.bham.ac.uk/back/special2/Ali_Fisher.pdf.

Fisher, Philip. *Hard Facts: Setting and Form in the American Novel*. New York: Oxford University Press, 1985.

———, ed. *The New American Studies: Essays from Representations*. Berkeley: University of California Press, 1991.

Fishkin, Shelley Fisher. "Crossroads of Cultures: The Transnational Turn in American Studies—Presidential Address to the American Studies Association, November 12, 2004." *American Quarterly* 57.1 (March 2005): 17–57.

———. "Interrogating 'Whiteness' Complicating 'Blackness': Remapping American Culture." *American Quarterly* 47.3 (September 1995): 428–66.

Flores, Juan, and Renato Rosaldo, eds. *A Companion to Latina/o Studies*. Malden, MA: Blackwell, 2007.

Floyd, Kevin. "Making History: Marxism, Queer Theory, and Contradiction in the Future of American Studies." *Cultural Critique* 40 (Autumn 1998): 167–201.

Ford, Richard Thompson. "What's Queer about Race?" *South Atlantic Quarterly* 106.3 (Summer 2007): 477–84.

Forrest Gump (dir. Robert Zemeckis). Paramount Pictures, 1994.

Foster, Eugene, M. A. Jobling, P. G. Taylor, P. Donnelly, P. de Knijff, Rene Mieremet, T. Zerjal, and C. Tyler-Smith. "Jefferson Fathered Slave's Last Child." *Nature* (November 5, 1998): 27–28.

———. "The Thomas Jefferson Paternity Case." *Nature* (January 7, 1999): 32.

Foucault, Michel, ed. "Sexual Choice, Sexual Act." In *Ethics, Subjectivity and Truth: Essential Works of Foucault 1954–1984*. Volume 1. Ed. Paul Rabinow. New York: New Press, 1997: 141–56.

———. "What Is Critique?" (1977). In *The Political*. Ed. David Ingram. Malden, MA: Blackwell, 2002: 191–211.

Fox, Claire F., ed. "Critical Perspectives and Emerging Models of Inter-American Studies." *Comparative American Studies* 3.4 (November 2005).

Franke, Katherine M. "Putting Sex to Work." In *Left Legalism/Left Critique*. Ed. Wendy Brown and Janet Halley. Durham, NC: Duke University Press, 2002: 290–336.

Frankenberg, Ruth, ed. *Displacing Whiteness: Essays in Social and Cultural Criticism*. Durham, NC: Duke University Press, 1997.

———. *White Women, Race Matters: The Social Construction of Whiteness*. Minneapolis: University of Minnesota Press, 1993.

Franklin, Sarah. "Romancing the Helix: Nature and Scientific Discovery." In *Romance Revisited*. Ed. Lynne Pearce and Jackie Stacy. London: Lawrence and Wishart, 1995: 63–77.

Freccero, Carla. *Queer/Early/Modern*. Durham, NC: Duke University Press, 2006.

Friedman, Susan Stanford. "(Inter)disciplinarity and the Question for the Women's Studies Ph.D." *Feminist Studies* 24.2 (Summer 1998): 301–25.

Frug, Mary Joe. *Postmodern Legal Feminism*. New York: Routledge, 1992.

Fuss, Diana. *Essentially Speaking: Feminism, Nature, and Difference*. New York: Routledge, 1989.

———. *Identification Papers*. New York: Routledge, 1995.

Gallop, Jane. *The Daughter's Seduction: Feminism and Psychoanalysis*. Ithaca, NY: Cornell University Press, 1984.

Gardner, Chris, with Quincy Troupe. *The Pursuit of Happyness*. New York: Amistad/HarperCollins, 2006.

Garvey, John, and Noel Ignatiev. "The New Abolitionism." *Minnesota Review* 47 (Fall 1996): 105–7.

Giardini, Federica. "Public Affects: Clues Towards a Political Practice of Singularity." *European Journal of Women's Studies* 6.2 (May 1999): 149–59.

Giddings, Paula. *When and Where I Enter: The Impact of Black Women on Race and Sex in America*. New York: William Morrow, 1984.

Giffney, Noreen. "Denormatizing Queer Theory: More Than (Simply) Lesbian and Gay Studies." *Feminist Theory* 5.1 (April 2004): 73–78.

Giles, Paul. "Reconstructing American Studies: Transnational Paradoxes, Comparative Perspectives." *Journal of American Studies* 28.3 (December 1994): 335–58.

———. "Transnationalism in Practice." *49th Parallel* 8 (Summer 2001): http://www.49thparallel.bham.ac.uk/back/issue8/giles.htm.

———. "Virtual Americas: The Internationalization of American Studies and the Ideology of Exchange." *American Quarterly* 50.3 (September 1998): 523–47.

———. *Virtual Americas: Transnational Fictions and the Transatlantic Imaginary.* Durham, NC: Duke University Press, 2002.

Gilkes, Cheryl Townsend. "From Slavery to Social Welfare: Racism and the Control of Black Women." In *Class, Race, and Sex: The Dynamics of Control.* Ed. Amy Swerdlow, Johanna Lessinger, and Hanna Lessinger. Boston: G. K. Hall, 1981: 288–300.

Gillman, Susan. "The New, Newest Thing: Has American Studies Gone Imperial?" *American Literary History* 17.1 (Spring 2005): 196–214.

Gillman, Susan, Kirsten Silva Gruesz, and Rob Wilson, eds. "Worlding American Studies." *Comparative American Studies* 2.3 (August 2004).

Gilmore, David. *Mankind in the Making: Cultural Concepts of Masculinity.* New Haven, CT: Yale University Press, 1990.

Gilmore, Glenda Elizabeth. *Gender and Jim Crow: Women and the Politics of White Supremacy in North Carolina, 1896–1920.* Chapel Hill: University of North Carolina Press, 1996.

Gilroy, Paul. *The Black Atlantic: Modernity and Double Consciousness.* Cambridge, MA: Harvard University Press, 1993.

Giroux, Henry A., and Peter McLaren, eds. *Between Borders: Pedagogy and the Politics of Cultural Studies.* New York: Routledge, 1994.

Giroux, Henry A., and Kostas Myrsiades. *Beyond the Corporate University: Culture and Pedagogy in the New Millennium.* Lanham, MD: Rowman and Littlefield, 2001.

Glenn, Evelyn Nakano. "Racial Ethnic Women's Labor: The Intersection of Race, Gender and Class Oppression." *Review of Radical Political Economics* 17.3 (1985): 86–108.

Glick, Elisa, Linda Garber, Sharon Holland, Daniel Balderson, and José Quiroga. "New Directions in Multiethnic, Racial, and Global Queer Studies." *GLQ* 10.1 (Winter 2003): 123–37.

Goldberg, David Theo, ed. *Multiculturalism: A Critical Reader.* Oxford: Blackwell, 1994.

Gordon, Avery, and Christopher Newfield, eds. *Mapping Multiculturalism.* Minneapolis: University of Minnesota Press, 1996.

Gordon, Lewis R., and Jane Anna Gordon, eds. *A Companion to African-American Studies.* Malden, MA: Blackwell, 2006.

Gordon-Reed, Annette. *The Hemingses of Monticello: An American Family.* New York: Norton, 2008.

———. *Thomas Jefferson and Sally Hemings: An American Controversy.* Charlottesville: University of Virginia Press, 1997.

Grayson, Deborah. "Mediating Intimacy: Black Surrogate Mothers and the Law." *Critical Inquiry* 24.2 (Winter 1998): 525–46.

Greene, Jack P. *The Intellectual Construction of America: Exceptionalism and Identity from 1493 to 1800.* Chapel Hill: University of North Carolina Press, 1993.

Grewal, Inderpal, and Caren Kaplan. "Global Identities: Theorizing Transnational Studies of Sexuality." *GLQ* 7.4 (Fall 2001): 663–79.

Gruesz, Kirsten Silva. *Ambassadors of Culture: The Transamerican Origins of Latino Writing.* Princeton, NJ: Princeton University Press, 2002.

Grunwald, Michael. "In Vitro, in Error—And Now, in Court: White Mother Given Black Couple's Embryos Will Give One 'Twin' Back." *Washington Post* (March 31, 1999): A1.

Gubar, Susan. "Feminist Misogyny: Mary Wollstonecraft and the Paradox of 'It Takes One to Know One.'" In *Feminism Beside Itself.* Ed. Diane Elam and Robyn Wiegman. New York: Routledge, 1995: 133–54.

———. "What Ails Feminist Criticism?" *Critical Inquiry* 24.4 (Summer 1998): 878–902.

Gunew, Sneja. "Feminist Cultural Literacy: Translating Differences, Cannibal Options." In *Women's Studies on Its Own.* Ed. Robyn Wiegman. Durham, NC: Duke University Press, 2002: 47–65.

———. *Feminist Knowledge as Critique and Construct.* London: Routledge, 1992.

Gutmann, Amy, ed. *Multiculturalism: Examining the Politics of Recognition.* Princeton, NJ: Princeton University Press, 1994.

Hagan, Kay Leigh, ed. *Women Respond to the Men's Movement: A Feminist Collection.* San Francisco: HarperSan Francisco, 1992.

Haggerty, George E., and Molly McGarry, eds. *A Companion to Lesbian, Gay, Bisexual, Transgender, and Queer Studies.* Malden, MA: Blackwell, 2007.

Hakim, Danny. "Church Rally Defies Klan." *Greenville News* (April 1, 1997): 2D.

———. "Redneck Shop Sticker Upsets Churchgoers." *Greenville News* (March 31, 1997): 1D.

Halberstam, Judith. "The Anti-social Turn in Queer Studies." *Graduate Journal of Social Science* 5.2 (2008): 140–56.

———. *Female Masculinity.* Durham, NC: Duke University Press, 1998.

———. "Reflections on Queer Studies and Queer Pedagogy." *Journal of Homosexuality* 45.2–4 (2003): 361–64.

———. "Shame and White Gay Masculinity." *Social Text* 23.3–4 (Fall–Winter 2005): 219–33.

Hale, C. Jacob. "Consuming the Living, Dis(re)membering the Dead in the Butch/FTM Borderlands." *GLQ* 4.2 (Spring 1998): 311–48.

———. "Introducing Transgender Studies into the Undergraduate Philosophy Curriculum." *APA Newsletter* 98.2 (Spring 1999): http://www.apaonline.org /publications/newsletters/v98n2_Lesbian_07.aspx.

Hale, Grace Elizabeth. *Making Whiteness: The Culture of Segregation in the South, 1890–1940*. New York: Vintage, 1999.

Hall, Donald E. *Reading Sexualities: Hermeneutic Theory and the Future of Queer Studies*. New York: Routledge, 2009.

Hall, Donald E., and Maria Pramaggiore, eds. *Representing Bisexualities: Subjects and Cultures of Fluid Desire*. New York: New York University Press, 1996.

Hall, Stuart. "Cultural Identity and Diaspora." In *Diaspora and Visual Culture: Representing Africans and Jews*. Ed. Nicholas Mirzoeff. New York: Routledge, 1999: 21–33.

Halley, Ian. "Queer Theory by Men." *Duke Journal of Gender, Law and Policy* 11.7 (Spring 2004): 7–53.

Halley, Janet. *Split Decisions: How and Why to Take a Break from Feminism*. Princeton, NJ: Princeton University Press, 2006.

Halley, Janet, and Andrew Parker, eds. "After Sex? On Writing since Queer Theory." *South Atlantic Quarterly* 106.3 (Summer 2007).

Halperin, David. "The Normalization of Queer Studies." *Journal of Homosexuality* 45.2–4 (2003): 339–43.

Halperin, David, and Valerie Traub, eds. *Gay Shame*. Chicago: University of Chicago Press, 2009.

Hammond, James T. "Legislators Want Stiffer Penalties for Hate Crimes." *Greenville News* (April 12, 1996): 1A.

Hancock, Ange-Marie. "Intersectionality as a Normative and Empirical Paradigm." *Politics and Gender* 3.2 (2007): 248–54.

Haraway, Donna. "A Manifesto for Cyborgs: Science, Technology, and Socialist Feminism in the 1980s." *Socialist Review* 80 (1985): 65–108.

———. "Situated Knowledges: The Science Question in Feminism and the Privilege of Partial Perspective." In *Simians, Cyborgs, and Women: The Reinvention of Nature*. New York: Routledge, 1991: 183–201.

Harding, Sandra, ed. *The Standpoint Reader: Intellectual and Political Controversies*. New York: Routledge, 2004.

Hardt, Michael. "Affective Labor." *boundary 2* 26.2 (Summer 1999): 89–100.

———. "The Militancy of Theory." *South Atlantic Quarterly* 110:1 (Winter 2011): 19–35.

Hark, Sabine. "Magical Sign: On the Politics of Inter- and Transdisciplinarity." *Graduate Journal of Social Science* 4.2 (2007): 11–33.

Harper, Phillip Brian. "Gay Male Identities, Personal Privacy, and Relations of Public Exchange: Notes on Directions for Queer Critique." *Social Text* 15.3–4 (Fall–Winter 1997): 5–29.

———. *Private Affairs: Critical Ventures in the Culture of Social Relations.* New York: New York University Press, 1999.

Harper, Phillip Brian, Anne McClintock, José Esteban Muñoz, and Trish Rosen, eds. "Queer Transexions of Race, Nation, and Gender." Special issue, *Social Text* 15.3–4 (Fall–Winter 1997).

Harris, Cheryl. "Whiteness as Property." *Harvard Law Review* 106.8 (June 1993): 1710–91.

Hartigan, John, Jr. *Odd Tribes: Toward a Cultural Analysis of White People.* Durham, NC: Duke University Press, 2005.

Hartman, Andrew. "The Rise and Fall of Whiteness Studies." *Race and Class* 46.2 (2004): 22–38.

Hartman, Joan E., and Ellen Messer-Davidow, eds. *(En)Gendering Knowledge: Feminists in Academe.* Knoxville: University of Tennessee Press, 1991.

Hartman, Saidiya. *Lose Your Mother: A Journey along the Atlantic Slave Route.* New York: Farrar, Straus, and Giroux, 2007.

———. *Scenes of Subjection: Terror, Slavery, and Self-Making in Nineteenth-Century America.* New York: Oxford University Press, 1997.

Hartouni, Valerie. "Breached Birth: Reflections on Race, Gender, and Reproductive Discourse in the 1980s." *Configurations* 2.1 (Winter 1994): 73–88.

Hartsock, Nancy. "The Feminist Standpoint: Toward a Specifically Historical Materialism." In *Money, Sex, and Power.* Boston: Northeastern University Press, 1985: 231–51.

Hausman, Bernice L. "Recent Transgender Theory." *Feminist Studies* 27.2 (Summer 2001): 465–90.

Hearn, Jeff. *The Gender of Oppression: Men, Masculinity and the Critique of Marxism.* New York: St. Martin's Press, 1987.

———. *Men in the Public Eye: The Construction and Deconstruction of Public Men and Public Patriarchies.* London: Routledge, 1992.

Hearn, Jeff, and David Morgan, eds. *Men, Masculinities, and Social Theory.* London: Unwin Hyman, 1990.

Hekman, Susan. "Truth and Method: Feminist Standpoint Theory Revisited." With commentaries by Nancy Hartsock, Patricia Hill Collins, Sandra Harding, and Dorothy Smith. In *Provoking Feminisms.* Ed. Carolyn Allen and Judith A. Howard. Chicago: University of Chicago Press, 2000: 9–69.

Hemmings, Clare. *Bisexual Spaces: A Geography of Sexuality and Gender*. London: Routledge, 2002.

———. "Invoking Affect: Cultural Theory and the Ontological Turn." *Cultural Studies* 19.5 (September 2005): 548–67.

———. "Telling Feminist Stories." *Feminist Theory* 6.2 (August 2005): 115–39.

———. "What's in a Name? Bisexuality, Transnational Sexuality Studies and Western Colonial Legacies." *International Journal of Human Rights* 11.1–2 (March 2007): 13–32.

Hennessy, Rosemary. "Queer Theory, Left Politics." *Rethinking Marxism* 7.3 (1994): 85–111.

———. "Queer Visibility in Commodity Culture." In *Social Postmodernism: Beyond Identity Politics*. Ed. Linda J. Nicholson and Steven Seidman. Cambridge: Cambridge University Press, 1995: 142–84.

———. "Women's Lives/Feminist Knowledge: Feminist Standpoint as Ideology Critique." *Hypatia* 8.1 (Winter 1993): 14–34.

Herdt, Gilbert. *Guardians of the Flutes Volume 1: Idioms of Masculinity*. Chicago: University of Chicago Press, 1981.

Heyes, Cressida J. "Reading Transgender, Rethinking Women's Studies." *NWSA Journal* 12.2 (Summer 2000): 170–80.

Higginbotham, Elizabeth. "Race and Class Barriers to Black Women's College Attendance." *Journal of Ethnic Studies* 13.1 (1985): 89–107.

Hill, Mike. *After Whiteness: Unmaking an American Majority*. New York: New York University Press, 2004.

———. "What Was (the White) Race? Memory, Categories, Change." *Postmodern Culture* 7.2 (January 1997): http://muse.jhu.edu/journals/postmodern _culture/v007/7.2r_hill.html.

———, ed. *Whiteness: A Critical Reader*. New York: New York University Press, 1997.

Hine, Darlene Clark, and Earnestine Jenkins, eds. *A Question of Manhood: A Reader in U.S. Black Men's History and Masculinity*. Bloomington: Indiana University Press, 1999.

Hollibaugh, Amber L. *My Dangerous Desires: A Queer Girl Dreaming Her Way Home*. Durham, NC: Duke University Press, 2000.

Holloway, Karla. "'Cruel Enough to Stop the Blood': Global Feminisms and the U.S. Body Politic, or: 'They Done Taken My Blues and Gone.'" *Meridians: feminism, race, transnationalism* 7.1 (2006): 1–18.

Hones, Sheila, and Julia Leyda. "Geographies of American Studies." *American Quarterly* 57.4 (December 2005): 1019–32.

———. "Toward a Critical Geography of American Studies." *Comparative American Studies* 2.2 (June 2004): 185–203.

hooks, bell. *Ain't I a Woman: Black Women and Feminism*. Boston: South End Press, 1981.

———. *Feminist Theory: From Margin to Center*. Boston: South End Press, 1984.

———. "Men: Comrades in Struggle." In *Feminist Theory: From Margin to Center*. Boston: South End Press, 1984: 68–83.

Howe, Florence. "Breaking the Disciplines." In *The Structures of Knowledge: A Feminist Perspective*. Ed. Beth Reed. Ann Arbor, MI: Great Lakes Colleges Association Women's Studies Program, 1979: 1–10.

Hull, Gloria T. "Researching Alice Dunbar-Nelson: A Personal and Literary Perspective." *Feminist Studies* 6.2 (Summer 1980): 314–20.

Hull, Gloria T., Patricia Scott Bell, and Barbara Smith, eds. *All the Women Are White, All the Blacks Are Men, but Some of Us Are Brave: Black Women's Studies*. Old Westbury, NY: Feminist Press, 1982.

Hurwitz, Ilana. "Collaborative Reproduction: Finding the Child in the Maze of Legal Motherhood." *Connecticut Law Review* 33.1 (Fall 2000): 127–180.

Hutchinson, Darren Lenard. "Identity Crisis: 'Intersectionality,' 'Multidimensionality,' and the Development of an Adequate Theory of Subordination." *Michigan Journal of Race and Law* 6.2 (Spring 2001): 285–317.

———. "Ignoring the Sexualization of Race: Heteronormativity, Critical Race Theory, and Anti-racist Politics." *Buffalo Law Review* 47.1 (Winter 1999): 1–116.

———. "Out Yet Unseen: A Racial Critique of Gay and Lesbian Legal Theory and Political Discourse." *Connecticut Law Review* 29.2 (Winter 1997): 561–645.

Ickstadt, Heinz. "American Studies in an Age of Globalization." *American Quarterly* 54.4 (December 2002): 543–62.

Ignatiev, Noel. *How the Irish Became White*. New York: Routledge, 1995.

Ignatiev, Noel, and John Garvey, eds. *Race Traitor*. New York: Routledge, 1996.

Ikemoto, Lisa C. "The In/Fertile, the Too Fertile, and the Dysfertile." *Hastings Law Journal* 47 (April 1996): 1007–61.

Ingraham, Chrys. "The Heterosexual Imaginary: Feminist Sociology and Theories of Gender." *Sociological Theory* 12.2 (July 1994): 203–19.

Irigaray, Luce. *This Sex Which Is Not One*. Trans. Catherine Porter. Ithaca, NY: Cornell University Press, 1985.

Izzo, Donatella. "Outside Where? Comparing Notes on Comparative American Studies and American Comparative Studies." *American Studies: An Anthology*. Ed. Janice A. Radway, Kevin K. Gaines, Barry Shank, and Penny Von Eschen. Malden, MA: Blackwell, 2009: 588–604.

Jackson, Stevi. "Gender, Sexuality and Heteronormativity: The Complexity (and Limits) of Heteronormativity." *Feminist Theory* 7.1 (2006): 105–21.

———. "Sexuality, Heterosexuality and Gender Hierarchy: Getting Our Priorities Straight." In *Thinking Straight: The Power, the Promise, and the Paradox of Heterosexuality*. Ed. Chrys Ingraham. New York: Routledge, 2005: 15–38.

Jacobson, Matthew Frye. *Whiteness of a Different Color: European Immigrants and the Alchemy of Race.* Cambridge, MA: Harvard University Press, 1998.

Jagose, Annamarie, and Don Kulik. "Thinking Sex/Thinking Gender." *GLQ* 10.2 (Spring 2004): 211–312.

James, C. L. R. *Beyond a Boundary.* 2nd ed. Durham, NC: Duke University Press, 1993.

Jameson, Fredric. *The Political Unconscious: Narrative as a Socially Symbolic Act.* Ithaca, NY: Cornell University Press, 1981.

Jardine, Alice, and Paul Smith, eds. *Men in Feminism.* New York: Metheun, 1987.

Jeffords, Susan. *Hard Bodies: Hollywood Masculinity in the Reagan Era.* New Brunswick, NJ: Rutgers University Press, 1994.

———. *The Remasculinization of America: Gender and the Vietnam War.* Bloomington: Indiana University Press, 1989.

Jeffreys, Sheila. "Heterosexuality and the Desire for Gender." In *Theorizing Heterosexuality: Telling It Straight.* Ed. Diane Richardson. Buckingham: Open University Press, 1996: 75–90.

Johnson, E. Patrick. " 'Quare' Studies, or (Almost) Everything I Know about Queer Studies I Learned from My Grandmother." *Text and Performance Quarterly* 21.1 (January 2001): 1–25.

Johnson, E. Patrick, and Mae G. Henderson, eds. *Black Queer Studies: A Critical Anthology.* Durham, NC: Duke University Press, 2005.

Johnson v. Calvert. 19 Cal. Rptr.2d, 506–18 (Cal. 1993); cert. denied, 113 S.Ct 206 (1993).

Jones, Howard Mumford. *The Pursuit of Happiness.* Cambridge, MA: Harvard University Press, 1953.

Jones, Jacqueline. *Labor of Love, Labor of Sorrow: Black Women, Work, and the Family from Slavery to the Present.* New York: Basic Books, 1985.

———. " 'My Mother Was Much of a Woman': Black Women, Work, and the Family Under Slavery." *Feminist Studies* 8.2 (Summer 1982): 235–69.

Jordan-Zachery, Julie S. "Am I a Black Woman or a Woman Who Is Black? A Few Thoughts on the Meaning of Intersectionality." *Politics and Gender* 3.2 (June 2007): 254–63.

Kadir, Djelal, ed. "America, the Idea, the Literature." *PMLA* 118.1 (January 2003).

———. "Defending America Against Its Devotees." *Comparative American Studies* 2:2 (June 2004): 135–52.

———. "Introduction: America and Its Studies." *PMLA* 118.1 (January 2003): 9–24.

Kammen, Michael. "The Problem of American Exceptionalism: A Reconsideration." *American Quarterly* 45.1 (March 1993): 1–43.

Kaplan, Amy. *The Anarchy of Empire in the Making of U.S. Culture.* Cambridge, MA: Harvard University Press, 2002.

———. "A Call for a Truce." *American Literary History* 17.1 (Spring 2005): 141–47.

———. "Manifest Domesticity." *American Literature* 70.3 (September 1998): 581–606.

———. "The Tenacious Grasp of American Exceptionalism: A Response to Djelal Kadir, 'Defending America Against Its Devotees.'" *Comparative American Studies* 2.2 (June 2004): 153–59.

Kaplan, Amy, and Donald E. Pease, eds. *Cultures of United States Imperialism.* Durham, NC: Duke University Press, 1993.

Katznelson, Ira. *When Affirmative Action Was White: An Untold History of Racial Inequality in 20th Century America.* New York: Norton, 2005.

Kaufman, Michael, ed. *Beyond Patriarchy: Essays by Men on Pleasure and Power.* Toronto: Oxford University Press, 1987.

Kaufman, Michael, and Michael A. Messner, eds. *Men's Lives.* New York: Macmillan, 1990.

Kazanjian, David. *The Colonizing Trick: National Culture and Imperial Citizenship in Early America.* Minneapolis: University of Minnesota Press, 2004.

Kelley, Robin D. G. "Contested Terrain." In *Race Rebels: Culture, Politics, and the Black Working Class.* New York: Free Press, 1994: 55–75.

Kennedy, Duncan. "Sexual Abuse, Sexy Dressing and the Eroticization of Domination." *New England Law Review* 26 (1991–92): 1309–93.

Kennedy, Elizabeth Lapovsky, and Agatha Beins, eds. *Women's Studies for the Future: Foundations, Interrogations, Politics.* New Brunswick, NJ: Rutgers University Press, 2005.

Kennedy, Liam. "Spectres of Comparison: American Studies and the United States of the West." *Comparative American Studies* 4.2 (June 2006): 135–50.

Khanna, Ranjana. *Dark Continents: Psychoanalysis and Colonialism.* Durham, NC: Duke University Press, 2003.

Kidwell, Clara Sue, and Alan Velie, eds. *Native American Studies (Introducing Ethnic Studies).* Lincoln: University of Nebraska Press, 2005.

Kim, Claire Jean. "The Racial Triangulation of Asian Americans." *Politics and Society* 27.1 (March 1999): 105–38.

Kimmel, Michael S. *Changing Men: New Directions in Research on Men and Masculinity.* London: Sage, 1987.

Kimmel, Michael S., and Michael Kaufman. "The New Men's Movement: Retreat and Regression with America's Weekend Warriors." *Gender Issues* 13.2 (June 1993): 3–21.

Kincheloe, Joe L., Shirley R. Steinberg, Nelson M. Rodriguez, and Ronald E. Chennault, eds. *White Reign: Deploying Whiteness in America.* New York: St. Martin's Press, 1998.

King, C. Richard, ed. *Postcolonial America*. Urbana: University of Illinois Press, 2000.

King, Deborah. "Multiple Jeopardy, Multiple Consciousness: The Context of a Black Feminist Ideology." *Signs* 14.1 (Autumn 1988): 42–72.

King, Mae. "The Politics of Sexual Stereotypes." *Black Scholar* 4.6–7 (1973): 12–23.

Kipnis, Laura. *Bound and Gagged: Pornography and the Politics of Fantasy in America*. New York: Grove Press, 1996.

———. *Ecstasy Unlimited: On Sex, Capital, Gender, and Aesthetics*. Minneapolis: University of Minnesota Press, 1993.

Kiss and Tell Collective. *Her Tongue on My Theory: Images, Essays, and Fantasies*. Vancouver: Press Gang, 1994.

Klein, Julie Thompson. "Blurring, Cracking, and Crossing: Permeation and the Fracturing of Discipline." *Knowledges: Historical and Critical Studies in Disciplinarity*. Ed. Ellen Messer-Davidow, David R. Shumway, and David J. Sylvan. Charlottesville: University of Virginia Press, 1993: 185–214.

———. *Crossing Boundaries: Knowledge, Disciplinarities, and Interdisciplinarities*. Charlottesville: University of Virginia Press, 1996.

———. *Interdisciplinarity: History, Theory, Practice*. Detroit, MI: Wayne State University Press, 1990.

Klein, Melanie. *The Collected Writings of Melanie Klein*. Volumes 1–4. London: Hogarth Press and the Institute of Psychoanalysis, 1975.

Kolasch, Oliver. *The Internationalisation of the Higher Education Industry: The Case of Universities in the U.S. and Canada*. Munich: GRIN, 2009.

Kolchin, Peter. "Whiteness Studies: The New History of Race in America." *Journal of American History* 89.1 (June 2002): 154–73.

Kousser, J. Morgan. *Colorblind Injustice: Minority Voting Rights and the Undoing of the Second Reconstruction*. Chapel Hill: University of North Carolina Press, 1999.

Kroes, Rob. *If You've Seen One, You've Seen the Mall: Europeans and American Mass Culture*. Urbana: University of Illinois Press, 1996.

———. "National American Studies in Europe, Transnational American Studies in America." In *American Studies in Germany: European Contexts and Intercultural Relations*. Ed. Günter H. Lenz and Klaus J. Milich. New York: St. Martin's Press, 1995: 147–58.

Kuczynski, Alex. "Her Body, My Baby." *New York Times Magazine* (November 20, 2008): 42–49, 64, 74, 78.

Kwan, Peter. "Intersections of Race, Ethnicity, Class, Gender and Sexual Orientation: Jeffrey Dahmer and the Cosynthesis of Categories." *Hastings Law Journal* 48.6 (August 1997): 1257–92.

Ladner, Joyce. *Tomorrow's Tomorrow: The Black Woman*. New York: Doubleday, 1971.

Lander, Eric S., and Joseph J. Ellis. "Founding Father." *Nature* 396 (November 5, 1998): 13–14.

Landrum, Cindy. "Jesse Jackson, Ministers Discuss the Redneck Shop." *Greenville News* (March 18, 1996): 2A.

Lane, Christopher, ed. *The Psychoanalysis of Race*. New York: Columbia University Press, 1998.

"Lasting Consequences." *Dateline NBC* (February 22, 2000). Transcript No. 1072. Livingston, NJ: National Broadcasting Company, 2000.

Lavery, David. " 'No Box of Chocolates': The Adaptation of Forrest Gump." *Literature/Film Quarterly* 25.1 (1997): 18–22.

Lawrence v. Texas (02-102) 539 U.S. 558 (2003).

Lee, Rachel. "Notes from the (Non)Field: Teaching and Theorizing Women of Color." In *Women's Studies on Its Own*. Ed. Robyn Wiegman. Durham, NC: Duke University Press, 2002: 82–105.

Lehman, Peter. *Running Scared: Masculinity and the Representation of the Male Body*. Philadelphia: Temple University Press, 1993.

Leiter, Samuel, and William Leiter. *Affirmative Action in Anti-discrimination Law and Policy: An Overview and Synthesis*. Albany: State University of New York Press, 2002.

Lenz, Günter H. "Internationalizing American Studies: Predecessors, Paradigms, and Dialogical Cultural Critique—A View from Germany." In *Predecessors: Intellectual Lineages in American Studies*. Ed. Rob Kroes. Amsterdam: VU University Press, 1999: 236–55.

———. "Toward a Dialogics of International American Culture Studies: Transnationality, Border Discourses, and Public Culture(s)." In *The Futures of American Studies*. Ed. Donald E. Pease and Robyn Wiegman. Durham, NC: Duke University Press, 2002: 461–80.

Leonardo, Zeus. "The Souls of White Folk: Critical Pedagogy, Whiteness Studies, and Globalization Discourse." *Race, Ethnicity and Education* 5.1 (March 2002): 29–50.

Levander, Caroline F., and Robert S. Levine, eds. "Hemispheric American Literary History." *American Literary History* 18.3 (Fall 2006).

Leverenz, David. *Manhood and the American Renaissance*. Ithaca, NY: Cornell University Press, 1989.

———. "The Politics of Emerson's Man-Making Words." *PMLA* 101.1 (January 1986): 38–56.

Lewis, Diane K. "A Response to Inequality: Black Women, Racism, and Sexism." *Signs* 3.2 (Winter 1977): 339–61.

Li, David Leiwei, ed. *Globalization and the Humanities*. Aberdeen, Hong Kong: Hong Kong University Press, 2004.

Liebler, Raizel. "Are You My Parent? Are You My Child? The Role of Genetics and Race in Defining Relationships after Reproductive Technological Mistakes." *DePaul Journal of Health Care Law* 5.15 (2002): 15–56.

Lipsitz, George. "Our America." *American Literary History* 17.1 (Spring 2005): 135–40.

———. *The Possessive Investment in Whiteness: How White People Profit from Identity Politics*. Philadelphia: Temple University Press, 1998.

———. "The Possessive Investment in Whiteness: Racialized Social Democracy and the 'White' Problem in American Studies." *American Quarterly* 47.3 (September 1995): 369–87.

Logue, Anne Marie. "'Telling America's Story to the World': U.S. Public Diplomacy, American Studies, and Cultural Productions of State." Master's thesis, Department of English, Duke University, 2009.

López, Ian F. Haney. *White by Law: The Legal Construction of Race*. New York: New York University Press, 1996.

Lorde, Audre. "Man Child: A Black Lesbian Feminist's Response." In *Sister Outsider*. Trumansburg, NY: Crossing Press, 1987: 72–80.

Lott, Eric. *Love and Theft: Blackface Minstrelsy and the American Working Class*. New York: Oxford University Press, 1993.

———. "White Like Me: Racial Cross-Dressing and the Construction of American Whiteness." In *Cultures of United States Imperialism*. Ed. Amy Kaplan and Donald E. Pease. Durham, NC: Duke University Press, 1993: 474–98.

Lovaas, Karen E., John P. Elia, and Gust A. Yep, eds. *LGBT Studies and Queer Theory: New Conflicts, Collaborations, and Contested Terrain*. New York: Routledge, 2007.

Love, Heather. "Epilogue: The Politics of Refusal." In *Feeling Backward: Loss and the Politics of Queer History*. Cambridge, MA: Harvard University Press, 2007: 146–64.

———. "'Oh, the Fun We'll Have': Remembering the Prospects for Sexuality Studies." *GLQ* 10.2 (Spring 2004): 258–61.

Lowe, Lisa. *Immigrant Acts: On Asian American Cultural Politics*. Durham, NC: Duke University Press, 1996.

———. "The International Within the National: American Studies and Asian American Critique." *Cultural Critique* 40 (Autumn 1998): 29–45.

Lubiano, Wahneema. "Black Ladies, Welfare Queens, and State Minstrels: Ideological War by Narrative Means." In *Race-ing Justice, En-gendering Power*, ed. Toni Morrison. New York: Pantheon, 1992: 323–63.

———. "Like Being Mugged by a Metaphor: Multiculturalism and State Narratives." In *Mapping Multiculturalism*. Ed. Avery Gordon and Christopher Newfield. Minneapolis: University of Minnesota Press, 1996: 64–75.

Lucas, Scott. "USA OK? Beyond the Practice of (Anti)-American Studies." *49th Parallel* 8 (Summer 2001): http://www.49thParallel.bham.ac.uk/back/issue8 /lucas.htm.

Lugones, Maria, and Joshua Price. "The Inseparability of Race, Class, and Gender in Latino Studies." *Latino Studies* 1.2 (July 2003): 329–32.

Lugones, Maria, and Elizabeth V. Spelman. "Have We Got a Theory for You! Feminist Theory, Cultural Imperialism, and the Demand for 'The Woman's Voice.'" *Women's Studies International Forum* 6.6 (1983): 573–81.

Luibhéid, Eithne. *Entry Denied: Controlling Sexuality at the Border*. Minneapolis: University of Minnesota Press, 2002.

———. "Heteronormativity and Immigration Scholarship: A Call for Change." *GLQ* 10.2 (Spring 2004): 227–35.

———. *Heteronormativity, Responsibility and Neo-liberal Governance in U.S. Immigration Control*. Cambridge, MA: Harvard University Press, 2005.

MacKinnon, Catherine A. "Feminism, Marxism, Method, and the State: An Agenda for Theory." *Signs* 7.3 (Spring 1982): 515–44.

Maddox, Lucy. *Locating American Studies: The Evolution of a Discipline*. Baltimore, MD: Johns Hopkins University Press, 1998.

Made in America (dir. Richard Benjamin). Warner Brothers, 1993.

Madsen, Deborah L. *American Exceptionalism*. Jackson: University Press of Mississippi, 1998.

Mahmood, Saba. "Feminism, Democracy, and Empire." In *Women's Studies on the Edge*. Ed. Joan Wallach Scott. Durham, NC: Duke University Press, 2008: 81–114.

Malloch, Theodore Roosevelt, and Scott T. Massey. *Renewing American Culture: The Pursuit of Happiness*. Salem, MA: M&M Scrivener Press, 2006.

Manalansan, Martin. *Global Divas: Filipino Gay Men in the Diaspora*. Durham, NC: Duke University Press, 2003.

Manegold, Catherine S. "The Citadel's Lone Wolf: Shannon Faulkner." *New York Times Magazine* (September 11, 1994): http://www.nytimes.com/1994/09/11 /magazine/the-citadel-s-lone-wolf-shannon-faulkner.html?scp=3&sq= catherine%20manegold&st=cse.

———. *In Glory's Shadow: The Citadel, Shannon Faulkner, and a Changing America*. New York: Vintage, 2001.

Marable, Manning. *Race, Reform, and Rebellion: The Second Reconstruction in Black America, 1945–1982*. Jackson: University Press of Mississippi, 1984.

Marginson, Simon. "The Rise of the Global University: 5 New Tensions." *Chronicle of Higher Education* (May 30, 2010): http://chronicle.com/article /The-Rise-of-the-Global/65694/.

Martin, Biddy. "Sexualities Without Genders and Other Queer Utopias." In *Femininity Played Straight: The Significance of Being Lesbian*. New York: Routledge, 1996: 71–96.

————. "Success and Its Failures." *differences* 9.3 (Fall 1997): 102–31.

Marx, Leo. "On Recovering the 'Ur' Theory of American Studies." *American Literary History* 17.1 (Spring 2005): 118–34.

Mattilda. "Gay Shame: From Queer Autonomous Space to Direct Action Extravaganza." In *That's Revolting: Queer Strategies for Resisting Assimilation.* Ed. Mattilda (Matt Bernstein Sycamore). Brooklyn, NY: Soft Skull Press, 2004: 268–95.

Maudlin, Amy Lyn. "Residents Rally Against Redneck Shop." *Greenville News* (April 27, 1996): 2A.

Maull, Samuel. "Oddly Enough: Judge Orders Psychological Exams for Babies in Embryo Mix-Up." *Portsmouth Herald* (June 29, 1999): http://archive .seacoastonline.com/1999news/6_300dd.htm.

McCall, Leslie. "The Complexity of Intersectionality." *Signs* 30.3 (Spring 2005): 1771–800.

McCallum, E. L. *Object Lessons: How to Do Things with Fetishism.* Albany: State University of New York Press, 1999.

McCarthy, Cameron. "Contradictions of Power and Identity: Whiteness Studies and the Call of Teacher Education." *International Journal of Qualitative Studies in Education* 16.1 (January/February 2003): 127–33.

McClure, Kirstie. "The Issue of Foundations: Scientized Politics, Politicized Science, and Feminist Critical Practice." In *Feminists Theorize the Political.* Ed. Judith Butler and Joan W. Scott. New York: Routledge, 1992: 341–68.

McCurry, Stephanie. *Confederate Reckoning: Power and Politics in the Civil War South.* Cambridge, MA: Harvard University Press, 2010.

McKee, Patricia. *Producing American Races: Henry James, William Faulkner, Toni Morrison.* Durham, NC: Duke University Press, 1999.

McMillen, Liz. "Lifting the Veil from Whiteness: Growing Body of Scholarship Challenges a Racial 'Norm.'" *Chronicle of Higher Education* 42.2 (September 8, 1995): A23.

McWhorter, Ladelle. "Where Do White People Come From? A Foucaultian Critique of Whiteness Studies." *Philosophy and Social Criticism* 31.5–6 (2005): 533–56.

Medovoi, Leerom. "Nation, Globe, Hegemony: Post-Fordist Preconditions of the Transnational Turn in American Studies." *interventions* 7.2 (July 2005): 162–79.

Mehta, Uday Singh. "The Essential Ambiguities of Race and Racism." In *Political Power and Social Theory 11.* Ed. Diane E. Davis. Stamford, CT: JAI Press, 1997: 235–46.

Mercer, Kobena. "Imaging the Black Man's Sex." *Photography/Politics: Two.* Ed. Patricia Holland. London: Camedia, 1987.

Messer-Davidow, Ellen. *Disciplining Feminism: From Social Activism to Academic Discourse.* Durham, NC: Duke University Press, 2002: 83–213.

Messner, Michael A. *Politics of Masculinities: Men in Movements*. Lanham, MD: AltaMira Press, 1997.

Michaels, Walter Benn, and Donald E. Pease, eds. *The American Renaissance Reconsidered*. Baltimore, MD: Johns Hopkins University Press, 1989.

Mies, Maria. *Patriarchy and Accumulation of a World Scale: Women and the International Division of Labor*. London: Zed Books, 1986.

Miller, Alice M. "Gay Enough: Some Tensions in Seeking the Grant of Asylum and Protecting Global Sexual Diversity." In *Passing Lines: Sexuality and Immigration*. Ed. Brad Epps, Keja Valens, and Bill Johnson González. Cambridge, MA: Harvard University Press, 2005: 137–87.

———. "Sexual but Not Reproductive: Exploring the Junction and Disjunction of Sexual and Reproductive Rights." *Health and Human Rights* 4.2 (2000): 69–109.

Miyoshi, Masao. "A Borderless World? From Colonialism to Transnationalism and the Decline of the Nation-State." *Critical Inquiry* 19.4 (Summer 1993): 726–51.

Moallem, Minoo. "'Women of Color in the U.S.': Pedagogical Reflections on the Politics of 'the Name.'" In *Women's Studies on Its Own*. Ed. Robyn Wiegman. Durham, NC: Duke University Press, 2002: 368–82.

Modleski, Tania. *Feminism Without Women: Culture and Criticism in a "Postfeminist" Age*. New York: Routledge, 1991.

Mohanram, Radhika. *Imperial White: Race, Diaspora, and the British Empire*. Minneapolis: University of Minnesota Press, 2007.

Mohanty, Chandra Talpade. "Under Western Eyes: Feminist Scholarship and Colonial Discourses." *Feminist Review* 30 (1988): 61–88.

Moorefield, April E. "Attorney: Man Charged in Redneck Shop Damage Not Malicious." *Greenville News* (April 5, 1996): 1D.

———. "Beasley Called Too Quiet on Racism." *Greenville News* (April 25, 1996): 2D.

———. "Change of Heart Closes Redneck Shop." *Greenville News* (July 9, 1996): 1A.

———. "Citizens Call for a Cautious Protest of Redneck Shop in Laurens County." *Greenville News* (March 11, 1996): 2A.

———. "City Would Deny Redneck Shop License." *Greenville News* (July 17, 1996): 1D.

———. "Help Close Redneck Shop, Jesse Jackson Urges Reno." *Greenville News* (March 19, 1996): 1A.

———. "Laurens Gives New License to Controversial Redneck Shop." *Greenville News* (November 21, 1996): 2D.

———. "Laurens Police Arrest Suspect in Front of Store." *Greenville News* (March 25, 1996): 1A.

———. "Man Sorry for His Role in Redneck Shop." *Greenville News* (July 11, 1996): 3D.

———. "New Klan 'Museum' Gets Chilly Reception." *Greenville News* (March 5, 1996): 2D.

———. "Ralliers Say Hate Belongs in Past." *Greenville News* (March 17, 1996): 1B.

———. "Redneck Shop Hits Roadblock." *Greenville News* (July 10, 1996): 1D.

———. "Redneck Shop Rally Slated to Be Just One of Many." *Greenville News* (April 28, 1996): 1B.

———. "Redneck Shop Reopens in Laurens Without Business License, Sues City." *Greenville News* (July 20, 1996): 2A.

———. "Reno to Review Request for Redneck Shop Probe." *Greenville News* (March 21, 1996): 1D.

———. "Ribbons Aim to Promote Racial Unity." *Greenville News* (March 14, 1996): 5D.

———. "Walk to Statehouse to Protest Redneck Shop." *Greenville News* (January 30, 1997): 2D.

Moorefield, April E., with James T. Hammond. "Suspect in Attack on Redneck Shop Decries Hate, Apathy." *Greenville News* (March 26, 1996): 1A.

Moraga, Cherríe, and Gloria Anzaldúa. *This Bridge Called My Back: Writings by Radical Women of Color*. New York: Kitchen Table/Women of Color Press, 1983.

More, Kate, and Stephen Whittle, eds. *Reclaiming Genders: Transsexual Grammars at the Fin de Siècle*. London: Cassell, 1999.

Morley, David, and Kuan-Hsing Chen, eds. *Stuart Hall: Critical Dialogues in Cultural Studies*. New York: Routledge, 1996.

Morrison, Toni. "Comment." *New Yorker* (October 5, 1998): http://www.newyorker.com/archive/1998/10/05/1998_10_05_031_TNY_LIBRY_000016504?currentPage=all.

———. *Playing in the Dark: Whiteness and the Literary Tradition*. Cambridge, MA: Harvard University Press, 1992.

Morton, Brian, ed. "Affirmative Action under Fire." *Dissent* (Fall 1995).

Morton, Donald. "Birth of the Cyberqueer." *PMLA* 110.3 (May 1995): 369–81.

———. "Global (Sexual) Politics, Class Struggle, and the Queer Left." *Postcolonial, Queer: Theoretical Intersections*. Ed. John C. Hawley. Albany: State University of New York Press, 2001: 207–38.

———. "The Politics of Queer Theory in the (Post) Modern Moment." *Genders* 17 (Fall 1993): 121–45.

Moya, Paula M. L., and Ramón Saldívar. "Fictions of the Trans-American Imaginary." *Modern Fiction Studies* 49.1 (Spring 2003): 1–18.

Muñoz, José Esteban. *Cruising Utopia: The Then and There of Queer Futurity*. New York: New York University Press, 2009.

————. *Disidentifications: Queers of Color and the Performance of Politics.* Minneapolis: University of Minnesota Press, 1999.

————. "Thinking Beyond Antirelationality and Antiutopianism in Queer Critique." *PMLA* 121.3 (May 2006): 825–26.

Murphy, Gretchen. *Hemispheric Imaginings: The Monroe Doctrine and Narratives of U.S. Empire.* Durham, NC: Duke University Press, 2005.

Murphy, Kevin P., Jason Ruiz, and David Serlin, eds. "Queer Futures." Special issue, *Radical History Review* 100 (Winter 2008).

Murphy, Peter Francis. *Feminism and Masculinities.* New York: Oxford University Press, 2004.

Murray, Pauli. "The Liberation of Black Women." In *Voices of the New Feminism.* Ed. Mary Lou Thompson. Boston: Beacon Press, 1970: 87–102.

Nadel, Alan. *Flatlining on the Field of Dreams: Cultural Narratives in the Films of President Reagan's America.* New Brunswick, NJ: Rutgers University Press, 1997.

Naffine, Ngaire. "The Legal Structure of Self-Ownership: Or the Self-Possessed Man and the Woman Possessed." *Journal of Law and Society* 25.2 (June 1998): 193–212.

Nakayama, Thomas K., and Judith N. Martin, eds. *Whiteness: The Communication of Social Identity.* Thousand Oaks, CA: Sage, 1999.

Namaste, Ki. " 'Tragic Misreadings': Queer Theory's Erasure of Transgender Subjectivity." In *Queer Studies: A Lesbian, Gay, Bisexual, and Transgender Anthology.* Ed. Brett Beemyn and Mickey Eliason. New York: New York University Press, 1996: 183–203.

Namaste, Viviane K. *Invisible Lives: The Erasure of Transsexual and Transgendered People.* Chicago: University of Chicago Press, 2000.

Nash, Jennifer C. "Re-thinking Intersectionality." *Feminist Review* 89 (June 2008): 1–15.

National Legal Research Group. "The Liability of Reproductive Laboratories for Mistakenly Provided Genetic Material." *Divorce Research Center* (July 2001): http://www.divorcesource.com/research/dl/paternity/01jul134.shtml.

"Nation's Blacks Freaked Out by All the People Smiling at Them." *The Onion* (February 16, 2009): http://www.theonion.com/content/news/nations_blacks_creeped_out_by_all.

Neale, Steven. "Masculinity as Spectacle: Reflections on Men and Mainstream Cinema." *Screen* 24.6 (November/December 1983): 2–16.

Nelson, Dana. *National Manhood: Capitalist Citizenship and the Imagined Fraternity of White Men.* Durham, NC: Duke University Press, 1998.

Nestle, Joan. *A Restricted Country.* New York: Firebrand Books, 1987.

Nestle, Joan, Clare Howell, and Riki Wilchins, eds. *GenderQueer: Voices from Beyond the Sexual Binary.* Los Angeles: Alyson Books, 2002.

Newfield, Christopher. "The Politics of Male Suffering: Masochism and Hegemony in the American Renaissance." *differences* 1.3 (Fall 1989): 55–87.

———. *Unmaking the Public University: The Forty Year Assault on the Middle
Class.* Cambridge, MA: Harvard University Press, 2008.

Newitz, Annalee. "White Savagery and Humiliation, or a New Racial Consciousness in the Media." In *White Trash: Race and Class in America.* Ed. Matt
Wray and Annalee Newitz. New York: Routledge, 1997: 131–54.

Newman, Andy. "Visiting Rights Denied in Embryo Mix-Up Case." *New York
Times* (October 27, 2000): http://www.nytimes.com/2000/10/27/nyregion
/visiting-rights-denied-in-embryo-mix-up-case.html?sec=&spon=.

Newman, Louise Michele. *White Women's Rights: The Racial Origins of Feminism
in the United States.* New York: Oxford University Press, 1999.

New York State Task Force on Life and the Law. "Assisted Reproductive Technologies: Analysis and Recommendations for Public Policy, Executive
Summary." New York State Department of Health. http://www.health.state
.ny.us/nysdoh/taskfce/execsum.htm.

Noble, Bobby Jean. *Masculinities Without Men? Female Masculinity in Twentieth-
Century Fictions.* Toronto: University of British Columbia Press, 2004.

———. "Refusing to Make Sense: Mapping the In-Coherence of *Trans.*" *Journal of
Lesbian Studies* 11.1 (2007): 167–75.

———. *Sons of the Movement: FtMs Risking Incoherence on a Post-Queer Cultural
Landscape.* Toronto: Women's Press, 2006.

Noble-Allgire, Alice M. "Switched at the Fertility Clinic: Determining Maternal
Rights When a Child Is Born from Stolen or Misdelivered Genetic Material."
Missouri Law Review 64.3 (Summer 1999): 517–94.

Nunokawa, Jeff. "Queer Theory: Postmortem." *South Atlantic Quarterly*
106.3 (Summer 2007): 553–63.

Nussbaum, Martha C. "The Professor of Parody." *New Republic* 220.8 (February
22, 1999): 37–45.

Omi, Michael, and Howard Winant. *Racial Formation in the United States, from
the 1960s to the 1980s.* New York: Routledge, 1986.

———. *Racial Formation in the United States, from the 1960s to the 1990s.* 2nd ed.
New York: Routledge, 1994.

Omolade, Barbara. "The Unbroken Circle: A Historical Study of Black Single
Mothers and Their Families." *Wisconsin Women's Law Journal* 3 (1987):
239–74.

"One Family's Roots, a Nation's History." *New York Times* (October 8, 2009):
http://roomfordebate.blogs.nytimes.com/2009/10/08/one-familys-roots-a
-nations-history/.

Ono, Kent A., ed. *Asian American Studies after Critical Mass.* Malden, MA:
Blackwell, 2005.

————. *A Companion to Asian American Studies*. Malden, MA: Blackwell, 2004.

Park, You-me, and Henry Schwarz. "Extending American Hegemony: Beyond Empire." *interventions* 7.2 (July 2005): 153–61.

Parker, Joe, Mary Romero, and Ranu Samantrai, eds. *Interdisciplinarity and Social Justice*. Albany: State University of New York Press, 2010.

Pascoe, Peggy. "Miscegenation Law, Court Cases, and Ideologies of 'Race' in Twentieth-Century America." *Journal of American History* 83.1 (June 1996): 44–69.

Patterson, Mark R. "Surrogacy and Slavery: The Problematics of Consent in Baby M, *Romance of the Republic*, and *Puddn'head Wilson*." *American Literary History* 8.3 (Autumn 1996): 449–70.

Patton, Cindy. "Stealth Bombers of Desire: The Globalization of 'Alterity' in Emerging Democracies." In *Queer Globalizations: Citizenship and the Afterlife of Colonialism*. Ed. Arnaldo Cruz-Malavé and Martin F. Manalansan IV. New York: New York University Press, 2002: 195–218.

————. "Visualizing Safe Sex." In *Fatal Advice: How Safe Sex Education Went Wrong*. Durham, NC: Duke University Press, 1996: 118–38.

Pease, Donald E. *National Identities and Post-Americanist Narratives*. Durham, NC: Duke University Press, 1994.

————. "National Identities, Postmodern Artifacts, and Postnational Narratives." *boundary 2* 19.1 (Spring 1992): 1–13.

————. *The New American Exceptionalism*. Minneapolis: University of Minnesota Press, 2009.

————, ed. *New Americanists: Revisionary Interventions in the Canon*. Durham, NC: Duke University Press, 1994.

————. "New Americanists: Revisionist Interventions into the Canon." *boundary 2* 17.1 (Spring 1990): 1–37.

————. "The Politics of Postnational American Studies." *European Journal of American Culture* 20.2 (2001): 78–90.

————. *Visionary Compacts: American Renaissance Writings in Cultural Context*. Madison: University of Wisconsin Press, 1987.

Pease, Donald E., and Robyn Wiegman, eds. *The Futures of American Studies*. Durham, NC: Duke University Press, 2002.

Penley, Constance, ed. *Male Trouble*. Minneapolis: University of Minnesota Press, 1993.

Pérez, Emma. "Queering the Borderlands: The Challenges of Excavating the Invisible and Unheard." *Frontiers: A Journal of Women's Studies* 24.2–3 (2003): 122–31.

Perez, Hiram. "You Can Have My Brown Body and Eat It, Too!" *Social Text* 23.3–4 (Fall–Winter 2005): 171–91.

Perry, Dale. "Klan Plans to Recruit in Laurens." *Greenville News* (March 2, 1997): 3B.

Perry-Rogers v. Fasano, 715 N.Y.S.2d 19 (App. Div. 2000).

Perry-Rogers v. Obasaju, 282 A.D.2d 231 (N.Y. App. Div. 2001).

Peterson, V. Spike. "Interactive and Intersectional Analytics of Globalization." *Frontiers: A Journal of Women's Studies* 30.1 (2009): 31–40.

Pfeil, Fred. *White Guys: Studies in Postmodern Domination and Difference.* New York: Verso, 1995.

Phelan, Peggy. "Feminist Theory, Poststructuralism, and Performance." *TDR* 32.1 (Spring 1988): 107–27.

Phillips, Adam. *On Kissing, Tickling, and Being Bored: Psychoanalytic Essays on the Unexamined Life.* Cambridge, MA: Harvard University Press, 1998.

———. *Winnicott.* Cambridge: Harvard University Press, 2004.

———. "Winnicott's Hamlet." *Promises, Promises: Essays on Psychoanalysis and Literature.* New York: Basic Books, 2002: 72–91.

Phoenix, Ann, and Pamela Pattynama. "Editorial." *European Journal of Women's Studies* 13.3 (2006): 187–92.

Poblete, Juan, ed. *Critical Latin American and Latino Studies.* Minneapolis: University of Minnesota Press, 2003.

Porter, Carolyn. "What We Know That We Don't Know: Remapping American Literary Studies." *American Literary History* 6.3 (Autumn 1994): 467–526.

Post, Robert, and Michael Rogin, eds. *Race and Representation: Affirmative Action.* Cambridge, MA: MIT Zone Books, 1998.

Povinelli, Elizabeth A., and George Chauncey, eds. "Thinking Sexuality Transnationally." Special issue, *GLQ* 5.4 (Fall 1999).

President's Council on Bioethics. "Beyond Therapy: Biotechnology and the Pursuit of Happiness." Washington, DC, 2003: http://www.bioethics.gov/topics/beyond_index.html.

Prosser, Jay. *Second Skins: The Body Narratives of Transsexuality.* New York: Columbia University Press, 1998.

Pryse, Marjorie. "Critical Interdisciplinarity, Women's Studies and Cross-Cultural Insight." *NWSA Journal* 10.1 (Spring 1998): 1–22.

———. "Trans/Feminist Methodology: Bridges to Interdisciplinary Thinking." *NWSA Journal* 12.2 (2000): 105–18.

Puar, Jasbir. "'I Would Rather Be a Cyborg Than a Goddess': Intersectionality, Assemblage, Affective Politics." http://eipcp.net/transversal/0811/puar/en.

———. "Mapping U.S. Homonormativities." *Gender, Place and Culture* 13.1 (February 2006): 67–88.

Pugliese, Joseph. "Race as Category Crisis: Whiteness and the Topical Assignation of Race." *Social Semiotics* 12.2 (August 2002): 149–68.

Radstone, Susannah. "Screening Trauma: Forrest Gump, Film, and Memory." In *Memory and Methodology*. Ed. Susannah Radstone. Oxford: Berg, 2000: 79–110.

Radway, Janice. "'What's in a Name?' Presidential Address to the American Studies Association, 20 November, 1998." *American Quarterly* 51.1 (March 1999): 1–32.

Radway, Janice, Kevin Gaines, Barry Shank, and Penny M. Von Eschen, eds. *American Studies: An Anthology*. Malden, MA: Blackwell, 2009.

Readings, Bill. *The University in Ruins*. Cambridge, MA: Harvard University Press, 1997.

Reddy, Chandan. "Asian Diasporas, Neoliberalism, and Family: Reviewing the Case for Homosexual Asylum in the Context of Family Rights." *Social Text* 23.3–4 (Fall/Winter 2005): 101–19.

———. "Time for Rights? Loving, Gay Marriage, and the Limits of Legal Justice." *Fordham Law Review* 76.6 (May 2008): 2849–72.

Reid-Pharr, Robert F. *Black Gay Man: Essays*. New York: New York University Press, 2001.

Reising, Russell J. *The Unusable Past: Theory and the Study of American Literature*. New York: Methuen, 1986.

Reynolds, David S. *Beneath the American Renaissance: The Subversive Imagination in the Age of Emerson and Melville*. New York: Knopf, 1988.

Reynolds, Michael, Shobha Shagle, and Lekha Venkataraman. *A National Census of Women's and Gender Studies Programs in U.S. Institutions of Higher Education: Final Report*. Chicago: National Opinion Research Center at the University of Chicago, 2008: http://www.nwsa.org/PAD/database/downloads/NWSA_Data_Report_08.pdf.

Rich, Adrienne. "Compulsory Heterosexuality and Lesbian Existence." In *Powers of Desire: The Politics of Sexuality*. Ed. Ann Snitow, Christine Stansell, and Sharon Thompson. New York: Monthly Review Press, 1983: 177–205.

Ridgeway, James. *Blood in the Face: The Ku Klux Klan, Aryan Nations, Nazi Skinheads, and the Rise of a New White Culture*. New York: Thunder's Mouth Press, 1990.

Riggs, Damien W., ed. "Why Whiteness Studies." Special issue, *borderlands* 3.2 (October 2004): http://www.borderlands.net.au/issues/vol3no2.html.

Roberts, Dorothy E. "The Genetic Tie." *University of Chicago Law Review* 62 (1995): 209–73.

———. *Killing the Black Body: Race, Reproduction, and the Meaning of Liberty*. New York: Vintage, 1998.

———. "The Nature of Blacks' Skepticism about Genetic Testing." *Seton Hall Law Review* 27.3 (1997): 971–79.

———. "Privatization and Punishment in the New Age of Reprogenetics." *Emory Law Journal* 54.3 (2005): 1343–60.

———. "Punishing Drug Addicts Who Have Babies: Women of Color, Equality, and the Right of Privacy." *Harvard Law Review* 104.7 (May 1991): 1419–82.

———. "Race, Gender, and Genetic Technologies: A New Reproductive Dystopia?" *Signs* 34.4 (Summer 2009): 783–802.

———. "Racism and Patriarchy in the Meaning of Motherhood." *American University Journal of Gender and the Law* 1.1 (1993): 1–38.

Robin, Ron. "The Outsider as Marginal Scholar: Reflections on the Past, the Foreign, and Comparative Studies in American History." *American Studies International* 31.1 (April 1993): 117–26.

Robinson, Sally. *Marked Men: White Masculinity in Crisis.* New York: Columbia University Press, 2000.

Rodgers, Daniel T. "American Exceptionalism Revisited." *Raritan* 24.2 (2004): 21–47.

Rodgers-Rose, LaFrances, ed. *The Black Woman.* Beverly Hills, CA: Sage, 1980.

Rodríguez, Juana María. "Gesture and Utterance: Fragments from a Butch-Femme Archive." In *A Companion to Lesbian, Gay, Bisexual, Transgender, and Queer Studies.* Ed. George E. Haggerty and Molly McGarry. Malden, MA: Blackwell, 2007: 282–91.

Roediger, David R. *Colored White: Transcending the Racial Past.* Berkeley: University of California Press, 2002.

———. *How Race Survived U.S. History: From Settlement and Slavery to the Obama Phenomenon.* London: Verso, 2008.

———. "Introduction." In *Towards a Bibliography of Critical Whiteness Studies.* Ed. Tim Engles. Urbana-Champaign: University of Illinois Center on Democracy in a Multicultural Society, 2006: 4–6: http://cdms.illinois.edu/pages/Research/06-07/CriticalWhiteness/Introduction.htm.

———. "A Response to Stoler." In *Political Power and Social Theory 11.* Ed. Diane E. Davis. Stamford, CT: JAI Press, 1997: 217–20.

———. *Towards the Abolition of Whiteness.* London: Verso, 1994.

———. *The Wages of Whiteness: Race and the Making of the American Working Class.* London: Verso, 1991.

———. *The Wages of Whiteness: Race and the Making of the American Working Class.* Rev. and exp. ed. London: Verso, 2007.

———. *Working Toward Whiteness: How America's Immigrants Became White: The Strange Journey from Ellis Island to the Suburbs.* New York: Basic Books, 2005.

Rohde, David. "Biological Parents Win in Implant Case." *New York Times* (July 17, 1999, late ed.): B3.

Romero, Lora. *Home Fronts: Domesticity and Its Critics in the Antebellum United States*. Durham, NC: Duke University Press, 1997.

Romero, Mary. "Disciplining the Feminist Bodies of Knowledge: Are We Creating or Reproducing Academic Structure?" *NWSA Journal* 12.2 (Summer 2000): 148–62.

Roseneil, Sasha. "Why We Should Care about Friends: An Argument for Queering the Care Imaginary in Social Policy." *Social Policy and Society* 3.4 (October 2004): 409–19.

Ross, Dorothy. "Liberalism and American Exceptionalism." *Intellectual History Newsletter* 24 (2002): 72–83.

Rotundo, E. Anthony. *American Manhood: Transformations in Masculinity from the Revolution to the Modern Era*. New York: Basic Books, 1993.

Rowe, John Carlos, ed. *A Concise Companion to American Studies*. Malden, MA: Blackwell, 2010.

———. "A Future for 'American Studies': The Comparative U.S. Cultures Model." In *American Studies in Germany: European Contexts and Intercultural Relations*. Ed. Günter H. Lenz and Klaus J. Milich. New York: St. Martin's Press, 1995: 262–78.

———. *The New American Studies*. Minneapolis: University of Minnesota Press, 2002.

———. "Post-nationalism, Globalism, and the New American Studies." *Cultural Critique* 40 (Autumn 1998): 11–28.

———, ed. *Post-nationalist American Studies*. Berkeley: University of California Press, 2000.

Rubin, Gayle. "Of Catamites and Kings: Reflections on Butch, Gender, and Boundaries." In *The Persistent Desire: A Femme-Butch Reader*. Ed. Joan Nestle. Boston: Alyson Publications, 1992: 466–82.

———. "Thinking Sex: Notes for a Radical Theory of the Politics of Sexuality." In *Pleasure and Danger: Exploring Female Sexuality*. Ed. Carole S. Vance. New York: Routledge, Kegan and Paul, 1984: 267–319. Reprinted in *The Lesbian and Gay Studies Reader*. Ed. Henry Abelove, Michéle Aina Barale, and David M. Halperin. New York: Routledge, 1993: 3–44.

———. "The Traffic in Women: Notes on the 'Political Economy' of Sex." In *Toward an Anthropology of Women*. Ed. Rayna R. Reiter. New York: Monthly Review Press, 1975: 157–210; and in *The Second Wave: A Reader in Feminist Theory*. Ed. Linda Nicholson. New York: Routledge, 1997: 27–62.

Russell, Michele. "Black-Eyed Blues Connections: Teaching Black Women." *Women's Studies Newsletter* 4.4 (Fall 1976): 6–7.

Rutherford, Charlotte. "Reproductive Freedoms and African American Women." *Yale Journal of Law and Feminism* 4 (1992): 255–90.

Sacks, Karen Brodkin. "Toward a Unified Theory of Class, Race, and Gender." *American Ethnologist* 16.3 (August 1989): 534–50.

Salamon, Gayle. *Assuming a Body: Transgender and Rhetorics of Materiality.* New York: Columbia University Press, 2010.

———. "Transfeminism and the Future of Gender." In *Women's Studies on the Edge.* Ed. Joan Wallach Scott. Durham, NC: Duke University Press, 2008: 115–36.

Saldívar, José David. *Border Matters: Remapping American Cultural Studies.* Berkeley: University of California Press, 1997.

———. *The Dialectics of Our America: Genealogy, Cultural Critique, and Literary History.* Durham, NC: Duke University Press, 1991.

Saldívar, Ramón. *The Borderlands of Culture: Américo Paredes and the Transnational Imaginary.* Durham, NC: Duke University Press, 2006.

Sanchez, George. "Reading Reginald Denny: The Politics of Whiteness in the Late Twentieth Century." *American Quarterly* 47.3 (September 1995): 388–94.

Saul, Stephanie. "Uncertain Laws on Surrogates Leave Custody at Issue." *New York Times* (December 13, 2009): A1.

Saxton, Alexander. *The Rise and Fall of the White Republic: Class Politics and Mass Culture in Nineteenth-Century America.* London: Verso, 1990.

Schlesinger, Arthur, Jr. "Human Rights and the American Tradition." *Foreign Affairs* 57.3 (1978): 503–26.

Schneider, David. *American Kinship: A Cultural Account.* Englewood Cliffs, NJ: Prentice-Hall, 1968.

Schor, Naomi. *Bad Objects: Essays Popular and Unpopular.* Durham, NC: Duke University Press, 1995.

Schueller, Malini Johar. "Postcolonial American Studies." *American Literary History* 16.1 (Spring 2004): 162–75.

Scott, Joan Wallach. "Deconstructing Equality-versus-Difference: Or, the Uses of Poststructuralism for Feminism." *Feminist Studies* 14.1 (Spring 1988): 33–50.

———. "Gender—A Useful Category of Analysis." *American Historical Review* 91.5 (December 1986): 1053–75.

———. "Introduction to *Women's Studies on the Edge.*" *differences* 9.3 (Fall 1997): i–iv.

———. *Only Paradoxes to Offer: French Feminists and the Rights of Man.* Cambridge, MA: Harvard University Press, 1997.

———, ed. *Women's Studies on the Edge.* Durham, NC: Duke University Press, 2008.

Scott, Jonathan. "Inside the White Corral." *Minnesota Review* 47 (Fall 1996): 93–103.

Scott, Steven D. "'Like a Box of Chocolates': Forrest Gump and Postmodernism." *Literature/Film Quarterly* 29.1 (January 2001): 23–31.

Sedgwick, Eve Kosofsky. *Between Men: English Literature and Male Homosocial Desire*. New York: Columbia University Press, 1985.

———. *Epistemology of the Closet*. Berkeley: University of California Press, 1990.

———. "Gender Studies." In *Redrawing the Boundaries: The Transformation of English and American Literary Studies*. Ed. Stephen Greenblatt and Giles Gunn. New York: Modern Language Association of America, 1992: 271–302.

———. "Melanie Klein and the Difference Affect Makes." *South Atlantic Quarterly* 106.3 (Summer 2007): 625–42.

———. Paranoid Reading and Reparative Reading." In *Touching Feeling: Affect, Pedagogy, Performativity*. Durham, NC: Duke University Press, 2003: 123–51.

———. *Tendencies*. Durham, NC: Duke University Press, 1993: 1–20.

———. *Touching Feeling: Affect, Pedagogy, Performativity*. Durham, NC: Duke University Press, 2003.

Segal, Lynne. *Slow Motion: Changing Masculinities, Changing Men*. New Brunswick, NJ: Rutgers University Press, 1990.

Segrest, Meg. *Memoir of a Race Traitor*. Boston: South End Press, 1994.

Seidler, Victor J. *Unreasonable Men: Masculinity and Social Theory*. New York: Routledge, 1994.

Seidman, Steven. "Deconstructing Queer Theory or the Under-theorization of the Social and Ethical." In *Social Postmodernism: Beyond Identity Politics*. Ed. Linda J. Nicholson and Steven Seidman. Cambridge: Cambridge University Press, 1995: 116–41.

———. "From Identity to Queer Politics: Shifts in Normative Heterosexuality and the Meaning of Citizenship." *Citizenship Studies* 5.3 (November 2001): 321–28.

Shafer, Byron E., ed. *Is America Different? A New Look at American Exceptionalism*. Oxford: Oxford University Press, 1991.

Shamir, Milette. "Foreigners Within and Innocents Abroad: Discourse of the Self in the Internationalization of American Studies." *Journal of American Studies* 37.3 (December 2003): 375–88.

Shapiro, Stephen. "Reconfiguring American Studies? The Paradoxes of Post-nationalism." *49th Parallel* 8 (Summer 2001): http://www.49thparallel.bham.ac.uk/back/issue8/shapiro.htm.

Shih, Shu-mei. "Comparative Racialization: An Introduction." *PMLA* 123.5 (October 2008): 1347–62.

Shukla, Sandhya, and Heidi Tinsman, eds. "Our Americas: Political and Cultural Imaginings." Special issue, *Radical History Review* 89 (Spring 2004).

Sielke, Sabine. "Theorizing American Studies: German Interventions into an Ongoing Debate." *European Journal of American Studies* (2006): http://ejas.revues.org/document470.html.

Silverman, Kaja. *Male Subjectivity at the Margins*. New York: Routledge, 1992.

Simons, Marlise. "Uproar over Twins, and a Dutch Couple's Anguish." *New York Times* (June 28, 1995): A3.

Singh, Nikhil Pal. *Black Is a Country: Race and the Unfinished Struggle for Democracy*. Cambridge, MA: Harvard University Press, 2004.

Slaughter, Sheila, and Gary Rhoades. *Academic Capitalism and the New Economy: Markets, State, and Higher Education*. Baltimore, MD: Johns Hopkins University Press, 2004.

Smith, Anna Marie. *Welfare Reform and Sexual Regulation*. New York: Cambridge University Press, 2007.

Smith, Barbara. "Doing Research on Black Women." *Women's Studies Newsletter* 4.2 (Spring 1976): 4–5, 7.

——, ed. *Home Girls: A Black Feminist Anthology*. New York: Kitchen Table/Women of Color Press, 1983.

——. "Racism and Women's Studies." *Frontiers: A Journal of Women Studies* 5.1 (Spring 1980): 48–49.

Smith, J. Douglas. *Managing White Supremacy: Race, Politics, and Citizenship in Jim Crow Virginia*. Chapel Hill: University of North Carolina Press, 2001.

Snitow, Ann. "A Gender Diary." In *Conflicts in Feminism*. Ed. Marianne Hirsch and Evelyn Fox Keller. New York: Routledge, 1990: 9–43.

Snitow, Ann, Christine Stansell, and Sharon Thompson, eds. *Powers of Desire: The Politics of Sexuality*. New York: Monthly Review Press, 1983.

Soto, Sandra K. *Reading Chican@ Like a Queer: The De-mastery of Desire*. Austin: University of Texas Press, 2010.

——. "Where in the Transnational World Are U.S. Women of Color." In *Women's Studies for the Future: Foundations, Interrogations, Politics*. Ed. Elizabeth Lapovsky Kennedy and Agatha Beins. New Brunswick, NJ: Rutgers University Press, 2005: 111–24.

Southern Poverty Law Center. "SPLC Urges Congress to Investigate Extremism in the Military." July 10, 2009: http://www.splcenter.org/news/item.jsp?aid=384.

Spelman, Elizabeth V. *Inessential Woman: Problems of Exclusion in Feminist Thought*. Boston: Beacon Press, 1988.

Spender, Dale, ed. *Men's Studies Modified: The Impact of Feminism on the Academic Disciplines*. London: Pergamon, 1981.

Spillers, Hortense. "'All the Things You Could Be by Now, If Sigmund Freud's Wife Was Your Mother': Psychoanalysis and Race." In *Black, White and in Color*. Chicago: University of Chicago Press, 2003: 376–427.

——. "Interstices: A Small Drama of Words." In *Pleasure and Danger: Exploring Female Sexuality*. Ed. Carole S. Vance. New York: Routledge, 1984: 73–100.

————. "Mama's Baby, Papa's Maybe: An American Grammar." *Diacritics* 17.2 (Summer 1987): 64–81.

————. "Women in/of the Academy." Address at the University of North Carolina–Duke Lecture in Women's Studies, Chapel Hill, NC, January 16, 2003.

Spivak, Gayatri. "Scattered Speculations on the Question of Cultural Studies." In *Outside in the Teaching Machine*. New York: Routledge, 1993: 255–84.

Spivak, Gayatri, and Sneja Gunew. "Questions of Multiculturalism." In *The Cultural Studies Reader*. Ed. Simon During. London: Routledge, 1993: 193–202.

Stacey, Judith. "Disloyal to the Disciplines: A Feminist Trajectory in the Borderland." In *Feminism in the Academy*. Ed. Domna C. Stanton and Abigail J. Stewart. Ann Arbor: University of Michigan Press, 1995: 311–29.

Staunæs, Dorthe. "Where Have All the Subjects Gone? Bringing Together the Concepts of Intersectionality and Subjectification." *Nora: Nordic Journal of Feminist and Gender Research* 11.2 (August 2003): 101–10.

Steady, Filomina Chioma. *The Black Woman Cross-Culturally*. Cambridge, MA: Schenkman, 1981.

Steinmetz, George. "Return to Empire: The New U.S. Imperialism in Comparative Historical Perspective." *Sociological Theory* 23.4 (December 2005): 339–67.

Stephens, Michelle. *Black Empire: The Masculine Global Imaginary of Caribbean Intellectuals in the United States, 1914–1962*. Durham, NC: Duke University Press, 2005.

Stoler, Ann Laura. "On Degrees of Imperial Sovereignty." *Public Culture* 18.1 (2006): 125–46.

————. "Racial Histories and Their Regimes of Truth." In *Political Power and Social Theory 11*. Ed. Diane E. Davis. Stamford, CT: JAI Press, 1997: 183–206.

————. "Tense and Tender Ties: The Politics of Comparison in North American History and (Post)Colonial Studies." *Journal of American History* 88.3 (December 2001): 829–65.

Stone, Sandy. "The Empire Strikes Back: A Posttranssexual Manifesto." In *Body Guards: The Cultural Politics of Gender Ambiguity*. Ed. Julia Epstein and Kristina Straub. New York: Routledge, 1991: 280–304.

Stowe, David W. "Uncolored People: The Rise of Whiteness Studies." *Lingua Franca* (September/October 1996): 68–77.

Streeby, Shelley. *American Sensations: Class, Empire, and the Production of Popular Culture*. Berkeley: University of California Press, 2002.

Stryker, Susan. "My Words to Victor Frankenstein above the Village of Chamounix: Performing Gender Rage." *GLQ* 1.3 (Summer 1994): 227–54.

————. "Transgender History, Homonormativity, and Disciplinarity." *Radical History Review* 100 (Winter 2008): 145–57.

———, ed. "The Transgender Issue." Special issue, *GLQ* 4.2 (Spring 1998).

———. "Transgender Studies: Queer Theory's Evil Twin." *GLQ* 10.2 (Spring 2004): 212–15.

Stryker, Susan, and Stephen Whittle, eds. *The Transgender Studies Reader*. New York: Routledge, 2006.

Sugg, John. "Inside the Secret World of White Supremacy." *Truthout Report* (October 18, 2006): http://www.truthout.org/article/john-f-sugg-inside-secret -world-white-supremacy.

Swain, Carol M., and Russ Nieli, eds. *Contemporary Voices of White Nationalism in America*. Cambridge: Cambridge University Press, 2003.

Swarns, Rachel L., and Jodi Kantor. "In First Lady's Roots, a Complex Path from Slavery." *New York Times* (October 8, 2009): http://www.nytimes.com/2009 /10/08/us/politics/08genealogy.html?_r=1.

Talbot, Margaret. "Getting Credit for Being White." *New York Times* (November 30, 1997): Sunday Magazine 116–19.

Tate, Claudia. *Black Women Writers at Work*. New York: Continuum, 1983.

———. "Nella Larsen's *Passing*: A Problem of Interpretation." *Black American Literature Forum* 14.4 (Winter 1980): 142–46.

Thelen, David. "The Nation and Beyond: Transnational Perspectives on United States History." *Journal of American History* 86.3 (December 1999): 965–75.

Thomas, Calvin. *Male Matters: Masculinity, Anxiety and the Male Body on the Line*. Urbana: University of Illinois Press, 1996.

Thomas-Lynn, Felicia. "Redneck Shop Operator Opens Klan Museum." *Greenville News* (September 26, 1996): 1D.

Tompkins, Jane. *Sensational Designs: The Cultural Work of American Fiction, 1790–1860*. New York: Oxford University Press, 1986.

Toribio, Helen C. "The Problematics of History and Location of Filipino American Studies within Asian American Studies." *Asian American Studies after Critical Mass*. Ed. Kent A. Ono. Malden, MA: Blackwell, 2005: 166–76.

Torres, Sonia. "US Americans and 'Us' Americans: South American Perspectives on Comparative American Studies." *Comparative American Studies* 1.1 (March 2003): 9–17.

Traister, Bryce. "The Object of Study; or, Are We Being Transnational Yet?" *Journal of Transnational American Studies* 2.1 (2010): http://escholarship.org /uc/item/864843hs.

Tuana, Nancy, William Cowling, Maurice Hamington, Greg Johnson, and Terrance MacMullan, eds. *Revealing Male Bodies*. Bloomington: Indiana University Press, 2002.

Twine, France Winddance. "Bearing Blackness in Britain: The Meaning of Racial Difference for White Birth Mothers of African-Descent Children." *Social Identities* 5.2 (1999): 185–210.

———. "Transracial Mothering and Antiracism: The Case of White Birth Mothers of 'Black' Children." *Feminist Studies* 25.3 (Fall 1999): 729–46.

Tyrrell, Ian. "American Exceptionalism in an Age of International History." *American Historical Review* 96 (October 1991): 1031–55.

Valdes, Francisco. "Sex and Race in Queer Legal Culture: Ruminations on Identities and Inter-connectivities." *Southern California Review of Law and Social Justice* 5.1 (Fall 1995): 25–71.

Valentine, David. "We're 'Not about Gender': The Uses of 'Transgender.'" In *Out in Theory: The Emergence of Lesbian and Gay Anthropology*. Ed. Ellen Lewin and William L. Leap. Urbana: University of Illinois Press, 2002: 222–45.

Valentine, Gill. "Theorizing and Researching Intersectionality: A Challenge for Feminist Geography." *Professional Geographer* 59.1 (February 2007): 10–21.

Vance, Carole S., ed. *Pleasure and Danger: Exploring Female Sexuality*. Boston: Routledge and Kegan Paul, 1984.

Viego, Antonio. *Dead Subjects: Toward a Politics of Loss in Latino Studies*. Durham, NC: Duke University Press, 2007.

———. "The Unconscious of Latino/a Studies." *Latino Studies* 1.2 (July 2003): 333–36.

Villarejo, Amy. "Tarrying with the Normative: Queer Theory and *Black History*." *Social Text* 23.3–4 (Fall–Winter 2005): 69–84.

Wacquant, Loïc J. D. "For an Analytic of Racial Domination." *Political Power and Social Theory 11*. Ed. Diane E. Davis. Stamford, CT: JAI Press, 1997: 221–34.

Wald, Priscilla. "Minefields and Meeting Grounds: Transnational Analyses and American Studies." *American Literary History* 10.1 (Spring 1998): 199–218.

Walker, Alice. *In Search of Our Mothers' Gardens*. New York: Harcourt Brace Jovanovich, 1983.

Walker, Cheryl. *Indian Nation: Native American Literature and Nineteenth-Century Nationalisms*. Durham, NC: Duke University Press, 1997.

Wallace, Michele. *Black Macho and the Myth of Super Woman*. (1979). London: Verso, 1990.

Walters, Barbara. "Losing Joseph." *20/20*. American Broadcasting Corporation, March 3, 2000.

Wang, Jennifer Hyland. "'A Struggle of Contending Stories': Race, Gender, and Political Memory in 'Forrest Gump.'" *Cinema Journal* 39.3 (Spring 2000): 92–115.

Ware, Vron. *Beyond the Pale: White Women, Racism, and History*. London: Verso, 1992.

Ware, Vron, and Les Back. *Out of Whiteness: Color, Politics, and Culture*. Chicago: University of Chicago Press, 2001.

Warner, Michael. "Introduction: Fear of a Queer Planet." *Social Text* 29 (1991): 3–17.

———. "The Mass Public and the Mass Subject." In *Habermas and the Public Sphere*. Ed. Craig Calhoun. Cambridge, MA: MIT Press, 1992: 377–401.

———. *The Trouble with Normal: Sex, Politics, and the Ethics of Queer Life*. New York: Free Press, 1999.

Washburn, Jennifer. *University Inc.: The Corporate Corruption of the University*. New York: Basic Books, 2005.

Weber, Lynn. *Understanding Race, Class, Gender, and Sexuality: A Conceptual Framework*. 2nd ed. New York: Oxford University Press, 2009.

Weedon, Chris. *Feminist Practice and Poststructuralist Theory*. Oxford: Basil Blackwell, 1987.

Weeks, Kathi. *Constituting Feminist Subjects*. Ithaca, NY: Cornell University Press, 1998.

Weinbaum, Alys, Lynn M. Thomas, Priti Ramamurthy, Uta G. Poiger, Madeline Yue Dong, and Tani Barlow, eds. *The Modern Girl Around the World: Consumption, Modernity, and Globalization*. Durham, NC: Duke University Press, 2008.

Weiner, Jon. "Arizona Bans Ethnic Studies—Update." *The Nation* (May 12, 2010): http://www.thenation.com/blog/arizona-bans-ethnic-studies-update.

———. "Fox News Defends Arizona Ethnic Studies Ban." *The Nation* (May 18, 2010): http://www.thenation.com/blog/arizona-ethnic-studies-ban-defended-fox-news.

Wesling, Meg. "Why Queer Diaspora?" *Feminist Review* 90 (2008): 30–47.

West, Robin. "Deconstructing the CLS-FEM Split." *Wisconsin Women's Law Journal* 2 (1986): 85–92.

Wexler, Laura. *Tender Violence: Domestic Visions in an Age of U.S. Imperialism*. Chapel Hill: University of North Carolina Press, 2000.

Whang, Selena. "The White Heterosexual Couple: On Masculinity, Sadism and Racialized Lesbian Desire." *College Literature* 24.1 (February 1997): 116–32.

White, Deborah Gray. *Ar'n't I a Woman? Female Slaves in the Plantation South*. New York: Norton, 1985.

"White Couple Gives Baby to His Black Genetic Parents in Embryo Mix-Up Case." *Jet* 96.2 (1999): 23.

Wiegman, Robyn. "Academic Feminism Against Itself." *NWSA Journal* 14.2 (Summer 2002): 18–37.

———. *American Anatomies: Theorizing Race and Gender*. Durham, NC: Duke University Press, 1995.

———. "The Ends of New Americanism." *New Literary History* 42.3 (Summer 2011): 385–407.

———. "Feminism, Institutionalism, and the Idiom of Failure." *differences* 11.3 (Fall 1999/2000): 107–36.

——. "Feminism's Apocalyptic Futures." *New Literary History* 31.4 (Autumn 2000): 805–25.

——. "Feminism's Broken English." In *Just Being Difficult: Academic Writing in the Public Arena*. Ed. Jonathan Culler and Kevin Lamb. Palo Alto, CA: Stanford University Press, 2003: 75–94.

——. "The Possibility of Women's Studies." In *Women's Studies for the Future: Foundations, Interrogations, Politics*. Ed. Elizabeth L. Kennedy and Agatha Beins. New Brunswick, NJ: Rutgers University Press, 2005: 40–60.

——. "What Ails Feminist Criticism: A Second Opinion." *Critical Inquiry* 25.2 (Winter 1999): 362–79.

——. "Whiteness Studies and the Paradox of Particularity." *boundary 2* 26.3 (Fall 1999): 115–50.

Wilcox, Lynne S., and William D. Mosher. "Use of Infertility Services in the United States." *Obstetrics and Gynecology* 82.1 (July 1993): 122–27.

Willett, Cynthia, ed. *Theorizing Multiculturalism: A Guide to the Current Debate*. Malden, MA: Blackwell, 1998.

Williams, Patricia. "Fetal Fictions: An Exploration of Property Archetypes in Racial and Gendered Contexts." *Florida Law Review* 42 (1990): 81–94.

Wilson, Elizabeth A. "Gut Feminism." *differences* 15.3 (Fall 2004): 66–94.

Wilson, Rob. *Reimagining the American Pacific: From South Pacific to Bamboo Ridge and Beyond*. Durham, NC: Duke University Press, 2000.

Winant, Howard. "Behind Blue Eyes: Whiteness and Contemporary U.S. Racial Politics." In *Off White: Readings on Race, Power, and Society*. 2nd ed. Ed. Michelle Fine, Lois Weis, Linda C. Powell, and L. Mun Wong. New York: Routledge, 2004: 3–16.

——. *The New Politics of Race: Globalism, Difference, Justice*. Minneapolis: University of Minnesota Press, 2004.

Winnicott, D. W. *The Child, the Family, and the Outside World*. (1964). New York: Perseus Books, 1992.

——. *Holding and Interpretation: Fragment of an Analysis*. (1986). With M. Masud R. Khan. New York: Grove Press, 1994.

——. *Playing and Reality*. (1971). New York: Routledge, 2005.

Winnicott, D. W., Clare Winnicott, Ray Shepherd, and Madeleine Davis. *Babies and Their Mothers*. Cambridge, MA: Da Capo, 1987.

Wise, Gene. "'Paradigm Dramas' in American Studies: A Cultural and Institutional History of the Movement." *American Quarterly* 31.3 (September 1979): 293–337.

Wise, Tim. *Affirmative Action: Racial Preference in Black and White*. New York: Routledge, 2005.

Wray, Matt. *Not Quite White: White Trash and the Boundaries of Whiteness*. Durham, NC: Duke University Press, 2006.

Wray, Matt, and Annalee Newitz, eds. *White Trash: Race and Class in America.* New York: Routledge, 1997.

Yanagisako, Sylvia, and Carol Delaney, eds. *Naturalizing Power: Essays in Feminist Cultural Analysis.* London: Routledge, 1995.

Yardley, Jim. "After Embryo Mix-Up, Couple Say They Will Give Up a Baby." *New York Times* (March 30, 1999): A1.

———. "Health Officials Investigating to Determine How Woman Got the Embryo of Another." *New York Times* (March 31, 1999): B3.

———. "Pregnant with Meaning." *Washington Post* (April 5, 1999): C2.

———. "Sharing Baby Proves Rough on 2 Mothers." *New York Times* (June 30, 1999): B1.

Yee, Shirley. "The 'Women' in Women's Studies." *differences* 9.3 (Fall 1997): 46–64.

Yingling, Thomas. "How the Eye Is Caste: Robert Mapplethorpe and the Limits of Controversy." *Discourse* 12.2 (Spring–Summer 1990): 3–28.

Young, Robert J. C. *White Mythologies: Writing History and the West.* New York: Routledge, 1990.

Yúdice, George. "Neither Impugning nor Disavowing Whiteness Does a Viable Politics Make: The Limits of Identity Politics." In *After Political Correctness: The Humanities and Society in the 1990s.* Ed. Christopher Newfield and Ronald Strickland. Boulder, CO: Westview Press, 1995: 255–85.

Yuval-Davis, Nira. "Intersectionality and Feminist Politics." *European Journal of Women's Studies* 13.3 (August 2006): 193–209.

Zack, Naomi. *Inclusive Feminism: A Third Wave Theory of Women's Commonality.* Lanham, MD: Rowman and Littlefield, 2005.

Zerilli, Linda. "Doing Without Knowing: Feminism's Politics of the Ordinary." *Political Theory* 26.4 (August 1998): 435–58.

Zimmerman, Bonnie. "Women's Studies, NWSA, and the Future of the (Inter) Discipline." *NWSA Journal* 14.1 (2002): viii–xviii.

INDEX

....

Ferguson, Roderick A., 334n34, 307n10

Field imaginary, 14–18, 25–35, 60–62, 68–69, 73n29, 78–90, 96n6, 140n2, 195, 205, 216–33, 237–38, 241, 326–35. *See also* Disciplinarity; Identity, knowledges

Field formation, as process, 16–17, 75–79, 82, 121–28, 202–8, 214–23, 231–38, 326–29. *See also* Disciplines; Disciplinarity

Fisher, Philip, 219n32

Forrest Gump (film), 141–43, 161–73, 180, 192, 287n81

Foucault, Michel, 19, 102n12, 329

Franklin, Sarah, 276

French feminism, 18, 155. *See also* Academic feminism; Feminism

Frug, Mary Joe, 114n21

Garvey, John, 177–78

Gay and Lesbian Studies, 40, 45–46, 48, 100, 117, 127n34, 191, 321, 329. *See also* Identity, knowledges; Queer Studies; Sexuality Studies; Transgender Studies

Gender, as object of study, 1, 2n2, 8, 10–12, 24, 25–26, 28–33, 38–40, 42, 44–62, 68–69, 78, 80, 83–90, 94–98, 102n13, 105–11, 114, 127n34, 129–32, 134–38, 246–49, 303–5, 308–26, 333n33, 336–38. *See also* Narrative, of progress; Race; Sex; Sexuality, as object of study; Transgender; Woman, monolithic figure of; Women, as object of study

Gender Studies, 25n26, 38n1, 40, 41n2, 43–61, 86–90, 322, 333n33. *See also* Identity, knowledges; Queer Studies; Sexuality Studies;

Transgender Studies; Women's Studies

Globalization, 6, 16, 82n37, 93n2, 198n1, 203n10, 207n15, 225, 236, 330

Grayson, Deborah, 272, 277–80

Grewal, Inderpal, and Caren Kaplan, 22n21

Halberstam, Judith, 26n27, 124n31, 131n38, 305n7, 311–12

Halley, Ian, 11, 27, 97, 104–25

Halley, Janet, 97, 103, 104n15, 310–12, 316

Halperin, David, 306n8, 331n32

Hark, Sabine, 71–71, 77n33

Harris, Cheryl, 166, 225

Hartman, Saidiya, 225, 278–79

Hartouni, Valerie, 272–73, 281–84, 286

Hemings, Sally, 255–56, 296

Heteronormativity, 21, 32–33, 131, 267, 282, 286, 286, 303–13, 316–29

Heterosexuality, 131n37, 268, 280, 288, 303–4, 307, 323, 335

Hill, Mike, 190

Holloway, Karla, 156n30

Homonormativity, 92. *See also* Antinormativity

Homosexuality, 21, 99, 155, 334n34, 339n38

Humanities. *See* Disciplines

Identification, 9n10, 28, 103, 163, 172, 175–76, 186, 256–57, 317n18, 331–32; disidentification and, 28–29, 96n6; refused, 28, 108, 200, 216–36, 339

Identity: knowledges, 1–10, 13–15, 17–19, 23–25, 35–37, 42, 50, 53n9, 61, 68, 79, 88–89, 91, 93–97, 100n10, 113n19, 118, 122, 124–27, 137–38, 188–89, 191, 197, 200–201, 203n8,

Masculinity: as object of study, 16, 38, 43, 45, 48–49, 56–59, 102n13, 139, 320; white, 155n29, 156n31, 158, 169, 286–87, 292–94; "without men," 58n14, 59, 131n38, 132–33, 139, 308, 311–12. *See also* Gender Studies; Paternity

Maternity, 253, 255, 258–85, 286n79, 288n83. *See also* Paternity; Reproduction; Race

Mattilda, 331n32

McCall, Leslie, 240

McClure, Kirstie, 34n32

Methodology, 73n29, 297, 334n34

Messer-Davidow, Ellen, 43n4, 78n35

Minoritization, 16–17, 23n23, 53n9, 62, 82n37, 86, 92, 120–22, 130, 138, 145–46, 163, 174–79, 183–87, 191, 199n2, 242, 258, 328, 335; *vs.* minority, 4n5. *See also* Race; Racialization

Model minority, 277n73

Modernity, 26–27, 29, 70, 119, 139, 225, 280, 334n34. *See also* Disciplines

Mohanram, Radhika, 156n30

Morrison, Toni, 23n23, 154n27, 156

Muñoz, José Esteban, 22n21, 96n6

Multiculturalism, 6, 36, 67, 147, 155, 227–28, 258, 289, 292–94. *See also* Nation

Multiracial, 6n7, 31n29, 249, 255, 265, 269–70, 279–80, 284–96; *vs.* interracial, 257–58

Narrative: of failure, 61, 81; of nation and national origin, 142, 169, 179–80, 198–200, 249, 314n16; of progress, 26, 37–42, 50–55, 61–67, 78–81, 83–90, 95–96, 118, 137–38,

214, 243–44, 280, 309; of race and kinship, 256n42, 257–58, 280, 286n79, 287–94; of white identity, 155–56, 162–71

Nash, Jennifer C., 244, 297–99

Nation: as object of study, 1, 4, 24–25, 29–30, 86, 197, 200–206, 210–11, 215n24, 218–20, 223–29, 233–34. *See also* American Studies; Internationalization; Narrative, of nation and national origin; Transnational

National Women's Studies Association, 31n29, 71n24

Newitz, Annalee, 182–85

Noble, Bobby Jean, 320–21

Noble-Allgire, Alice M., 265n57, 288n83

Nussbaum, Martha C., 43n4

Obama, Barack, 193, 236n55, 256n42

Object relations, 4–5, 8, 20, 89, 91, 96, 98, 104, 135, 137, 188, 206, 336. *See also* Identity, knowledges

Omi, Michael, 151n24, 152n25

Paradigmatic reading, 32, 241–43, 246–49, 263, 265, 267–68, 276, 283–85, 287–88, 297–98, 302, 328

Paternity, 163–65, 170, 172, 255, 268, 279, 283–96. *See also* Masculinity

Patriarchy, 57n12, 133, 271

Pease, Donald E., 14–15, 212, 213n23, 219–23, 228, 230, 232–34

Perry-Rogers v. Fasano, 250n20, 252–54, 260, 272–76, 284–85, 294, 297

Political imaginary, 69, 78n35, 94n4, 125, 195, 217, 233, 263, 314n16, 334n34, 336. *See also* Field formation; Identity, knowledges

Sexuality, as object of study, 12n13, 22–23, 27, 33, 30–39, 46–48, 50–51, 58, 64n17, 96–98, 102n13, 105–28, 132–36, 240n3, 303–4, 308–43. *See also* Gender; Sex

Slavery, 147, 150n21, 167, 178, 183, 187, 256–57, 266, 268, 270, 275–89, 293, 295–96, 334n34. *See also* White supremacy

Social construction theory, 38n1, 48, 57–58, 65, 139–40, 159, 161, 174–76, 180–82, 187, 218, 291

Social movements, 5–7, 11, 17, 27–28, 37, 39, 61–62, 76, 81, 92, 94–95, 100n9, 104, 116, 117–18, 121, 125–27, 134, 191, 196, 199n2, 213, 217, 221–22, 233, 311, 327. *See also* Civil Rights; Identity, politics; University

Soto, Sandra K., 16n16

Spillers, Hortense, 66–67, 99–101, 117–18, 121, 260n48, 286n79

Spivak, Gayatri, 6n7, 244

Standpoint theory, 34, 65, 118n25, 245.

Stoler, Ann Laura, 199n3, 266n58

Theory/practice divide, 84–85, 189, 263–64, 316–17

Transferential idealism, 40, 43–45, 51–53, 69, 80–81, 88–90

Transgender: as object of study, 3, 44n6, 101, 122–23, 127n34, 131n37, 308–9, 315–20, 333. *See also* Gender; Sex

Transgender Studies, 101n11, 320–23. *See also* Gay and Lesbian Studies; Identity, knowledges, Queer Studies

Transnational: as analytic, 3, 22, 25–26, 40, 44n6, 86–88, 198n1, 202, 203n10,

207, 212–13, 222, 224, 226, 228, 235–36, 238, 274n67, 314n16; commodity circuits, 169–72, 276n70. *See also* Internationalization

University: social movements and, 5–7; U.S., 1n1, 11, 13–14, 16, 38n1, 52, 70, 73, 75–78, 99–101, 117–18, 121, 123, 127, 200–207, 210n21, 215n24, 216–17, 236, 240n3, 264n54, 274–75, 328, 330n31

Viego, Antonio, 22–24

Warner, Michael, 303–4, 324n25, 330n31

"We," in academic criticism, 13

White supremacy, 23n23, 28–29, 139–42, 146–53, 157, 171–88, 249, 257, 282, 286–88, 295. *See also* Ku Klux Klan; Segregation; Whiteness

Whiteness: historical formation, 141–42, 143–45, 147–55, 159, 164–67, 257; as object of study, 4, 16, 24, 28–29, 50, 139, 145–47, 156–58, 166–67, 196, 255, 285–87. *See also* Antiracism; Race; Racialization; Racism; White supremacy

Whiteness Studies, 3, 4, 8, 9, 28–29, 138–43, 156–60, 171–96, 199–200, 202. *See also* Ethnic Studies, Identity, knowledges

Wilson, Elizabeth A., 38n1

Winant, Howard, 151–53, 172, 191–93

Woman, monolithic figure of, 47, 62, 66, 114, 133, 244, 245n13, 247

Women, as object of study, 10, 24, 25–26, 37–42, 44–45, 47–69, 73, 76, 78, 82n38, 85–90, 103–6, 117, 119,

ROBYN WIEGMAN is Professor of Women's
Studies and Literature at Duke University.
She is the author of *American Anatomies:
Theorizing Race and Gender* and the editor
of *Women's Studies on Its Own: A Next Wave
Reader in Institutional Change*, both also
published by Duke.

Library of Congress Cataloging-in-Publication Data
Wiegman, Robyn.
Object lessons / Robyn Wiegman.
p. cm. — (Next wave)
Includes bibliographical references and index.
ISBN 978-0-8223-5146-7 (cloth : alk. paper)
ISBN 978-0-8223-5160-3 (pbk. : alk. paper)
1. Critical theory.   2. Feminist theory.   3. Queer
theory.   4. Race.   5. Whites—Race identity.
I. Title.   II. Series: Next wave.
HM480.W54 2012
301.01—dc23   2011038526